Contemporary
Graphic Artists

ISSN 0885-8462

Contemporary Graphic Artists

A Biographical, Bibliographical, and
Critical Guide to Current Illustrators,
Animators, Cartoonists, Designers,
and Other Graphic Artists

Maurice Horn
Editor

Volume 2

Gale Research Company • Book Tower • Detroit, Michigan 48226

STAFF

Maurice Horn, *Editor*
Richard Calhoun, Javier Coma, Pierre Horn, Leonid Krizek,
Frederik Schodt, Dennis Wepman, *Contributors*
Thomas M. Bachmann, Paul Gallagher, *Assistant Editors*

Roger D. Hubbard, *Graphic Arts Coordinator*
Charles Hunt, *Cameraman*

Special acknowledgment is due to Diane L. Dupuis for her assistance
in the preparation of this volume.

Frederick G. Ruffner, *Chairman*
J. Kevin Reger, *President*
Dedria Bryfonski, *Publisher*
Ellen T. Crowley, *Associate Editorial Director*
Christine Nasso, *Director, Biography Division*
Linda S. Hubbard, *Senior Editor, Contemporary Graphic Artists*

Every effort has been made to trace copyright for the illustrations in this
volume, but if omissions have been made, please contact the publisher.

ISBN 0-8103-2190-4
ISSN 0885-8462

Computerized photocomposition by
AMTEC Information Services, Inc.
Lakewood, California

Contents

Artists Featured in This Volume

John Groth—His friend and confidant Ernest Hemingway once said of this illustrator, "He looked more like an artist than any good artist I ever knew." In the 1930s Groth helped launch the maiden issue of *Esquire*, contributed to the success of the *New Republic* and the *Nation,* and reported on every major upheaval from Mexico to Russia. Later, he became one of the most celebrated graphic reporters of World War II.

In addition to his illustrations for Hemingway's *Men Without Women* and a number of the author's magazine pieces, Groth is also known for illustrating John Steinbeck's *The Grapes of Wrath,* Leo Tolstoy's *War and Peace,* Margaret Mitchell's *Gone with the Wind,* Erich Maria Remarque's *All Quiet on the Western Front,* and a score of other books. Also a painter and etcher of note, Groth says of his work, "If I fail to communicate, . . . I feel the work is a distinct failure."

Harvey Kurtzman—Best known as the creator of the satirical magazine *Mad,* Kurtzman first made his mark as the editor, illustrator, and writer of EC's celebrated "New Trend" comic books, notably *Two-Fisted Tales* and *Frontline Combat,* two war comics in which he articulated a clear anti-war message. Hailed as "a major innovator who has influenced at least two generations of comic book artists," Kurtzman is noted for his writings in *Mad* and other magazines, and for his invention of such characters as the cretinous Alfred E. Neuman ("What . . . Me Worry?"). He is also the creator and writer of *Little Annie Fanny,* the irrepressible sexual parody that has enchanted *Playboy*'s readers since 1962.

M. G. Lord—As a woman in a field almost entirely dominated by men, Lord is a rarity among editorial cartoonists. Her acerbic wit and barbed commentary have delighted, and sometimes shocked, *Newsday* readers since 1978 and national audiences since 1984. Ready when necessary to offend rather than compromise her principles, Lord unabashedly explains, "I like drawing vicious pictures of people." Among her targets have been President Ronald Reagan, Secretary of Defense Caspar Weinberger, and former Secretary of the Interior James Watt, as well as South African apartheid and the nuclear arms race.

Lord accepts the criticism directed at her graphic commentary with equanimity, terming it "water off the back of a very morally committed duck." This attitude has won her the loyalty of her many readers and the respect of her colleagues; Garry Trudeau, for example, noted that her work shows "a wonderful seditiousness that hasn't been seen since the days of Watergate," while Jules Feiffer has called her "smart, tough, funny, and original."

Don Martin—Few artists' personal styles are as readily identifiable as this cartoonist's has become in the course of his long association with *Mad* magazine. Nicknamed "*Mad*'s maddest artist," Martin is the master of outrageously graphic slapstick, and the proud inventor of a number of preposterous characters, including the devious, unshaven, shrimpish Fester Bestertester and his gigantic, pinheaded companion Karbunkle, the perennially feckless superhero Captain Klutz, and the irresistibly named psychiatrist Dr. Fruitcake P. Fonebone. These and other of Martin's outlandish characters have entered the lexicon of American youth and made their creator a cult figure in many circles.

His cartoons have been called surrealistic, Dadaistic, and anarchistic, but Martin disclaims any intellectual connotations his work might suggest. "The purpose of my cartoons," he states, "has simply been to be comical, both visually and in content. I have never intended any social or political commentary and have only wanted to be funny—the sillier the better."

Norman McLaren—Highly regarded by his peers, McLaren exhibited a fascination with animation beginning in his high school days. He was one of the pioneers of direct drawing on film, having started his work in this vein in 1936 in Britain. Later, while in New York City on commission from the Guggenheim Museum, he made his first abstract, cameraless films. To fit some of his abstract motion patterns, he painted directly on the soundtrack portion of the film, generating percussive musical rhythms and inventing one of his most acclaimed techniques.

McLaren's name became almost synonymous with that of the National Film Board of Canada, with which he was associated beginning in 1941. He made many of his most famous films in Canada, including *Canon, Pas de Deux,* and *Neighbors,* which garnered scores of prestigious awards, including an Oscar and the top prizes at the Venice, Cannes, and London film festivals. McLaren invented "pixilation," a technique for animating live models, and made successful animated films to illustrate complex classical forms in music. His is the most respected name in contemporary animated and experimental film.

Fabian Melgar—The recipient of awards in every major area of his profession, Melgar numbers among his honors seven gold Clio awards, a Society of Illustrators merit award, three gold New York Art Directors Club awards, seven Advertising Club of New York awards, and more than seventy other awards that together acknowledge his work in packaging, advertising, and brochure, poster, and logo design. "I have no specialty," Melgar says. "I do everything in the creative field."

Melgar's most spectacular success came in 1982, when he helped design a small, portable, high-intensity reading lamp intended to be attached to a book. Creating the name "itty bitty book light," he organized an advertising campaign that resulted in a sales phenomenon described as "one of the most remarkable marketing successes in recent years."

Bretislav Pojar—One of the most internationally respected names in the field of animation filmmaking, this Czech animator has made scores of cartoon, cut-out, and puppet films that have delighted children and adult audiences alike. Pojar is a remarkable example of a versatile filmmaker who approaches his creations from two directions simultaneously—that of animator and that of graphic artist. His filmography is outstanding in its consistency and in its abundance of important works, such as *A Drop Too Much, The Lion and the Song, Bombomania, Boom,* and *If.* The recipient of many prestigious awards, including first prizes at the Oberhausen, Venice, Mamaia, and Annecy film festivals, Pojar is the only three-time winner of the coveted Golden Palm in the history of the Cannes Film Festival.

Mort Walker—The creator of *Beetle Bailey,* Walker is currently producing five nationally syndicated newspaper strips that appear daily—a feat unparalleled in the entire history of the comics. In addition to the top-ranked *Beetle Bailey,* they include *Hi and Lois, Boner's Ark, Sam and Silo,* and *The Evermores.* Besides working as a comic strip artist, Walker has found time to pen his humorous memoirs, *Backstage at the Strips,* and, in 1974, to found the Museum of Cartoon Art, which houses and maintains an extensive collection of original comic strips and cartoons, as well as thousands of animated films and an important research library.

In the public mind, however, Mort Walker's name remains permanently linked to that of Beetle Bailey. Walker created the lackadaisical private in 1950, and the strip soon gained unprecedented popularity, earning its author many awards as well as a loyal following. Camp Swampy, Beetle's home base, has become possibly the world's best-known U.S. military outfit, thanks to such outrageous characters as "Sarge" Orville Snorkel, the inept Lieutenant Fuzz, the hapless General Halftrack, and his buxom secretary, Miss Buxley. Consistently ranked among the top five newspaper features, *Beetle Bailey* appears in almost two thousand newspapers around the world.

Chuck Werner—With a cartoon forecasting the fate of Czechoslovakia a week before the signing of the Munich Pact, Werner became the youngest cartoonist to win journalism's highest award, the Pulitzer Prize, in 1939. Having thus established a national reputation as a perceptive and independent-minded political commentator, Werner has maintained and reinforced his standing for a half century with a steady flow of dynamic and expressive editorial cartoons.

Associated with the *Indianapolis Star* since 1947, Werner has received virtually all the awards his profession offers. He is clear about his objectives, stating that a political cartoon must be "a ridicule, a jab, a kick in the pants at a person, place, or thing. You have to go after the negative, the controversial, the dark side of life, yet still try to make a reader smile in the process." Werner's mastery of his craft has earned him the title of "cartoonist's cartoonist."

Gahan Wilson—One of the most distinctive and original comic artists of our time, Wilson has established a reputation as "the mirthful master of the macabre." His cartoons range from such conventional devices as the visual pun to some of the most outlandish grotesques ever committed to paper. In almost all of his work the bizarre predominates: he delights in depicting weird creatures with bulging eyes and hypertrophied heads engaging in gruesome activities. He is the creator of the most frighteningly hilarious gallery of freaks and monsters ever to stride or crawl across a magazine page. Wilson's style—deceptive in its seeming simplicity yet easily recognizable in periodicals from the *New Yorker* to *Playboy*—has helped him become a cultural institution, as firmly placed in the national consciousness as any cartoonist in memory.

Preface

Within recent years, the work of illustrators, animators, cartoonists, designers, and other graphic artists has emerged as an important and lively development in contemporary art. Since their works influence our lives in countless ways each day, graphic artists of all types are subjects of high interest—humor cartoonists drawing for newspapers or for magazines; editorial cartoonists of the left, right, or center; theatrical and televisual animators whose creations are intended for entertainment or commerce; newspaper comic strip artists and story strip creators; comic book and magazine artists; book, magazine, or newspaper illustrators; cover and poster designers; and even artists in developing fields such as computer graphics. Unfortunately, comprehensive biographical and critical information on these popular artists, presented in an easy-to-use format and enhanced with numerous illustrations of their work, is often difficult to find. With the publication of *Contemporary Graphic Artists (CGA)*, Gale Research Company has taken a step toward meeting this need.

Scope

CGA is a comprehensive new biographical, bibliographical, and critical guide that provides detailed information about the lives and accomplishments of noteworthy graphic artists. With more than 100 entries in each annual volume, *CGA* includes biographies on a wide variety of graphic artists—illustrators, animators, cartoonists, designers, and other graphic artists whose work appears in books, newspapers, magazines, film, and other media. Since graphic art shares with fine art the use of symbolic imagery and the broad goals of enlightening, beautifying, and persuading, a number of the artists covered in *CGA* move with equal ease between the commercial art scene and the fine arts.

Primary emphasis is given to modern-day American artists. *CGA* includes major, established figures whose positions in artistic history are assured, as well as new and highly promising individuals, some of whom have yet to be discovered by the public at large. Among the artists featured in *CGA*, Volume 2, are the following:

Graphic designers—Charles Goslin, Fabian Melgar, and Don Weller

Editorial cartoonists—Jim Borgman, L. Draper Hill, Dick Locher, M. G. Lord, Ben Sargent, and Chuck Werner

Magazine cartoonists—Rick Geary, Richard Hess, Bruce John Kleinsmith ("Futzie Nutzle"), Don Martin, and Gahan Wilson

Illustrators of books, magazines, and other publications—Bascove, Bill Charmatz, Alan E. Cober, John Groth, Frances Jetter, and Mel Odom

Newspaper comic strip artists—Zack Mosley, W. B. Park, Jerry Scott, and Mort Walker

Comic book artists—Bernard Krigstein, Harvey Kurtzman, Scott McLeod, and Joshua Quagmire

Animators, animation directors and producers—Howard Beckerman, Norman McLaren, and Bretislav Pojar

To round out this survey of contemporary art, *CGA* also includes foreign artists whose work is well known in the United States, such as Japanese illustrator Hajime Sorayama, Canadian editorial cartoonist Merle R. Tingley, Spanish illustrator Sanjulian (Manuel Perez Clemente), and German-born woodcut artist Dorothea Wiedemann, who is now a citizen of Brazil. To add historical perspective to the series, selected *CGA* sketches record the achievements of outstanding artists of the past whose influence is widely acknowledged by contemporary practitioners. William Hogarth, the eighteenth-century English artist whose works were the first to be called cartoons, the nineteenth-century French caricaturist Honore Daumier, and the illustrator

Howard Pyle and the comic strip artist F. B. Opper from the early twentieth century are examples of such important historical figures. All are included in this volume.

With its broad coverage and detailed entries, *CGA* is designed to assist a variety of users—researchers seeking specific facts, librarians fielding questions, students preparing for classes, teachers drawing up assignments, or general readers looking for information about a favorite artist. Individually, *CGA* sketches present a concise but detailed record of the achievements of a variety of graphic artists. Collectively, *CGA* entries provide a survey of comic art, cartoons, caricature, design, illustration, and animation in their historical, aesthetic, cultural, sociological, ideological, and commercial contexts. It is the editors' hope that from this and future volumes will emerge not only a record of contemporary artistic achievement but also a "bird's eye" view of our times as reflected through the artistic sensibility.

Compilation Methods

The editors make every effort to secure information directly from the artists through questionnaires, correspondence, telephone calls, and, in many cases, personal meetings. If artists of special interest to *CGA* users are deceased or fail to reply to requests for information, material is gathered from other reliable sources. Biographical dictionaries and art encyclopedias are checked, as are bibliographical sources such as *Cumulative Book Index*. Published interviews, feature stories, and reviews are examined, and often material is supplied by the artists' agents, publishers, syndicates, or studios. All sketches, whether prepared from questionnaires or through extensive research, are sent to the artists for review prior to publication.

The editors recognize that entries on particularly active artists may eventually become outdated. To insure *CGA*'s timeliness, future volumes will provide revisions of selected sketches when they require significant change.

Format

CGA entries, modeled after those in the Gale Research Company's highly regarded *Contemporary Authors* series, are written in a clear, readable style with few abbreviations and no limits set on length. So that a reader needing specific information can quickly focus on the pertinent portion of an entry, typical *CGA* listings are clearly divided into topical sections with descriptive rubrics, among them the following:

    Entry Heading—Cites the complete form of the listee's name, followed by birth and death dates, when available. Pseudonyms or name variations under which the artist has issued works are included within parentheses in the second line of the entry heading.

    Personal—Provides date and place of birth, family data, and information about the subject's education, politics, and religion. Home, office, studio, and agent addresses are noted, when available.

    Career—Indicates past and present career positions, with inclusive dates, as well as civic activities and military service.

    Member—Lists professional and social organizations to which the artist belongs.

    Awards, Honors—Notes artistic awards as well as writing awards, military and civic honors, and fellowships and honorary degrees received.

    Writings—Lists published books, syndicated features, illustrated works, and contributions to periodicals, with pertinent bibliographic data.

    Films—Highlights all film work, whether as animator, director, producer, designer, or in some other capacity, along with film production data.

    Exhibitions—Reports both group shows and one-person shows in which the artist's work has been represented, with locations and dates.

    Work in Progress—Notes artistic activity in progress and other projects of all kinds, some of which may result in future publication.

Sidelights—Provides a comprehensive overview of the artists' careers, achievements, and contributions to their chosen fields.

All *CGA* sketches contain sidelights, written by contributors who are knowledgeable about the artists' particular fields and often personally acquainted with the biographees. By filling in the details that make for fascinating biography, sidelights add a personal dimension to the listings and provide informative and enjoyable reading.

Biographical/Critical Sources—Lists newspaper and magazine articles and books containing additional information about the artists and their work.

Illustrations

To provide a visual sampling of the artists' themes and styles, the majority of *CGA* entries are accompanied by numerous illustrations, often chosen by the listees themselves as being among their most representative work. Reflecting the diverse graphic arts covered in these pages, this volume contains a multitude of illustrations—newspaper, magazine, sports, and political cartoons; caricatures; posters; animation frames and sequences; magazine and book illustrations; comic book pages; and newspaper strips. In most cases, these illustrations and the textual material are further complemented by a photogaph or self-portrait of the artist. And some of the self-portraits are unique to *CGA*, having been drawn specially for this series. Among the never-before-published self-portraits included in this volume are those created for *CGA* by M. G. Lord, Scott McLeod, Leonard Rifas, and Karel Saudek. Together, the portraits and copious illustrations that enliven the text not only offer a visual guide to the careers of the artists profiled in *CGA* but also allow for hours of pleasant browsing.

Obituary Notices Make *CGA* Timely and Comprehensive

To be as timely and comprehensive as possible, *CGA* publishes brief obituary notices on recently deceased artists within the scope of the series. These notices provide dates and places of birth and death, highlight the artist's career and works, and list other sources where additional biographical information and obituaries may be found. To distinguish them from full-length sketches, obituaries are identified with the heading "Obituary Notice."

Cumulative Indexing Begins With This Volume

To best serve the needs of a wide variety of users by providing access to the entries in a number of ways, beginning with this volume *CGA* contains cumulative artist, occupation, and subject indexes.

Cumulative Artist Index—Lists alphabetically the names of biographees with their birth and death dates, when available, followed by the number of the volume in which their sketches appear. Obituary notices are clearly identified as such. Cross-references lead the user from pseudonyms or familiar forms of the artists' names to the full names used in the entry headings.

Cumulative Occupation Index—Cites artists, with appropriate volume numbers, alphabetically under their major fields of activity. A reader can thus scan a range of editorial cartoonists, for example, from the conservative Tom Curtis to the liberal Jimmy Margulies or check to see who is active in computer graphics. As the series grows, *CGA*'s detailed, illustrated entries will provide an increasingly comprehensive overview of the major fields within the graphic arts.

Cumulative Subject Index—Who created the Green Giant advertising symbol? Whose animation has won an Academy Award? What cartoonists are responsible for giving birth to the characters Captain Klutz and Alfred E. Neuman? Which artists have been associated with Push Pin Studio? Answers to these and numerous other questions can be found through the Cumulative Subject Index.

This index includes references to well-known characters and works, major awards, key syndicates representing the artists, and important studios, publications, and associations cited in *CGA* entries. Under each subject heading in the index are listed those artists who have had a significant connection with each topic and the volume number in which their entries appear. With citations ranging from "Academy Awards" to "Yogi Bear," the Cumulative Subject Index not only allows users to answer specific questions when they lack an artist's name to start their search but also invites browsing, permitting readers to discover topics they may wish to explore further.

Acknowledgments

The editor would like to extend special and sincere thanks to Mr. Terry Brown of the Society of Illustrators for his help in recommending American illustrators for inclusion in *CGA*.

Suggestions Are Welcome

If readers would like to suggest people to be covered in future *CGA* volumes, they are encouraged to send these names (along with addresses, if possible) to the editor. Other suggestions and comments are also most welcome and should be addressed to: The Editor, *Contemporary Graphic Artists*, Gale Research Company, 150 E. 50th St., New York, NY 10022.

Contemporary
Graphic Artists

Contemporary Graphic Artists

ADDISON
   See WALKER, (Addison) Mort(on)

* * *

ANDERSON, William T. 1936-

PERSONAL: Born December 13, 1936, in Minneapolis, Minn.; son of Bill Robert (an activities coordinator) and Evelyn (Marsh) Anderson; married Carolyn Kiegly (an artist and teacher), May, 1978; children: Susanne, Chris, Joel Giedt, Annie, Brighton, Brandon. *Education:* Attended El Camino College, 1959-60; Chaffey College, A.A., 1964; California State College (now University) at Los Angeles, B.A. and M.A., 1967. *Politics:* Republican. *Religion:* Church of Jesus Christ of Latter-Day Saints. *Home:* 1451 Stromberg Ave., Arcata, Calif. 95521. *Office:* Art Department, Humboldt State University, Arcata, Calif. 95521.

CAREER: Artist and printmaker, 1959—; professor, 1967—, chairman of art department, 1983—, Humboldt State University, Arcata, Calif. Chief reader for Educational Testing Services, 1984—.

MEMBER: Redwood Art Association, Ink People Printmaking Club.

AWARDS, HONORS: Awards include honorable mention from Los Angeles Printmaking Society, 1967; Best of Show Award from Redwood Art Association, 1970 and 1982; Museum Purchase Award from Downey Museum of Art, 1972; Juror's Choice selection by Springville Museum of Art, 1984.

EXHIBITIONS—All one-man shows: Ingomar Gallery, Eureka, Calif., 1968; College of the Redwoods, Eureka, 1968; Humboldt Gallery, San Francisco, Calif., 1969; Graphics Gallery, San Francisco, 1970, 1972, and 1974; Media Gallery, Orange, Calif., 1971; University of Montana, Missoula, Mont., 1973; Graphics Gallery, Los Angeles, Calif., 1974; Jambalaya, Arcata, Calif., 1976, 1977, and 1978; Main Gallery, University of Puget Sound, Tacoma, Wash., 1979; "Travels in the Far West: A William T. Anderson Retrospective," Coastlands Gallery, Eureka, 1986.

Group shows include those at Lytton Center for the Visual Arts, Los Angeles, Calif., 1967; Boller Gallery, San Francisco, Calif., 1971; Whitney Museum of American Art, New York City, 1972; Brooklyn Museum, Brooklyn, N.Y., 1972; International Graphics Exhibition, Ljubljana, Yugoslavia, 1972, 1973; Cincinnati Art Museum, Cincinnati, Ohio, 1973; Springfield Art Museum, Springfield, Ill., 1973; Print Club of Philadelphia, Philadelphia, Pa., 1973; Biennial Exhibition

WILLIAM T. ANDERSON

of Graphic Art, Segovia, Spain, 1974; International Art Fair, Cologne, Germany, 1977. Represented in "The National Screenprint Show," which originated at Old Dominion University Gallery, Norfolk, Va., in 1985 and will tour the United States for two years.

WORK IN PROGRESS: A continuing series of mixed media painting/prints; a series of slide lectures on the work of American landscape artist Thomas Moran; a slide lecture on native American bead work; "an investigation of the causes of *Artificeum Recombinant Tribulatus Syndrome* or A.R.T.S.—this research hopes to answer the universal question that has puzzled mankind for ages: namely, why do some people become artists."

SIDELIGHTS: A printmaker, painter, educator, and lecturer for two decades, William T. Anderson is best known for his depictions of the Old West, the West of myth and legend as well as of actual geography. His larger-than-life prints reflect the larger-than-life place this region occupies in the American psyche; he likes to quote American filmmaker John Ford's admonition, "If myth and reality conflict, print the myth." Anderson's work in this domain has received

Wild Flowers and Desert Tenements, **ca. 1980** (© William T. Anderson. Reprinted by permission.)

considerable attention and has been widely exhibited in the United States and abroad.

Anderson's primary medium since the late 1960s has been the silkscreen. He works through the technique of reverse printing/painting on clear sheets of plexiglass, using inks of acrylic lacquer especially formulated for plastics. (Because he is working on the "back" side, everything is in reverse. He applies the foreground or "front" image first, working toward the "background." As the work progresses, the successive images are covered over with opaque masking; only when the work is completed does the artist remove the front masking to reveal the whole.) In addition to silkscreen, he uses other image-making processes, such as air-brush through stencil, collage, and transfer techniques.

In a statement about his work (self-mockingly titled "In Which I Expose Some of My Profoundest Thoughts and Deepest Fantasies about the Western Mystique") Anderson wrote: "George Catlin had been a practicing artist before 1824, but it wasn't until the summer of that year, when a delegation of Indians from the wilds of the Far West visited Philadelphia that he determined to make his lifework the recording of 'the history and custom of such a people, preserved by pictorial illustration.' Like George Catlin I can determine the beginning of my art career almost to the day and hour: in 1945, at about the age of nine, while living in

Arizona with my uncle, I saw for the first time the great Fourth of July Indian Dances at Flagstaff. I have been drawing Indians ever since.

"In those happy pre-population boom days Arizona was still 'old Arizona.' The Navahoes in their traditional dress would arrive in town for the annual celebration in endless lines of covered wagons stretched out along Highway 66. Many old-timers would drop by our house and tell tall tales about 'the good old days' long into the night: I didn't get much sleep during those times as I had to crane my head through the bedroom doorway in order to listen in.

"Down in the red rock of Oak Creek Canyon near Sedona, John Wayne was just finishing his latest Western movie, *The Angel and the Badman.* Even with all that Hollywood hubbub Oak Creek was still a quiet place with few people around; and Sedona was definitely a one-street town with only a couple of old buildings along the road. We could fish for trout almost anywhere along the creek, and we could even drink the water. Although much has changed, my annual pilgrimage to this fantasyland is still like going home."

Anderson reflected on the relation of past and present: "The more rapidly we race toward the stars, the more ancient our recent past becomes. Like fence posts that blur together as they recede into the distance, the early Hollywood Westerns seem so much closer to the times they depict; and, like Buffalo Bill's Wild West shows, the early Western films had real cowboys and old-time Indians among their cast. It is good to know that many authentic westerners have helped to create the myths we enjoy so much today.

"The blurring of the real and the unreal, the new and the old, contrasting opposites, and the effortless transitions between them are what my work is about. Specifically I try to recapture that undefinable neutral zone where neither fantasy nor reality is firmly established, yet where both appear one. At least I hope the best of my work contains some of that elusive quality."

BIOGRAPHICAL/CRITICAL SOURCES: Who's Who in American Art, Bowker, 1984; Les Krantz, *American Artists*, Facts on File, 1985.

* * *

ASHER, Lila Oliver 1921-

PERSONAL: Born November 15, 1921, in Philadelphia, Pa.; daughter of Benjamin O. (a physician) and Mollie (Finkelstein) Oliver; married Sidney S. Asher, May 5, 1946 (died, February 28, 1974); married Kenneth P. Crawford, April 26, 1980; children: (first marriage) Bonnie Asher Doar, Warren Oliver. *Education:* Graduated from Philadelphia College of Art, 1943; studied at Graphic Sketch Club and with Frank B. A. Linton in Philadelphia, and with Gonippi Raggi in Orange, N.J. *Home:* 4100 Thornapple St., Chevy Chase, Md. 20815. *Office:* College of Fine Arts, Howard University, Washington, D.C. 20059.

LILA OLIVER ASHER

Persephone II, **a collagraph, ca. 1982** (© Lila Oliver Asher. Reprinted by permission.)

CAREER: Painter and printmaker, 1946—; instructor in art, Howard University, Washington, D.C., 1947-51; instructor in art, Wilson Teachers College, Washington, D.C., 1953-54; instructor, 1961-64, assistant professor, 1964-66, associate professor, 1966-71, professor of art, 1971—, Howard University, Washington, D.C. Guest artist at University of Texas, 1972. Gave lectures and workshop demonstrations in Japan and India under auspices of U.S. Information Agency, 1973-74. *Wartime service:* Volunteer for United Service Organizations (U.S.O.) camp shows during World War II; did over thirty-five hundred charcoal sketches of members of the U.S. Armed Forces.

MEMBER: American Association of University Professors, Artists Equity, Society of Washington Artists, Washington Print Club, Print Club of Philadelphia.

AWARDS, HONORS: Invited to live and work in Wolfsburg Castle by City of Wolfsburg, Germany, 1968, 1971, 1975, and 1981; honoree of School Graphics Exhibit at National Museum of American Art, Washington, D.C., 1981.

EXHIBITIONS—One-woman shows: Barnett-Aden Gallery, Washington, D.C., 1951; William C. Blood Gallery, Philadelphia, Pa., 1955; Arts Club, Washington, D.C., 1957; Collectors Gallery, Washington, D.C., 1959; Garrett Park Public Library, Garrett Park, Md., 1960; Art Shop, Silver Spring, Md., 1961; Burr Galleries, New York City, 1963; Potters House, Washington, D.C., 1963; Gallery Two Twenty Two, El Paso, Tex., 1967; Thomson Gallery, New York City, 1968; B'nai B'rith Headquarters, Washington, D.C., 1969.

University of Virginia, Charlottesville, Va., 1970; Green-Field Gallery, El Paso, Tex., 1972; (retrospective) Franz Bader Gallery, Washington, D.C., 1972; American Club, Tokyo, Japan, 1973; U.S. Information Service, Bombay, India, 1974; Iran-American Society, Teheran, Iran, 1974; (retrospective) Fisk University, Nashville, Tenn., 1974; U.S.

Mother and Child IV, **a linoleum block print, ca. 1983**
(© Lila Oliver Asher. Reprinted by permission.)

Information Service, Calcutta, Bombay, and Madras, India, 1975; U.S. Information Service, Karachi, Lahore, and Islamabad, Pakistan, 1975; U.S. Information Service, Ankara and Adana, Turkey, 1976; Via Gambaro Gallery, Washington, D.C., 1976; Gallery Kormendy, Alexandria, Va., 1978; (retrospective) Howard University, Washington D.C., 1978; Washington Hebrew Congregation, Washington, D.C., 1979; Northeastern University, Boston, Mass., 1980; National Museum of History, Taipei, Taiwan, 1982; Kastrupsamlingen Museum, Copenhagen, Denmark, 1982; Gallaudet College, Washington, D.C., 1985; Mickelson Gallery, Washington, D.C., 1986.

Group shows include those at Pennsylvania Academy of Fine Arts, Corcoran Gallery of Art, Library of Congress, Baltimore Museum of Art, and Rochester Museum. Work represented in permanent collections of the National Museum of American Art, the Corcoran Gallery, and the National Museum of History in Taipei, Taiwan.

SIDELIGHTS: If there is a constant in Lila Oliver Asher's art, it is her strong yet subtle depiction of universal themes, whether derived from mythology, the Bible, or the common well of human experience: *Joseph and His Brethren, Eve, Jacob and Esau,* and *Narcissus* are indicative titles of some of her prints. One of her most recurrent themes is that of mother and child, which she treats without mawkishness and with grace and understatement. Working in the medium of the linoleum cut (in which the image from a previously cut and inked piece of linoleum is transferred to paper), Asher displays a sharp line and a simple, uncluttered way of handling her subjects, while her figures express a definite rhythm in pose and gesture.

Asher's work has been widely exhibited in this country and abroad. In the mid-1970s the U.S. Information Agency arranged for a series of shows in India, Pakistan, and Turkey, where her prints were well received and favorably reviewed. She has also done portraits of notable Americans, including Congressman James Auchincloss and Justice Harold H. Burton. Asher's work is represented in the permanent collections of museums in the United States and Taiwan and is displayed in the U.S. embassy buildings in Mexico City and Tel Aviv. In addition, her murals can be seen in many public and private buildings throughout the eastern United States.

BIOGRAPHICAL/CRITICAL SOURCES: Dictionary of International Biography, International Publications Service, 1980; *Who's Who of American Women,* Marquis, 1984; *Who's Who in American Art,* Bowker, 1984.

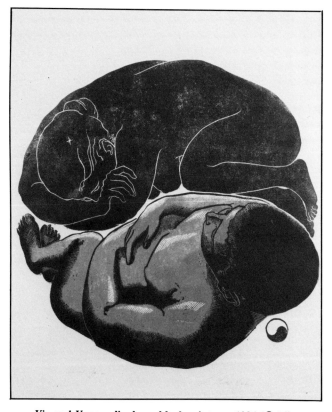

Yin and Yang, **a linoleum block print, ca. 1984** (© Lila Oliver Asher. Reprinted by permission.)

An editorial cartoon by Ed Ashley, ca. 1983 (© *Toledo Blade*. Reprinted courtesy of *Toledo Blade*.)

ASHLEY, Ed(ward J.)   1922-

PERSONAL: Born May 5, 1922, in Milan, Ohio; son of George (a railroad engineer) and Dorothy (Stein) Ashley; married Audrey Zinser (an artist) in 1949. *Education:* Pratt Institute, B.A., 1953. *Politics:* Independent. *Home:* 4390 E. Terrace Circle, Port Clinton, Ohio 43452. *Office:* Toledo *Blade*, 541 Superior St., Toledo, Ohio 43660.

CAREER: Commercial artist, *Toledo Blade*, Toledo, Ohio, 1946-49; artist and cartoonist, Denver, Colo., 1953-66; commercial artist, *Toledo Blade*, Toledo, 1966-72, editorial cartoonist, 1972-85, staff artist, 1985—. *Military service:* U.S. Army Air Forces, 1942-46.

SIDELIGHTS: After graduating from Pratt Institute, Ed Ashley lived a dozen years in Colorado, sometimes working as staff artist in the advertising department of the *Denver Post*, until he returned to the *Toledo Blade* in 1966 as one of their commercial artists. In 1972 he took over the editorial cartoonist's job left by Larry Barton, a position he held until 1985.

Much influenced by fellow cartoonists C. D. Batchelor, Jim Berryman, and Bill Mauldin, Ashley's drawings cover the whole range of social and political subjects, whether infla-

tion and the high cost of groceries, fuel shortages, worthless job retraining programs, or inane solutions to problems, as in the 1983 cartoon of what to do with five billion Carter-era gasoline coupons: "We'll print up five billion 'Null and Void' stickers and paste 'em on each one!" More moving is his depiction of boxer Jack Dempsey at the Pearly Gates asking for his formidable opponent Gene Tunney.

Ed Ashley has the sharpness of a born observer and an unerring eye for detail, as well as the no-nonsense directness of caption brevity: Husband to wife looking at a flying saucer in night sky declares, "They *must* be intelligent! They never land."

The man who describes himself as "generally obstreperous and unpleasant" perhaps took Bill Mauldin's prescription for the effective cartoonist too much to heart ("Indignation, sorrow, wrath, and even remorse should so disquiet a good cartoonist's mile-and-a-half of intestines that he will rush through the darkness looking for the bastards"), for following a dispute over editorial policy Ashley was replaced on the editorial page by Kirk Walters, although he still remains at the paper in another artistic capacity.

BIOGRAPHICAL/CRITICAL SOURCES: Syd Hoff, *Editorial and Political Cartooning*, Stravon, 1976.

Self-portrait of Ed Ashley (© Ed Ashley. Reprinted by permission.)

B

BACALL, Aaron 1939-

PERSONAL: Born April 4, 1939, in Brooklyn, N.Y.; son of Saul (a furrier) and Yetta (Schwartz) Bacall; married Linda Gold (a teacher), May 2, 1965; children: Darron. *Education:* City College of the City University of New York, B.S., 1961; New York University, M.S., 1963; attended Art Students League, New York, 1964; New York University, M.A., 1971. *Home:* 204 Arlene St., Staten Island, N.Y. 10314.

CAREER: Research chemist, Hoffman–LaRoche Laboratories, Nutley, N.J., 1961-68; chemistry teacher, 1963—, curriculum researcher, 1974-77, Brooklyn Board of Education, Brooklyn, N.Y. Free-lance cartoonist and humorous illustrator, ca. 1965—; creator of self-syndicated business cartoon panel, 1985—.

MEMBER: Graphic Artists Guild, Cartoonists Association.

WRITINGS: (Illustrator) Durk Pearson and Sandy Shaw, *Life Extension,* Warner Books, 1982; (contributor of cartoons) Sam Gross, editor, *Why Are Your Papers in Order? Cartoons for 1984,* Avon, 1983; (illustrator) Pearson and Shaw, *Life Extension Companion,* Warner Books, 1984; (contributor of cartoons) S. Gross, editor, *Cats, Cats, Cats,* Harper, 1985.

Author of monthly "Toontalk" column for *Modern Cartooning,* 1981—. Contributor of cartoon panels to *Staten Island Advance.*

EXHIBITIONS: Federal Plaza Building, New York, N.Y., 1983; Snug Harbor Newhouse Gallery, Staten Island, N.Y., 1983-84; Master Eagle Gallery, New York City, 1984; Cambridge Library Art Gallery, Harvard University, Cambridge, Mass., 1984; Master Eagle Gallery, May-June, 1985.

WORK IN PROGRESS: Contributing cartoons to *Dogs, Dogs, Dogs,* edited by Sam Gross, publication by Harper expected in 1986.

SIDELIGHTS: Aaron Bacall has carved out for himself a special niche in the little-worked area of big-business humor. His cartoons on the subject appear in many newspapers and magazines in the United States, including both such specialized periodicals as the *Wall Street Journal* and popular newspapers like the *National Enquirer* and the Westchester, N.Y., Gannett newspapers. Since May, 1985, he has syndicated his business-oriented panels and distributed them to newspapers across the nation. Cartoons and humorous illustrations from what New York's *Staten Island Advance* calls Bacall's "skilled pen and bright imagination" have appeared in *Popular Mechanics, Saturday Evening Post, Psychology Today, Saturday Review,* and *Woman's World,* as

well as in such trade and technical journals as *Medical Economics, American Bar Association Journal, National Law Journal,* and *Datamation.*

A lover of cartoons since early childhood, Bacall used to write fan letters to cartoonists and still treasures a reply he received from Mort Walker. An original *Beetle Bailey* comic strip that Walker sent the admiring youngster hangs on the wall in Bacall's home on Staten Island.

After receiving an M.S. degree in chemistry from New York University in 1963, Bacall determined to become a professional cartoonist and enrolled at the Art Students League in New York. A year of study there enabled him to make his first sale, a cartoon purchased by a religious publishing company for ten dollars. It was a humble beginning, but it encouraged him to persevere.

Bacall's training as a chemist provided him with a secure financial setting for his artistic aspirations. He worked as a

Courtesy of Aaron Bacall

AARON BACALL

research chemist for seven years before accepting a position teaching chemistry in a Brooklyn high school. He continues to teach, but his work as a cartoonist and illustrator has increasingly grown to become a full second career. In addition to his cartoons, he provides illustrations for industry and business, all in a cartoon-like style. His clients include such prestigious firms as Citicorp, Warner-Lambert, Metropolitan Life Insurance, Hearst Publishing, and Harper & Row. In his hometown newspaper, the *Staten Island Advance*, he publishes a regular cartoon panel in the Sunday "Perspective" section and another in the Tuesday business section. Since 1981 he has contributed a monthly column, "Toontalk," to the trade journal *Modern Cartooning*.

"I most enjoy doing cartoons with a business slant," Bacall reports, and the largest share of his work features business as its theme. A banker in a typical Bacall cartoon offers a couple an "hourly-adjustable mortgage," for example. In another a patient asks his doctor if his blood pressure is bullish or bearish. The cliches of big business are employed in unlikely contexts that reveal the emptiness underlying many of them.

Business is not the only subject of Bacall's cartoons however. His work features a complete spectrum of cartoon topics including many traditional ones, though often with a contemporary twist. Parents have the usual problems with their adolescent children. ("My son is away at college," one matron confides to another in a Bacall cartoon. "He's majoring in communications, but he never writes or calls!") Television intrudes on our consciousness. ("Good evening

"Remember, this is only a stock tip and is neither an offer to sell nor a solicitation of an offer to buy these securities. Such an offer is made by the prospectus only."

A humor cartoon (© 1984, Aaron Bacall. Reprinted by permission.)

and welcome to public television," an announcer says from the box. "Our programming begins right after this message of guilt.")

Bacall does rough sketches in soft pencil before attempting a final inked version. He is constantly searching for the perfect drawing pen, and has tried "about a million" different kinds in his quest. He now uses Koh-i-noor's Roto-ring art pen, a refillable sketch pen with a flexible nib which gives him control of the width of line.

Whether dealing with business or with other themes, Bacall uses his art to make a point. What he values in his profession is the opportunity to make a direct statement efficiently, with the economy that only a graphic medium affords. He told *CGA*: "Cartooning is such an 'immediate' art form. That's what I like most about it. It cuts through the excess verbiage and tells the story, often in one picture. When I sit down to create a cartoon, all stress vaporizes. The creative process seems to call forth the brain's natural opiates. I most love cartoons that prick the balloons that society sends up in an effort to self-glorify its actions." In all his work in cartooning and humorour illustration, Becall takes advantage of the chance to make his satirical point with precision, economy, and wit.

* * *

"Is my blood pressure bullish or bearish?"

A humor cartoon (© 1980, Aaron Bacall. Reprinted by permission.)

BADIA ROMERO, Enrique 1930-
(Enrique Romero)

PERSONAL: Born April 24, 1930, in Barcelona, Spain; son of Enrique (an urban planner) and Camila (Romero) Badia; married Anna Maria Ejarque Barderi (an office worker),

A strip from *Axa* by Enrique Badia Romero (© 1980, Romero Associates. Reprinted by permission.)

February 8, 1958; children: Enrique, Anna, Ricardo, Alberto. *Education*: Studied business administration at a private school, Barcelona, 1948-50.

Home: Junta de Comercio, 18, 08001 Barcelona, Spain. *Agent*: Bardon Art, Avenida de las Cortes Catalanas, 806, Barcelona, Spain; Selecciones Ilustradas, Diagonal, 325, 08009 Barcelona, Spain; Herb Spiers, S.I. International, 43 E. 19th St., New York, N.Y. 10003.

CAREER: Comic strip artist under the name Enrique Romero, Barcelona, Spain, 1951—, for series including *Lillian, azafata del aire* (title means "Lillian, Daredevil of the Air"), 1958-61, *World*, 1967-69, *Modesty Blaise*, 1970-78, *Eric Keller*, 1974-76, *Rahan*, 1975-83, *Axa*, 1978-85, *Wendy and Kathy*, 1986—. Also worked as director of a correspondence course in cartoon and comic drawing, 1951, collecting card illustrator, 1955-57, fashion illustrator, 1959, and advertising artist, 1960-62. *Military service*: Spanish Army, 1950-53, served in Engineer Corps.

AWARDS, HONORS: Award from Society of Strip Illustration, London, England, 1979.

WRITINGS—All books of comics: (With Peter O'Donell) *Modesty Blaise*, Ken Pierce, 1980; (with Donne Avenell) *Axa*, Vols. 1-7, Ken Pierce, 1981-86.

WORK IN PROGRESS: Developing a new comic strip for the British market; doing illustration work.

SIDELIGHTS: As did so many other Spanish artists, Enrique Romero worked mainly for foreign publishers during the 1960s, and especially for the British market, where he specialized in romance comics with no artistic pretensions. But, unlike the great majority of his compatriots at the time, he promptly succeeded in imposing himself as a first-class artist in this market, breaking into the newspaper comics field, and maintaining his position for a very long time.

Romero had previously drawn such series as *Lillian, azafata del aire* (title means "Lillian, Daredevil of the Air") for publication in Spain and *World* for release in England. Upon the death in February, 1970, of Jim Holdaway, the artist on the famous daily strip *Modesty Blaise*, the London newspaper *Evening Standard* signed up Romero (who was then drawing a daily panel, *Isometrics*, on a physical exercise theme) to succeed him. Romero adapted himself perfectly to the style of his predecessor (this had been a primary requirement for the task) and brilliantly continued to depict Modesty's adventures until 1978. The international fame that he garnered thereby helped him get work from other countries, such as *Satana* (1973) which he did for Marvel Comics and *It Returns!* (1974) for Warren, both in the United States, as well as the series *Eric Keller* for Germany and *Rahan* for France.

Romero's apprenticeship in the field of romance comics, with its emphasis on the female face and the female body, stood him in good stead when he came to draw *Modesty Blaise*, and the strip, in return, confirmed him as an expert in both the craft of drawing a daily strip and the skill of depicting a feminine protagonist. This in turn brought about a new series that demonstrated both these talents.

Romero himself explains how this came about: "In early 1978 I began work on a creation of my own. I've always wished, as every professional does, to design a story in my own way, without getting instructions from an editor or a scriptwriter. I started to cook up an idea about a new character whose adventures would take place in a world devastated by a nuclear holocaust. After sketching out a synopsis of the story I drew a poster in which I expressed my ideas graphically. The London daily *Sun* accepted my outline, but with a substantial twist: the protagonist had to be a woman with a great deal of sexiness, fearlessness, adorableness, rebelliousness, as well as a total lack of inhibitions."

Romero's English representative persuaded him to enlist the services of a good scriptwriter, and Donne Avenell took up the writing of the *Axa* series, which debuted in the *Sun* on July 4, 1978. Romero found it impossible to draw two different daily strips at the same time, and he soon abandoned *Modesty Blaise* to devote himself fully to his new creation, which rapidly gained in popularity and started getting distribution outside of Britain.

Axa combined eroticism (through the constant half-nakedness of its beautiful heroine) and fantasy adventure, with sword-and-sorcery and science-fiction elements thrown in. Romero's graphic style followed the classic line of such masters of British comic art as Frank Bellamy and Jim Holdaway; its major virtue lay in its ability to create bold compositions, with much imaginative use of black-and-white contrasts to increase tension and enhance the dramatic power of the narrative. These qualities had already existed in his treatment of *Modesty Blaise*, but they found their perfect expression in *Axa*.

In the meantime, however, attacks upon *Axa*'s alleged immorality and display of violence had steadily mounted, and despite its success, on November 16, 1985, the *Sun* decided to drop the strip in mid-episode (a prose epilogue was hastily concocted). This cavalier treatment brought protests from Axa's admirers in Europe and in the United States (where reprints of her adventures had appeared with great success in book form), and the feature may yet be revived in some other format.

Currently Romero is doing a series of weekly comic pages based on a new character, *Dark*, for an Italian magazine. He has also created a daily strip, *Wendy and Kathy*, which runs in a Spanish tourist publication called *Holiday Maker & Resident News*; the daily is supplemented by a weekly page of drawings of women titled *Romero y sus Chicas* (title means "Romero and His Girls").

BIOGRAPHICAL/CRITICAL SOURCES: Javier Coma, editor, *Historia de los Comics*, Toutain (Barcelona), 1983.

* * *

BARRETT, Jack
  See BARRETT, John

* * *

BARRETT, John 1929-
  (Jack Barrett)

PERSONAL: Born November 5, 1929, in Pittsburgh, Pa.; son of John Samuel (a banker) and Mary Margaret

JOHN BARRETT

Photograph by Tony Lopez, St. Petersburg Times-Evening Independent. Courtesy of John Barrett.

(McBride) Barrett; married Louise Monique Ladouceur (a registered nurse), February 23, 1985; children: (by a former wife) Stephanie Centanni. *Education:* Attended Carnegie Institute, 1944-45; graduated from the Art Institute of Pittsburgh, 1954. *Home:* 5729 Calais Blvd., St. Petersburg, Fla. 33714. *Office:* News Art Department, *St. Petersburg Times*, P.O. Box 1121, St. Petersburg, Fla. 33701. *Agent:* Salomon's Fine Arts Gallery, St. Petersburg, Fla.

CAREER: Advertising artist, Reuter & Bragdon Advertising Agency, Pittsburgh, Pa., 1955-57; free-lance advertising artist and illustrator at various agencies and art studios, 1957-65; illustrator, Mel Richman Advertising Agency, Philadelphia, Pa., 1965-66; instructor, Ivy School of Art, Pittsburgh, Pa., 1966-69; illustrator, *St. Petersburg Times*, St. Petersburg, Fla., 1969—. Free-lance illustrator for *Congressional Quarterly*, 1975-1980. *Military service:* U.S. Marine Corps, 1948-52, served in Korea; became sergeant; awarded the Purple Heart.

MEMBER: National Cartoonists Society, Art Center of St. Petersburg, Fla.

AWARDS, HONORS: First Award, for Satirical Art, Pittsburgh Advertising Artists, 1959; First and Third Awards in Newspaper Illustration, *St. Petersburg Times*, 1971, 1972, 1973, 1975; First Award in the Florida Newspaper Illustrations and Cartoonist Contest, University of Florida College of Journalism and Communications, 1985.

WRITINGS: Hands Down (book of cartoons), Ivy School of Art, n.d.; *Laxative* (book of cartoons), Ivy School of Art, n.d.; (illustrator) Roy Peter Clark, editor, *Best Newspaper*

Writing (annual vols.), Modern Media Institute, 1981—. Contributor of cartoons and illustrations to periodicals.

EXHIBITIONS: St. Petersburg Art Center, St. Petersburg, Fla., 1982; Salomon's Fine Arts Gallery, St. Petersburg, 1983; Salomon's Gallery, Door County, Wisconsin, 1985.

WORK IN PROGRESS: Preparing a one-man show of expressionist paintings and drawings of people and night life of St. Petersburg, planned for 1986.

SIDELIGHTS: Jack Barrett's diversified body of work has included news feature illustration, sports cartoons, political caricatures, show business portraits, and humorous art, as well as "serious" paintings. His style ranges as widely as his subjects, from meticulous representationalism to free expressionism and from subtle caricature to the broadest "bigfoot" cartooning. If there is a unifying theme in all of his many-faceted work, it is the artist's constant striving to capture and fix the transient. "What art is about," Barrett states, is "to record a likeness [or] a gesture in a dramatic spontaneous moment."

Barrett has drawn continuously since the age of seven. Drawing is his primary artistic discipline; his principal advice to those about to enter the field is: "To begin, you must have a foundation in drawing." He first studied drawing in a special program for artistic youngsters at the Carnegie Institute in Pittsburgh, while still in his early teens, and went on from there to the Art Institute of Pittsburgh. After graduation with a solid academic foundation in art, Barrett became an advertising artist, and for ten years he freelanced for various advertising agencies and art studios. A sense of the dramatic always pervaded his work and his artistic outlook. In 1965 his theatrical instincts were given a practical outlet when he played one of the "living dead" in George Romero's cult classic film *Night of the Living Dead*.

In 1966, he left the uncertainties of the free-lance art world to begin a three-year stint as an instructor at the Ivy School of Art in Pittsburgh. During this time he published two collections of cartoons, *Hands Down* and *Laxative*. It was in 1969, however, that Jack Barrett found the natural outlet for his varied and distinctive talents. In that year he became an illustrator for the *St. Petersburg Times* in Florida, and he has remained in this post ever since. His work has also appeared in such national periodicals as the *Congressional Quarterly*. Since 1981 his portraits have been featured in the annual publication *Best Newspaper Writing*.

It is the human face that fascinates Barrett above all and receives his major attention. He renders his portraits expressively and dramatically, with bold lines and forceful modeling. The faces that appear in his work may be precisely rendered with finely detailed tonal cross-hatching and subtle shading, suggestive of the caricatures of David Levine, or they may be done in a free expressionistic style when the subject seems to call for it. Barrett is never locked into a mannered style. Another piece of advice he offers beginners is: "Be yourself, and of course have something to say." His portraits fully obey both injunctions, making forceful statements or ironic digs with their incisive lines and dynamic modeling. Even in his whimsical caricatures of show business personalities he adds such ironic cartoonist-touches as depicting Johnny Carson leaning insouciantly on a pile of money bags. His weekly illustrations for the *St. Petersburg Times* TV Guide section affords him the opportunity to employ his gifts at such fanciful portraiture.

Described by Ken Muse in *The Total Cartoonist* as "a master of his profession . . . to be admired by those who enter the profession," Barrett has developed a highly organized and methodical procedure for his work. He never works on more than one drawing at a time, and paces his work to produce one piece a day or more as needed. He works with a 4H pencil and a soft eraser for preliminary sketches if he has time, using ink directly on board or four-

ply Strathmore if he doesn't. He uses a Crowquill penpoint for drawing and a Speedball for lettering, and applies wash with number 2 to 4 brushes if required. He never traces on a light box, but resorts to benday shading when it is appropriate. He is a fully professional newspaperman, and adapts his medium, style, and work schedule to the demands of the assignment. If there is no time to make sketches, Barrett composes in his mind, and he reports that he seldom makes

A portrait of Bishop Desmond Tutu (© 1984, J. Barrett. Reprinted by permission.)

roughs. His work, however, is not facile, and a single panel may take him as long as five hours to produce.

Painstaking as he is, however, he is deeply involved with his work and finds his profoundest personal expression in it. He names drawing and painting as his hobbies. A lover of travel, he takes yearly painting trips to Haiti, Ireland, England, and Canada. Barrett told *CGA:* "I draw and paint because I must. It is all-consuming, a compulsion."

The precision of Barrett's draughtsmanship and his mastery of line appear even in his most ephemeral work and reveal the attention he gives to accuracy of representation. Never superficial even when most loose and spontaneous in style, his portraits are carefully conceived and executed. "The artist is best served," he states, "by a study of past traditions and disciplines." Although he has dedicated himself to the exacting task of capturing the fleeting moment on paper, his work clearly reveals the devotion he feels for past tradition and the great personal discipline he brings to it.

BIOGRAPHICAL/CRITICAL SOURCES: National Cartoonists Society Album, 1980; Ken Muse, *The Total Cartoonist*, Prentice-Hall, 1983; Roy Paul Nelson, *Humorous Illustration and Cartooning: A Guide for Editors, Advertisers, and Artists*, Prentice-Hall, 1984.

—*Sketch by Dennis Wepman*

* * *

BASCOVE 1946-

PERSONAL: Known professionally by surname alone; born April 4, 1946, in Philadelphia, Pa.; daughter of Leonard and Lillian (Hechter) Bascove. *Education:* Attended Philadelphia Museum College of Art, 1964-68. *Studio:* 319 E. 52nd St., New York, N.Y. 10022.

CAREER: Graphic designer, artist, and illustrator, 1967—. Contributing artist for department of anthropology and staff artist for Peabody Museum at Yale University, 1970-72; project manager and contributing artist for U.S. Department of Education in Washington, D.C., 1974-75.

AWARDS, HONORS: Silver Medal from New York Art Directors Club, 1975; numerous awards for excellence from Society of Illustrators, New York City; many other awards.

WRITINGS—Illustrator: Marlo Thomas et al., *Free to Be . . . You and Me*, McGraw, 1974; Fyodor Dostoevsky, *Crime and Punishment*, Eastern Press, 1975; Euslin, *The Green Hero*, Four Winds, 1975; Anton Chekhov, *Short Stories*, Franklin Library, 1986. Cover illustrator for books by Macmillan, Doubleday, Crown, Random House, Viking, and other publishers.

Contributor of illustrations to U.S. and foreign periodicals, including *Atlantic Monthly, Harper's, Redbook, New York Times, Esquire, Ms., Fortune,* and *Marie-Claire.*

EXHIBITIONS—All group shows unless otherwise noted: (One-woman show) Art Directors Club, New York City, 1980; "Political Art Exhibition," Marymount College, New York City, 1982; Martin-Molinary Art & Design Gallery, New York City, 1982 and 1983; Facchetti-Burke Gallery, New York City, 1983; Barron Arts Center, Woodbridge, N.Y., 1985; Galerie du Soir, Paris, France, 1985 and 1986;

BASCOVE

James Hunt Barker Gallery, Nantucket, Mass., 1985, Palm Beach, Fla., 1986.

SIDELIGHTS: The definitive qualities of a Bascove illustration—a concern with hidden or repressed feelings, a sophisticated sense of humor, and an impressive command of the vocabulary of visual metaphor—are all abundantly in evidence in her book jackets and drawings. Frequently working in woodcuts, Bascove expresses her attraction to this medium in terms that suggest an aggressive rather than a passive temperament: "It's a very sensual medium. You're actually working on a piece of sculpture which is three-dimensional even though the finished product is only two-dimensional. I find that physical involvement very satisfying." Moreover, the woodcut look has also influenced her development as a pen-and-ink draftsman and painter (in watercolors, gouache, and oils).

In the last analysis, however, discussions of style and possible formative influences (early twentieth-century German artists Kathe Kollwitz and Georg Grosz or the Expressionists) are really beside the point. What sets Bascove apart from her more easily classifiable peers is, after all, the substance of her work, not her technique or choice of format. Judged by this criterion, she shows an intelligence and acuity that make hers a truly individual eye. The primary role of ideas in her art is made trenchantly apparent in a cover design done for the March-April, 1973 issue of *Print:* a literal "brain child" embryo tucked into a woman's cranial cavity and linked umbilically to the figure's eye. Likewise, in her announcement for the 1980 Art Directors' Club Show, a complex intellectual conceit is proposed with

A woodcut sequence from "My Animal,", a story published in *Esquire* (© 1979, Bascove. Reprinted by permission.)

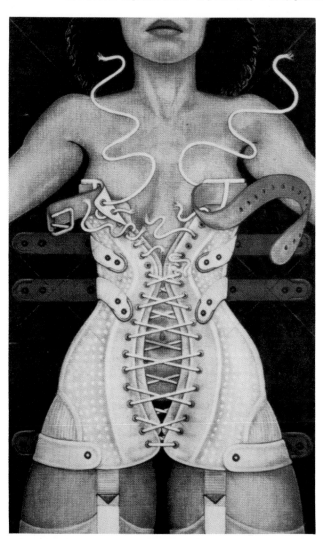

Announcement for a Bascove show at the Art Directors Club (© 1980, Bascove. Reprinted by permission.)

striking economy and power. It is this gift that has made her such a sought-after designer of book jackets and prolific editorial illustrator, particularly among art directors who require that texts be graphically complemented by artists who will intellectually come to grips with the material, and whose illustrations will reflect an understanding of it. Bascove satisfies such demands with her highly individual, occasionally harsh or shocking, but always arresting images.

It is not surprising to learn that her commissions have included book covers for such eminently cerebral authors as Fyodor Dostoevsky, Ivan Turgenev, Virginia Woolf, Amos Oz, and Italo Calvino, and editorial illustrations for pieces about such physical and emotional phenomena as menopause, depression, anxiety, masochistic fantasies, and phobias. As a studio painter Bascove is said to be especially concerned with the interpretation of dreams. Ultimately the reason that her work does not lend itself to standard classification relates precisely to the connection it requires between the eye and the brain, and the intellectual/emotional speculations that touches off. A phrase attributed to another provocative American artist-illustrator, Brad Holland, however, does seem applicable to the art of Bascove: it is indeed "beyond illustration."

BIOGRAPHICAL/CRITICAL SOURCES: Print, March-April, 1973, December, 1982; *Graphis*, November-December, 1981.

* * *

BECKERMAN, Howard 1930-

PERSONAL: Born December 25, 1930, in the Bronx, N.Y.; son of Saul M. and Minnie (Gottlieb) Beckerman; married Iris Funk (an animation artist), December 30, 1951; children: Mara, Sheri, Amy. *Education:* Attended Art Students League, 1950, and City College (now City College of City University of New York), 1950-51. *Office:* Howard Beckerman Animation, Inc., 45 W. 45th St., New York, N.Y. 10036.

CAREER: Assistant, Terrytoons (animation studio), New York City, 1949-50; in-betweener, Paramount/Famous Studios, New York City, 1950-51; storyman and animator, working for United Producers of America (U.P.A.), Ernest Pintoff, Electra, and other animation studios, 1953-63; designer, Norcross Greeting Card Co.. New York City, 1964-66; animator and storyman, Paramount Cartoons (formerly Paramount/Famous Studios), New York City, 1966-67; free-lance animator, 1967-70; owner and operator, Howard Beckerman Animation, New York City, 1970—.

Creator, with Carl Memling, of daily comic strip *Miss Chipps*, distributed by Sponsored Comics, 1958-59. Instructor at School of Visual Arts and Parsons School of Design. *Military service:* U.S. Army, 1951-53, served in Korea.

MEMBER: ASIFA (international vice-president, 1985—), National Cartoonists Society.

AWARDS, HONORS: Awards from ASIFA-East, 1972, for *How the Zebra Came to Be*, 1975, for *Wilderness*, 1976, for *A Fuzzy Tale*, 1983, for *Boop-Beep*; Best Children's Film Award from *Learning* magazine, 1973, for *The Most Marvelous Cat;* "Best in Animation" awards from National Cartoonists Society, 1976 and 1984.

WRITINGS: Scriptwriter for many animated short subjects. Contributor of monthly articles to *Filmmakers Newsletter*, 1972-1982, and weekly articles to *Back Stage*, 1982—.

FILMS—All as animator and storyman; all animated short subjects: *The Trip*, Paramount, 1967; *How the Zebra Came to Be*, National Broadcasting Co. (NBC), 1972; *The Most Marvelous Cat*, Xerox Corp., 1973; (also producer and director) *Wilderness*, Howard Beckerman Animation, 1975; (also producer and director) *A Fuzzy Tale*, Beckerman, 1976; (also producer and director) *Boop-Beep*, Beckerman, 1983; (also producer and director) *Cadence*, Beckerman, 1986.

EXHIBITIONS: Special screening of all major works held at Astoria Motion Picture and Television Foundation, Astoria, N.Y., 1980; screening of *Boop-Beep* at Museum of Modern Art, New York City, 1984. Exhibits at Museum of Cartoon Art, Rye Brook, N.Y., 1978 and 1984.

WORK IN PROGRESS: "Developing new scripts for educational and entertainment films."

SIDELIGHTS: "Cartooning reveals us to ourselves," Howard Beckerman wrote *CGA*. "Animation extends this insight into an observation of how life appears in motion. Much of today's humorous and illustrative art depicts

A frame from *Boop-Beep* (© 1984, Howard Beckerman Animation. Reprinted by permission.)

people and animals in static poses, a reflection of our sedentary contemporary habits. In actuality we are always in motion, and even the most minute movements and gestures have meaning and provide a reflection on our character and mood."

Beckerman has been immersed in drawing and animation from his earliest days. At age six he had his first lesson from his friend Marvin Fox who showed him how to draw a World War I biplane. "Marvin was full [of information] on how to draw sailors and Santa Clauses," he later recalled. "He could make the most wondrous things out of commonplace items." This skill transfixed the young Beckerman, who from the beginning knew he would become a cartoonist. While a student at New York's famed School of Industrial Art (now High School of Art and Design) he decided to focus on animation, figuring he could always go back to cartoon drawing later. It was then that he became fascinated with the history of animation and all the possibilities of the medium.

After graduation he served an apprenticeship of sorts at the Terrytoons animation studio, before going over to Paramount/Famous studios as an in-betweener; there he stayed less than one year, the Korean War having broken out in the meantime. After serving two years in the Army, he came back with the firm intention of becoming a full-status animator; he free-lanced for a variety of studios, took a two-and-one-half-year job with the Norcross Greeting Card Company, but came back to animation for good in 1966, when he returned to Paramount as an animator and storyman.

Once more Beckerman experienced the vagaries of the animation business when Paramount closed the doors of its animation unit in 1967. This time he determined to weather the storm, and after a period of freelancing, he set up his own animation studio. Since then his clients have included Public Television's *Sesame Street*, the Xerox Corporation, Exxon, and Black Flag insecticide (for which he has done the memorable "Roach-Motel" commercials). His best work, however, is done in what he calls "personal anima-

HOWARD BECKERMAN

tion," in which he serves in the multiple capacities of director, layout man, scriptwriter, and producer. Beckerman's short films of this type have garnered a fair number of awards and have also received popular and critical acclaim. Perhaps the best-liked of his films is *Boop-Beep*, an endearing little fable about a cat, a miser, and an old woman; the whole story is deftly visualized to the on-and-off rhythm of a lighthouse beacon.

In addition to his credits as an animator Beckerman is also the creator of the short-lived comic strip *Miss Chipps*, about a Chaplinesque female character. Of longer duration has been Beckerman's own experience as a teacher, and his courses at the School of Visual Arts and Parsons School of Design have helped form a whole generation of young animators. Of equal influence have been Beckerman's monthly articles in *Filmmakers Newsletter*, and later his weekly contributions to *Back Stage*, in which he shared his detailed knowledge of the history and techniques of animation with his readers. His column has included series of essays that comprise an "Animation Kit" (covering such topics as "Creating Motion," "The Cel," "The Pencil Test," and "Teaching Animation,"), recognized as standard texts for any student of the medium.

Beckerman is ably assisted in most facets of his work by his wife, Iris, who explained her role to the author of *Animation: The Art and the Industry:* "I work in a unique situation with my husband, Howard, in a studio that is usually made up of just the two of us. . . . My job is the handling of the production once it leaves the animation stage and before it goes to camera." She could have added that she also takes care of the day-to-day running of the studio, thus leaving her husband free to devote his full time to his creative activities, which involves doing everything in his films, from writing the storyline to drawing of the actual animation.

BIOGRAPHICAL/CRITICAL SOURCES: Cartoonist Profiles, March, 1974, March, 1978; Leonard Maltin, *Of Mice and Magic,* McGraw, 1980; Thomas W. Hoffer, *Animation:*

Model sheet for *Stuffin* (© 1982, Howard Beckerman. Reprinted by permission.)

A Reference Guide, Greenwood Press, 1981; Susan Rubin, *Animation: The Art and the Industry,* Prentice-Hall, 1984.

* * *

BECKLER, Rochelle Emilie   1955-
**   (Shelley Beckler)**

PERSONAL: Born April 30, 1955, in Washington, D.C.; daughter of David Zander (an international consultant on science and technology policy) and Harriet (Levy) Beckler; married Rohit Modi (a graphic designer), July 14, 1984; children: Shaun Zander. *Education:* Rhode Island School of Design, B.F.A., 1977. *Home:* 470 Second Ave., New York, N.Y. *Office:* Modi & Beckler Design, 271 Madison Ave., New York, N.Y. 10016.

CAREER: Graphic designer, Gips & Balkind, New York City, 1978-80; graphic designer, Danne & Blackburn, New York City; graphic designer, Student Book Program, Random House, New York City, 1979-80; partner, Modi & Beckler, New York, N.Y. 1980—.

MEMBER: American Institute of Graphic Arts, Graphic Artists Guild.

AWARDS, HONORS: Desi Award, Graphic Design USA, 1983, for the *Fear of Filing,* cover design; selection in a competition for design of the 1986 greeting card, UNICEF, 1984; Desi Award, Graphic Design USA, 1984, for a logotype design for the Frank Spencer Heart Research Foundation.

SIDELIGHTS: Since graduating from the Rhode Island School of Design, Shelley Beckler has been working as a graphic designer in New York City. In 1979 and 1980 she worked with the Student Book Program at Random House, helping to design children's books and promotional literature. In 1980 she founded her own firm with Rohit Modi, an Indian-born designer then working in New York. Four years later, the two married.

As a partner of Modi & Beckler Design, Beckler continues to work in the same way, but now a good portion of her work is done jointly with her husband. Her experience with children's books and their promotion led her to handle an account for Scholastic, Inc. She designed *See Saw,* a promotional magazine for teachers and students in kindergarten and the first grade, and then switched to Scholastic's magazine for second- and third-grade students, *Lucky,* designing the issues for the 1985-86 school year.

A large percentage of Modi & Beckler Design's work is devoted to packaging design and to logotypes and promotional material for magazines, brochures, and posters. In its first five years the firm earned some notable awards and distinctions. The mayor of New York honored the partners in a special ceremony for their 1983 poster for the City of New York's Human Resources Administration, Agency for Child Development. The poster design, supporting city day care centers, was contributed to the city without charge.

Consistent with her sensitivity to educational programs, Shelley Beckler feels very strongly about the moral responsibilities of her work. "One word sums up M & B designs:

"Dreams of a New Year" (© 1984, Modi & Beckler Design. Reprinted by permission.)

Integrity," her brochure reads, and if she and her husband do not believe in the product or service of a prospective client, they will reject the account. A few years ago, for example, they declined to design a dealership magazine for a cigarette company because they disapprove of smoking, even though they would have made from fifteen to twenty thousand dollars from the job. Much of their work is for organizations in whose positions they support, among them UNICEF, the City of New York Agency for Child Development, the Frank Spencer Heart Research Foundation, the New York State Council on Economic Education, and Volunteer Lawyers for the Arts. One of their most highly admired designs is the logo for the Institute for the Advancement of Health. This striking symbol, twining two human faces around a caduceus, effectively conveys the complex idea of cooperation in the medical field and appears on the cover of the Institute's quarterly journal.

Modi and Beckler employ two additional artists in their offices on Madison Avenue. The cheerful quarters are bustling with activity and enhanced by the presence of their infant son. Surrounded as he is by the creative atmosphere of a busy design agency, the alert child seems likely to fulfill the prediction made for him by an Indian astrologer that he was destined to grow up to be an artist.

Despite her busy pace as a mother and working professional, Shelley Beckler does not lose sight of her goals as a graphic designer and does not compromise her standards. "Good design conveys quality," she states, and the output of her successful young firm bears the precept out.

BIOGRAPHICAL/CRITICAL SOURCES: Wylie Davis, *AIGA: American Institute of Graphic Arts Journal of Graphic Design,* April, 1983; *Overseas Times,* October 21, 1983; *SPAN* (U.S. Information Service Journal; New Delhi, India), December, 1983.

* * *

BECKLER, Shelley
See BECKLER, Rochelle Emilie

BORGMAN, James Mark   1954-
(Jim Borgman)

PERSONAL: Born February 24, 1954, in Cincinnati, Ohio; son of James (a commercial artist) and Marian (Maly) Borgman; married Lynn Goodwin in 1977; children: Dylan. *Education:* Kenyon College, B.A. (summa cum laude), 1976. *Office:* Cincinnati Enquirer, 617 Vine St., Cincinnati, Ohio 45201. *Syndicate:* King Features Syndicate, 235 E. 45th St., New York, N.Y. 10017.

CAREER: Editorial cartoonist, *Cincinnati Enquirer,* 1976—. Contributor, *Newsweek's Cartoon-A-Torial,* 1978-81.

MEMBER: Association of American Editorial Cartoonists, National Cartoonists Society.

AWARDS, HONORS: Sigma Delta Chi Award in Editorial Cartooning, 1978; Thomas Nast Prize, 1980; Post-Corbett Award, 1981; Best of Gannett in Editorial Commentary, 1982 and 1984; finalist, Pulitzer Prize for editorial cartoon, 1985; Best of Gannett, Special Citation, 1985; second prize, Fischetti Competition, 1985.

WRITINGS: Smorgasborgman (collection of cartoons), Armadillo Press, 1982; *The Great Communicator* (collection of cartoons), Colloquial Books, 1985.

EXHIBITIONS: University of Cincinnati, Cincinnati, Ohio, 1980; Kenyon College, Gambier, Ohio, 1981; International Salon of Cartoons, Montreal, Canada, 1981; Haslem Gal-

JAMES MARK BORGMAN

lery, Washington, D.C., 1982 and 1983; Courthouse Gallery, Pittsburgh, Pa., 1983; Mount St. Joseph College, Cincinnati, 1984; Art Pac Shows, 1984 and 1985.

SIDELIGHTS: Born and raised in a traditional German Catholic family in a blue-collar, conservative Democratic neighborhood of Cincinnati, Jim Borgman has never lost sense of his origins, especially in his local cartoons. Some of these attack city or state officials all too eager to dig into taxpayers' pockets for ever wilder boondoggles, while others satirize poorly thought-out issues, as in his dig at a proposed anti-smoking ordinance: first-graders, smoking and puffing away, come out of the boys' room, their hands raised, and march off to jail under the suspicious eye of several beefy cops.

Borgman has been drawing since grade school, but became truly interested in cartooning only in his senior year at Kenyon College where he majored and received high honors in fine arts. A grassroots understanding of the man-in-the-street mentality, a natural talent, and a straight-forward sense of humor quickly landed him the job of editorial cartoonist at the conservative *Cincinnati Enquirer*. His early political cartoons show the influence of such greats as Pat Oliphant, Jeff MacNelly, and Mike Peters, and deal with the usual topics and themes. After this on-the-job apprenticeship, however, Borgman developed his personal view of the world and a forceful style that is completely his own.

Because Jim Borgman considers his role as attracting readers to the editorial page, he wants his cartoons to tell a story in a funny way and thus lead to more thoughtful reflection. This explains why the paper's editors understand and support his often liberal stand, not only on politics but also on civil rights and the environment. (As a matter of fact, he declared in a television interview, since the birth of his son, many issues, like the budget deficit and arms control, have become more personalized for him.) In order to report and comment on the news, he may present for ridicule President Reagan trying on a chastity belt as the sole government-approved and funded method of birth control; a woman looking at a gigantic bun (labeled "Promises") and a minuscule black blob and asking short-order cook Walter Mondale, "Where's the beef?"; or a map of the United States with an electric outlet dangerously overloaded with Japanese audiovisual equipment compared to one lone television set, made in the United States—

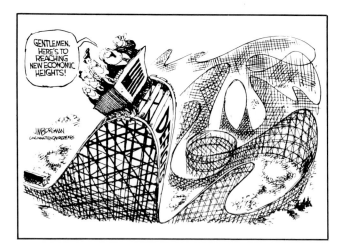

An editorial cartoon by Jim Borgman (© 1985, *Cincinnati Enquirer*. Reprinted by permission.)

disconnected from an outlet on the map of Japan. Lately, though, Borgman's social satire has begun to reveal a more pointed philosophical outlook, whether in his depiction of hackers' unethical conduct or of Yuppies' quest for the good but empty life. May of his editorial cartoons were reprinted in a 1982 collection, *Smorgasborgman*, and in its 1985 sequel, *The Great Communicator*.

Borgman's drawings all have a beautiful balance among protagonists, setting and action, with the right dramatic buildup for maximum suspense, impact and knowing irony. His style and wit have made him, according to a *Time* writer, the uncontested leader of a new breed of cartoonists who view their art as a highly personal form of expression. It is no wonder, then, that Jim Borgman was a 1985 finalist for a Pulitzer Prize and that his cartoons are syndicated in over two hundred newspapers and magazines, including *Newsweek, Time, Business Week, Washington Post*, and the "Week in Review" section of *New York Times*.

Veteran editorial cartoonist Mike Peters calls Borgman "one of today's best caricaturists."

BIOGRAPHICAL/CRITICAL SOURCES: Cartoonist Profiles, March, 1979; *Ohio Magazine*, February, 1984; *Who's Who in America 1984-85,* Marquis, 1984.

* * *

BORGMAN, Jim
    See BORGMAN, James Mark

* * *

BOWLER, Joe
    See BOWLER, Joseph, Jr.

* * *

BOWLER, Joseph, Jr. 1928-
    (Joe Bowler)

PERSONAL: Born September 4, 1928, in Forest Hills, N.Y.; son of Joseph (a real estate operator and newspaper reporter) and Catherine (Bowdish) Bowler; married Marilyn Carscallen Crang (an artists' representative), June 16, 1950; children: Jolyn Louise, Brynne Wakefield. *Education:* At-

An editorial cartoon by Jim Borgman (© 1985, *Cincinnati Enquirer*. Reprinted by permission.)

tended Art Students League, New York City, 1949-50. *Studio and office:* 9 Baynard Cove Rd., Hilton Head Island, S.C. 29928. *Agent:* Marilyn C. Bowler, 9 Baynard Cove Rd., Hilton Head Island, S.C. 29928.

CAREER: Office assistant, Barry Stevens (an artists' representative), New York City, 1946-47; office assistant, Kling Studios, New York City, 1947-48; staff artist, Charles E. Cooper's Studio, 1949-66; free-lance portraitist and illustrator, 1966—. Instructor at Parsons School of Design, 1968-72, and Syracuse University, 1980-85. Regularly contributes paintings for charitable organizations to benefit arts education, youth, and the environment.

MEMBER: Society of Illustrators.

AWARDS, HONORS: Named Artist of the Year by Artists Guild, New York City, 1967.

EXHIBITIONS: Society of Illustrators, New York City, 1978.

WORK IN PROGRESS: Commissioned portraits.

SIDELIGHTS: Joseph Bowler, American illustrator and portrait artist, was born in Forest Hills, New York, in 1928. A passion for drawing surfaced early—his first sustained efforts came at the age of three—and, unchallenged by more "practical" urges, grew increasingly strong as he grew older. Upon graduation from high school, Bowler took a job as an office assistant for noted artists' and illustrators' representative Barry Stevens, and there he began what would ultimately become a lifelong course of self-instruction. At Stevens's office Bowler "borrowed" clients' work overnight; he would take it home, then sit up copying until two and three a.m. in order to get the materials back to the office the following morning before they were missed. Under this regimen, Bowler not only became an adept copyist, but obviously learned first hand about the tyranny of deadlines.

When Chicago's Kling Studios opened a New York City shop, Bowler used his portfolio of copies to land a job there doing spot work and making copies. It was the sort of apprenticeship that has today been largely supplanted by formal art school training, and he made good use of it. Bowler remained with Kling until 1948, when he moved to Charles E. Cooper's Studio. Although this meant something of a demotion (from regular assignments to general backup as staff artist), Bowler eagerly took the new job for it gave him the opportunity to observe the techniques of some of the finest American illustrators then working, including Coby Whitmore, Tran Mawicke, and Bernard D'Andrea. "For three months," he recalled in an interview in 1967, "I matted pictures, cleaned Coby Whitmore's paint tray every day, and looked over everybody's shoulder." He also took a night course in drawing at the Art Students League during this period, but as usual found the on-the-job training much more helpful in developing his artistic skills and instincts. Soon promoted to a regular drawing board, the nineteen-year-old Bowler scored his first success when Coby Whitmore arranged for the publication of one of his drawings in *Cosmopolitan.* It showed the head of a girl in the Whitmore style. This marked the beginning of a period of unbroken success as a magazine illustrator that lasted through the 1950s and well into the 1970s. Affiliated with the Cooper studio for advertising work until it shut down in the mid-1960s, Bowler freelanced as an illustrator from 1959.

JOSEPH BOWLER, JR.

A sampling of Bowler's work as cover artist and editorial illustrator for such major mass circulation periodicals as *Saturday Evening Post, Time, McCall's, Good Housekeeping,* and *Woman's Day* reveals a traditional representational artist with a marked ability to evoke moods. Laying thin coats of transparent glaze with a wet or dry brush over carefully done pencil drawings on gessoed surfaces, Bowler achieved his results with the kind of discipline that had more in common with the old masters of the seventeenth century than with contemporary experimentalists. As he explained at this point in his career, "I guess I'm kind of square, I still have that need to be a craftsman. Oh, I keep up with all the new media, the new techniques. Like everybody else I use acrylics. I experiment with collage and all sorts of accidental effects. I use camera and projection equipment. But I'm always myself. I don't let any of this take over and become technique for its own sake. For a change of pace, I still paint some of my illustrations in oils—something that almost nobody does anymore—and I paint portraits and figures for fun."

With the decline of the mass circulation periodical market in the 1970s, Bowler found his "quirks" (i.e., classical style, penchant for mood, obsessive craftsmanship, labor-intensive technique, and personal fascinations with the portrait genre and the medium of oil) nudging him in a new direction—as a commission portraitist. In the contemporary art world portraiture is regarded as regressive and synonymous with hack work; indeed, it has not been a respected genre in Europe since the photographic age was ushered in during the nineteenth century, and in America since the New York Armory Show of 1913 which introduced so many modern

art concepts. Thus, in pursuing portraiture Bowler was separating himself even further from his contemporaries, both in the trendy world of illustration and the more rarified circles of fine art. That he has so distanced himself is undeniable; yet the corollary—that he has become hack limner of beautiful folk and their offspring—is by no means a defensible criticism of the work he has produced.

As a magazine cover artist, Bowler had already produced many portrait studies—Jackie Onassis, Rose Kennedy, French President Charles De Gaulle, and a portrait of David and Julie Nixon Eisenhower—while his editorial work had given him a thorough grounding in the sort of gentle quietism of mood especially suited to the portrait genre. These abilities, along with his technical mastery, willingness to accept the camera as a creative partner, and an honest commitment to a branch of art not seriously practiced since the era of John Singer Sargent at the turn of the century, have brought Bowler more than a continuing flow of lucrative commissions. They have also won him a measure of critical respect. In an appreciation written for the *Christian Science Monitor*, critic Theodore F. Wolff placed Bowler's work in the tradition of European old masters Velasquez, Rubens, and Vermeer, and their nineteenth-century descendants Renoir and Sargent, calling attention to its "breathing likeness" and the painterly skill with which the artist creates an "overwhelmingly 'realistic' illusion." Singling out *The Eyelet Dress*—a full-length portrait of a regal little girl who might as easily date from seventeenth-

The Eyelet Dress, an oil painting (© 1983, Joe Bowler. All rights reserved. Reprinted by permission.)

century Flanders as twentieth-century America—Wolff saw in it "a humanity, a celebration of the good life, tenderness, a display of sumptuous painting and subtle color, and a very special quality called art." Other examples of Bowler's portraiture collected in a portfolio published in the magazine *Southern Accents* (winter, 1982) offer equally fine demonstrations of what this neglected, not to say scorned genre can be in capable hands.

"Producing a portrait," Bowler has said, "is more challenging than any other form of painting, because I must achieve a likeness, please the client, and satisfy myself as an artist." He added (characteristically), "Every year I become more aware of how much I have yet to learn."

BIOGRAPHICAL/CRITICAL SOURCES: Don Holden, "Joe Bowler," *American Artist*, November, 1967; Cory SerVaas, "Artist in the White House," *Saturday Evening Post*, summer, 1972; "The Southern Artists—Joe Bowler," *Southern Accents*, winter, 1982; Theodore F. Wolff, "The Many Masks of Modern Art," *Christian Science Monitor*, January 6, 1983; *Who's Who in American Art*, Bowker, 1984.

—*Sketch by Richard Calhoun*

* * *

BREISACHER, George 1939-

PERSONAL: Surname is pronounced "*Bry*-socker"; born August 24, 1939, in Toledo, Ohio; son of Melvin and Ruth (Hertzler) Breisacher; married Jayne Welch, June 16, 1961; children: Jeffrey, Jimmy, Tammy. *Education:* Graduated from high school in Grand Blanc, Mich., 1957. *Home:* 1800 Progress Ln., Charlotte, N.C. 28205. *Office: Charlotte Observer*, 600 S. Tryon St., Charlotte, N.C. 28232.

CAREER: Worked for the U.S. Post Office, 1957-62, before beginning his art career. Layout artist, Sears, Roebuck & Co., Flint, Mich., 1965-66; layout artist, Hamady Brothers (foodstore chain), Flint, 1966-67; staff artist, *Oakland Press*, Pontiac, Mich., 1967-73; newsroom artist, *Charlotte Observer*, Charlotte, N.C., 1973—. Comic strip artist and writer for *Channel One* (also called *Knobs*), United Feature Syndicate, 1978-80, and *Mutt & Jeff*, Field Newspaper Syndicate, 1981-83. *Military service:* U.S. Army, 1963-65, served as clarinetist in Army Band.

MEMBER: National Cartoonists Society, Winterfield Boosters Club (vice-president, 1980 and 1983; president, 1981 and 1985).

AWARDS, HONORS: Finalist for the Charles M. Shultz Award, Scripps-Howard Foundation, 1984; Award of Excellence, Society of Newspaper Design, 1985.

SIDELIGHTS: George Breisacher has been dedicated to the arts for most of his working life. A musician for two years with a U.S. Army band ("traveling around Kentucky giving the clarinet a bad name," as he modestly expresses it), he entered graphic art as a layout man for Sears, Roebuck & Co., in Flint, Michigan, in 1965, and the next year continued in the same field with Hamady Brothers foodstore chain in the same city. In 1967 the Ohio-born, Michigan-raised Breisacher took his first newspaper job with the *Oakland Press* in Pontiac, Michigan, as a staff artist. Six years later, in

GEORGE BREISACHER

1973, he left Michigan for a job as newsroom artist with the *Observer* in Charlotte, North Carolina. Although loyal to his new state, he admits to remaining "a die-hard Tiger fan."

A die-hard comics fan as well, Breisacher has been drawing cartoons since he began with the *Oakland Press* in 1967. He started his first daily strip, *Knobs,* also known as *Channel One* (the only channel the Federal Communications Commission never assigns), in 1978. A television spoof, *Channel One* made gentle fun of the medium and was distributed nationally by United Feature Syndicate until 1980. The next year, Breisacher began a stint drawing Bud Fisher's classic gag strip *Mutt & Jeff,* a comics-page institution which began in 1907; he continued drawing it for the Field Newspaper Syndicate until 1983. Although never formally educated in art, Breisacher has always commanded a skillful pen and achieved a droll style. His Mutt and Jeff adhered to the classic pattern of these characters, but his own creations are distinctive in conception and execution. Loose and spontaneous in appearance, his graphic work is well-balanced and imaginatively conceived.

As much a sports fan as a comics fan, Breisacher says that he "spends far too much time away from the drawing board playing softball, coaching and organizing kids' sports," and that he "considers a successful round of golf one where injury is avoided." The vigor and vitality of the sportsman are apparent in the free-wheeling line and light touch of the comic artist.

BIOGRAPHICAL/CRITICAL SOURCES: National Cartoonists Society Album, 1980.

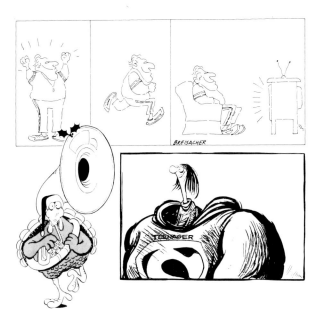

A cartoon montage (© 1986, George Breisacher. Reprinted by permission.)

* * *

BROTHERS, Barry 1955-

PERSONAL: Born January 18, 1955, in Brooklyn, N.Y.; son of James and Blanche Brothers. *Education:* Brooklyn College of the City University of New York, B.S., 1977, M.F.A., 1980. *Home and studio:* 1922 E. 18th St., Brooklyn, N.Y. 11229.

CAREER: Free-lance painter, muralist, illustrator, photographer, and graphic artist, 1974—. Works include two triptych murals for the new building complex of American Broadcasting Co. in New York City, 1985-86.

MEMBER: Graphic Artists Guild.

AWARDS, HONORS: Charles G. Shaw Memorial Award in Painting from Brooklyn College, 1979; Certificate of Distinction from *Art Direction,* 1981; Publication Design Award (art) from Society of Publication Designers, New York, N.Y., 1982.

EXHIBITIONS: (One-man show) Brooklyn College Fine Arts Gallery, 1976 and 1977; "Photographers Forum," Milwaukee Center for Photography, 1978; "New Realists," Adelphi University Art Gallery, 1982; "Brooklyn '83," Brooklyn Museum, 1983; "Charles G. Shaw Memorial Award Recipients 1978-80," Museum of the Borough of Brooklyn, 1983; "Twelve Year Retrospective," Museum of the Borough of Brooklyn, 1984; "The Brooklyn Landscape," Ammo Artists Exhibition Space, Brooklyn, 1984; "Brooklyn '85," Brooklyn Museum, 1985; Henry Hicks Gallery, Brooklyn, 1986.

WORK IN PROGRESS: Paintings, new murals.

SIDELIGHTS: An initial glib generalization about the artist Barry Brothers might hold him a kind of high-tech inheritor of the legacy of the American painter Edward Hopper. The unpopulated settings, the flat, restrained colors, the way light suggests temperature and space, and the careful attention to form and organization all recall the work of the earlier American master, even as Brothers's typical preoccupation with television imagery, oil refineries, and towering cityscapes give his work a distinctly space-age tone. Then, as with most glib generations, this impression begins to fade, to be replaced by a sense that any resemblance to Hopper is strictly coincidental and that Brothers's style is really very much his own, an intriguing fusion of geometry and imagination.

It is not surprising to learn that during his first two years at Brooklyn College, Brothers was a math and science major. Shifting his major to art, he took the usual painting, drawing, and design courses, but his dominant interest early on was photography. At first Brothers's photographs showed him as a recorder of social behavior. However, as he told Carol Stevens in *Print*, a part-time job in a studio on the upper floor of a Madison Avenue building introduced him to a new environment: rooftops and architecture as viewed (in the manner of the late photographer Andre Kertesz) from the detached vantage point of roofs and upper windows. This, in turn, suggested new areas of exploration as a painter. The use of photography as a basis for painting is hardly unique—photorealist painters are devoted to such synthesis of art and technique—but Brothers takes a definite Bauhaus approach to his blending of the two expressive media. As Stevens describes it in *Print*: "Brothers is an accomplished photographer but his dramatic black-and-white shots of industrial locations and urban environments are merely stepping stones to what is for him a more compelling product—an idealized, tranquil vision of that same world, rendered in oil. In Brothers' paintings, the

East River, the right panel of Barry Brothers's triptych mural for the American Broadcasting Co., (© 1985, Barry Brothers and ABC, Inc. Reprinted by permission.)

clutter and dirt of man-made precincts have been excised. The pavements are clean; architectural details have been eliminated; there are no people." Less may not have become more, but it certainly provides an alternative perspective. "I am interested," Brothers has said, "in using concrete visual data of the environment as a springboard to abstract thought, in isolating the basic geometric order and rhythm in our contemporary environment."

A case in point is the portfolio he did for *Fortune* entitled "Refineries Refined," a cover and a six-painting series based on photographs of the largest, smallest, and oldest oil refineries in the United States. "By reducing the visual to its essential form, ridding it of obscuring detail," he explains, "one can see the true relations, the patterns, more clearly." The results are cool-hued, rather stark schematics drawn from the shapes—tanks, piping, catwalks, chimney stacks, and storage sheds—that appear in detail in the accompanying photos, and bear about the same relationship to the originals as tinker toy models of them would. Yet there is a purity in these highly distilled images that lead one back to the original photos with an enhanced awareness of the symmetry that informs what at first glance seems little more than confusion. Besides the simplification, Brothers rearranges or edits his photos to focus on certain details that interest him, and his color is, by his own definition, "improvisatory"—i.e., "not to describe the scene as it really is, but rather as it makes me feel."

A lucidly detached imagination pervades Brothers' work. This is in part a result of his deliberate dependence on photographic imagery for inspiration for many of his works, but it also reflects the influence of an analytical geometrician's temperament. The degree of abstraction in his work, however, seems largely a function of perspective and logic—the closer one stands to a confusing environment, the more puzzlement it provokes—and distance does give his paintings a more representative cast. Consider his paintings of Manhattan as seen from each of its three rivers—Hudson, East, and Harlem. Done as one of two triptych murals commissioned by the American Broadcasting Company for its new studio complex, Brothers portrays Gotham as a kind of clean, distant ideal. Bathed in wintry light, the city's clamor is stilled, its harshness gentled. It is not, to be sure,

BARRY BROTHERS

On Air, **the center panel of Barry Brothers's triptych mural for the American Broadcasting Co., Inc.** (© 1985, Barry Brothers and ABC, Inc. Reprinted by permission.)

the romantic Hopperesque vision of a quiet Sunday morning in New York, but it captures in its own way much of the mythical ambiance of the great metropolis in 1986.

In the last two years, the predominance of architectural landscapes has somewhat diminished in favor of a new-found interest in exploring a softer, more delicate natural environment. The inspiration for these paintings ranges from the shores of Montauk, Long Island, to the valleys, mountains, and reservoirs of the Catskill region in upper New York. Brothers's view is expanding in order to convey a diligently detailed picture of the state of New York in its

totality. The simplified perspective remains intact in these latter works, but the harder, flat areas of color are being replaced with softened, suggestive shapes through greater modulation of tone.

BIOGRAPHICAL/CRITICAL SOURCES: Fortune, January 12, 1981; *Print,* March-April, 1984; Les Krantz, *American Artists,* Facts on File, 1985; *Gran Bazaar* (Milan, Italy), June-July, 1985; *Corporate Showcase 5,* Corporate Showcase, 1986.

—Sketch by Richard Calhoun

C

CASSADY, Jack
 See CASSADY, John R.

* * *

CASSADY, John R.   1940-
 (Jack Cassady)

PERSONAL: Born April 26, 1940, in Orlando, Fla.; son of John R. and Louise M. (Pruckner) Cassady; married Judith Lynne Tompkins, 1962; children: Carol Marie, Richard Brannen. *Education:* Furman University, B.A., 1962, M.A., 1972; attended Memphis State University, 1984—. *Religion*: Protestant. *Office*: P.O. Box 28766, Memphis, Tenn. 38128. *Agent*: Jack Albert, 3 E. 54th St., New York, N.Y. 10022.

CAREER: Technical illustrator, Boeing Aircraft, Melbourne, Fla., 1957-58; military officer, U.S. Army, 1962-84; served in Vietnam and Laos; became lieutenant-colonel; served as senior staff officer and department chief responsible for planning, organizing and conducting advertising and public relations activities related to Army Reserve Officers' Training Corps in a seventeen-state region. Free-lance illustrator and cartoonist, 1960—. Lecturer and instructor in cartooning. Producer and host of a series on cartooning for WDCN-TV, Nashville, Tenn. Management consultant for various graphic art firms.

MEMBER: Cartoonists Guild (secretary, 1982-83), Graphic Artists Guild, Cartoonists Association, National Cartoonists Society, Museum of Cartoon Art, Special Forces Association, Association of the U.S. Army, American Running and Fitness Association, Rotary Club.

AWARDS, HONORS—Military: Bronze Star, three Meritorious Service Medals, five Air Medals, Army Commendation Medal, Presidential Unit Citation, Meritorious Unit Citation. Civilian: South Carolina Collegiate Press Award, for best editorial cartoon, 1962; Maxwell Award for Excellence in Art, 1962.

TELEVISION: (Producer and host) *Funny Business: The Art in Cartooning* (a thirteen-program series), WDCN-TV, Nashville, Tenn., 1985.

EXHIBITIONS: Festival of Cartoon Art, Ohio State University, 1984; Museum of Cartoon Art, Port Chester, N.Y., 1985; Illustrators South 85, Memphis, Tenn., 1985.

WORK IN PROGRESS: Humorous illustration and magazine cartooning; research in high resolution computer graphics for television, at Memphis State University, completion expected in 1987.

JOHN R. CASSADY

Photograph by Tom Lawson, WDCN-TV. Courtesy of John R. Cassady.

SIDELIGHTS: Jack Cassady managed to combine his interest in art and cartooning with a long career in the military during which he taught art (along with courses in leadership development, educational psychology, management, and assessment technology) at four major colleges and universities over an eight-year period. He also sharpened the cartooning skills he had acquired in his college years (when he was editorial cartoonist on his campus newspaper) and published a line of full-color comic art sports and military prints that were retailed nationally. His cartoons of military life were mildly satirical, but also sympathetic and understanding, as could be expected from an insider.

After his discharge from the Army, Cassady embarked full-time upon a career as cartoonist, illustrator, and lecturer. He is an exponent of the "bigfoot" style of drawing, in which the characters are drawn with caricatural features (hence the name) and seen in exaggerated situations. One of his cartoons, for example, shows a caveman eye doctor (from the light-mirror on his forehead) giving an eye examination to a patient using rows of pictograms on a stone tablet; another one (for *Family Circle*) depicts two obviously out-of-shape men surrendering themselves to an employee of the President's Council on Physical Fitness. The humor in these and other drawings is gentle and unassuming, certainly unexpected from a man with such a long military career.

Jack Cassady's cartoon look behind the scenes of his public television series, *Funny Business* (© 1985, John R. Cassady. Reprinted by permission.)

A gag cartoon (© 1985, John R. Cassady. Reprinted by permission.)

It is perhaps as a historian and explainer of the cartooning arts that Cassady shines brightest. He has moderated a number of panel discussions on the subject and has appeared as guest speaker at numerous civic clubs, organizations, universities, schools, and television talk shows throughout the South. His public television series, *Funny Business: The Art in Cartooning*, which he produced and hosted, received national attention. In thirteen half-hour segments it explored such aspects of the profession as "Which Comes First, the Drawing or the Caption?," "Humorous Illustration in Advertising," and "Women in Cartooning." It also boasted an array of guest celebrities, including magazine cartoonist George Booth, comic strip artist Mort Walker, and political cartoonist Jerry Robinson.

BIOGRAPHICAL/CRITICAL SOURCES: Personalities of the South, bicentennial edition, American Biographical Institute, 1976; *Dictionary of International Biography,* Rossman, 1977.

BILL CHARMATZ

CHARMATZ, Bill   1925-

PERSONAL: Surname is pronounced "charm-ats"; born November 15, 1925, in New York, N.Y.; son of Morris and Brana Charmatz; children: Katrina. *Education:* Studied with Howard Trafton at Art Students League; studied with Stuart Davis and Alexei Brodovitch at Ecole des Beaux Arts, Fontainebleau, France, 1948; attended Academie de la Grande Chaumiere, Paris, France, 1950-52. *Home and studio:* 25 W. 68th St., New York, N.Y. 10023.

CAREER: Free-lance illustrator, painter, and author, 1946—. Advertising and direct corporate art work for such clients as Exxon, American Express, IBM, AT&T, Bonwit Teller, and Price Waterhouse, and for national and international advertising agencies. Instructor at School of Visual Arts in the 1960s. *Military service:* U.S. Navy, 1944-46.

MEMBER: Society of Illustrators, Illustrators Guild (founding member), Graphic Artists Guild (founding and charter member; former vice-president).

AWARDS, HONORS: "Recipient of over fifty awards from professional graphic arts organizations, both in this country and abroad."

WRITINGS: Author and illustrator of more than ten books for adults and children, including *The Little Duster*, 1967, *The Cat's Whiskers*, 1969, *Endeerments* (Ballantine), 1971, and *Troy St. Bus*, 1977; all for Macmillan except as noted. Also contributor to *New York Times*, *New Yorker*, *Time*, *Playboy*, *TV Guide*, and other periodicals.

EXHIBITIONS: "Work represented at most professional exhibitions nationwide; [has] had a number of private showings of [his] paintings, both in group and one-man shows."

SIDELIGHTS: Bill Charmatz defines himself "as an image maker using words and pictures to convey feelings and meanings." The images in which he deals are simple, ebullient, and colorful, and they express his feelings and meanings with a childlike charm and whimsicality. This approach not only serves him as a commercial and editorial illustrator, but also contributes to his success as an author and illustrator of children's books. His impulsive broad-line drawings, done in a kind of primitive expressionist fashion and frequently daubed with bright, flat colors, bring to mind the work of American comic artists William Steig and Charles Saxon. Aside from some minimal similarity in styles, Charmatz, like Steig and Saxon, takes a strongly conceptual approach to graphic communication and gives technique a subordinate role.

"My ideal," he has written, "is for my words and pictures to move as one, and walk and talk to my reader, creating its own reality." Indeed, motion seems to be central to his effort, and it is this quality that he captures most faithfully in his drawings. The figures themselves are cartoonish—long-limbed dumplings with exaggerated facial features—but the sense of movement they evoke with their running, jumping, and dancing poses is so deft that one accepts the anatomical crudities as simply part of the illusion, if not its center. That is obviously the "reality" Charmatz wants his art to create.

A humorous illustration (© 1986, Bill Charmatz. Reprinted by permission.)

A humorous illustration (© 1972, Bill Charmatz. Reprinted by permission.)

In his advertising work, Charmatz's style often works as a deliberate counterweight to the material he is graphically supplementing. In his own promotional piece, for example, two executives are shown dancing what appears to be a tango (one with a rose in his mouth) before an easel supporting a dry-looking bar graph. "Whimsy," the accompanying copy reminds the art director, "lightens what might otherwise be a heavy corporate tale." Exxon, Esso, Bell Telephone, and Price Waterhouse are among the accounts that have found this a persuasive argument over the years.

In his children's books Charmatz adds a whimsical narrative and demonstrates what he means when he talks about having his "words and pictures move as one." His volume *The Cat's Whiskers* tells the story of a cat with long whiskers who uses his peculiar assets to do "many useful things." In adventures which involve the cat's adoption by, abduction from, and reunion with his little mistress, these amazing whiskers become, variously, fishing lines, the strings of a musical instrument, wings, parachute cords, and the ropes of a swing. In fact, these whiskers are simply a linear extension of Charmatz's own imagination, expressed in warm and endearing fashion.

His most elaborate creations, if "elaborate" is ever exactly the right word for a Charmatz work, appear to be his editorial illustrations. Although his minimal, suggestive style is consistent, he is able within its constraints to produce surprisingly dense, rich tapestries of color and motion—bright and lively quasi-impressionist watercolors of river

traffic on the Seine; a "March on Washington" in which democracy is portrayed as an orderly convergence of citizens on the Capitol steps—and to sum up the essence of an article in a few lines and blobs of color (as in his work for *Fortune*).

Charmatz is not as well-known outside the field as many of his colleagues, nor has his work been featured in the prestigious magazines devoted to the graphic arts, but his general anonymity may be as much a matter of personal choice as of public neglect. Such an inference might be drawn at any rate from one of his portfolio pieces which displays a typically blob-like figure seated at a drawing board, pouring bright colors haphazardly from a gardener's watering can onto the board and over the floor below: how can anything this impulsive, and this much fun (he seems to be saying) possibly be taken seriously? Less circumstantial evidence of his professional status is the respect he enjoys among his peers, having served as vice-president and director on the board of the Graphic Artist's Guild and been a founding member of the Illustrators' Guild.

AVOCATIONAL INTERESTS: "Avid cross-country skier and race walker, often seen in the company of a shaggy dog anywhere from the Alps to the wilds of Central Park. Indefatigable renovator of ruined barns and collector of primitive furniture and assorted cabinetry."

BIOGRAPHICAL/CRITICAL SOURCES: Something about the Author, Vol. 7, Gale, 1975; *Contemporary Authors,* Vol. 29-32R, Gale, 1978.

CLEAVER, Elizabeth (Mrazik)   1939-1985

OBITUARY NOTICE: Born November 19, 1939, in Montreal, Quebec, Canada; died of cancer, July 27, 1985, in Montreal. Illustrator Elizabeth Cleaver started her distinguished career in the late 1960s after studies at various universities and colleges in her native Canada and in Hungary. Using the medium of torn paper collage she illustrated such diverse books as a collection of poems by Mary Alice Downie and Barbara Robertson, *The Wind Has Wings*, and William Toye's *The Mountain Goats of Temlaham*, a folk tale. Her illustrations of children's books won many awards from Canadian associations. Cleaver also adapted and illustrated legends from Hungary and other eastern European countries, including *The Golden Hind* and *Petrouchka*. The artist represented Canada in many international competitions and art exhibitions. Her many puppet shows often re-enacted native Indian and Eskimo legends, and Cleaver taught puppetry courses for both children and adults. Her reputation reached far beyond the boundaries of Canada, and she illustrated a number of books for such American publishers as Atheneum and Macmillan. Her works are on permanent exhibition at McGill University and in the Toronto Public Library.

OBITUARIES AND OTHER SOURCES: Contemporary Authors, Vol. 97-100, Gale, 1981; *Publisher's Weekly,* August 23, 1985.

* * *

CLEMENTE, Manuel Perez
See PEREZ CLEMENTE, Manuel

* * *

JUDY CLIFFORD

CLIFFORD, Judy   1946-

PERSONAL: Born December 23, 1946, in Orange, Calif.; daughter of John Landon (a chemical engineer) and Nancy (a model; maiden name, Payton) Broughten; married Philip Clifford (a certified public accountant), April 19, 1969. *Education:* University of Washington, B.A. (with honors), 1968; attended Academy of Art, San Francisco, Calif., 1971-74. *Home:* 24 W. 90th St., New York, N.Y. 10024. *Studio:* 35 W. 71st St., New York, N.Y. 10023. *Agent:* Bernstein & Andriulli, 60 E. 42nd St., New York, N.Y. 10017.

CAREER: Buyer, Liberty House (a department store), Honolulu, Hawaii, 1969-71; staff artist, Artworks, San Francisco, Calif., 1975-76; staff artist, Compendium Inc., San Francisco, 1976-77; free-lance illustrator, New York, N.Y. 1978—.

MEMBER: Society of Illustrators, Alliance Francaise.

AWARDS, HONORS: Award of Distinctive Merit, Western Art Directors Show, 1974; Awards of Merit, Western Art Directors Show, 1975, 1976, Society of Illustrators of Los Angeles, 1975, San Francisco Society of Communication Arts, 1976, Society of Illustrators, 1976, 1978, 1980, 1985, New York Art Directors Show, 1979; winner of International Competition, Women in Design, 1981; Award of Merit, Fifth Annual Exhibition of Fine Art in Children's Book Illustration, New York City, 1984; Award of Excellence in package design from New York Art Directors Club, for Scarborough & Co. tea packages, 1985.

WRITINGS—Illustrator: Joan Harris, *The Schoolmouse and the Hamster*, Warne, 1979; Eve Bunting, *The Empty Window*, Warne, 1980. Contributor of illustrations to books and periodicals.

EXHIBITIONS: International Exhibition of Botanical Drawings, Hunterdon Art Center, Hunterdon, N.J., 1977; "Gallery 3," Society of Illustrators, New York City, 1984.

WORK IN PROGRESS: Contributing recipes and illustrations to *Food and Architecture*, a cookbook scheduled for publication in 1986; *The Sky Shop*, an illustrated children's book co-authored with Cooper Edens; *Drawing Your Baby*, a how-to book; and "Living in the Visual World," a new approach to perspective and the psychology and physiology of seeing.

SIDELIGHTS: After graduation with a B.A. in English literature and a stint as a buyer for a Honolulu department store, Judy Clifford went back to study at the San Francisco Academy of Art (where she won the Richard Stephens Merit Scholarship Award in 1972). In 1974 she felt she was ready for a career in illustration. Working first in California, she designed and illustrated promotional material, annual reports, and posters for such corporations and institutions as Del Monte, Levis, Crown-Zellerbach, and the San Francisco Ballet Company. In 1978 she moved to New York City, and her career rapidly went soaring.

While she has worked for corporate clients ranging from Almay Cosmetics to American Express, Judy Clifford is best noted as an illustrator for books and such magazines as *Reader's Digest, Redbook,* and *Cosmopolitan.* Her drawings display a freshness (almost an exuberance) in outlook and a whimsical quality that are probably most apparent in her

An illustration from "Food City," published in *Review*, **February, 1984.** (© 1984, Judy Clifford. Reprinted by permission.)

celebrated "Food and Architecture" series of paintings. In 1984 *Review* presented a portfolio of her works, prefacing it thus: "Most people look at New York City skyscrapers and see glass and steel. When Judy Clifford looks at them, she sees strawberry shortcakes, banana splits, and bacon and

mushroom sandwiches." The article compared her work with that of the sixteenth-century Italian painter Giuseppe Arcimboldo, and the reference is most apt; but while Arcimboldo used fruits and vegetables to paint his "composite heads," Clifford uses the same ingredients to create composite buildings, perhaps suggesting that to modern man the cityscape has replaced the human face as the metaphor for human existence.

"There are many areas of outside interest that inspire my work," Judy Clifford wrote *CGA*. "For instance: I am a gourmet cook, therefore I am interested in developing visually exciting food concepts; for the past three years I have studied French and traveled to France, thus a series of watercolors based on French life. Right now I'm pregnant, so it's logical that I'd be working with a publisher in developing a new book, *Drawing Your Baby*."

BIOGRAPHICAL/CRITICAL SOURCES: Henry C. Pitz, *200 Years of American Illustration*, Random House, 1977; "Food City," *Review*, February, 1984; "Food and Architecture," *Vanity* (Italy), fall, 1984; Lester Krantz, *American Artists*, Facts on File, 1985.

* * *

COBER, Alan E(dwin) 1935-

PERSONAL: Born May 18, 1935, in New York, N.Y.; son of Sol Walter (an attorney) and Mollie (Spitzer) Cohen; name legally changed; married Ellen L. Ross, November 17, 1961; children: Leslie (daughter), Peter. *Education:* Attended University of Vermont, 1952-54; School of Visual Arts, 1954-56. *Home:* Ossining, N.Y. *Agent:* Harvey Kahn Associates, 50 E. 50th St., New York, N.Y. 10022.

CAREER: Artist and illustrator, 1960—. Instructor, Silvermine College of Art, Conn., 1966, and Parsons School of Design, New York City, 1969. President of Illustrators Workshop. *Military service:* U.S. Army, 1958-60.

MEMBER: Society of Illustrators (vice-president, 1968); American Institute of Graphic Arts.

AWARDS, HONORS: Named Artist of the Year by Artists Guild of New York, 1965; *Winter's Eve* and *Mr. Corbett's Ghost* appeared on *New York Times* list of best-illustrated books of the year, 1968 and 1969; Hamilton King Award from Society of Illustrators, 1968; Gold Medal from Society of Illustrators, 1969, 1972, 1974, 1976, and 1977; Gold Medal from Art Directors Club of New York 1973, 1976, 1977, 1981, 1982, and 1983. More than 250 awards from various institutions since 1961.

WRITINGS—All as illustrator: George Sanderlin, *First Around the World*, Harper, 1964; Sanderlin, *Eastward to India*, Harper, 1965; Madeleine Polland, *The White Twilight*, Holt, 1965; Robert P. Smith, *Nothingatall, Nothingatall, Nothingatall*, Harper, 1965; Julia Cunningham, *Viollet*, Pantheon, 1966; Carl Withers, adapter, *The Tale of the Black Cat*, Holt, 1966; Phyllis LaFarge, *The Gumdrop Necklace*, Knopf, 1967; Leon Garfield, *Mr. Corbett's Ghost*, Pantheon, 1968; Withers, adapter, *The Wild Ducks and the Goose*, Holt, 1968; Robert Nye, *Beowulf* (retold), Hill & Wang, 1968; Natalia M. Belting, *Winter's Eve* (poem), Holt, 1969; Florence Melman White, *Your Friend, the Tree*, Knopf, 1969.

Jean-Pierre Abraham, *The Pigeon Man*, Quist, 1972; Susan Cooper, *The Dark Is Rising*, Atheneum, 1973; Ted Hughes, *The Tiger Bones*, Viking, 1973; Cober, *The Forgotten Society*, Dover, 1974; Franz Kafka, *The Trial*, Limited Editions Book Club, 1975; James Joyce, *Ulysses*, Franklin Library, 1976; Edgar Allan Poe, *Poe's Poems and Essays*, Franklin Library, 1977; Kurt Vonnegut, *Slaughterhouse 5*, Franklin Library, 1977; Norman Mailer, *The Naked and the Dead*, Franklin Library, 1978; Vonnegut, *Jailbird*, Franklin Library, 1979; *Cober's Choice*, Dutton, 1979; Albert Camus, *Exile and the Kingdom*, Franklin Library, 1980; *Alan E. Cober; The Sketchbook*, Neenah, 1981.

Contributor of illustrations to *Time, Newsweek, Sports Illustrated, Inside Sports, Ladies Home Journal, New York Times*, and other periodicals.

EXHIBITIONS—One-man shows: Society of Illustrators, New York City, 1966, 1969, 1981; Terry Dintenfass Gallery, New York City, 1970, 1975; Katonah Gallery, Katonah, New York, 1970, 1975; Albrecht Museum, St. Joseph, Mo., 1975, 1981; Springfield Museum, 1976; Utah State University, Logan, Utah, 1978; Brigham Young University, Provo, Utah, 1978; F.A.R. Gallery, New York City, 1978; Ringling Museum of Art, Sarasota, Fla., 1979; North Carolina State University, Raleigh, N.C., 1980; Art Center College of Design, Los Angeles, Calif., 1981.

Participated in numerous group shows, including Whitney Museum of American Art, New York City, 1975, and New York Historical Society, 1976. Represented in the permanent collections of many museums.

SIDELIGHTS: The work of Alan Cober does not lend itself to glib appreciations or facile generalizations. Its range is too broad. In the first twenty-five years of his professional career, Cober won recognition as an advertising artist in areas as diverse as men's fashion and corporate editorial, as an illustrator of children's books, and as a journalistic reporter in venues from *Newsweek* to the *New York Times* op-ed page. His work has too many facets, too many influences have been absorbed with too much individuality, to allow it to be easily categorized. He has been praised as "a first class artist" (*Gebrauchsgraphik*) with an "innate sense of design" (*American Artist*) and the courage to "use his talent in the expression of his own social consciousness" (*Print*). Even a cursory review of his output over the years brings to mind artists as widely varied in time, substance, and style as Albrecht Durer, Honore Daumier, William Hogarth, James Ensor, George Grosz, and Ben Shahn. Few illustrators currently working have been examined from as many different perspectives; but then few have deserved the compliment of such varied analysis.

In a revealing reminiscence, Cober has recalled that as a boy he was a slow reader of limited comprehension (later called learning disabled), but could remember every film he saw, not only as a visual experience but in the social context of its viewing (i.e., where he saw it, who accompanied him, etc.). This faculty he has called "total recall as a social experi-

"The Coloseum," an illustration (© 1975, Alan E. Cober. Reprinted by permission.)

ALAN E. COBER

ence," indicative of a mind more impressed with ambiance than detail and a memory more dependent on sensation than fact. It is not surprising, then, that his earliest inclinations were more toward the fine than the liberal arts; but his father, a successful lawyer, discouraged such inclinations in favor of a professional career. In fact, it was not until Cober completed two years of pre-law studies at the University of Vermont that he was encouraged by the positive comments of an art instructor to take up the formal study of art. He transferred to the School of Visual Arts, where he studied under Al Werner and Robert Frankenberg, and later under Chaim Gross at the New School. As avid readers read, committed writers write, and compulsive talkers talk, the freshly liberated Cober produced an explosion of drawings in his quest to develop a distinctive style. His first employment came in the area of fashion illustration, where his naturally breezy linear expressiveness was perfectly suited to the requirements of the trade, but the real process of stretching his capacities as an illustrator began in earnest when he was commissioned by the editors of *Parents Magazine* to provide a set of drawings for their reissue of Rudyard Kipling's *Jungle Book*.

The resulting work caught the eye of Ursula Nordstrom, children's book editor at Harper & Row, and opened up the area of juvenile literature illustration for him. His free-lance

career thus proceeded satisfactorily through the late 1950s and 1960s, with commissions regularly coming in from *Ladies' Home Journal*, *Harper's*, and *Sports Illustrated*; corporate accounts like IBM, CBS, and Standard Oil of New Jersey; and numerous publishers of children's books. By the mid-1960s he had acquired a reputation as one of the more versatile and inventive of graphic artists working on the advertising scene, most notably for his success in blending descriptive penmanship with the imperatives of design. As he told critic Henry Pitz in 1966: "I love to draw. . . I keep searching, keep looking for new ways. I try to see things differently each time I draw. I'm always looking for new things to do; I would love to try films or a mural." This remark, in conjunction with Pitz's observation that Cober didn't seem "particularly drawn toward the elegant or the chic" strikes one, in retrospect, as being remarkably prescient.

In 1971, Cober was asked to do some drawings to accompany a *Newsweek* cover story entitled "Justice in America." The assignment took him on a Cook's tour of New York state and city penal institutions, police stations, and courthouses, and inspired an outpouring of stark, spidery, ink-line images: looming guard-towers, dingy tank cells, cops, cons, judges, even a grim rendering of the electric chair at Sing-Sing. It was his first headlong plunge into socially conscious reportage, and his subsequent justification of the effort is revealing: "It was what was happening at the time, and I wanted to document it." This idea of visual documentation, of artist as social historian was to become even more important in his next journalistic undertaking.

In 1973, as the broadcast media particularly were breaking the story of deplorable conditions at the Willowbrook Institute, a state-run custodial facility for the mentally retarded on Staten Island, the *New York Times* hired Cober to illustrate an op-ed page piece on the subject. In the course of this assignment, Cober found himself becoming personally committed. The resulting work projected an empathy he had failed to communicate in his powerful but comparatively detached prison sketches. For three days he prowled the institution, smelling the stench, listening to the cacophony, observing the human jetsam, and bearing witness as an artist to it all. What emerged was a series of more than fifty drawings—nervous, electric, abrupt, often angry outcries in ink—many including urgently scrawled notations "to com-

Self-portrait of Alan E. Cober (© 1979, Alan E. Cober. Reprinted by permission.)

"The Alamo," an illustration (© 1977, Alan E. Cober. Reprinted by permission.)

municate things that can't be drawn." It was an exhausting, painfully depressing, yet profounding touching experience. "That kind of confrontation made my involvement a total thing," he told an interviewer for *Print* in 1973, "but it was good. I needed it." These works, along with the prison sketchbook and later drawings done in various old age homes, were published in 1974 in a volume entitled *The Forgotten Society.*

In 1981, Cober's skills as a narrative artist (sharpened by his social reportage and children's book illustration) won him a commission from the Smithsonian Institution to do a mural depicting George Washington's early life in colonial Virginia for its Museum of American History. His charge was to produce an annotated map of the vicinity of the Mount Vernon as it must have been in 1753, when Washington was twenty-one years old. Again Cober was putting himself in the familiar role of historian, but in this case passion was replaced by scholarly preparation and mood subordinated to design. His original study measured twenty-five by sixty inches (one-sixth the final scale) and constituted more than anything else a test of his technical skill. "You realize that any decision you make about one element affects everything else," he explains; "You have to multiply the effect of your decision not by ten but by one hundred. The weight of even small adjustments must be related to the rest of the mural and to the mural six times the size you're working in." In all respects from design to execution, this work provides a showcase for the narrative flair, fineness of line, evocative use of color, and calligraphic notation that Cober has

perfected over the past two-and-a-half decades; it also confirms the continuing appeal of the mural form for socially and politically conscious artists.

BIOGRAPHICAL/CRITICAL SOURCES: Gebrauchsgraphik, September, 1965; *American Artist*, June, 1966; *Print*, May/June, 1973, January/February, 1982; *Communications Arts*, January/February, 1975; *People*, March 3, 1975; *Atlantic*, June, 1979; *Something About the Author*, Vol. 7, Gale, 1975; *Who's Who in American Art*, Bowker, 1984; *Who's Who in America, 1984-85*, Marquis, 1984; *How Magazine*, November-December, 1985.

—*Sketch by Richard Calhoun*

*   *   *

COLIN, Paul 1892-1985

OBITUARY NOTICE: Born June 27, 1892, in Nancy, France; died June 18, 1985, at his home in Nogent-sur-Marne, near Paris. Poster and set designer, painter, illustrator, and educator, Paul Colin ranks alongside Henri de Toulouse-Lautrec, Jules Cheret, and Cassandre, as one of the supreme French masters of the art of the poster. He began his career shortly after World War I, and his design for posters of entertainment celebrities and fashionable places in the mid- and late-1920s made him famous. Blending Art Deco lines with Expressionist elements, such posters as the one of Josephine Baker (1925), "Bal Negre"

(1927), and "Nuit du Theatre a Luna Park" (1928), have become classics. After the outbreak of World War II he designed many patriotic posters; and in 1944 he created the poster commemorating the Liberation of Paris. He also did many posters protesting war atrocities, the most celebrated one being "Varsovie" (1945). At the time of his retirement in the 1970s he had more than forty-five hundred posters to his credit; he had also designed over seven hundred stage and film sets. Colin was a respected painter who exhibited widely, and his art school trained several generations of French poster designers and illustrators. He himself illustrated many French classics and travel books. He was a Chevalier of the Legion of Honor, and had many retrospective shows honoring him, the last one being at the Sorbonne in 1982. As John Barnicoat wrote, "[His] excellent design clearly relates the poster to decorative painting of the time."

BIOGRAPHICAL/CRITICAL SOURCES: John Barnicoat, *A Concise History of Posters*, Oxford University Press, 1972; Emmanuel Benezit, *Dictionnaire des Peintres, Sculpteurs, Dessinateurs et Graveurs*, Grund (Paris), 1976.

OBITUARY SOURCES: New York Times, June 21, 1985.

* * *

CORNELL, J.
    See CORNELL, Jeff(rey W.)

* * *

CORNELL, Jeff(rey W.)   1945-
    (J. Cornell)

PERSONAL: Born September 22, 1945, in Bridgeport, Conn.; son of Arthur William (in lumber business) and Mary-Jo (Madiloni) Cornell; married Janice Builter (a high school aide), December 31, 1966; children: Todd, Kelly, Evan. *Education:* Attended Paier School (now College) of Art, 1968-72. *Home and studio:* 58 Noyes Rd., Fairfield, Conn. 06430. *Agent:* Gail Thurm, Jeff Palmer Art Co., 227 Godfrey Rd., Weston, Conn. 06883.

CAREER: Free-lance illustrator, signing his work J. Cornell or Jeff Cornell, 1969—; waiter, Peppermill Restaurant, Milford, Conn., 1969-74; instructor, Paier College of Art, 1981-83. *Military service:* U.S. Air Force, 1964-68, served in Vietnam; became sergeant.

MEMBER: Society of Illustrators.

AWARDS, HONORS: Designed commemorative stamps for U.S. Postal Service, 1979 and 1985.

WRITINGS—All as illustrator: Richard Peck, *Through a Brief Darkness*, Viking, 1973; Elizabeth Witheridge, *Just One Indian Boy*, Atheneum, 1975; Witheridge, *May I Cross Your Golden Bridge*, Atheneum, 1975; Steven Rayson, *The Crows of War*, Atheneum, 1975; John McPhee, *Deltoid Pumpkin Seed*, Ballantine, 1975; John P. Marquand, *The Late George Apley*, Franklin Library, 1976; Thomas McGuane, *Nobody's Angel*, Ballantine, 1984; Alice Walker, *Meridian*, Pocket Books, 1985; Oscar Hijuelos, *Our House in the Last World*, Pocket Books, 1985.

Illustrator; all by Herman Wouk, all for Pocket Books, 1985: *Aurora Dawn*; *Youngblood Hawke*; *Marjorie Mornings-*

JEFF CORNELL

tar; *City Boy*; *This Is My God*.

Contributor of illustrations to *Redbook*, *Reader's Digest*, and other national magazines.

EXHIBITIONS: Society of Illustrators, New York, N.Y., 1974; G.W.S. Gallery, Southport, Conn., 1983, 1986; Marks Gallery, Atlanta, Ga., 1985, 1986; Griffin-Haller Gallery, Washington, Conn., 1985, 1986.

SIDELIGHTS: "Until 1980 or so," Jeff Cornell wrote *CGA*, "illustrators were 'commercial.' Now they are asked to do their 'own thing'; they are consulted about projects, and their feelings and points of view are taken into respectful consideration. This gives the illustrator great freedom, as clients don't come in with preconceived ideas anymore. I am therefore always searching for clients whose projects can be molded around my own way of thinking."

So far Cornell's clients have constituted an impressive list that includes such organizations as the American Stock Exchange, Bell Telephone, RCA Records, NBC-TV, General Electric, Texaco, Bell Communications Research, and Exxon. He has illustrated projects as diverse as company promotions, advertising campaigns, and corporate reports. His assignments are noted for the impressionistic flair which the artist brings to the solution of tricky illustrative challenges. His illustrations appear in many popular magazines, including *Reader's Digest*, *Good Housekeeping*, *Redbook*, and *Golf Magazine*.

Portrait of Herman Melville by Jeff Cornell (© 1980, Franklin Library. Reprinted by permission.)

It is, however, as a book illustrator that Cornell is best noted. Starting with covers for "gothic horror" paperback novels, he has gradually worked up to more and more demanding assignments. His cover illustrations for Isaac Bashevis Singer's novels have been praised for their fidelity to the spirit of their author—a not inconsiderable feat since the artist's experience is far removed from those of the Eastern European Jews whose lives the author depicts in his tales. "I love illustrating," Cornell says, and he credits three great illustrators—Bernie Fuchs, Mark English, and Bob Heindel—whom he met during his years as an art student, for his present vocation. His love of illustration can be seen in the many books he has illustrated for publishers as diverse as Dell, Pocket Books, Atheneum, Viking, Ballantine, and Macmillan; and on the covers of many other publishers. He

has been chosen to illustrate limited editions of classics published by the Franklin Library, and his portrait of American literary giant Herman Melville in particular has been noted for its brooding intensity. In 1979 Cornell's illustration work earned him a commission from the U.S. Postal Service to design a commemorative stamp honoring the Summer Special Olympic Games; and in 1985 he designed the commemorative stamp honoring the Winter Special Olympics.

BIOGRAPHICAL/CRITICAL SOURCES: Something about the Author, Vol. 11, Gale, 1977; Walt and Roger Reed, *The Illustrator in America 1880-1980,* Madison Square Press, 1984.

CROCKETT, Linda 1948-
(Linda Crockett-Hanzel)

PERSONAL: Born June 14, 1948, in Slater, S.C.; daughter of Robert Roy (a fire fighter) and Karrie Mae (Cobb) Crockett; married Andrew John Hanzel, September 11, 1971 (divorced, 1983); married Steven Robert Blassingame (a writer), October 12, 1985. *Education:* Attended Cleveland Institute of Art, 1966-67; also attended Cleveland State University, Cooper School of Art, and Illustrators Workshop. *Home and studio:* 2103 Granville Rd., Franklin, Tenn. 37064 *Agent:* Crockett, 796 E. 222nd St., Euclid, Ohio 44123.

CAREER: Advertising assistant, Bob Craig Advertising, Cleveland, Ohio, 1967; clothing designer for professional rock musicians, Mantalk Men's Store, Cleveland, 1967; layout artist, Sterling-Lindner (a department store), Cleveland, 1968; artist, American Greetings Corp., Cleveland, 1968-71; free-lance illustrator, designer, and art director, 1971—; creative coordinator for gift wrap design, CPS Industries, Franklin, Tenn., 1985—. Instructor at Macomb County Community College, Warren, Mich., and Akron University. Special lecturer at Lakeland Community College, Mentor, Ohio; University of Miami; and Center for Creative Studies, Detroit, Mich.

MEMBER: Society of Illustrators.

AWARDS, HONORS: Desi Awards for illustration and book cover design, from Graphics: USA, 1979; Margaret Bevier Wright Memorial Award, for painting, Cooperstown Art Association, 1979; honorable mention, International Society of Artists, 1979; Gold Medals for editorial and book illustration, from Society of Illustrators, 1982; Special Mention, for painting, Grand Prix International d'Art Contemporain of Monte-Carlo, 1983; Special Painting Award, Cleveland Museum of Art, 1983.

EXHIBITIONS: "Illustrators Workshop Exhibit," Master Eagle Gallery, New York City, 1978; (one-woman show) Brigham City Museum Gallery, Utah, 1978; Society of Illustrators, 1978; "Illustrators Workshop Retrospective Show," Master Eagle Gallery, 1980; Museum of American Illustration, New York City, 1983; Cleveland Museum of Art, 1983; Lorillard Gallery, New York City, 1984; Eagle Gallery of Children's Book Illustrations, New York City, 1985; Society of Illustrators, 1985. Many other exhibitions and gallery showings.

WORK IN PROGRESS: A series of paintings about English life; a series of sculptures; sculpture-collages depicting figures of historical costuming; a triptych on punk rock.

An illustration by Linda Crockett

Photographic self-portrait of Linda Crockett (© Linda Crockett)

CROCKETT-HANZEL, Linda
See CROCKETT, Linda

* * *

CRUISE, S(haron) 1947-

PERSONAL: Born November 13, 1947, in Pomona, Calif.; daughter of Val D. (an insurance agent) and Marie A. (Cassidy) Ridge; married Lawrence J. Cruise (an artist), September 1, 1973. *Education:* Chaffey Junior College, A.A., 1981, A.S., 1981. *Office:* Artara Co., P.O. Box 1367, Upland, Calif. 91785.

CAREER: Bookkeeper, office manager, and assistant manager, San Bernardino Business Men's Association, San Bernardino, Calif., 1965-71; supervisor and executive secretary, Transamerica Title Insurance Co., Riverside, Calif., 1971-74; free-lance artist and illustrator, 1977-86; manager and artist, Artara Co. (illustration, fine arts, stained glass, and sand-etchings), Upland, Calif., 1986—. Editor in chief and art consultant to Yeh's Center of Natural Medicine, Upland; International Order of Rainbow Girls (line officer, 1960-65).

Self-portrait of S. Cruise (© 1986, S. Cruise. Reprinted by permission.)

SIDELIGHTS: In the commercial art field since 1967, Linda Crockett has steadily risen in proficiency and acceptance over the years. In 1982 she was awarded two Gold Medals by the Society of Illustrators, the first woman to be so honored in the twenty-four-year history of the event; the medals were for both editorial and book illustration, and highlighted Crockett's artistic range. She has also received awards in other artistic fields, from book design to painting, which further evidences her versatility and adaptability.

Linda Crockett (who from 1972 to 1982 was known as Crockett-Hanzel) has variously worked as greeting card designer, illustrator, art director, and fashion designer. Among her present and former clients are prestigious magazines and publications of the order of *Atlantic Monthly, Fortune, New York Times,* and *Playboy,* and publishers such as the Literary Guild, Ballantine, and Scholastic Books. Her illustrations, moody and evocative, always perfectly suit her subject matter. For instance, to illustrate an article on the life of a newspaperman titled "A Ringside Seat for Life," she used a shadowy profile nursing a glass of beer in front of a bar window, a newspaper spread on the table before him— an ironic comment on the supposed glamour of a journalist's life. Her paintings also precisely delineate in mood and setting a particular moment in life; a young girl gravely contemplating a photograph, two old ladies whiling the time away in a tearoom, these are telling vignettes that aim at recapturing small remembrances of things past.

BIOGRAPHICAL/CRITICAL SOURCES: Illustrators 24, Hastings House, 1982; *Communication Arts,* July-August, 1982; *Cleveland Museum Bulletin,* May, 1983.

MEMBER: National Wildlife Association, Smithsonian Institution, San Bernardino County Museum and Fine Arts Association, Genealogical Society of Pennsylvania, Los Angeles County Museum and Arts Association.

AWARDS, HONORS: Honorable Mention from San Bernardino County Fine Arts Institute, 1983, for colored pencil drawing "Grey Squirrel," and 1984, for colored pencil drawing "Imperiled Canis rufus."

WRITINGS: Illustrator and contributor to local and national art journals and periodicals.

EXHIBITIONS: San Bernardino County Fine Arts Institute, Redlands, Calif., 1983, 1984; Ontario Museum and Gallery, Ontario, Calif., 1985.

WORK IN PROGRESS: Editing, research, artwork, and some writing for the quarterly journal of Yeh's Center of Natural Medicine; portrait painting.

SIDELIGHTS: Sharon Cruise wrote *CGA*: "As the recipient of degrees in fine arts and advertising I enjoy working in both fields. My husband and partner in Artara Company is also an artist. We tend to motivate each other in all aspects of our careers and in other fields as well. Lawrence has a beautiful gift for design, color, and drawing; in combining his and my own talents we have started a small art business together. As of the present we are involved in stained glass, sand-etching, advertising, design, illustration, painting, and drawing; we expect to expand eventually into the fields of ceramics, sculpture, glass blowing, woodworking, weaving, and other media, and to bring together other talented artists into what we hope will become a full teaching and experimental studio.

"I have always drawn, as far back as I can remember: drawing has been my first love. Although I did not become seriously involved in art until I met my husband, who is also interested in many facets of the arts, I taught myself as much as I could, then went on to college to further my education. It is while in college that I also became fascinated with advertising, design, and illustration; and I decided to get an additional degree in that field. I was the first, at that particular college, to get two degrees at the same time. While I enjoy working in many fields of art, my mediums of choice are pencil (black-and-white and color), pen-and-ink (black-and-white and color), acrylics, and oils."

Sharon Cruise has been drawing and painting through her entire life, even when a painful illness kept her bed-ridden for more than a year. Her depictions of animals and especially of wildlife (red-tailed hawks, owls, harp seals, roadrunners) are minutely detailed and almost naturalistic. As she stated, "I normally draw and paint in a very realistic style, but I am capable of a different approach." This can be seen in some other, more fanciful works, such as the montage "The World of Art and Artist" and "Cornucopia," in which she combines a certain whimsicality of treatment with a great delicacy of line.

AVOCATIONAL INTERESTS: Reading, photography, sculpture, genealogy, music, dancing, playing and learning to play instruments, swimming, and bicycling. Cruise told *CGA*: "I have traveled extensively across the United States and Canada since I was very young. I never get enough of seeing our beautiful country, but I also have a desire to see parts of Ireland, Germany, and Europe, where my ancestors originally came from."

* * *

"Transition" (© 1984, S. Cruise. Reprinted by permission.)

CURTIS, Thomas P. 1938-
(Tom Curtis)

PERSONAL: Born June 10, 1938, in New York, N.Y.; son of Thomas (a civil servant) and Elizabeth (a portrait painter; maiden name, Longfellow) Curtis; married Denise Dietrich Willman, November 18, 1972; children: Elizabeth L., Thomas J., Marguerite W., Andrew W. *Education:* Harvard College, A.B., 1960; attended Corcoran School of Art, Washington, D.C., 1966-67; graduated from U.S. Army Command and General Staff College, 1979. *Religion:* Episcopalian. *Home:* 758 E. Day Ave., Milwaukee, Wis. 53217. *Agent:* William Van DeLind, 933 N. Mayfair Rd., Milwaukee, Wis. 53226.

CAREER: Editorial cartoonist, *National Review*, New York, N.Y., 1967—; editorial cartoonist, *Milwaukee Sentinel*, Milwaukee, Wis., 1969-83; art director, PM Advertising, Milwaukee, 1984-85; president, Curtis Studio (oil portraits, illustrations, art, cartoons), Milwaukee, 1985—. Teacher of history of art at Brookfield Academy (upper school), 1986—. Chairman of Transient Task Force, Central City Churches, Milwaukee, 1976-78. *Military Service:* U.S. Army Corps of Engineers, active duty 1960-65; U.S. Army Reserves, 1966—, with rank of lieutenant colonel; received Army Commendation Medal.

MEMBER: Association of American Editorial Cartoonists (president, 1977-78).

AWARDS, HONORS: Silver Ink Bottle Award, Association of American Editorial Cartoonists, 1983; George Washington Honor Medal, Freedoms Foundation at Valley Forge, 1970, 1971, 1975, 1977; Highway Safety Award, 1975; Best Editorial Cartoon of 1976, Milwaukee Press Club, 1976.

WRITINGS—All collections of editorial cartoons: (With Allan Brownfeld) *Obadiah and the Decline of the Great Society*, privately printed, 1968; *The Turn of the Decade*, Heritage Press, 1970; *Curtis in Profile: Fourteen Years of Editorial Cartoons in the Milwaukee Sentinel*, Heritage Features Syndicate, 1983.
Contributor of cartoons: Charles Brooks, editor, *Best Editorial Cartoons of the Year*, Pelican, 1972, (not published 1973) 1974-85; Stephen Hess and Milton Kaplan, *The Ungentlemanly Art: A History of American Political Cartoons*, Macmillan, 1975; Syd Hoff, *Editorial and Political Cartooning*, Stravon, 1976.

EXHIBITIONS: Charles Allis Art Library, Milwaukee, Wis., editorial cartoons, 1970.

WORK IN PROGRESS: A series of large oil paintings and pen drawings of the U.S. Cavalry in the West during the 1870s, completion expected in 1986.

THOMAS P. CURTIS

SIDELIGHTS: Tom Curtis is cut from the classic pattern of editorial cartooning, with his work placing him firmly in the great nineteenth-century tradition of the illustrator-cartoonist going back to Thomas Nast. Growing up in an artistic household (his mother was a portrait painter) and educated at Harvard in the exacting discipline of architecture, Curtis approaches his profession soberly and with due respect for the responsibilities it carries. Always ingenious and often witty, Curtis is never frivolous or facetious; he is a commentator, not a comic. His art is employed in the service of his ideas, and he takes his ideas seriously.

That his work is taken seriously by others is proved by the wide use that has been made of it beyond his own newspaper. His cartoons have been included in many standard text and reference books, such as *The Ungentlemanly Art: A History of American Political Cartoons* by Stephen Hess and Milton Kaplan and *Editorial and Political Cartooning* by Syd Hoff. Charles Brooks's annual series *Best Editorial Cartoons of the Year* has included examples of Curtis's work every year since it started in 1972. In 1983 the Association of American Editorial Cartoonists, of which he had been president in 1977 and 1978, awarded him its highest prize, the Silver Ink Bottle Award.

With an architectural degree from Harvard, Curtis entered the U.S. Army at twenty-two and served for five years in the Corps of Engineers before finding his way into the art world. In 1967 he became a regular editorial cartoonist for the *National Review* and two years later took on the same post with the *Milwaukee Sentinel*. During the fourteen years he held this position, he published three collections of his cartoons. The first, *Obadiah and the Decline of the Great Society*, covered the last days of President Lyndon Johnson's administration, with a text by Allan Brownfeld; the second, *The Turn of the Decade*, was a report at the end of the 1960s; and in 1983 the U.S. Industrial Council gave him a grant for *Curtis in Profile*, a retrospective of his decade-and-a-half with the *Milwaukee Sentinel*. With this gesture of farewell, Curtis left the newspaper for a one-year stint as art director of a Milwaukee advertising agency, and in 1985 opened his own studio.

Curtis Studio brings the portrait painter's son full circle. Here he offers illustrations, cartoons, and portraits and does serious historical paintings and drawings in oils or ink. When the work load becomes heavy enough, he employs help, but generally he does all the work, issuing a steady stream of illustrations for publications, portraits in oil, and his regular editorial cartoons for the *National Review*. For some time he has had a special interest in the American West and has been engaged in a series of large oils and drawings dealing with the U.S. Cavalry on the frontier during the 1870s.

In all of Curtis's work, the tight discipline of his formal training is apparent. His clean, simple drawing is masterful and his composition is always balanced and pleasing. His economy of line exemplifies the ideal of the cartoonist's art, to convey complex ideas succinctly. Often he accomplishes his goal by his drawing alone, without need of words, as in his eloquent and moving obituary drawing for ventriloquist Edgar Bergen, showing the solitary and silent Charlie McCarthy with a tear in his unmonocled eye. Curtis claims the influence of the early twentieth-century German caricaturists Eduard Thony and Bruno Paul, both regular contributors to the German satirical review *Simplicissimus*, and the elegant, clean style of Curtis's cartoons surely owes something to Paul, whose sinuous line and strong contrasts of black and white were powerful influences on the cartoon style of Europe and the United States in the 1920s and 1930s. Curtis also acknowledges a debt to English cartoonist David Low. But the Milwaukee artist has gone far beyond his German and English masters in his simplicity of line, reducing his forms often to mere outlines. In an inside joke on Curtis's graphic minimalism, *Chicago Tribune* editorial cartoonist Wayne Stayskal has drawn a man looking at a completely blank rectangle signed "Curtis" and exclaiming, "How I love the simplicity of a Curtis cartoon." Curtis so appreciated the gag that he had it printed on the back cover of his last book.

Curtis is that rare phenomenon among political cartoonists, a witty conservative. For almost two decades he has contributed commentary in graphic form to America's leading conservative magazine, *National Review*. But despite his Ivy-League background, he is no crusty reactionary. He identifies his political philosophy as "what [British columnist John] Chamberlain once called libertarian conservatism," and like any honest political cartoonist, he is flexible. Never a cruel caricaturist, he portrays even his greatest villains with dignity. During President Nixon's final months in office, there was more tragedy in Curtis's depictions of him than in those of most cartoonists; a particularly haunting one showed the President strangling in a spider web of White House tapes.

A man of deep religious beliefs, Curtis has been active in church work in his community and for many years has included a graceful little fish—an ancient Christian symbol—in his signature. For a time an editor banished this expression of the artist's faith from his cartoons, but since Curtis changed jobs, it has swum back into his panels and remains a tasteful testimony to his convictions.

Curtis's essentially painterly style directs him to the classical tools of the artist. Like the American master Winsor McCay, whose cartoons Curtis's sometimes resemble, he almost always uses a brush and black ink for his cartoons, using a pen only for lettering. He draws on board at 175 percent of the size of the published cartoon. For his painting he prefers oils and leans toward representational depictions of his subjects. His favorite illustrator, not surprisingly, is the popular American realist N. C. Wyeth.

Curtis speaks Spanish fluently and claims smatterings of French, German, Russian, and Latin. These accomplishments seem appropriate to a man of his traditionalist tastes, as does his ability to play the bagpipe and his interest in genealogy. Bill Janz of the *Milwaukee Sentinel* described him in 1983 as "a professional American square, in the best sense of those dimensions," and says of him, "Tom is sensitive. And, in his dedication to the art of cartoonery, he is serious to a point that his work will sometimes squeeze frowns out of readers." To Curtis, "An editorial cartoon is like a laser beam. It can cut deep and sharp. . . . The editorial cartoonist plays an important role in shaping the

" These tapes may further damage my case." —Nixon

An editorial cartoon by Tom Curtis (© 1974, *Milwaukee Sentinel*. Reprinted by permission.)

A magazine illustration by Tom Curtis, ca. 1983 (© *Triumph.*)

complexion of the editorial page. The cartoonist is not just a graphic artist for the editorial writers." He regrets that so few editorial cartoonists are willing to make strong political statements about the news. Profoundly aware of the potential power of his position, he states: "A good cartoonist is far more than an illustrator. He is a keen political analyst with a well developed political philosophy. . . to make the daily cartoon the effective and powerful instrument that it ought to be." Add to this description a distinctive personal style and a keen sense of visual metaphor, and you have a portrait of Tom Curtis.

BIOGRAPHICAL/CRITICAL SOURCES: Dan Kelly, "Portrait of a Conservative Cartoonist," *Bugle American,* June 25, 1975; Syd Hoff, *Editorial and Political Cartooning,* Stravon, 1976; Bill Janz, "Introduction," Tom Curtis, *Curtis in Profile,* Heritage Features Syndicate, 1983.

—*Sketch by Dennis Wepman*

* * *

CURTIS, Tom
    See CURTIS, Thomas P.

* * *

CUSACK, Margaret   1945-

PERSONAL: Born August 1, 1945, in Chicago, Ill.; daughter of Harold Milton (an expediter) and Catherine (an executive secretary; maiden name, Lynch) Weaver; married Frank Cusack (an art director), December 27, 1969; children: Katie. *Education:* Pratt Institute, B.F.A. (cum laude), 1968. *Politics:* Democrat. *Home:* 124 Hoyt St., Brooklyn, N.Y. 11217.

CAREER: Art director, Richard Manoff Co., New York City, 1968-70; art director, Bailey Deardorf & Bowen (advertising agency), Washington, D.C., 1970; art director, WETA-TV, Washington, 1970-71; art director, C. Richard Hatch Associates (design studio), New York City, 1971-72; co-owner, Margaret & Frank & Friends, Brooklyn, N.Y., 1972—. Member of Hoyt Street Association (president, 1974-78).

MEMBER: Graphic Artists Guild, American Crafts Council.

AWARDS, HONORS: Emmy Award, National Academy of Television Arts and Sciences, 1971, for set design; Andy Award, 1975, for set design; award from Society of Publication Designers, 1976; awards from Society of Illustrators, 1981, 1982, 1984, and 1985.

WRITINGS—Self-illustrated: *The Christmas Carol Sampler,* Harcourt, 1983.

EXHIBITIONS: Handwork Gallery, New York City, 1973, 1974; Mari Gallery, Mamaroneck, N.Y., 1974, 1975; Fairtree Gallery, New York City, 1974, 1975; Calhoun Crafts Exhibition, Yale University, New Haven, Conn., 1975; Brooklyn College, Brooklyn, N.Y., 1975; Philadelphia Art Alliance, Philadelphia, Penn., 1975, 1976; Elizabeth Fortner Gallery, Santa Barbara, Calif., 1976; New York Bicentennial Exhibition, New York City, 1976; Artspace Invitational Fibre Exhibition, Milwaukee, Wis., 1977; "Women's Art Symposium," Indiana State University, 1977; Intersew Exhibition, Monte Carlo, Monaco, 1978; Thrasher-Orth Gallery, Seattle, Wash., 1979.

Olympic Village Exhibit, Lake Placid, N.Y., 1980; Louise Himelfarb Gallery, Southampton, N.Y., 1981; "Contemporary Graphics," Maryland Institute, Baltimore, Md., 1981; "Circus," Castle Gallery, College of New Rochelle, N.Y., 1981; "Mythic Machines," America House, Tenafly, N.J., 1982; "Art Space," Swan Galleries, Philadelphia, Penn., 1982; "20th Century Images of George Washington," Fraunces Tavern Museum, New York City, 1982; "The Christmas Carol Sampler," Art Directors Club, New York City, 1983; "Currents 84," Middle Tennessee State University, Murfreesboro, Tenn., 1984; "Texture, Form, and Style," Hartwick College, Oneonta, N.Y., 1984; "New York State of Mind," The Gallery at 15 Steps, Ithaca, N.Y., 1984; "The Christmas Carol Sampler," Skera Gallery, Hadley, Mass., 1984; "New York Society of Illustrators Exhibition to Japan," Tokyo, Japan, 1984; "American Politics and the Presidency," Renwick Gallery, Washington, D.C., 1984; "Masks, Masques, Masx," Gallery Mesa, Mesa, Ariz., 1984; "Contemporary Illustration," College d'Enseignement General et Professionnel de Sainte Foy, Quebec, Canada, 1985; "Quilting: New Images from Old Traditions," Gallery at Hastings-on-Hudson, N.Y., 1985; "Currents 1986," Murfreesboro, Tenn., 1986.

WORK IN PROGRESS: A poster-map of the United States for American Express Co.; a series of full-page ads for Peek Freans cookies; *The Hoyt Street Garden,* written with

MARGARET CUSACK

husband Frank Cusack, to be published by Harcourt in 1987.

SIDELIGHTS: Applique artist/illustrator Margaret Cusack, like so many who chose creative metiers in the spontaneity-drenched era of the 1960s, does "her own thing." It is not something she set out to do, nor was it a part of any formal study curriculum at her alma mater, Brooklyn's Pratt Institute; but insofar as her educationally formative years occurred during an era in which primacy was given to the generation of ideas and technique was relegated to support status, the result of her conceptual freelancing— i.e., three-dimensional illustration—is perfectly in character. Her major at Pratt, in fact, was design, a strongly concept-oriented discipline which places emphasis on organization and tends to require acquaintance with a broad range of graphic skills rather than a mastery of any one genre, while encouraging experimentation in various mediums. Despite all this, however, her current professional success owes a great deal to chance.

For four years after graduation, Cusack worked at a series of hectic, high-pressure design jobs in New York and Washington, D.C. Despite her success (including an Emmy Award for set design in 1971), in 1972 she found herself simultaneously out of work and physically exhausted. At this point, she recalls, "I decided that my first priority should be to get healthy." It was during her recuperation period that she began to explore texture and design by doing appliqued pillows (portraits and landscapes) for friends. The response was so encouraging that she was soon selling them to various New York City boutiques. An artists' representative whom

she'd met through her husband, art director Frank Cusack, suggested that she put together a portfolio of what had by now evolved into a hybrid of fabric collage and soft sculpture, and her new career as a free-lance illustrator was soon thriving.

Producing one of her applique works begins with a postcard-sized sketch which is then blown up to work-size—"I tend to work small," [fourteen by seventeen inches generally] she notes; "Any larger you lose the texture"—and a pattern is traced out on a light box. This pattern is then used to cut out the fabric shapes that will make up the completed illustration. The component pieces are cut from spray-starched fabric to ensure that they hold their shapes, then affixed to the background with spray glue before finally being stitched into place using an ordinary zig-zag sewing machine. An article on her work in *Print* described her appliques as "tightly designed, exactly constructed compositions. There are no rough edges, no rags or frays, no loose ends trailing off the finished composition. Instead areas of color begin and end as they might in a silk screen printing. Each gradation of pattern and color suggests the lights and shadows that might realistically define a figure or a scene. To obtain her subtle shadings, Cusack often dyes her own complementing shades."

She makes no pretense to skill as a seamstress—"I can't even sew a zipper" she told a *New York Times* interviewer in 1975—and confesses that the final stitching process is the

July Statue of Liberty, **fabric collage for 1986 Avon calendar** (© Margaret Cusack. Reprinted by permission.)

least creative part and that she has to psych herself up to do it sometimes. The creative, spontaneous aspect of her work depends, however, not on technique but largely upon her selection and deployment of materials which, beside fabric, include wood, metals, old jewelry, and buttons. Considerations of texture—corduroy, burlap, dotted swiss, lace—as well as color and pattern figure in her choice of fabric, while the selection of three-dimensional items allow for wit and invention. Thus, when an apple pie illustration seemed inadequately bumpy, she ripped up the top crust and threw in a handful of pebbles from her backyard; elsewhere the red fruit on a tree bears a suspicious resemblance to little cinnamon hearts. The overall effect of these efforts is one of warmth and individuality, of ingenuousness, of an almost childlike simplicity and accessibility.

With a designer's savvy, Cusack (whom the *New York Times* called a "noted fabric collage artist") knows how to exploit this special quality by choosing her subjects with great care. Good examples are her book *The Christmas Carol Sampler* and her 1986 calendar for Avon Cosmetics, each of which contain a number of sampler-style works suggesting influences as diverse (and yet as related) as Currier and Ives, Grandma Moses, Norman Rockwell, Vincent Van Gogh, and Henri Rousseau. Certainly her work has proved attractive to advertisers from Ciba-Geigy and Mobil Oil to Perrier and Peek Freans, as well as to editorial outlets as varied as *Emergency Medicine, Seventeen, Yankee, Epicure,* and *Reader's Digest.* She also does applique portraiture on a commission basis, and her work has been part of many gallery shows and is represented in a number of public and private collections.

BIOGRAPHICAL/CRITICAL SOURCES: Print, December, 1973, September, 1985; *New York Times,* January 21, 1975; *Art Direction,* August, 1979; *Prattfolio,* spring, 1984.

Ochre Skyscape, **a fabric collage** (© 1979, Margaret Cusack. Reprinted by permission.)

D

DALY, Tom 1938-

PERSONAL: Born October 11, 1938, in New York, N.Y.; son of Harold (in merchant marine) and Dorothy (a cook; maiden name, Devenney) Daly. *Education:* Attended Art Students League, 1957-61, and School of Visual Arts, 1961-63. *Politics:* "None." *Religion:* "None." *Home and studio:* 47 E. Edsel Ave., Palisades Park, N.J. 07650.

CAREER: Free-lance artist and illustrator, 1960—. *Military service:* U.S. Army Reserve, 1960-67.

MEMBER: Society of Illustrators, Graphic Artists Guild.

AWARDS, HONORS: Award of Excellence from Society of Illustrators, 1963, for record album cover *Nippon-Soul*; nominated for Grammy Award for Best Record Album Cover by National Academy of Television Arts and Sciences, 1964; Gold Medal from New York Art Directors Club, 1966, for "Painted Woman" announcement poster.

WRITINGS: (Illustrator) Helga Sandburg, *Joel and the Wild Goose*, Dial, 1964.

SIDELIGHTS: Designer/illustrator Tom Daly made it very difficult, if not impossible, to top himself rather early in his career. It was in the mid-1960s that he employed the varied skills of conceptual artist, graphic artist, and designer to come up with one of the most characteristic images from that bumptious slice of recent history referred to as the "sixties" (though in fact the era spilled well over into the 1970s). Against a backdrop of electric rock music, Carnaby Street fashion, experimental arrangements in living and loving, and drugs (especially of the hallucinogenic variety), Daly created his "Call for Entries" poster for the 1966 New York Art Directors Club Show. So perfectly did this piece sum up all the varied "liberations" and excesses of contemporary hip culture that it remains to this day a virtual anthropological artifact, a document for social historians to cite in their reconstructions of the period.

Originally conceived in a twelve-by-sixty-three inch format, the piece started out as a nude, the curving contours of whose body were decorated from face to foot, using a mixture of greasepaint and plastic pigment, with a colorful plethora of psychedelic imagery (paisley shapes, stylized flowers, rainbows, sunbursts, etc.) and lettered in art nouveau block with the title of the event being advertised. The scroll began at the knee on the model's right leg and ended with the word "Show" molded around the right side of her right breast (which was itself tipped with a cunningly devised flower-nipple). She was then posed in a modified prone position, head in full profile, pelvic area full front, holding the Club logo, and photographed, forelit with spots

TOM DALY

to accent the design while artfully sustaining her feminine mysteries in shadow. In sum, it is hard to know which aspect of the production to praise most highly. As a concept it is stunning, as humor it is deft, in execution it is faultless, and as an achievement with more than transient value it possesses a rare distinction. At the time, Daly was twenty-eight.

The years since 1966 have hardly been unkind to Tom Daly—he has continued to work steadily as an illustrator for some of the top advertising accounts in the country, winning his share of awards and honors in the process. Most recently he has moved into the area of video animation. In his print work, design still seems as important as technical virtuosity; but an esthetic that was very contemporary in the 1960s seems in the intervening years to have been replaced by a retreat into the art deco past. What feeling there once was in his work for gritty realism (for example, his album cover for *Lenny Bruce Live at Carnegie Hall*) appears to have given way to a colorful, cheery, sophisticated kind of imagery reminiscent of the 1930s and 1940s—a ruddy-cheeked, freckled, Norman Rockwellesque little boy, a red waistcoated waiter with a pillbox hat (recalling the bellhop in the old

A silhouette drawing, ca. 1980 (© Tom Daly)

Philip Morris Co. ads), even silhouette figures, which of themselves seem to reflect an art deco emphasis on mass rather than detail. He shows a distinct preference for rounded forms and metallic sheens in his color painting, which is bold and ingenuous, as well as a fondness for the visual experience offered by *Saturday Evening Post* layouts of forty years ago. As a style, it is more evocative than original, but it is also lively, competently executed, eye-catching stuff, and may, after all, owe more to Daly's current interest in video animation than to earlier mixed-media successes like the famous "Painted Lady."

BIOGRAPHICAL/CRITICAL SOURCES: Print, January/February, 1967; *Horizons*, autumn, 1967; *Twenty Years of Award Winners*, Hastings House, 1981.

* * *

DAUMIER, Honore (Victorin)   1808-1879

PERSONAL: Born February 26, 1808, in Marseilles, France; died February 10, 1879, in Valmondois, France, and buried in Paris; son of Jean-Baptiste (a glazier) and Cecile-Catherine (Philip) Daumier; married Marie-Alexandrine Dassy (a dressmaker), April 16, 1846. *Education:* Received little formal education; took art lessons in Paris from Alexandre Lenoir and in the studios of artists Suisse and Eugene Boudin.

CAREER: Errand boy in law offices and in a Palais-Royal bookstore, Paris, France, 1822; lithograph-stone preparer for print publisher A. Belliard, mid-1820s; free-lance contributor to lithograph and print shops, 1825-29; contributor of cartoons and drawings to several periodicals published by Charles Philipon, including *La Silhouette*, 1829-30, *La Caricature*, 1830-35, and *Le Charivari*, 1832-72, as well as to other illustrated papers; painter, watercolorist, and sculptor, 1850-79.

AWARDS, HONORS: Chevalier of the French Legion of Honor, 1870 (refused).

WRITINGS—All collections of drawings and cartoons: *Hunting and Fishing*, Leon Amiel, 1975; *Daumier: One Hundred Twenty Lithographs*, Dover, 1978; *Lawyers and Justice*, Vilo, 1981; *Doctors and Medicine*, Vilo, 1981; *Liberated Women*, Vilo, 1982; *Businessmen and Finance*, Vilo, 1983; *Daumier and Music*, Da Capo, 1983; *Drawings of Daumier*, Borden, n.d.

EXHIBITIONS: Work represented in numerous exhibitions, including those at Ecole des Beaux-Arts, Paris, France, 1901; Museum of Modern Art, New York City, 1930; Musée de l'Orangerie, Paris, 1934; Philadelphia Museum of Art, Philadelphia, Pa., 1937; Tate Gallery, London, England, 1961. Daumier's work is represented in all the great collections of the world.

SIDELIGHTS: Honore Daumier's cartoons have been in print continuously from the century of his birth down to our own time. They have been anthologized in books published in his native France, in English-speaking countries, and elsewhere—a feat paralleled by very few other graphic artists and excelled by none. His satires of the professional classes, businessmen, politicians, bluestockings, and other social and human types are as relevant today as they were in his own time. In compositions favoring the universal over the anecdotal, the artist made his characters symbols of human behavior and human folly in all times and nations.

Moreover, Daumier possessed a directness of vision and a lack of sentimentality that are more of our time than of his own. His images, so realistic in their rendition, are almost abstract in their impact; they usually illustrate a concept that transcends their prosaic context. Daumier was not the only artist to attempt this, but he is the one who did so most successfully—and the long roll call of cartoonists and social illustrators who invoke his example and inspiration attest to the permanence of his vision. As long as there will be corruption to expose, injustices to denounce, and abuses to combat, Daumier will remain as timely as today's (and tomorrow's) headlines.

From the time his practical-minded mother and aspiring-author father moved the family from Marseilles to the Latin Quarter of Paris, Daumier roamed the city streets, first leading the free life of the street urchin, then running errands as a *saute-risseau* (gutter-jumper) for various lawyers. He also briefly worked in a bookstore. After Daumier decided to become a painter, he studied under Alexandre Lenoir, a noted authority on medieval art, who instilled in the young artist a deep and lasting appreciation of such masters as Michaelangelo, Rubens, and Rembrandt. At the same time Daumier discovered the progressive political ideals of Jean-Jacques Rousseau and Jean de La Fontaine, which were to shape his own political and social views.

Although Daumier worked for several publishers and merchants of lithographs, it was not until he met Charles Philipon that his creative career really took off. Philipon, who was a born opposition man by temperament, knew how to inspire Daumier to attack the bourgeois monarchy of Louis-Philippe for the publisher's *La Caricature*, a weekly journal. There, at first, Daumier drew caricatures (for instance, a whole family finding shelter under Finance Minister d'Argout's nose) and satirized the entire administration (especially Premier Francois Guizot and the diminutive Minister of Foreign Affairs Adolphe Thiers). He continued Philipon's practice of using the pear as symbolic representation of the king. Daumier went too far, however, with his 1831 cartoon "Gargantua," for it depicted Louis-Philippe devouring tons of money, while sitting on his throne-commode and defecating patronage, appointments, and subsidies to eager supporters, while the masses are starving and in rags. Brought to trial in February, 1832, Daumier was fined and condemned to a six-month jail sentence in Ste-Pélagie, a prison which, according to a

The Orchestra While Tragedy Is Being Played, **a lithograph by Daumier, 1852**

A lithograph by Daumier from *French Types*, 1835

Daumier print, one entered a healthy man and exited in a coffin. (In fact, the artist only served two months and then was transferred to a sanatorium.)

In December, 1832, Philipon founded *Le Charivari*, and this daily became the main outlet for Daumier's talents. To make his research easier and also to have permanent access to his political models, Daumier sculpted thirty-eight terra-cotta exaggerated portrait busts of ministers and other important personages, which were so good that poet Charles Baudelaire, an early admirer, wrote: "Every little meanness of spirit, every absurdity, every quirk of intellect, every vice of the heart can be clearly seen and read in these animalized faces; and at the same time everything is broadly and emphatically drawn. Daumier combined the freedom of an artist with the accuracy of a Lavater [founder of the science of physiognomy, character analysis through interpretation of facial features]." Daumier would then use these faces in his printed lithographs, either singly or in a group, as in the superb "The Legislative Belly," cited by Howard Vincent as "the satiric climax of Daumier's campaign [and] an artistic triumph." The drawing presents thirty-five deputies in four semicircular rows, chatting, sleeping, daydreaming, reading—all symbolizing too well the regime's graft and corruption.

In addition to this cartoon, Daumier contributed four other prints (all dated 1834) to be sold through Philipon's *L'Association mensuelle* (a kind of Print-of-the-Month Club): they included the uninteresting *Very Naughty and*

Very Mighty Legitimist Brats (about the royal family); *Freedom of the Press*, an early example of proletarian art; *The Funeral of La Fayette* shows Louis-Philippe's hypocritical sorrow at the passing of "a true friend of liberty"; and the powerful masterpiece of the series, perhaps influenced by Jacques-Louis David's portrait of the revolutionary *Marat*, *Rue Transnonain*. Charles Philipon wrote an excellent description of this portrayal of the massacre of innocent citizens by royalist troops run amok: "This lithograph is shocking to see, frightful as the ghastly scene which it relates. . . In creating this drawing, Daumier raised himself to a high eminence. He has made a picture which, though executed in black on a sheet of paper, will not be the less esteemed nor will it be the less enduring. The murders of the Rue Transnonain will be a permanent blot of shame on all who allowed them to happen. This lithograph which we cite will be the medal struck at the time to perpetuate the recollection of the victory won over fourteen old men, women, and children." In the picture, Daumier used his favored triangular pattern of composition, with a strong, accented figure in the foreground while crowded vignettes are represented in the rear left and right corners.

When stringent censorship laws were passed in 1835, Daumier decided to limit his satire to the middle-class and the professions, whether in the famous *Robert Macaire* series of one hundred prints (1836-38) that illustrate the prototypical con man's various unpunished swindles ("Does one ever arrest a millionaire?" Macaire cynically asks in one caption), or in his drawings of landlords, politicians, shopkeepers, citizen-militiamen, and of hordes of clerks and civil servants forever scratching paper and mailing tax assessments. Among the professions, none is more martyred than the pathetic schoolteacher (*Teachers and Students*). Nor is any more greedy or arrogant than the thousands of lawyers and judges of all types (*Men of Law*, 1845-48)—after all, whatever the outcome, the lawyers at least always win. The family too is the butt of his humor, particularly, the paterfamilias as lord and master, and of course women (*Bluestockings, Divorcing Women, The Female Socialists*) are good targets for his antifeminist ridicule.

Most of these series were quite successful financially, and Daumier was able to marry a glazier's daughter fourteen years his junior and move to the île St.-Louis, where he rented an apartment and studio from 1846 to 1862. He also enjoyed press freedom after the 1848 revolution overthrew Louis-Philippe. (The king, however, was not to live in abject poverty; Daumier depicted Louis-Philippe arriving in exile in England with a cashbox under his arm. The caption reads: "All is lost, except the cashbox!")

More and more, though, Daumier turned to painting, some allegorical (*The Republic*), others dramatic and very moving, like *The Uprising*, "one of the greatest paintings of all time" according to Duncan Phillips. Often using his lithograph subjects for his oils, watercolors, and pen-and-wash pieces, much of his art shows the influence of Eugene Delacroix and Theodore Gericault, as well as the chiaroscuros of Rembrandt, the carnal exuberance of Rubens, the haunted look of Goya (e.g., *The Fugitives*). Most critics agree that *The Third-Class Carriage* is his masterpiece for its mood that is at once massive and sensuous, for its parabolic power, for its "somber but sure affirmation of life, good and evil, wrung from the infinite ambiguities of human experience," in the words of Howard Vincent.

A lithograph by Daumier from *Professor and Kids,* 1845

All the while Daumier was also contributing drawings that satirized Second-Republic politicians and, after Louis-Napoleon's coup d'etat on December 2, 1851 brought the reimposition of censorship, the artist introduced the character of Ratapoil (literally, hairy rat). Just as Robert Macaire came to symbolize Louis-Philippe and his regime, so Ratapoil does Napoleon III. In his rumpled frock coat and weather-beaten top hat he embodies the nasty agent provocateur, rabble-rouser, and street-thug leader; armed with a cane-bludgeon he is ready to "beat up any Parisian who won't shout with me 'Vive l' Empereur!" (Daumier's caption). Rodin, on seeing the statuette Daumier had crafted of this imperial supporter, exclaimed in awed admiration, "What a sculptor!"

Once more unable to comment on the political scene, Daumier poked fun at the bourgeois of the Second Empire, typified by the stereotype of the middle class, Joseph Prudhomme; the artist lampooned their fads and fashions, from crinolines to antique collecting, from spiritism to balloon flights ("Nadar Elevating Photography to the Height of Art"), from museum visitors to train travelers. He also drew the worlds of the theater and the open-air circus, with their actors and actresses, jugglers, clowns, dancers, spectators, claques. Many of these appeared in *Le Boulevard, Le Charivari* (under new ownership after Philipon's death in 1862), and *Le Journal amusant;* Daumier also contributed several drawings of drunkards, which are later highly praised by the painter Vincent Van Gogh.

When press restrictions were lifted in 1865, Daumier regained a new vigor in his political cartoons, although he now preferred broad allegories of Peace, Diplomacy, War, and Death, to pointed caricatures: "European Equilibrium," "Sisyphus and the Budget," "Peace, an Idyl." Moreover, he was inspired by the works of such authors as La Fontaine, Moliére, and Cervantes, whose Don Quixote attacks the follies of his age, much as did Daumier. Failing eyesight, however, forced him to retire from regular lithographic assignments with one final drawing. "Monarchy Is Dead" (September 24, 1872) shows a shrivelled old woman in her shroud, lying in a coffin against a black background, and the caption, "And during all this time they continued to assert that she never was in better health."

Despite his reduced output Daumier lived moderately well at Valmondois, a little village some twenty miles north of Paris in the Oise River valley where he had gone in 1872. He was able to sell his artworks, many to American collectors. The artist died there on February 10, 1879, from a stroke, leaving behind five thousand prints and several hundred pictures. His body was later removed to the Pére Lachaise cemetery in Paris, where a tombstone was erected: "People, Here lies Daumier, a good man, great artist, great citizen"— a fitting epitaph for a modest and shy man of great talent and simple pleasures: "What do I need?" he once remarked to a friend. "Two fried eggs in the morning and at night a cutlet or a herring. Add a glass of Beaujolais and tobacco to fill my pipe. Anything more would be too much."

Honore Daumier's cartoons of slumlords, corrupt politicians, military aggression, political assassination, and imprisonment are still pertinent in today's world of gulags and terrorism, of apartheid and dictatorship, of stupidity and meanness. It is no wonder, therefore, that "the Michelangelo of caricature" (in historian Jules Michelet's phrase) has had so many of his works reprinted in the last fifty years, either in book form or singly (especially those dealing with physicians and lawyers). The *Washington Times'* cover of *Insight* magazine (February 3, 1986) uses one of Daumier's cartoons to depict the failure of modern French Socialism ("The operation was a success, but the patient died").

BIOGRAPHICAL/CRITICAL SOURCES: Jean Adhemar, *Honore Daumier,* (Paris) 1954; Oliver W. Larkin, *Daumier: Man of His Time,* McGraw, 1966; Howard P. Vincent, *Daumier and His World,* Northwestern University Press, 1968; Thieme and Becker, editors, *Allgemeines Lexikon der Bildenden Kunstler,* Vol. 8, Seemann, (Leipzig) 1970; *The World Encyclopedia of Cartoons,* Chelsea House, 1980; Roger Passeron, *Daumier,* Poplar, 1981.

—*Sketch by Pierre Horn*

* * *

DAY, Robert (James) 1900-1985

OBITUARY NOTICE: Born September 25, 1900, in San Bernardino, Calif.; died February 7, 1985, in St. Louis, Mo. Cartoonist and illustrator Robert Day studied at the Otis Art Institute in Los Angeles, while holding a job in the art department of the *Los Angeles Times* from 1919 to 1927. After working for the *Los Angeles Examiner* for three more years, he moved to New York and a position on the staff of the *Herald-Tribune* in 1930. A prolific cartoonist, he contributed to every major American magazine, including *Collier's, Saturday Evening Post, Look, Saturday Review, Sports Illustrated, This Week,* and *Liberty,* as well as to *Punch* in London, from the early 1930s until his retirement in the late 1970s. It is with the *New Yorker,* however, that he is most associated. His first cartoon appeared there in September, 1931; his last one on May 24, 1976. In the forty-five years of his connection with the magazine he drew hundreds of cartoons and a number of covers. His work has been widely reproduced in the many collections of *New Yorker* cartoons that have come out through the years; and his cartoons have also been exhibited in shows across the United States and in Europe. In addition to his books of cartoons and humor, such as *All Out for the Sack Race* (1945), *Fun Fare* (1949), *Mad World of Bridge* (1960), and

Rome Wasn't Burnt in a Day (1972), he also illustrated *Little Willie* by Arthur Godfrey (1953). In the *World Encyclopedia of Cartoons* Richard Calhoun said of Day, "He was certainly one the most published cartoon artists of the century." The artist's most famous cartoon is inarguably a 1933 *New Yorker* piece in which a coal-miner at the bottom of a darkened pit incredulously exclaims to his companion: "For gosh sakes, here comes Mrs. Roosevelt!"

BIOGRAPHICAL/CRITICAL SOURCES: Brendan Gill, *Here at the New Yorker*, Random House, 1975; *The World Encyclopedia of Cartoons*, Chelsea House, 1980.

OBITUARY SOURCES: New York Times, February 12, 1985; *New Yorker*, March 4, 1985.

* * *

DI FATE, Vincent 1945-

PERSONAL: Born November 21, 1945, in Yonkers, N.Y.; son of Victor George (an aeronautical designer) and Carmina (Sgueglia) Di Fate; married Roseanne Panaro (a teacher), March 10, 1968; children: Christopher, Victor. *Education:* Phoenix School of Design (now Pratt-Manhattan Center), New York City, certificate in illustration, 1967. *Politics:* Democrat. *Religion:* Roman Catholic. *Home and studio:* 12 Ritter Dr., Wappingers Falls, N.Y. 12590.

CAREER: Art teacher, Sts. John and Paul School, Larchmont, N.Y., 1967-68; assistant animator, Krantz Films, New York City, 1968-69; free-lance illustrator, 1969—. *Military service:* U.S. Naval Reserve, 1966-69.

MEMBER: Society of Illustrators, Graphic Artists Guild, Science Fiction Writers of America, World SF (a science fiction organization).

AWARDS, HONORS: Science Fiction Achievement Award, 1978, for Best Professional Artist; Frank R. Paul Award, 1978, for Outstanding Achievement in Science Fiction Art; Hugo Award, 1979, for science fiction illustration.

WRITINGS: (With Ian Summers) *Di Fate's Catalogue of Science Fiction Hardware*, Workman, 1980; (contributor) *The Science Fiction Reference Book*, Starmont Press, 1981. Contributing editor and columnist, *Science Fiction Chronicle*, 1976—. Contributor of illustrations to *Analog, Cinefantastique, Future Life, Magazine of Fantasy & Science Fiction, Omni, Reader's Digest*, and other periodicals.

EXHIBITIONS—All group shows, except as indicated: (One-man show) "Visions of Space/Time," Reading Public Museum, Reading, Pa., 1977-78; New Britain Museum of American Art, New Britain, Conn., 1980; Bronx Museum of the Arts, Bronx, N.Y., 1980; "Kunst und Kosmos," Stadthalle Gallerie, Limburg, West Germany, 1980; Kent State University School of Art, Kent, Ohio, 1981; Museum of the Surreal and Fantastique, New York City, 1981; "Omni Group Show," Picture Galleries, Chicago, Ill., 1981; Bryce Gallery, Moore College of Art, Philadelphia, Pa., 1981; (one-man show) Museum of Science and Natural History, St. Louis, Mo., 1982; Pendragon Gallery, Annapolis, Md., 1983-84; Worcester Science Center, Worcester, Mass., 1984-85; group show of NASA artists, Museum of Science, Cleveland, Ohio, 1984-85; "Future Scapes," New Jersey State Museum, Trenton, N.J., 1985.

A science-fiction illustration (© 1983, Vincent Di Fate. Reprinted by permission.)

WORK IN PROGRESS: "Ongoing research into fantastic art, particularly of a scientific rather than a mystic nature; science fiction art history; science fiction in film and television."

SIDELIGHTS: "The ability to represent technology and environments that either do not exist or are currently beyond the human experience is still unique among visual artists," observes illustrator Vincent Di Fate; "I find the challenge of this type of work stimulating." Like many boys of his post-war generation, he fondly recalls Saturday afternoons at the cinema being thrilled and chilled by such films as *Forbidden Planet, Invaders From Mars*, and *War of the Worlds*. But this son of an aeronautical engineer took more than damp palms away from the movie houses of his youth; he also developed a fascination with the fantastic technology projected on their screens. One might attribute such an interest to heredity but for Di Fate's confession that he was a terrible math student.

With the option of following in his father's footsteps thus foreclosed, Di Fate had to find another outlet for his fascination with aerospace technology. An innate talent for drawing and excellent visual recall supplied a useful means of expression. Initially Di Fate would race home from the theatre and set himself to reproducing, on paper or in clay, copies of the spaceships and machines he'd just seen; then

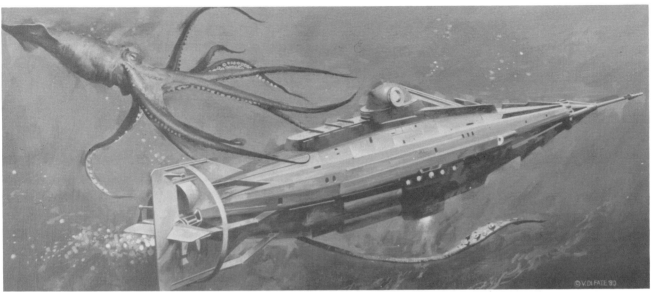

"**Nautilus Submarine**," **an illustration** (© 1980, Vincent Di Fate. Reprinted by permission.)

later when he graduated to science-fiction literature he likewise graduated to the task of visualizing machines and environments described by writers like Jules Verne, Robert Heinlein, and H. G. Wells. The fact that his father's work gave him access to blueprints and models ensured that these efforts retained a logic and verisimilitude, even as they remained very much works of imagination.

Committed to the profession of art, Di Fate attended the Phoenix School of Design in New York City, from which he graduated in 1967. He taught art for a year before landing a job in Ralph Bakshi's animation studio, where he worked briefly on the children's television series, *Spiderman.* When the abrupt cancellation of that show (for excessive violence) put him out of work, Di Fate embarked upon a free-lance career out of sheer necessity. His first notable success as a science fiction illustrator came in 1971 when he was hired to do the cover for a novel entitled *Broke Down Engine.* After that, the commissions began to flow steadily in, and what had begun as a post-Saturday afternoon matinee avocation became a livelihood.

Di Fate did the usual assignments—a series of covers for the venerable pulp magazine *Analog* won him a devoted following among sci-fi buffs. Signet Books tapped him as cover artist for its paperback reissue of the classic novels of Robert Heinlein—and in 1979 he was honored with a Hugo Award, the genre's highest, for his work as an illustrator. But along with these achievements came other forms of recognition. In 1975 he was commissioned as the Smithsonian's artist for NASA's Apollo-Soyuz launch. Since 1976 his work has been annually represented in various group shows with science/technology themes. And his paintings have been the subject of two one-man shows and have been acquired as part of the permanent collections at the Smithsonian's National Air and Space Museum and the New Britain Museum of Scientific Art in Connecticut.

Di Fate's success in elevating his work above the standards usually set for illustrators working in the science-fiction/fantasy milieu—one reviewer calls him "a kind of visual guru in the field"—rests on three apparent strengths. First,

he is clearly a competent, well-schooled painter in acrylics and oils and an appropriately restrained colorist. Secondly, he is an able problem solver in an area of illustration that depends to a large extent on satisfying the often impossibly literal demands of editors and art directors. (He once managed to give an insistent editor an overall view of a "chaos machine" as big as a solar system and powered by "four black holes" while also including closeup studies of the story's principal characters, all in one frame.) Thirdly, he brings to his work a desire to produce honest, credible images even in the most unlikely of contexts. "What is important is atmosphere and making it look like it exists," he explains, "or making people believe it exists."

A handy compendium of his work, *Di Fate's Catalogue of Science Fiction Hardware,* was published by Workman in 1980. In it Di Fate tackles the job of translating literary concepts from Jules Verne's *Nautilus* submarine and H. G. Wells's Martian war machines to proton-driven faster-than-light ships and the "Alien Educator," a huge, floating, computerized library. Describing his goal as one of "visual generalization," Di Fate has taken on the challenge of reproducing the purely fanciful notions of old-fashioned romantic fantasists like Verne as well as the reality-based concepts of modern writers like Joe Haldeman while giving to each as much scientific veracity as he can. But this commitment to scientific truth notwithstanding, he remains at heart very much the artist. His favorite writers are fantasists and poets who, like Ray Bradbury, truly "sing the body electric." He claims to share with them a reassuring "Victorian" faith in the essential benevolence of the machine; a sense he finds missing in the work of some modern "hard-edged" writers, who are at once more technologically sophisticated and mistrustful of technology. "We get in trouble," he insists, "when we fail to use machines responsibly." In this respect he regards his function, at least in part, as one of forwarding through illustration this sense of collective accountability. As he puts it in his foreword to the *Catalogue,* "If science fiction ideas in words and pictures are not a part of the high art our time, they at least compel us to consider the consequences of our actions and to seek our solutions beyond the obvious." It is this philosophical conviction underlying his approach to his work, as much as the technical competence with which he executes it, that elevates the result above the common, largely evanescent mean.

BIOGRAPHICAL/CRITICAL SOURCES: Future Life, March, 1979; Omni, May, 1981; St. Louis Post-Dispatch, June 1, 1981; Who's Who in American Art, Bowker, 1984.

—Sketch by Richard Calhoun

*   *   *

DINH, Vo
    See VO-DINH, Mai

*   *   *

DOBBIN, Ol'
    See DOBBINS, James Joseph

*   *   *

DOBBINS, James Joseph 1924-
    (Jim Dobbins, Ol' Dobbin, E. Quine)

PERSONAL: Born August 12, 1924, in Woburn, Mass.; son of William John (a leather worker) and Delia (Feeney) Dobbins; married Dorothy Esther Fitzpatrick, January 20, 1951; children: Patricia Osborn, William, Mary Hintlian, James Joseph, Jr., Rita McGoldrick, Mark, Dorothy Claflin, Christopher, John, Maura. Education: Attended Cornell College, Mount Vernon, Iowa, 1945; Massachusetts College of Art, B.S., 1951; graduate study at Boston University, 1951-52. Politics: Democrat. Religion: Roman Catholic. Home: 1 Swan Rd., Winchester, Mass. 01890. Office: 1½ Swan Rd., Winchester, Mass. 01890. Agent: Lordly & Dame, 51 Church St., Boston, Mass. 02116.

CAREER: Artist, Woburn Press, Woburn, Mass., 1945-46; artist, Woburn Daily Times, 1947-51; teacher, Boston Public School System, Boston, Mass., 1952; editorial cartoonist,

Lowell Sun, Lowell, Mass., 1952-53; editorial cartoonist, New York Daily News, New York City, 1953; editorial cartoonist, Boston Post, Boston, 1953-56; editorial cartoonist, Boston Herald-Traveler, 1956-72; editorial cartoonist, Boston Herald-American, 1972-76; editorial cartoonist, Manchester Union Leader, Manchester, N.H., 1977—. Director of Marr Boys and Girls Club, Dorchester, Mass; president of Community Safety Education Program, Boston, Mass.; trustee of Catholic Charities for the Diocese of Boston. Military service: U.S. Navy, 1943-45, served as aviation radioman and gunner; awarded Distinguished Flying Cross and Air Medal.

MEMBER: Association of American Editorial Cartoonists, National Cartoonists Society, Boston Press Club (president, 1966-68), Ecumenical Council of Archdiocese of Boston, Winchester Country Club.

AWARDS, HONORS: Fourteen Honor Medals, Freedoms Foundation at Valley Forge; National Safety Council Award, 1957, 1959, and 1961; named Outstanding Young Man of the Year, Boston Jaycees, 1957; Christopher Literary Award, 1958; First Prize, Freedoms Foundation at Valley Forge, 1960 and 1964; Grand Prize, International Competition, Wayne State University, 1960; Certificate of Merit, Syracuse University, 1969.

WRITINGS: Dobbins Diary of the New Frontier (collection of editorial cartoons), Bruce Humphries, 1964; Collectors Series (series of caricatures and drawings), Boston Herald Traveler, 1970; (illustrator) Cornelius Dalton, Leading the Way, Massachusetts Department of State, 1985; (contributor) Charles E. Brooks, editor, Best Editorial Cartoons of the Year, Pelican, 1975—.

SIDELIGHTS: Jim Dobbins began his career as a newspaper artist with the Woburn Press in 1945 and in the four decades since then has drawn editorial cartoons for seven other newspapers in the northeast. His loosely-drawn, vigorous cartoons have been widely reprinted and have become well known throughout the country for their

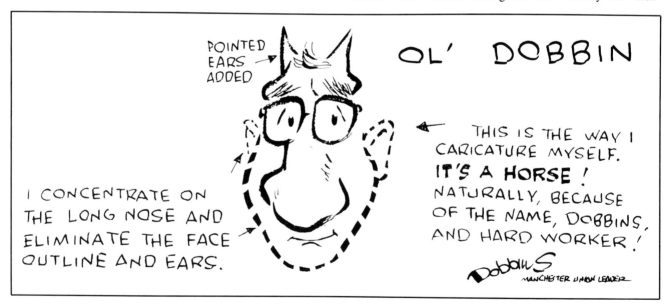

Self-portrait of James Joseph Dobbins as "Ol' Dobbin" (© Jim Dobbins. Reprinted by permission.)

MARLBORO COUNTRY-1986

An editorial cartoon (© 1986, James J. Dobbins, *Manchester Union Leader*. Reprinted by permission.)

spontaneous style and sharp wit. His caricatures of public figures in politics, sports, and entertainment, originally a Sunday feature of the *Boston Herald-American*, were taken up by a large department store in Boston and sold separately in 1970. He has also made a reputation for himself as a courtroom and political-convention artist and illustrated a book on Massachusetts history with over three hundred pen-and-ink drawings.

First attracted to his profession by an interest in sports, Dobbins hoped to become a sports cartoonist like Willard Mullins or Bob Coyne. He became an editorial cartoonist while in art school and contributed work to the weekly *Woburn Press*. While still at the Massachusetts College of Art he was hired to do a weekly cartoon panel for the *Woburn Daily Times* illustrating local events and drawing community figures. After receiving a bachelor's degree, he decided to go on to the Boston University Graduate School of Education, to assure himself of a living in case his chosen profession did not have a place for him immediately. While he studied there he continued sending and selling drawings to various papers around Massachusetts. The *Lowell Sun* bought several and when he graduated and began teaching in the Boston public schools, the paper invited him to do three drawings a week on a regular basis. In 1952 the *Sun* asked him to join Tom Flannery as a full-time cartoonist. "It was probably the smallest paper in the country that had two full-time editorial cartoonists," Dobbins comments.

The next year, he was asked to replace Pulitzer prize-winner

C. D. Batchelor at the *New York Daily News* for four-and-a-half weeks when Batchelor was on vacation, and for four more months he continued to do Batchelor's Sunday feature. Later that year he became the editorial cartoonist for the *Boston Post*, and for the next twenty-three years he served that and other Boston newspapers. In 1977 he joined the staff of the *Manchester Union Leader* in Manchester, New Hampshire, where he has remained ever since.

Dobbins's artistic mascot—a self-portrait as a bespectacled horse named "Ol' Dobbins" (Jimmy Durante's nickname for the cartoonist; the artist also uses the horsey pseudonym E. Quine)—appears with an ironic comment in the corners of many of his cartoons as the spokesman of his own opinions. Always completely his own man, Dobbins reports that he never shows rough sketches of his cartoons to his editor before sending them in to the engraver. "I try to decide the best subject myself," he says. "I used to attend editorial conferences but don't anymore." He has little respect for those cartoonists who "just repeat their editors' ideas," and he advises young editorial cartoonists to seek independence. "[A]s soon as they get their own identity away from the paper's policy," he says, "the better off they'll be."

A confirmed Democrat on a staunchly conservative newspaper, Dobbins has never compromised his own independence. "I suppose I agree with the paper seventy-five percent of the time," he states, "but I don't wait to see how they feel before I do a cartoon." When his paper supported Nixon, for example, and he did not, he continued to draw his cartoons as he saw fit, and his publisher agreed that "you have to kick both doors, and you have to be fair about various issues." Dobbins sees three stages in the career of a political cartoonist: when he just wants to see his cartoons in print, when he wants to please his editor and himself, and when he wants to please his public and himself. Dobbins has been at this last stage for many years.

Active in community affairs, Dobbins gives his time freely to many social causes. He is a member of the Roman Catholic Ecumenical Council, a trustee of the Catholic Charities Bureau, and president of the Community Safety Education Program in Boston, and a member of the Board of Directors of the Marr Boys and Girls Club of Dorchester, Massachusetts, as well as a member of the Association of American Editorial Cartoonists and the National Cartoonists Society and a former president of the Boston Press Club. He appears often on television and is on a lecture circuit doing chalk-talks for many fund-raising events.

Dobbins reports that he spends two-and-a-half to three hours on an average cartoon, but this takes no account of the work and time that must go into developing an idea or researching an illustration. He reads extensively—the *New York Times, New York Daily News,* the Boston newspapers, *Editor and Publisher, Time, Newsweek, U.S. News and World Report*—and never allows himself to spend an idle moment. The father of ten children and a man with an active professional life, he uses his time to its best possible advantage. He modestly estimates that "perhaps twenty-five percent is inherited drawing ability and. . . the other seventy-five percent of a cartoonist's success is due to the time he has put in on his profession." Surely the success of his own prodigiously productive career bears witness to his dedication, energy and discipline. "If there is a free minute," he wrote to *CGA,* "I have something to do for that minute, if there is a free hour, I do an hour's project; a free afternoon, then I do a big job I've been holding for such an occasion. Credo: Life is but a second on the clock of eternity, we can't afford to waste any of it."

BIOGRAPHICAL/CRITICAL SOURCES: Cartoonist Profiles, May, 1970, March, 1972, December, 1973; *National Cartoonists Society Album,* 1980; *The World Encyclopedia of Cartoons,* Chelsea House, 1980; *Bostonian Magazine,* May, 1984; *Who's Who in America 1984-85,* Marquis, 1984.

—Sketch by Dennis Wepman

* * *

DOBBINS, Jim
    See DOBBINS, James Joseph

* * *

DUKE, Chris(tine) 1951-

PERSONAL: Born June 12, 1951, in Detroit, Mich.; daughter of Jay William (an automotive engineer) and Inga (Ahlbom) Duke; married Stanley Russell Hunter (a commercial artist), December 1, 1972; children: Stanley Russell II, Inga-britt. *Education:* Received certificate from Parsons School of Design, 1972. *Religion:* Episcopalian. *Home and studio:* East Maple Ave., P.O. Box 471, Millbrook, N.Y. 10022.

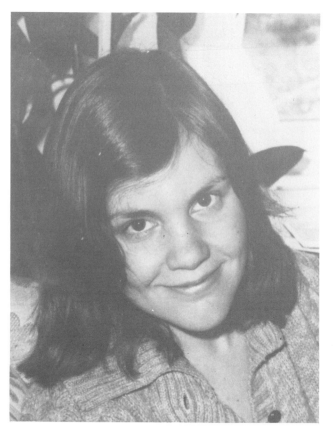

CHRIS DUKE

An illustration by Chris Duke for Jane Austen's *Pride and Prejudice* (© 1981, Franklin Library. Reprinted by permission.)

CAREER: Free-lance illustrator, 1972—. Clients have included American Airlines, American Express, Borg-Warner, General Electric, and Columbia Broadcasting System.

AWARDS, HONORS: Awards from Society of Illustrators, Graphic Artists Guild, and *Communication Arts.*

WRITINGS—All as illustrator, all for Franklin Library: Henrik Ibsen, *Six Plays,* 1977; Edith Wharton, *The Age of Innocence,* 1977; Louisa May Alcott, *Little Women,* 1980; Jane Austen, *Pride and Prejudice,* 1981.

WORK IN PROGRESS: "Doing five portraits for Eli Lilly, nineteen pieces for Charles of the Ritz, and some illustrations for the magazine *People.*"

SIDELIGHTS: "In my more personal work," Chris Duke wrote *CGA,* "I put stress on personal symbolism which I try to represent in painting. Inspired by the Swiss philosopher, Carl Jung, and a personal journal, I try to incorporate the richness of personal imagery and the ephemeral quality of memories. Portraiture interests me in this respect."

Duke's artistic goals are reflected in the dual aspect of her illustration work. On the one hand she loves powerful imagery and the virile order of an almost exclusively masculine world: assembly-line workers hunched over the controls of monstrous machines, truck-drivers piloting their massive rigs, soldiers firing the weapons of war. This is even further accented by her inclusion of diagrams of machinery, weaponry, and conveyances such as tugboats, motor launches, and cantilever bridges, accompanying her illustrations. On the other hand, her illustrations for literary classics like Jane Austen's *Pride and Prejudice* show her sensitivity to mood and character, especially in her portraits of the protagonists.

Living in a Victorian house in a small town of upstate New York, Duke is now considering seriously offers from galleries to have her work exhibited. Considering that the artist is only in her early thirties, it is a fair assumption that more will be heard from her in the future.

BIOGRAPHICAL/CRITICAL SOURCES: Les Krantz, *American Artists,* Facts on File, 1985.

E

EMIL
   See NOVAK, Emil, Jr.

*   *   *

ENGLEHART, Bob
   See ENGLEHART, Robert, Jr.

*   *   *

ENGLEHART, Robert, Jr. 1945-
  (Bob Englehart)

PERSONAL: Born November 7, 1945, in Fort Wayne, Ind.; son of Robert Wayne and Shirley (Rogers) Englehart; married Judith King, February 20, 1965 (divorced, 1986); children: Mark Allen, Sherri Lynn. *Education:* Attended

ROBERT ENGLEHART, JR.

American Academy of Art, Chicago, Ill., 1964-66. *Home:* West Hartford, Conn. *Office: Hartford Courant*, 285 Broad St., Hartford, Conn. 06115.

CAREER: Staff artist, *Chicago Today*, Chicago, Ill., 1966-72; editorial cartoonist, *Fort Wayne Journal Gazette*, Fort Wayne, Ind., 1972-75; owner, Englehart & Associates (an art studio), 1972-75; editorial cartoonist, *Journal Herald*, Dayton, Ohio, 1975-80; editorial cartoonist, *Hartford Courant*, Hartford, Conn., 1981—.

MEMBER: Association of American Editorial Cartoonists, National Cartoonists Society.

AWARDS, HONORS: First runner-up, Pulitzer Prize for editorial cartoon, 1979.

WRITINGS—Collections of cartoons: *Never Let the Facts Get in the Way of a Good Cartoon*, Journal Herald, 1979; *A Distinguished Panel of Experts,* Hartford Courant, 1985.

WORK IN PROGRESS: "Writing short stories, essays."

SIDELIGHTS: Bob Englehart reports that as a child he used to read the Famous Artists School ads in the magazines and fantasize. Today, he adds, he is living that fantasy. But if his dream of a career as an editorial cartoonist has come true, it has not been by fantasizing about it that he has brought it about. He has earned his position by serious application to his craft, a wide range of experience, and a thoroughly professional approach to his work.

After a complete grounding in art at the American Academy of Art in Chicago, Englehart entered the newspaper world at age twenty-one as a staff artist with *Chicago Today.* When that evening paper folded five years later, he moved his wife and two young children to Fort Wayne, Indiana, where for the next three years he held the position of editorial cartoonist with the *Journal Gazette* while directing his own commercial art studio, Englehart & Associates. Moving on to Dayton, Ohio, in 1975, he took the position of editorial cartoonist with the *Journal Herald,* and five years later exchanged it for the same post with the *Hartford Courant* in Connecticut. Here his steady eastward migration has come to an end, and for the past five years he has built a growing reputation in Hartford as one of the sharpest pens in the East.

His exposure to a broad range of editors, editorial policies, and working conditions has provided Englehart with a flexibility and a responsiveness that make themselves apparent in his work. "I've worked for a gaggle of editors," he observes, "and have learned how to cope with just about every situation an editor can invent. I've had my cartoons

An editorial cartoon by Bob Englehart (© 1986, Copley News Service. Reprinted by permission.)

approved by a committee, a liberal Socialist, two conservative Reaganauts, a closet psychotic, a Victorian patriarch, a nit-picker and the role model for TV's Lou Grant." Such an apprenticeship is bound to produce an alert and adaptable journalist, and Englehart admits that this assorted gallery of bosses have taught him the newspaper business.

Englehart's work is basically "cartoony," and he never passes up an opportunity to be funny. The influence of the cartoonist he acknowledges as his "biggest influence," Mike Peters, can be seen in his approach to his subjects, but his spare, clean style is strictly his own. Other cartoonists whom he also singles out as favorites, but whose work seems to have had little influence on Englehart, include Jeff MacNelly, Doug Marlette, Tony Auth, Arnold Roth, Don Wright, Pat Oliphant, Dwane Powell, and Paul Conrad. His own work is probably simpler in execution and conception than most of this list. "My favorite kind of cartoon," he states, "is a single panel that reflects my belief and has an underlying, devastating smart-ass attitude. My least favorite is a multi-paneled epic that takes the reader twice around the hen house before it gets to the point."

The impact of Englehart's work derives in large measure from this very simplicity of approach. But it also depends on his keenness of wit and essentially comic outlook. When Interior Secretary James Watt made his famous gaffe about having a black, a woman, two Jews, and a cripple on a committee, most of the country's cartoonists pounced on him; Englehart revealed that the cripple in Watt's office was the Secretary himself, having just shot himself in both feet.

Englehart's cartoons are carefully composed, ingeniously conceived, and precisely executed. The artist works very methodically, using a variety of pen points according to the effect he seeks to produce: Crowquill, Hunt number 22, Speedball C-5, C-3, or FB-6. He prefers a series 7 number 2 Winsor-Newton brush, Pelikan waterproof india ink (which he calls "the only kind"), and Dr. Martin's Pen-White and Pro-White inks, along with Cel-Vinyl white, which he can draw over when it dries. He finds rapidograph pens "too high-tech" for him.

Bob Englehart has increasingly freed himself from "looking similar to the other guys" and developed a distinctive voice and style of his own. As the range of both his art and his ideas has grown, he has emerged as one of the wittiest and most versatile workers in the field of editorial cartooning.

BIOGRAPHICAL/CRITICAL SOURCES: Best Editorial Cartoons of the Year, Pelican, 1976; *Cartoonist Profiles,* December, 1983.

* * *

ENRIC
      See **TORRES PRAT, Enric**

* * *

ENRICH
      See **TORRES PRAT, Enric**

* * *

ESTES, James 1942-

PERSONAL: Born January 23, 1942, in Pasadena, Tex.; son of James Loron (a food broker) and Virginia Mae (Kelley) Estes; married Martha Ella Hudgens (a registered nurse), January 24, 1964; children: Robert, Kelley (daughter), Paige (daughter). *Education:* Amarillo College, A.A., 1962; attended University of Texas, 1962-64; West Texas State University, B.S., 1966. *Politics:* Independent. *Religion:*

JAMES ESTES

A magazine cartoon by James Estes, ca. 1980 (© *Boy's Life.*)

Church of Christ. *Home and studio:* 1103 Callahan, Amarillo, Tex. 79106-4201.

CAREER: Field interviewer, A. C. Nielsen Co. (a market research firm), Chicago, Ill., and Houston, Tex., 1966-67; assistant manager, Better Business Bureau, Amarillo, Tex., 1967-70; free-lance cartoonist, 1970—. Artist and writer of *Sonny Pew* newspaper strip for Syndicated Newspaper Services, 1981-82. Deacon in the Church of Christ, 1970-78; P.T.A. historian, 1981-82; West Point Parents Club of Amarillo (president, 1983—).

MEMBER: Museum of Cartoon Art, National Cartoonists Society.

WRITINGS: Put a Smile in Your Eyes (a book on eye care), Eyecare Communications, 1981. Contributed cartoons to *Good Housekeeping, National Enquirer, Woman's World, Boy's Life, Wall Street Journal, Fort Worth Star-Telegram,* and other periodicals.

WORK IN PROGRESS: Drawing cartoons for publications, developing a new comic strip.

SIDELIGHTS: James Estes had always enjoyed drawing, so when he became assistant manager of the Better Business Bureau in Amarillo and was put in charge of the *BBB Bulletin,* the organization's newsletter, he promptly started drawing cartoons for each issue. As his cartoons began to be picked up by other *BBB Bulletins* around the country, in 1970 he decided to try his hand at a full-time cartooning career.

Estes started contributing cartoons to such publications as the *Wall Street Journal, Good Housekeeping, Boy's Life,* and others; but his ambition was to draw a nationally syndicated comic strip. In 1973-74 he tried out his first comic strip idea, *Sea Rations,* for the Fort Worth Star-Telegram Syndicate, which was followed by a daily panel, *Classy Ads,* for the same syndicate, in 1974-75. In 1981 he created a strip about a preacher, which he sold to the newly formed Syndicated Newspaper Services. Titled *Sonny Pew,* it was a sweetly funny feature centering around Sonny, his father Reverend John Pew, his mother Martha, his adopted sister Cecilia, his dog Shadrach, Cecilia's cat Hymnlet, and Sonny's friend Robert. "Although John Pew is a minister, *Sonny Pew* is not a religious strip," Estes declared in 1982. "It has no axes to grind and espouses no doctrine—I am careful to keep it very ecumenical." Despite its endearing qualities, *Sonny Pew* folded in 1982, following the demise of its syndicate.

Estes draws in a direct, uncluttered style, and his gags, which often derive from his own experiences, are funny and to the point. His family is both a source of comfort and inspiration to him; he is indeed very much a family man who declares that above all he enjoys "reading, going to movies, long walks with Martha, family picnics, and other family activities." With his son Robert being a student at the U.S. Military Academy at West Point, Estes is also particularly interested in watching the Army versus University of Texas football games.

BIOGRAPHICAL/CRITICAL SOURCES: Cartoonists Profiles, June, 1982.

F

FEARING, Jerry
See FEARING, Walter Jerome

* * *

FEARING, Walter Jerome   1930-
(Jerry Fearing)

PERSONAL: Born July 16, 1930, in St. Paul, Minn.; son of Walter C. (a laborer) and Delphine (Kashuba) Fearing; married Dolores M. Kulhanek, July 12, 1952; children: Jodie, Vickie, Scott, Mark. *Education:* Attended art schools in St. Paul and Minneapolis, Minn., 1952-55. *Home:* 20200 Quinnell Ave., Scandia, Minn. 55073. *Office: St. Paul Pioneer Press-Dispatch*, 345 Cedar St., St. Paul, Minn. 55101.

CAREER: Artist in advertising department, staff artist, and editorial cartoonist, *St. Paul Pioneer Press-Dispatch*, St. Paul, Minn., 1949—. Drew the comic strip *Rooftop O'Toole* with Bill Farmer, 1975-80 (syndicated by United Feature Syndicate, 1977). *Military service:* U.S. Marine Corps, 1950-52, served in Korea; member of the Marine Corps Reserves, with rank of sergeant, 1952-62.

WRITINGS: The Sioux Uprising, N.W. Publications, 1962; *The Story of Minnesota*, N.W. Publications, 1964; *Fearing Revisited* (collection of editorial cartoons), St. Paul Pioneer Press-Dispatch, 1981.

WORK IN PROGRESS: Sculpting a series of statues called "Cartoons in Clay"; working with a new comic strip concept.

SIDELIGHTS: Jerry Fearing has remained close to his beginnings in Minnesota, but his mind and his pen have ranged widely. For nearly four decades he has provided a stream of genial and expert artwork for the same newspaper, the *St. Paul Pioneer Press-Dispatch* in his own home town, but the Minnesota capital has provided him with a window on the national and the international scene as well as on his state.

After finishing high school in St. Paul, Fearing attended art schools there and in the twin city of Minneapolis. At nineteen he began work in the advertising art department of the *Pioneer Press-Dispatch*. After a two-year interruption to serve in the U.S. Marine Corps, from 1950 to 1952, during which he had active duty in Korea, he returned to his old job at the *Pioneer Press-Dispatch*, and he has been there ever since, although he retained his connection with the Marine Corps as a reservist for ten years, holding the rank of sergeant. His job drawing advertising pictures soon grew to

Self-portrait of Jerry Fearing (© Jerry Fearing. Reprinted by permission.)

include the larger scope of a staff artist, and he began doing feature illustrations, rotogravure covers, and Sunday color comic pages. At last he reached his goal when he was appointed to the post of editorial cartoonist.

Since then he has been turning out six political cartoons a week, commenting on everything from local politics to international summit meetings and from conditions in St. Paul to problems in South Africa. For five years, 1975-80, he and co-author Bill Farmer did a comic strip (syndicated nationally by United Feature Syndicate after six months in the *Pioneer Press-Dispatch*). The daily gag strip entitled *Rooftop O'Toole* featured a White House paper boy who served as the foil and straight man. The strip was more of a political cartoon than a conventional comic strip, projecting its ironic points about the facts of political life in the nation's capital (always identified, in the classic political-cartoon fashion, by the White House or the Capitol building in the background.) The strip made its points pithily and with

An editorial cartoon by Jerry Fearing (© 1985, Fearing, *St. Paul Pioneer Press & Dispatch*. Reprinted by permission.)

considerable wit through the eyes of its ingenuous young protagonist Rooftop, and its genial commentary on the foibles of the Washington scene humorously complemented the artist's regular daily editorial cartoons in the *Pioneer Press-Dispatch*. During its five-year run, *Rooftop O'Toole* had a loyal, though not a large, national following.

Although he works in the state capital, Fearing and his family live in an old farm house set on eighteen wooded acres on the St. Croix River, forty miles north of St. Paul. He enjoys wilderness camping and has taken eight trips to the Arctic region. When he can find the time in his busy life, he goes canoeing in the Canadian border area.

In his cartoons, Fearing works with bold, heavy lines and large patches of shade or black, producing striking effects. His generally balanced and pleasing compositions draw the eye to the focal point he intends. But although his cartoons

A *Rooftop O'Toole* strip by Jerry Fearing and Bill Farmer (© 1979, United Feature Syndicate. Reprinted by permission.)

create dramatic visual impact, it seems less to the solar plexus than to the funny bone that Fearing directs his most forceful efforts.

The pleasure that Fearing takes in his work comes through clearly in the good-natured humor of his art. Although he has created an antediluvian Ronald Reagan, the president is never caricatured caustically or unkindly, and even South Africa's Premier P. W. Botha seems rather foolish than evil. Uncle Sam is depicted as a bewildered, rather touching old man. Fearing does not make his points with acerbity or melodrama, but with good-humored satire and a pleasant sense of fun. "I've always enjoyed drawing," the cartoonist reports, "and since it also pays the bills, I'll keep at it." The readers of Minnesota's newspapers have reason to be glad of it.

BIOGRAPHICAL/CRITICAL SOURCES: National Cartoonists Society Album, Museum of Cartoon Art, 1980.

* * *

FILIPPUCCI, Sandra   1953-

PERSONAL: Surname is pronounced "Filleepoochi"; born September 17, 1953, in Brooklyn, N.Y.; daughter of Vincent (an Army finance officer) and Beatrice May (Ward) Filippucci. *Education:* Attended Paier School of Art, New Haven, Conn., 1971-73; Peabody Museum, Yale University, 1973; Maryland Institute of Art, Baltimore, 1974-76 ("no B.F.A."). *Home and studio:* 270 Park Ave. S., New York, N.Y. 10010. *Agent:* (For advertising only) Dale Eldridge & Associates, 393 N. Euclid Ave., St. Louis, Mo. 63108.

CAREER: Scientific illustrator, New Haven, Conn., and Baltimore, Md., 1973-76; free-lance illustrator and designer, 1975—; songwriter and singer, New York, N.Y., 1978-80; actress on television, stage, and in film, New York City, 1979-1982; design consultant, International Robotics, Inc., New York City, 1982-85.

MEMBER: Society of Illustrators.

AWARDS, HONORS: Evergreen Merit Award from Johns Hopkins University, 1975; named "Upcoming Illustrator" by *Art Direction*, 1979; Gold Medal from New Jersey Art Directors Club, 1980; award from Society of Publication Designers, 1982; third place for graphics, International Juried Art Competition, 1985; award from *Communication Arts* (a magazine), 1985.

EXHIBITIONS: "*Sports Illustrated* Artists Show," Spectrum Gallery, New York City, 1979; Eagle Gallery, New York City, 1983; "The Fine Art of Illustration," Castle Gallery, New York City, 1985; Society of Illustrators, New York City, 1985.

WORK IN PROGRESS: Preparing a show tentatively titled "Interfaces," exclusively about robots with a view towards "humanizing" them, expected date of completion; 1988.

SIDELIGHTS: Sandra Filippucci wrote *CGA:* "It is this need I have to tell stories that made me choose to become an illustrator and not a painter. Like a painter, however, I try to channel my emotions into my assignments in the hope that the viewer will respond from the heart and not just through the retina. My pictures are considered 'mysterious,' which I appreciate. There are no simple answers, after all.

SANDRA FILIPPUCCI

"It has always seemed to me—and it still does—that those of us who are engaged in the graphic arts have taken on a responsibility to the countless thousands exposed to our work. I particularly despise stereotyped images of anyone, and especially images demeaning to women; I also find gratuitous violence extremely disturbing. We have a responsibility *not* to perpetuate those images. My goal is to make pictures with humor and insight.

"1986 is a great time in which to be an illustrator. People are tired of being constantly underestimated, and over-exposed to screaming, manipulative headlines, billboards, and posters. As a consequence they have grown more appreciative of personal visions and points of view in visual imagery. Life has become far more dangerous and subtle than ever before, and we all feel the need to have our own humanity reinforced."

While still a student in art school, Filippucci was hired as a scientific illustrator and assistant to Louise Demars, the head of design at the Peabody Museum of Yale University. This left a lasting imprint on the young artist. "This was an honor, to say the least," Filippucci commented. "Pulitzer Prize winners leaned over my shoulder to correct me; professors were never without comment. They taught me standards of excellence and, to this day, I struggle to live up to their expectations, which were considerable."

These expectations have led Sandra Filippucci into many fields, including a career in singing and songwriting, and to an acting career on stage and in daytime soap-operas, while pursuing at the same time her goals as a professional illustrator—a profession she was finally able to take up full-time in the early 1980s. As can be expected from her

A robot illustration (© 1984, Sandra Filippucci. Reprinted by permission.)

A poster for the Museum of Science and Industry (© 1985, Sandra Filippucci. Reprinted by permission.)

scientific background, Filippucci's illustrations often have either a science or a science-fiction slant. She has been able to paint in one telling image both the benefits and the costs (economic and emotional) of bypass surgery, and her depictions of robots (some of which she helped design) have a romantic as well as a primitive appeal. Another one of her fascinations is the relation of volumes in space (one of her posters actually bears the title "Spatial Relations"), and her compositions of geometric masses against a stark background recalls Italian artist Giorgio di Chirico's surreal paintings of deserted palaces and empty piazzas.

Filippucci's professional reputation has been steadily rising, as evidenced by the number of awards she has garnered in recent years. Her illustrations have appeared in publications ranging from scientific periodicals such as *Postgraduate Medicine, Science '86, Sports Medicine,* and *Video Magazine* to general readership journals like *Time, Psychology Today, Sports Illustrated,* and the *New York Times.* She has also created visuals and designs for such corporations as Ceiba-Geigy and International Robotics. Her posters are nationally sold through Springfield Graphics.

BIOGRAPHICAL/CRITICAL SOURCES: "Robert Weaver's Illustration Issue of the Unusual," *Print,* November-December, 1979; *Graphis Annual,* Graphis Press, 1983; *Illustrators 26,* Madison Square Press, 1984; *American Showcase,* American Showcase, 1985; Art Directors Index, Rotovision, 1985; "Examining the World of Today's Illustration," *New York Times,* September 22, 1985.

* * *

FISHGOLD, Susan   1949-

PERSONAL: Born February 13, 1949, in New York, N.Y.; daughter of Abraham (in the garment industry) and Ruth (a draftswoman; maiden name, Miklowitz) Fishgold; married Jay Molishever (a writer), November 17, 1974. *Education:* Queens College of the City University of New York, B.A., 1973; attended Brooklyn Museum Art School, 1976, Art Students League, 1977; Brooklyn College of the City University of New York, M.A., 1977. *Home:* 132 Remsen St., Brooklyn, N.Y. 11201. *Studio:* 70 Willoughby St., Brooklyn, N.Y. 11201. *Agent:* Fred Dorfman Gallery, 831 Broadway, New York, N.Y. 10003.

CAREER: Artist in New York City, 1977—.

MEMBER: World Print Council, Brooklyn Artists Registry, Brooklyn Museum, New York Artists Equity Association.

WRITINGS: (Collaborating artist) Susan Chapman, *Conversations with Dracaena* (poetry), Word Merchant Press, 1982.

EXHIBITIONS: (One-woman show) Work of Art Gallery, Brooklyn, N.Y., 1978; The Gallery at 112 Greene St., New York City, 1979; Custom House Gallery, New York City, 1979; Work of Art Gallery, 1979; "Femailable Art," Muse Gallery, Philadelphia, Pa., 1980; "Brooklyn '80" Show, Brooklyn Museum, 1980; 14th Annual Arkansas Exhibition, Pine Bluff, Ark., 1981; "New Talent Show," Allan Stone Gallery, New York City, 1981; "21 Women Artists," Cork Gallery, New York City, 1981; 11th National Print and Drawing Exhibition, Minot College, North Dakota, 1982; (one-woman show) "Dancing Tulips," Fred Dorfman Gallery, New York City, 1983; "Repeating Image," Rotunda

Photograph by Jay Molishever, © 1984. Courtesy of Susan Fishgold.

SUSAN FISHGOLD

Gallery, Brooklyn, 1983; (one-woman show) "Tiger Lilies," Satellite Gallery, Bronx Museum of the Arts, Bronx, N.Y., 1984; "Summer Mail Art, '84," Dallas Museum of Art, Dallas, Tex., 1984; "Monoprints," Fred Dorfman Gallery, 1984; "The Painted Print," Fred Dorfman Gallery, 1984; National Paperwork Show, Las Vegas Museum of Art, Las Vegas, Nev., 1984; "Echo," International Mail Art Show, Diverse Works Gallery, Houston, Tex., 1985; IBM Corporation Conference Center, Thornwood, N.Y., 1985.

SIDELIGHTS: Among the most innovative and imaginative of New York area graphic artists, Susan Fishgold has in the past five years produced a distinguished body of work in a form largely original to herself, multi-layered monotypes with crayon.

The child of an artistic family, Fishgold has devoted herself to art all her life. Her mother, a draftswoman who has done mechanical drawings for such major firms as Sperry-Rand and General Electric, imbued her with a sense of the discipline and precision underlying even the most spontaneous artistic expression, while her father, in the garment industry, instilled in her a feeling for style. She earned an undergraduate degree in art education, and, after further study at the Brooklyn Museum Art School and the Art Students League in New York, received a master's degree in painting and drawing at Brooklyn College in 1977. With a solid grounding in both theory and technique, Fishgold began exhibiting in New York galleries.

Her early work was in the traditional vein in oils and pastels, and she revealed a firm command of both of those media. A 1978 one-woman exhibition of her figure paintings and portraits at the Work of Art Gallery in Brooklyn won her the commendations of local reviewers for the technical proficiency of her workmanship and the sensitivity of her insight. "Fishgold fully achieves the portraitist's tasks— representation of both the individual and the universal. . . . The facial expressions she has managed to capture in most of her pictures are amazingly subtle and evocative," wrote Jay Molishever in the *Brooklyn Paper*. Miriam Kuznets, in the *Phoenix*, noted Fishgold's feeling for color and concluded, "The show is definitely an outstanding start."

The elements of Fishgold's style observed in this first exhibit have remained apparent in all of her subsequent work. Although her restless imagination has explored technical innovations, her passion for color and the intensity of her personal vision have continued to attract the attention of critics. By 1981 she was experimenting with monotypes, and her vivid orange and blue work in that medium at the Cork Gallery in New York was described as "executed with fervor." In her *Artspeak* review, "The Inner Eye of the Figurative Artist," Renee Phillips spoke enthusiastically of Fishgold's "plant like forms which appear to sway and gurgle underwater." The capacity of the medium to convey a sense of motion has prompted much of her work in the years since then and been effectively explored in several subsequent series.

A monotype is, as its name suggests, a unique print taken from a metal or glass plate on which a picture has been made and which is then pressed against canvas or paper. In the last five or six years, Susan Fishgold has been developing her own monotype process, using oil-based inks and painting on glass. By overprinting with several plates containing different colors, and then heightening the effect with drawing in vivid crayon, she produces brilliant and luminous images with profound vitality and movement.

In 1983, she and poet Susan Chapman produced a book, *Conversations with Dracaena*, in which Chapman's poems were set against eight of Fishgold's color monotypes. The tropical houseplant dracaena, an African lily whose Greek name translates "she-dragon" but whose African name means "fire-dance," is perceived by both artists as a symbol of life, growth, and movement. The repeated monotype images of its sinuous dancing leaves complement the poems, both media working in their own ways to convey the artists' idea. Called by the *New Brooklyn Quarterly* "a unique hybrid," the chapbook was warmly received; a poetry magazine in India, *Skylark*, stated that "The two mediums support each other by giving a more complete expression to the ideas and feelings. . . . [A] worthy contribution and a fine expression of very old thoughts." Award-winning poet

Portrait of a Woman (© 1978, Susan Fishgold. Reprinted by permission.)

Rainbow Dracaena II, **a monotype** (© 1980, Susan Fishgold. Reprinted by permission.)

and novelist May Sarton wrote of Fishgold's "glowing monotypes" and said that the poems and the art in this little book made "a vibrant whole."

The "vibrancy" Sarton notes is an accurate expression of the artist's experience in the creative act. The making of monotypes is a sensually exciting process for Fishgold, who says she loves the spontaneity of the form and takes acute pleasure in the sense of total participation she has with it. The overprinting of several transparent layers of ink produces a richly luminous effect and a texture that is almost sculptural. The relief on her monotypes can be quite distinct, each block with its own clearly raised veins of ink and thus its own unique character and shape. In 1985, the IBM Corporation commissioned Fishgold to produce sixty of these layered monotype prints for their new conference center in Thornwood, New York.

As the direct product of her hand, Fishgold's work grows out of her immediate personal involvement with her materials. "It's the consistency of the ink, which I can control by the amount of pressure that I apply to the plate," she reported to the *East Villager* in 1983, adding that she follows up the transfer process with crayon drawing because she "like[s] to break up spaces, and the negative spaces are very exciting." This excitement is the key to her work. The motion captured by her art expresses, she says, "the essence of life, the flowing of energy, the spirit, the strength of these forms." It is the ardor with which she transmits this life and energy, the passion with which she conveys the essential motion of life which she finds in forms, that conveys the intense excitement that she experiences in her work and inspires in her audience.

Fishgold does not identify herself with any style, movement, or school of art. She is dedicated to graphic creation in terms

of her own personal aesthetic. Printmaking is, for her, an intensely involving process, sometimes requiring her to mold or wipe the paint directly with her hands on the glass plate or paper. It is, she says, "like dancing with paint."

BIOGRAPHICAL/CRITICAL SOURCES: Miriam Kuznets, "One Woman Show," *Phoenix,* January 13, 1978; Jay Molishever, "Review: Current Gallery Exhibits," *Brooklyn Paper,* October 30, 1978; Jeanette Walls, "Group Show at Work of Art," *Phoenix,* July 13, 1979; Jay Molishever, "Five Showcases of Atlantic Avenue Art," *Brooklyn Paper,* October 19, 1979; *WIA: Women in the Arts Bulletin,* Summer, 1981; Renee Phillips, "The Inner Eye of the Figurative Artist," *Artspeak,* April 9, 1981; Bernd A. Klugman, "Review," *Skylark* (India), Number 53/54, 1982; *New Brooklyn Quarterly,* spring, 1983; John Korcz, "Repeating Changes," *East Villager,* March 1-14, 1983; *Brooklyn Heights Press,* March 3, 1983; Brooklyn Museum of the Arts Satellite Gallery Program, *Catalogue,* October, 1985.

—*Sketch by Dennis Wepman*

* * *

FLU, Jerry
See PFLUGH, Gerald J.

* * *

FORNARI, C. L.   1950-

PERSONAL: Born September 8, 1950, in Colorado Springs, Colo.; daughter of James H. (an educator) and Janice (a designer; maiden name, Grey) Albertson; married Daniel J.

C. L. FORNARI

Fornari (a geologist), 1972. *Education:* Attended University of Wisconsin, 1968-72, and Penland School of Crafts, 1975. *Home and studio:* Pratt Hill Rd., Chatham, N.Y. 12037.

CAREER: Free-lance textile designer, 1972-80; artist, illustrator, and lecturer, 1980—.

EXHIBITIONS: "Painted Warp—C. L. Fornari," Threadbare Gallery, New York, N.Y., 1977; "Fiber Invitational," Artspace Gallery, Milwaukee, Wis., 1978; "Art in Modern Handcrafts," Museum of Art, Carnegie Institute, Pittsburgh, Pa., 1979; "New Faces," Incorporated Gallery, New York City, 1980; "Pyramid National," Pyramid Art Center, Rochester, N.Y., 1982; "Electrostatics," Image Resource Center, Cleveland, Ohio, 1984; (one-woman show) Park Row Gallery, Chatham, N.Y., 1984; "Photography/Xerography," Pinnacle Gallery, Rochester, N.Y., 1985; (one-woman show) Berkshire Art Gallery, Pittsfield, Mass., 1985.

WORK IN PROGRESS: Photo-generated collages, including collage portraits; greeting cards and illustrations.

SIDELIGHTS: A 1972 graduate of the University of Wisconsin—whose Madison campus was during that period virtually an epicenter for all sorts of rebellion—C. L. Fornari began her artistic career as a weaver and "fiber artist." During the turbulent 1960s and early 1970s few college fine arts majors embraced the methods, let alone the conventions, of the traditional arts curriculum and the result was a blurring of the distinctions between art and craft, touching off an explosion of new techniques and novel experimentations in form as well as media. The medium-as-message dictum may be acceptable in communications, but it can be the asphyxiation of creativity in art, as Ms. Fornari

came to realize in about 1980: "I got to the point where there was no reason for the pieces to be in fiber—they should have been on paper."

Her most recent work, known as "photo-generated collage" (a term she prefers over its alternative "xerography"), is very much within the mixed-media, art-as-process vernacular of the 1960s-bred artist. Using the collage format, Ms. Fornari's state-of-art creations employ photography, photocopying (in color and black-and-white) and pastel tinting. As she explains it, the process uses "images from slides and photographs I have taken. These images are often used in combination with pictures of objects taken by placing the objects [themselves directly] on the copy machine. Drawing on the collage is done with ink or prismacolor pencils and black-and-white copies are often tinted with pastels. Copies are made on acid-free paper and a neutral ph adhesive is used to bond images to 100% rag watercolor paper."

Characteristic of process-oriented artists, Ms. Fornari's favorite themes are themselves reflections of the larger mixed media clutter of everyday life. Images associated with the shopping mall, television, and the general commercial environment of twentieth-century American life recur in her pieces, but in a manner that is affectionate rather than critical. "I do like," she confesses, "what my pieces are about." One work in particular seems to sum up this feeling: a before/after study of the Statue of Liberty as a problem in cosmetology. Entitled "Miss Liberty's Makeover," it is at once a send up of the commerciality with which the restoration project has become invested and a gently satirical swipe at the notion that a woman can be made anew by paints and powders, a notion given universal currency by the cosmetic manufacturers and their Madison Avenue allies. "I work a lot with popular symbols," she says, "and the whole beauty industry is very pervasive and full of interesting ideas."

That such high-tech methodology as Ms. Fornari's might ever become significant in an advertising or general editorial context is doubtful, and in fact in declaring herself a commission artist she appears to have cast her lot with the fine rather than the decorative/communications arts. But the currency and inspiration of the imagery that informs her work places it nonetheless within the graphic art tradition.

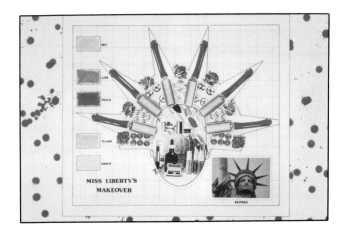

Miss Liberty's Makeover (© 1983, C. L. Fornari. Reprinted by permission.)

On her commission work C. L. Fornari commented: "I am always interested in doing collage work on a commission basis. Because the work begins with photographs that I take, a collage about a specific person, place, or thing can be made."

"Subjects that currently interest me are: architecture (especially American commercial architecture), clothing, gardens, shrines, parties, television, and romance. I am always exploring new themes, however, and will consider other subjects as well."

BIOGRAPHICAL/CRITICAL SOURCES: "Inspiration by Combination," *The Paper*, August 9-September 12, 1984.

* * *

FOWLER, Eric N.   1954-

PERSONAL: Born February 14, 1954, in Morristown, N.J.; son of Nicholas John (an executive) and Estelle (Sullivan) Fowler; married Palma Gradone (a commodities clerk), October 6, 1985. *Education:* Attended Syracuse University, 1972-74; Pratt Institute, B.F.A. (with honors), 1978. *Home:* Lambertville, N.J. *Studio:* 122 N. Union St., Lambertville, N.J. 08530.

CAREER: Graphic designer, Hall Graphics, Miami, Fla.; free-lance artist, illustrator, and photographer, 1977—; staff

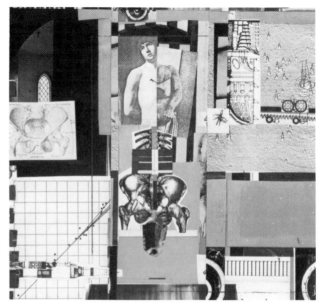

Elements of Impotence, **a collage** (© 1983, Eric H. Fowler. Reprinted by permission.)

designer and illustrator, Backes Graphics, Hopewell, N.J., 1986—.

MEMBER: Society of Illustrators.

AWARDS, HONORS: Scholarship from Illustrators Workshop, New York City, 1977; awards from *Art Direction* magazine, 1981, and Society of Publication Designers, 1983; Certificates of Merit from Society of Illustrators, 1983 and 1986; award from Graphis Annual, 1984.

WRITINGS: (Illustrator) Randal C. Douglas, *Joy of Stuffed Preppies,* Holt, 1982.

EXHIBITIONS: One-man show, Gallery 3, Society of Illustrators, 1986. Numerous group shows in New York and New Jersey, including Studio 53, New York City, 1978-79; Diaz-Marcial Gallery, New York City, 1984; Westport Gallery, Westport, Conn., 1985; Loft Gallery, Princeton, N.J., 1985; Gallery 3, Society of Illustrators, New York City, 1986.

WORK IN PROGRESS: A poster for the 1986 Bucks County (Pennsylvania) Arts Council's Festival of the Arts.

SIDELIGHTS: Eric Fowler has had his eye firmly set on a career in art since he was a child and still continues to explore new avenues of expression in it. Originally directed toward a career in architecture, he found in college that he didn't like the mathematics it required, and turned to a major in communications with a strong emphasis on commercial art. This combined theory, history, and technique to provide a broad, balanced foundation for a professional career. He took a bachelor of fine arts degree with honors from Pratt Institute in New York City in 1978, but even before he graduated he had already begun to make some impression in the field. The year before he finished at Pratt he was the first winner of the Society of Illustrators' scholarship to an illustrators workshop in Easton, Connecticut.

Self-portrait of Eric H. Fowler (©Eric H. Fowler. Reprinted by permission.)

An illustration for *The Physician and Sportsmedicine* (© 1985, Eric N. Fowler. Reprinted by permission.)

Fowler works in many media—oils, pastels, crayon, pen and ink, and collage, as well as in mixed media. Refusing to be locked into a fixed style, his eclectic pen and brush range widely and freely across the spectrum, drawing what is appropriate to his subject from many sources. Since early in 1986 he has been working with Backes Graphics as a staff illustrator and book designer, doing page design and chapter heads for such prestigious publications as the *Ontario Review*. He also continues to do book jackets and other advertising art and illustration on a free-lance basis, and carries his portfolio to show art directors. His command of the medium is so diverse that he does not hesitate to undertake any assignment in the field.

Increasingly, Fowler is turning to gallery painting as his success in commercial art permits him to grow personally. Thoroughly founded in the history of art, he draws his inspiration and influence from all periods and styles, but admits to a particular predilection for the work of American Edward Hopper. Although more electric and contemporary than his model, Fowler has much in common with him. Like Hopper, Fowler is as much an illustrative painter as a painterly illustrator.

BIOGRAPHICAL/CRITICAL SOURCES: Les Krantz, *American Artists*, Facts on File, 1985.

* * *

Recognizing that it was almost impossible to make a living as a painter—a dream which has not left him, but which he realistically defers for the present—Fowler entered the profession of illustration in 1977, with a deliberate mind and a trained eye and hand, and has since built a solid reputation in the periodicals field for a vivid, highly contemporary style, a versatile command, and a sensitive control of both form and content. His illustrations have appeared in the *New York Times, Psychology Today, Redbook, Sports Illustrated, Penthouse, Tennis Magazine*, and many trade journals in the medical field, including *Emergency Medicine, Postgraduate Medicine*, and *The Physician and Sportsmedicine*. Illustrating trade journals does not pay as much as other illustration work, but it is more plentiful and Fowler finds it offers him a wide range of experiment in developing his graphic style. His illustrations have also been used by a wide variety of national companies, including IBM, Ziff-Davis, American Express, RCA Records, Columbia University, and Holt, Rinehart & Winston.

An ardent fan and collector of jazz, rock-and-roll, and rhythm-and-blues records from the 1950s and 1960s, Fowler was selected by Verve records to do the cover of an album of Ella Fitzgerald's renderings of Duke Ellington's songs in 1980. His stylized pastel portrait of Ms. Fitzgerald on the album cover (with a smaller portrait of Ellington inset) is luminous in pink and blue; its loose impressionistic style captures the spirit of both the singer and her music eloquently. Like much of Fowler's work, the effectiveness derives in great measure from his masterly and sensitive use of color.

Photographic self-portrait of Allen R. Freeman (© 1985, Allen R. Freeman. Reprinted by permission.)

FREEMAN, Allen R. 1956-

PERSONAL: Born August 9, 1956, in Owensboro, Ky.; son of Harry Ray (a fire fighter) and Gerry (a contract administrator with General Electric; maiden name, Holder) Freeman; married Beth Rae Butler, February 21, 1980; children: Dustin Todd, Alaina Michelle. *Education:* Western Kentucky University, B.F.A., 1978. *Home:* 109 Elizabeth St., Frankfort, Ky. 40601. *Studio:* Freeman Illustrations, 125 Laralan Ave., Frankfort, Ky. 40601.

CAREER: Graphic artist and retoucher, Hitchcock, Fleming & Associates, Akron, Ohio, 1978-83; graphic artist and illustrator, Freeman Illustrations, Frankfort, Ky., 1983—.

MEMBER: Arts Council of Frankfort.

AWARDS, HONORS: Jury's Merit Award, 14th Annual Coca-Cola Art Show, 1984, for painting *1000CC Down Main*; national finalist, American Artist National Art Competition, 1985, for painting *The Magical Toy Chest.*

WRITINGS: Contributor to many small-press comic book series, including *Sensawunda!, Realm of Adventure, Slam Bang,* and *Shrinkage.*

EXHIBITIONS: Grand Central Galleries, New York City, 1985.

SIDELIGHTS: "I have worked with one of the leading airbrush artists in America," Allen Freeman told *CGA*, "and with this experience I have studied and worked with the airbrush in order to create paintings of superrealism. I am most interested in doing the kind of commercial art that would motivate people to stop and think. I am also working in the cartooning field and publishing small-press publications, an experience designed to extend my creative boundaries."

One of the many practitioners in the field of superrealism (or photorealism), Freeman has made a reputation for himself with his depictions of powerful machines seen from slightly ominous angles. Thus *1000CC Down Main* posits the motorcycle-rider as an outrider from an alien, threatening

The Magical Toy Chest, **a print** (© 1983, Allen R. Freeman. Reprinted by permission.)

A caricature of actor Jim Varney (© 1985, Allen R. Freeman. Reprinted by permission.)

order; while *At the Car Show*, another one of Freeman's paintings, contemplates a sleek automobile as if it were some futuristic spaceship. Yet the artist doesn't feel beholden to the naturalistic discipline of superrealism: *The Magical Toy Chest* gives us a child's eye view of a toyshop universe, and in *Wildcats* he is able to convey an image of cheerleaders that is both tongue-in-cheek and affectionate.

Such whimsy is perhaps even more strongly expressed in Freeman's black-and-white prints, as in his slightly caricatural portrait of actor Jim Varney, or in his brooding rendering of the 1930s pulp-magazine hero The Shadow. His love of old comic books (which he avidly collects) is reflected in his publication of a number of comic pamphlets in which elements of fantasy and reality are even more intricately blended together.

BIOGRAPHICAL/CRITICAL SOURCES: Airbrush Digest, October, 1984; *American Artist,* July, 1985; *Fandom Forum,* Number 1, 1986.

G

GAMBLE, Ed 1943-

PERSONAL: Born May 12, 1943, in Morristown, Tenn.; son of James Vernon (in government) and Anna (a newspaper columnist; maiden name, Hill) Gamble; married Saundra Lancaster, June 28, 1964. *Education:* University of South Florida, B.A., 1970. *Religion:* Methodist. *Home:* 2485 Bernice Dr., Jacksonville, Fla. 32217. *Office: Florida Times-Union*, One Riverside Ave., Jacksonville, Fla. 32217.

CAREER: Editorial cartoonist, *Nashville Banner*, Nashville, Tenn., 1972-1980; editorial cartoonist, *Florida Times-Union*, Jacksonville, Fla., 1980—. Syndicated by the Register and Tribune Syndicate (now Cowles Syndicate) 1973—.

AWARDS, HONORS: Dragonslayer Award, U.S. Industrial Council, 1976; Small Business Association Awards, 1978 and 1979; Freedoms Foundation George Washington Award, 1980; Tennessee School Bell Award, 1980; Metro Nashville Teachers Award, 1980.

WRITINGS—Contributor: *Peek at the Great Society*, Whitehaven Press, 1965; Carew Papritz, editor, *100 Watts: The James Watt Memorial Cartoon Collection*, Khyber Press, 1983; Charles E. Brooks, editor, *Best Editorial Cartoons of the Year*, Pelican Publishing, 1972—.

SIDELIGHTS: As the son of a government official and the nephew of newspaper owners, Ed Gamble was born and raised in an atmosphere of journalism and absorbed both the discipline of the newspaperman and the political commitment of a concerned citizen from his earliest years. His uncles owned and operated a daily newspaper in his home town of Morristown, Tennessee, and his mother wrote a daily column for it. His twin brother John was a reporter with United Press International for a time before going on to study law, and now serves as a attorney and agent for the Bloom Agency in Hollywood, California. A first cousin, Jane Wagner, is a playwright and television writer, as well as a stage director.

An editorial cartoon by Ed Gamble (© 1985, *Florida Times-Union*. Reprinted by permission.)

From his childhood, Ed Gamble aspired to express his ideas in graphic form and calls the position of editorial cartoonist he now holds his "life-long goal." He began drawing as a child on rolls of copy paper his mother brought home from the family newspaper, and he won his first art award, for a city-wide beautification and clean-up contest, at the age of nine. The sketching pencil was never very far from his hand after that, and a steady stream of cartoons issued from him for his high-school and college newspapers during the next few years.

Gamble worked as a reporter and sports editor on a number of daily newspapers after receiving his bachelor's degree from the University of South Florida, serving as sports cartoonist as well for several, until 1972. In that year editorial cartoonist Jack Knox of the *Nashville Banner* retired, and Gamble accepted the position. The following year he was syndicated by the Register and Tribune Syndicate in Des Moines, Iowa. In 1980 he moved to the *Florida Times-Union* in Jacksonville, where he has been the editorial cartoonist ever since.

During the past thirteen years, Gamble has acquired a growing reputation and won a string of awards, both local and national, for his hard-hitting political cartoons. His work has appeared in numerous collections and has been included in every edition of *Best Editorial Cartoons of the Year* since 1972. Two of his cartoons appeared in *100 Watts*, a collection attacking the policies of U.S. Secretary of the

Interior James Watt in 1983. Gamble's concern for environmental issues was reflected in the vigor of his assaults. One cartoon, originally published in 1981, shows a group of quaking forest creatures learning that Watt has received the Interior post. "Don't. . . don't anybody panic. . .," urges a terrified raccoon, "but I've got grave news."

Although a *People* review of *Best Editorial Cartoons of the Year: 1983* refers to Gamble as a "crusty conservative," his editorial cartoons cover a wide spectrum of positions, and it would be difficult to assign him a specific political stance. As an editorial voice, Gamble is always his own man. In 1981 he depicted President Ronald Reagan as a mobster preparing to commit a St. Valentine's Day massacre on such social programs as Medicaid and food stamps, and in another cartoon of that year he lashed out at the bankruptcy of the Social Security System. His work is often witty and cutting, but it is always instilled with human sympathy.

Gamble works in great detail and displays full backgrounds, highlighting the droll, simply sketched faces of his characters. A powerful use of black and shaded areas gives his compositions great dramatic force, and the striking contrasts featured in his work strengthen the impact of his message.

BIOGRAPHICAL/CRITICAL SOURCES: "Picks and Pans," *People*, June 13, 1983.

* * *

GARLAND, Michael 1952-

PERSONAL: Born July 16, 1952, in New York, N.Y.; son of Thomas C. (a policeman) and Margaret (Carney) Garland; married Margaret McDermott, June 28, 1980; children: Katherine Anne, Alice Jeanne. *Education:* Pratt Institute, B.F.A., 1974. *Home:* 78 Columbia Ave., Hartsdale, N.Y. 10530.

CAREER: Commercial illustrator, New York, 1974—. Member of Steering Committee, Graphic Artist Guild Book; judge for Society of Illustrators annual shows; member of Advisory Committee, Children's Book Council.

MEMBER: Society of Illustrators, Graphic Artist Guild.

AWARDS, HONORS: Awards from Society of Illustrators, New York City, 1981-85; Communications Design Show, New York City, 1983; *American Artist* Annual Show, New York City, 1985; Pratt Alumni Exhibition, Brooklyn, N.Y., 1985; *Communication Arts* Annual Award, New York City, 1985. Also received honors for original art of children's books, 1981-83.

EXHIBITIONS: (One-man show) Society of Illustrators, New York, 1985; Miniature Show, GSW Gallery, Southport, Conn., 1985; Artist on Location, Garrison Art Gallery, 1985; American Artist Annual Show, Grand Central Gallery, 1985; Pratt Alumni Exhibition, 1985; (one-man show) Hudson River Gallery, 1986.

WORK IN PROGRESS: "A series of more personal landscapes and still lifes to be shown in galleries or reproduced as limited-edition prints. Preparing an article on bridging the gap between illustration and fine arts as viewed from a personal and historic perspective to be published by a national art publication."

Self-portrait of Ed Gamble, specially drawn for *Contemporary Graphic Artists* (© 1986, Ed Gamble.)

SIDELIGHTS: An example of the new generation of commercial illustrators, Michael Garland combines the skills of a layout designer, a portrait painter, and an advertising man. The range of his work extends well beyond that of the old-style advertising artist, as his many and varied awards attest.

Solidly grounded in the mechanics and technique of art by his studies at New York's prestigious Pratt Institute, Garland began his career as a free-lance commercial illustrator immediately after graduating in 1974 and has achieved a growing professional reputation during the decade since. His technical proficiency has enabled him to work with many firms in a wide variety of product-areas, and his range of affiliations has been impressive. His clients have included the J. Walter Thompson Agency, AT&T, IBM, General Electric, *Forbes, Ladies Home Journal*, Estee Lauder, *Cosmopolitan, Parents Magazine*, McGraw-Hill, Scribners/Atheneum Publishers, Fawcett Publications, Bantam Books, ABC, Ballantine Books, NBC, and *Woman's Day*, along with many specialized trade and technical journals.

The subjects Garland treats as a commercial illustrator are as varied as the assignments he undertakes, ranging from architecture to medicine, electronics to labor, athletics to industry, but in all he displays the same precision of style and firm grasp of formal detail. His faces, whether of public figures or imagined characters, have an almost photographic realism. The sharp-edged clarity and vivid color of his images produce arresting pictures, and the combination of his command of external appearance with the imaginative use of composition and symbol results in always memorable illustrations. Particularly striking are his imaginatively set portrait illustrations of musical celebrities like James Galway and Luciano Pavarotti.

Despite his proficiency in portraying the human face, Garland feels a special affinity for both still lifes and landscapes, and incorporates both as elements in some of his commercial illustrations. His personal paintings employ these traditional subjects with great skill, and he is currently working on a series of still life and landscape paintings.

Garland has sought to bring the creative energies of the fine

Stuyvesant Landing, **an oil painting** (© 1985, Michael Garland. Reprinted by permission.)

artist to his work as a commercial illustrator and indicates that his present goal is "to merge [his] personal painting with [his] commercial illustration." Indeed, for him the two strands of his artistic life have not been widely separated. An imaginative and creative aspect may be seen in his commercial work, setting it apart from the purely perfunctory work of others who work on assignment, and the same technical gifts found in his formal advertising art are apparent in his personal paintings.

As a landscape painter, Michael Garland displays a lyrical realism that calls to mind the work of John Constable, and he shares the early nineteenth-century English master's devotion to simplicity and the gentle aspects of nature. In his landscape painting, Garland permits himself some freedom in loose, impressionistic brushwork which might be considered too painterly for advertising art, but the same controlled draftsmanship and assured mastery of his material and technique pervade it. In this regard, the personal and the commercial art of Michael Garland may be said to form a single body of highly professional work.

BIOGRAPHICAL/CRITICAL SOURCES: Society of Illustrators Annual, 1981-85; RSVP, Numbers 1-10, 1974-85; Graphic Artist Guild Directory, 1985; Communication Arts Annual, 1985.

MICHAEL GARLAND

* * *

GEARY, Rick   1946-

PERSONAL: Born February 25, 1946, in Kansas City, Mo.; son of Edward Vernon (a banker) and Helen Louise (Brooks) Geary; married Nancy J. Wiegand, May 8, 1971 (divorced, 1973). *Education:* University of Kansas at Lawrence, B.F.A., 1968, M.A., 1971. *Home:* 918 Felspar St., San Diego, Calif. 92109. *Studio:* P.O. Box 99835, San Diego, Calif. 92109. *Agent:* David Scroggy Agency, 2124 Froude St., San Diego, Calif. 92107.

CAREER: Free-lance cartoonist and illustrator, 1976—; director, San Diego International Film Festival, 1978—. Author and artist, *The Perfect Couple*, single-panel newspaper strip, syndicated by Copley News Service, 1985—.

AWARDS, HONORS: Inkpot Award, San Diego Comics Convention, 1980.

WRITINGS—Collections of cartoons: *Nine Views, Various Electrical Appliances, Young Eisenhower (Rick Geary's Mini-Comix, Set Number 1)*, privately printed, 1977; *Television*, Schanes & Schanes, 1978; *San Diego Transit, American Motels (Rick Geary's Mini-Comix, Set Number 2)*, privately

An illustration (© 1984, Michael Garland. Reprinted by permission.)

printed, 1978; *Hello from San Diego*, Schanes & Schanes, 1978; *Farewell to Charlie Chaplin, The Shopping Mall Book* (*Rick Geary's Mini-Comix, Set Number 3*), privately printed, 1979; *Ike and Mamie, Book of Falling* (*Rick Geary's Mini-Comix, Set Number 4*), privately printed, 1979; *Fly with Us, Let's Get Organized, Book of Condos, Six Remarkable Innovations* (*Rick Geary's Mini-Comix, Set Number 5*), privately printed, 1980; *This New Age, Von Stroheim Directs* (*Rick Geary's Mini-Comix, Set Number 6*), privately printed, 1980; *Byting Back*, Valleyware Publications, 1983; *True Crimes of Passion*, privately printed, 1984; *At Home with Rick Geary: Collected Stories 1977-85*, Fantagraphics, 1985; (contributor) Harvey Kurtzman, *Nuts!* I and II, Bantam, 1985; (illustrator) Byron Preiss and Michael Sorkin, *Not the Webster's Dictionary*, Wallaby/Simon & Schuster, 1983.

EXHIBITIONS: A group show of local artists at a San Diego shopping center, 1986.

WORK IN PROGRESS: A short animated film entitled *Murder at the Hollywood Hotel* in pre-production.

SIDELIGHTS: Rick Geary has for the last few years been best known to the general public for his evocative and stylish monthly cartoons in *National Lampoon*, but for a decade he has had a devoted following in the esoteric world of "Newave" comics. This genre, which carries on the independent tradition of the old, now largely silent underground comics but without their violent, revolutionary spirit of iconoclasm, is characterized by freedom from graphic or thematic conventions and an often quirky individuality of styles, ranging from the deliberate crudeness of stick figures to elaborately ornamental parodies of nineteenth-century engravings. But as idiosyncratic as the styles of the Newave are, few of its practitioners are more immediately recognizable in print than Rick Geary.

Although he sold his first piece of advertising art in Wichita, Kansas, in 1973, Geary has been calling himself a free-lance artist and illustrator only since 1976, a year after he moved to San Diego, California, to pursue a career in art. In 1977 he published the first of his highly original little sets of booklets, *Rick Geary's Mini-Comics*, because as he explains, "at first, no one else would." Self-publication—a typical feature of the Newave comics industry—is a natural expression of the highly personal nature of its art, and Geary's finely executed sets represented the highest standard not only of originality in art and content but in quality of production. Entirely under his own control, each of these tiny "mini-comics" is a complete, self-contained feature, sometimes a narrative and sometimes merely a thematically linked collection of drawings. The fifteen booklets, grouped in six sets and issued from 1977 to 1980, established Geary's reputation in the Newave market and beyond it.

As an undergraduate at the University of Kansas, studying commercial art as a path of least resistance, Geary thought he would become an editorial cartoonist, although he admits he is "not comfortable with point-making." The sly, oblique commentary that emerges from his cartoons is rather psychological than sociological or political, and his art remains more personal than public. As a child, he reports, he seldom showed his cartoons to friends and never to his family. "My parents still don't understand anything I do," he says. "They don't see how I'm able to make a living with this stuff." A master's degree in film reflected a deeper

affinity, however, and one which has not faded. Since 1978 Geary has been a director of the San Diego International Film Festival, where he works in selection and programming. Not all of his involvement with the cinema is vicarious: he is currently working on an animated film of one of his off-beat stories, "Murder at the Hollywood Hotel."

In addition to his extensive self-published output during his decade in the field, Geary has appeared in a score of newspapers and magazines. Along with such fringe journals as *Snarf, Bop, Raw,* and *Bizarre Sex*, his outlets include *San Diego Magazine, Los Angeles Magazine*, and such national periodicals as *Heavy Metal, National Lampoon,* and *Rolling Stone*. In 1983 his clean, crisp line-drawings illustrated Preiss and Sorkin's collection of humorous neologisms *Not the Webster's Dictionary* for Simon & Schuster, and in 1985 some of his pieces appeared in Harvey Kurtzman's two volumes of *Nuts!* Of the latter the *Comics Journal* stated, "The only thing that saves *Nuts* from mediocrity is the incandescent Rick Geary." Also in 1985, Fantagraphics Books brought out a retrospective collection, *At Home with Rick Geary: Collected Stories 1977-85*.

There is seldom a clearly defined narrative in Geary's strips, although a thread of development runs through most of them. It is not as a storyteller that he gets his effects, but as a patient compiler of small, isolated details which compose a situation or an attitude. There is something indefinably but chillingly funny in his scrapbook approach to the icons of contemporary (and nineteenth-century) America. His book *Television*, for example, presents a page of drawings of

Self-portrait of Rick Geary (© Rick Geary. Reprinted by permission.)

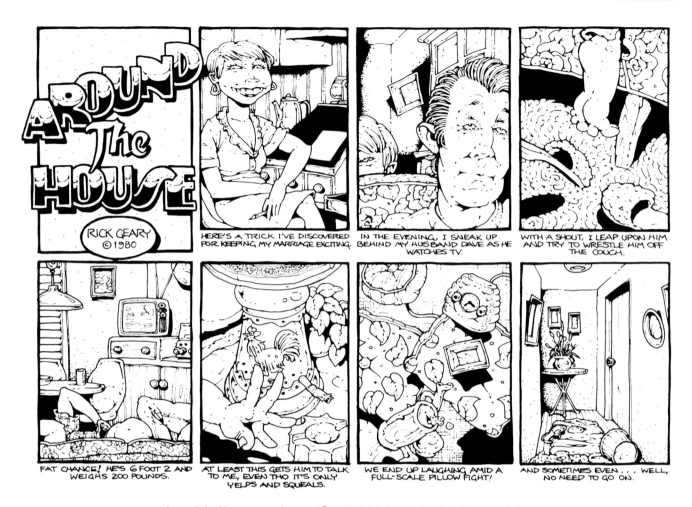

***Around the House,* a comic page** (© 1980, Rick Geary. Reprinted by permission.)

television dinners, simply listing their ingredients like a sales brochure; or a series of parts of sets, magnified details of a common household object; or antennas, or test patterns; by the simple act of meticulously depicting them, he dramatizes the almost totemic position television has come to assume in our lives, and the result is both startling and hilarious. In 1983 he did the same for computers in *Byting Back.*

Geary's work is never the same twice, although the clean, elegant line is always an unmistakable trademark. He never re-uses the same characters, and indeed points out that he never even draws the same character twice; even within the same story, the character's face rarely appears more than once. He is continuously experimenting and varying the composition and layout of his page, breaking them up into all sorts of new and original patterns. His panels may be square, or round, or lozenge-shaped; they may appear in neat symmetry or at odd angles. Also constantly changing and growing are his professional outlets; in addition to the ever-growing body of unique cartoons, he has since 1973 done a wide variety of work for local advertising agencies. Last year the Southern California Exposition at Del Mar called on Geary for artwork which included a huge cartoon map of the fairgrounds.

Variously called "lyrical," "sinister," "petulant," and "engaging," Geary's beautifully controlled style ultimately

defies classification. His uncanny eye and ear for the banal, coupled with his stylish drawing and highly personal organization of material, enable him to capture the underlying strangeness in the everyday and open our eyes to layers of meaning beyond words in the commonplace. The obscurely cinematic effect evident in his work is no accident. The artist has written to *CGA:* "The cinema is very important to me; I think I'm probably a frustrated filmmaker, and it comes out in my work in various forms." Geary acknowledges the inspiration and "indirect" influence of several artists and illustrators: Edward Gorey ("I like the quaintness of it."), Saul Steinberg, Gluyas Williams, and Robert Crumb. "But," he adds, "being a movie junkie, I think my visual and storytelling sense has been influenced as much if not more by certain film directors, notably Hitchcock, Welles, Bunuel, and Kurosawa." These filmmakers may have added something to his technique, but the odd angle of vision with which Geary sees our world is uniquely his own. "All I've sought is to convey my own bemused and detached view of life," he reports. In a decade of distinctive and distinguished work he has accomplished his goal notably.

BIOGRAPHICAL/CRITICAL SOURCES: [Untitled], *Comics Buyer's Guide,* August 25, 1978; Bob Getz, "Was Magazine Lampooning Wichita's Finest?," *Wichita Eagle Beacon,* November 21, 1980; Nanette Wiser, "Funny Pictures," *Downtown* (San Diego, Calif.), July 19, 1982; Dale

Humorous illustrations by Rick Geary (clockwise from upper left, © 1980, 1981, 1983. Reprinted by permission.)

Luciano, "Nostalgia, Mice, and Ducks," *Comics Journal*, September, 1982; "Hello from San Diego," *San Diego Hill Courier*, October, 1983; Lois Horowitz, "Books/Writers: Local Artists Crack Kids' Book Field," *San Diego Tribune*, December 9, 1983; Heidi MacDonald, "Fight Scenes, Fight Scenes Everywhere, Nor Any Stop to Think," *Comics Journal*, December, 1983; R. Fiore, "Funnybook Roulette," *Comics Journal*, February, 1985, September, 1985; Dale Luciano, "Newave Comics Survey," *Comics Journal*, March, 1985, April, 1985; [untitled], *Antique Trader*, November 20, 1985; Scott McCloud, "Small Press Watch," *Amazing Heroes*, January 15, 1986; Divina Infusino, "New Wave Comics," *San Diego Union*, February 5, 1986; [untitled], *Comics Buyer's Guide*, February 14, 1986.

—*Sketch by Dennis Wepman*

* * *

GORSLINE, Douglas (Warner)   1913-1985

OBITUARY NOTICE: Born May 24, 1913, in Rochester, N.Y.; died June 26, 1985, in Dijon, France, of a stroke. An artist and illustrator, Douglas Gorsline illustrated more than fifty books in his forty-year career, from Izaak Walton's classic *The Compleat Angler* to Dale Eunson's *The Day They Gave Babies Away.* His forte, however, was the West, which he depicted with vigor and zest in such works as Fred Reinfeld's *Trappers of the West* and Louise D. Rich's *First Book of the Early Settlers*, as well as in the series of books (*North American Indians, Cowboys, Pioneers*, etc.) which he did in the late 1970s and early 1980s for Random House. He also took up the daunting task of illustrating Clement C. Moore's poem *The Night Before Christmas*, some ninety years after Thomas Nast's celebrated version. Among the other books illustrated by Gorsline are Louisa May Alcott's *Little Men* and Bernardine Kielty's *Marie Antoinette*. Gorsline was the author of *Farm Boy*, a self-illustrated juvenile, and put together the witty compilation, *What People Wore: A Visual History of Dress from Ancient Times to Twentieth-Century America.* As a painter he had many one-man shows in galleries in the United States and Europe; he was represented in numerous private and public collections. Gorsline received awards and honors from such groups and organizations as the American Academy of Arts and Letters, the American Watercolor Society, Audubon Artists, and the National Arts Club. A citizen of the world, he traveled extensively through Europe and Asia; for the last fifteen years before his death he lived in France.

BIOGRAPHICAL/CRITICAL SOURCES: Contemporary Authors, New Revision Series, Vol. 9, Gale, 1983.

OBITUARY NOTICES: New York Times, July 10, 1985.

* * *

GOSLIN, Charles   1932-

PERSONAL: Born February 23, 1932, in Attleboro, Mass.; son of Herbert Hyland (a silversmith) and Florence Pauline (an artist; maiden name, Guyot) Goslin; married Caroline Millicent Ryder, August 5, 1955 (divorced January 25, 1966). *Education:* Rhode Island School of Design, B.F.A., 1954. *Home and studio:* 264 Garfield Pl., Brooklyn, N.Y. 11215.

CAREER: Graphic designer, William J. Small Advertising Agency, Boston, Mass., 1954-55; graphic designer, Lester Beal Graphic Design, Brookfield Center, Conn., 1955-58; free-lance graphic designer, Brooklyn, N.Y., 1958—; adjunct professor of graphic design, 1966—, chairman of department of communications design, 1973-74, Pratt Institute, Brooklyn, N.Y. Instructor in advanced graphic design at School of Visual Arts; guest lecturer in graphic design at Parsons School of Design. Contributing reviewer for *Idea*, 1974—.

MEMBER: Graphic Artists Guild, United Federation of College Teachers, Rhode Island School of Design Club of New York, Unitarian Universalist Service Committee, National Association for the Advancement of Colored People (NAACP), Long Island Historical Society.

AWARDS, HONORS: Awards of merit from Art Directors Club of Boston, 1954, American Institute of Graphic Arts, 1955 and 1964, Art Directors Club of New York, 1956, and Society of Illustrators, 1960.

EXHIBITIONS: Work represented in many exhibitions in New York, West Germany, Czechoslovakia, and Japan, including those at Brownstone Gallery, Brooklyn, N.Y., 1975; Bienniales of Graphic Design, Brno, Czechoslovakia, 1976, 1978, 1980, 1982, 1984, and 1986; and Staatliches Museum fur Angewandte Kunst, Munich, West Germany, 1983.

WORK IN PROGRESS: Working on a collection relating Goslin's material to the work of his great-grandfather, a Swiss steel engraver.

CHARLES GOSLIN

A promotion piece (© 1986, Charles Goslin. Reprinted by permission.)

SIDELIGHTS: Charles Goslin has stated his professional ideal clearly and concisely as being "to speak with style," and his wide critical acclaim on three continents attests to his success at establishing a recognizable personal style. Few contemporary designers speak more forcefully or with a more distinctive graphic voice than Goslin. In 1963 he was already identifiable as a significant new figure and was named by the Japanese journal *Graphic Design* as part of "the new wave" in design. The trend he signaled then toward direct emphatic statement and simple, muscular form did not become established for many years, and since then tastes have come and gone, but through the sometimes precious or whimsical vogues of the 1960s and 1970s Charles Goslin has never wavered from his own stern discipline and austere good taste. For three decades his sturdy, sinewy designs have been a ringing statement of his aesthetic principles.

Goslin's artistic creed emerges from a heritage of earlier generations of artistic craftsmanship. The son of a silversmith and the great-grandson of a master steel engraver, Goslin comes by both his aesthetic principles and the strict discipline and control of his craft naturally, and he has reinforced his natural gifts with a rigorous training in his field. After obtaining a degree in fine arts from the Rhode Island School of Design in 1954, he worked for an advertising agency in Boston for a year and then spent four years with graphic designer Lester Beal, a period he still regards as an apprenticeship. From Beal he learned many things, Goslin reports, not least of them "a fine set of values." Beal never did anything vulgar and never stinted on time according to his former student. Goslin recalls doing 125 variations on the trademark for one of his clients with Beal before the job was considered finished, and he continues to dedicate himself to every project with the same tireless perfectionism.

In addition to Beal and his own family, three other designers figure among the inspirations which Goslin recognizes. Like his great-grandfather, all are Swiss: Ernst Keller, whom he considers "the father of modern Swiss design"; Pierre Gauchat, a French-Swiss designer and typographer with the rare honor of having his name appear on his country's currency, which he designed; and Hans Hartmann, who still designs postage stamps for Switzerland, among other areas of design. These three men represent both the Swiss tradition of masterful craftsmanship and a breadth of activity that Goslin finds impressive.

Goslin sets no boundaries on his own work. He will, he states, design anything, and has done book jackets, album covers, theater posters, trademarks, packaging, and, recently, a pair of cuff links. Among his most distinguished accomplishments is the design of the 1958 "Freedom of the Press" postage stamp, a four-cent commemorative issued on the centennial of the opening of the first school of journalism in the United States. He still gets first-day covers with requests for his autograph for that design. He has done album covers for Decca and Columbia Records, and clients for his book covers have included Random House, Simon & Schuster, Atheneum, Franklin Watts, and Harper & Row. Theater posters have always figured prominently among his projects; although he admits they are not very lucrative, he cannot resist requests to do them because of his love for the theater and for the freedom of artistic expression they permit him. Other major clients include Chase Manhattan Bank, the accounting firm of Price Waterhouse, Pfizer pharmaceuticals, and Robbins Awards, a very large awards jewelry company.

Goslin's work has been exhibited and reviewed in many countries. Since 1976 it has been displayed in every biennial exhibition of graphic art at Brno, Czechoslovakia, and articles about his work have appeared in *Print* (U.S.), *Graphic Design* and *Idea* (Japan), *Novum Gebrauchsgraphik* (Germany), and *Modern Publicity* (Great Britain). He has contributed a number of reviews of others' work to *Idea* since 1974.

Goslin's unmistakable style, described by Katzumie Masaru in *Graphic Design* as "pure and intellectual," has remained remarkably constant during his long creative career. As Heribert Zahn observed in *Novum Gebrauchsgraphik* in 1985, "It was in the early seventies that he drew attention with his unusual work. . . Even then the basic design approach was recognizable which still characterizes his work today." Typically austere and unembellished, his designs convey a powerful conciseness. "I hate excess," he reported to *Graphis* in 1983. "It's vulgar. I'm a practical man. I love economy in all things." Although his highly personal technique seems to owe no debt to tradition, his Swiss background surely emerges in the practicality and economy that runs so continuously throughout the body of his work.

Also evident in his work is his early training in and life-long love of typography. Alphabets appear regularly in Goslin's designs and always form an organic part of the composition. The designer shows a keen appreciation of the abstract forms of letters and utilizes them as integral elements of his design. "I use the alphabet creatively," he states, "as a supportive part of the whole picture." However, he is not dependent on typography, and may relinquish it when his

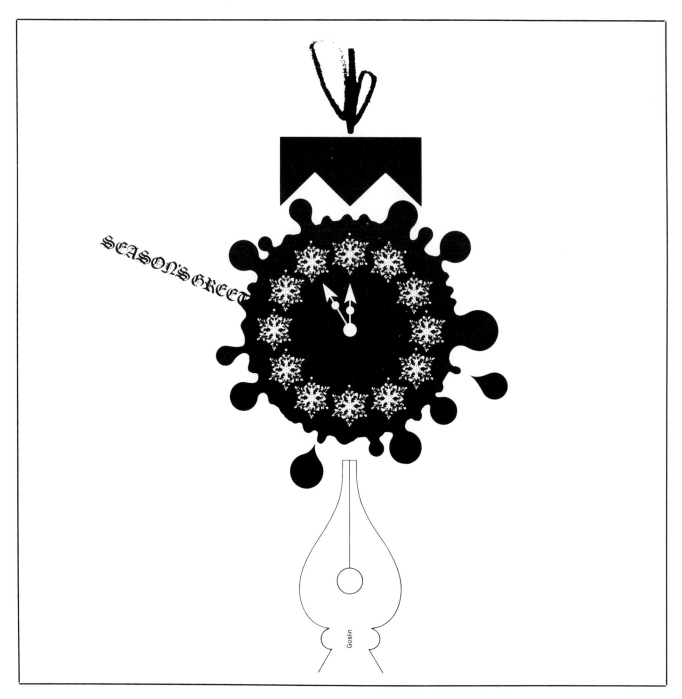

A greeting card design (© 1986, Charles Goslin. Reprinted by permission.)

message may be better expressed without it. A crossword-puzzle collection published by Simon & Schuster, for example, featured a cover by Goslin depicting an abstract key-and-keyhole motif which eloquently conveyed the information with no distraction from letters of the alphabet.

Goslin considers himself an "applied artist," but draws from models when necessary. Most of his work is done in collage using photostats and cut paper, often incorporating pencil drawing. His pencil work reveals fine detail produced by a very sharp point, recalling the engraving tools of his Swiss ancestor. In this as in other ways, Goslin perceives a

continuity between his work and that of his forebear which he is exploring in a forthcoming collection that will include his own work and what he has been able to preserve of his great-grandfather's. He hopes to bring this volume to completion in 1988.

Despite the wide range of professional assignments which Goslin accepts, he has since 1966 been a dedicated teacher and has given as fully of his energies to the classroom as to the designing board. He has taught graphic design at Pratt Institute (where he served as chairman of the department of communications design in 1973-74) and at the School of

Visual Arts and has been a guest lecturer at Parsons School of Design. Successful professionals often teach as a minor sideline, for a little extra money or as the fulfillment of a duty to pass their expertise on to their juniors, but Goslin takes his academic life seriously as an equal element of his professional career. "I am interested in the interaction of my careers as artist and teacher," he reported to *CGA*. "The necessity for a single set of standards for my students' work and my work is vital. . . . The artist/teacher must have a single set of standards. . . which are rigorously applied to himself first and foremost." The strength of his principles as a teacher are evident also in his creative work as a designer,

and the artistic and moral integrity which he brings to his teaching may be seen as a unifying force in his always powerful graphic design.

BIOGRAPHICAL/CRITICAL SOURCES: Gebrauchsgraphik, June, 1962; *Idea*, December, 1963, May, 1974; *Graphic Design*, October, 1963, March, 1981; *Print*, September-October, 1968; *Novum Gebrauchsgraphik*, January, 1972, November, 1985; *Graphis*, May-June, 1983; *Who's Who in the East 1983-84*, Marquis, 1983.

—Sketch by Dennis Wepman

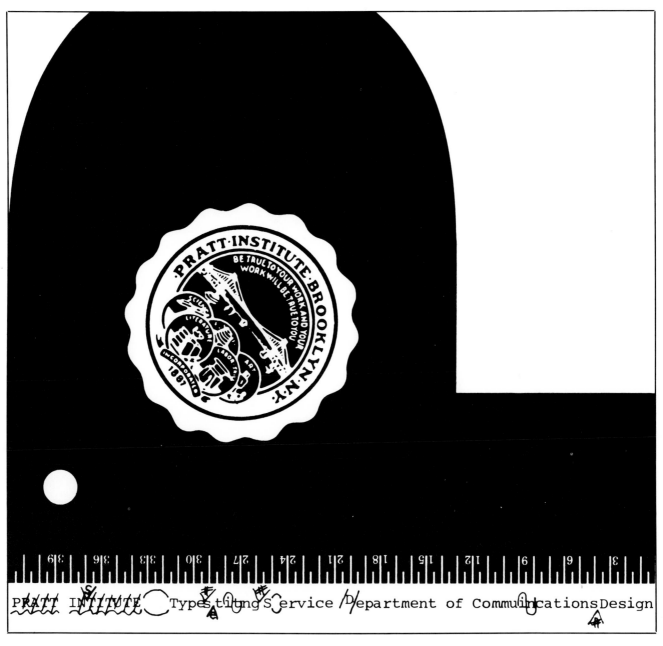

Logo for the Pratt Institute Department of Communication Design (© 1986, Charles Goslin. Reprinted by permission.)

A greeting card design (© 1986, Charles Goslin. Reprinted by permission.)

* * *

GROTH, John 1908-

PERSONAL: Surname is pronounced "Growth"; born February 26, 1908, in Chicago, Ill.; son of John (a store owner) and Ethel (Bragg) Groth; divorced; children: Tamara Collins. *Education:* Attended Chicago Art Institute, 1927-28, and Art Students League of New York, 1936-37. *Politics:* Democratic. *Religion:* Protestant. *Studio:* 12 E. 86th St., New York, N.Y. 10028.

CAREER: Artist, illustrator, and journalist, 1927—. Art director, *Esquire*, Chicago, Ill., 1933-37; art director, *Parade*, New York City, 1941-45; art director and staff artist, *Esquire*, 1953-64. Instructor at Art Students League of New York, 1946—, Pratt Institute, Brooklyn, N.Y., 1952-55; art instructor at Parsons School of Design, New York City, 1954-55, National Academy of Design, New York City, 1962-63; artist-in-residence at University of Texas, Austin, 1970. War correspondent in Europe for Chicago Sun Syndicate, 1944-45, in French Indo-China for Metropolitan Group Syndicate, 1951, in Asia for *Sports Illustrated*, 1954, in Congo and Central Africa for U.S. Air Force, 1960, in Dominican Republic, 1965, and in Vietnam for U.S. Marine Corps, 1967.

MEMBER: National Academy of Design (associate), Overseas Press of America, American Watercolor Society, Society of Illustrators, Explorers Club, Lotos Club.

AWARDS, HONORS: Citations from U.S. Air Force, 1960, for Congo action, U.S. Marine Corps, 1967 and 1968, for Vietnam action. Honorary bachelor of arts, Eastern Michigan University, 1977.

WRITINGS—Self-illustrated: *Studio: Europe*, Vanguard, 1945; *Studio: Asia*, World Publishing, 1952; *John Groth's World of Sport*, additional text by Pat Smith, Winchester Press, 1970.

Illustrator: (And author of introduction) Ernest Hemingway, *Men Without Women*, World Publishing, 1946; John Steinbeck, *The Grapes of Wrath*, World Publishing, 1947; Harford Willing Hare Powel, *Good Jobs for Good Girls*, Vanguard, 1949; Leo Tolstoy, *War and Peace*, Heinemann, 1961; Leon Uris, *Exodus*, Doubleday, 1962; Anna Sewell, *Black Beauty*, Macmillan, 1962; Charles Dickens, *A Christmas Carol*, Macmillan, 1963; O. Henry, *The Stories of O. Henry*, Heritage, 1966; Margaret Mitchell, *Gone With the Wind*, Heritage, 1968; Mark Twain, *War Prayer*, Harper, 1968; Erich Maria Remarque, *All Quiet on the Western Front*, Limited Editions Club, 1969.

Maia Wojciechowska, *Life and Death of a Brave Bull*, Harcourt, 1972; Giles Tippette, *The Brave Men*, Macmillan, 1972; Twain, *Pudd'nhead Wilson*, Limited Editions Club, 1974; John Graves, *The Last Running*, Encino Press, 1974; Arnold Gingrich, *The Fishing in Print*, Winchester Press,

JOHN GROTH

Boar Hunt near Moulins, **a watercolor** (© 1969, John Groth, Reprinted by permission.)

1974; Kurth Sprague, *The Promise Kept*, Encino Press, 1975; Alice Hopf, *Biography of an American Reindeer*, Putnam, 1976; Captain Elijah Petty, *Journey to Pleasant Hill*, University of Texas, 1982.

Sole illustrator of *Short Story International*, 1964-66 and 1977-80. Contributor of illustrations to *Collier's, Esquire, Vogue, Saturday Evening Post, New Yorker, Fortune, Sports Illustrated, Holiday*, and other periodicals.

WORK IN PROGRESS: Oil paintings; Civil War battle scenes; various assignments for magazines.

SIDELIGHTS: "He looked," Ernest Hemingway once observed of John Groth, "more like an artist than any good artist I ever knew." If by "good artist" Hemingway meant the undernourished, garret-dwelling surrealists of his Paris days in the 1920s, then indeed the athletic and fearless Chicagoan Groth must have seemed a marked improvement to the "Papa Bear." About the young graphic journalist's sketches of the taking of Berlin, the celebrated author noted with approval, "If John would have made them from any closer up, he would have had to sit in the Krauts' lap." Hemingway is better known for his judgments of men than for his judgments of art, but his remarks on John Groth the

man do provide a useful insight into the work of John Groth the artist.

Born in 1908, the young Groth was a gifted athlete who at one time had hopes of a career in professional football. When this hope was shattered, along with his right shoulder, on the playing field, he turned to the drawing board. Enrolling at the Chicago Institute of Art in 1926, he soon found that formal studio classes were not to his activist taste.

He did, however, find inspiration in the school's library, where he pored over the prints of Francisco Goya and Honore Daumier and studied closely their economy of line and use of chiaroscuro effects to convey mood and emphasis. Having found a genre that appealed to his temperament, Groth set out to master it through persistence and concentration. This regimen included private study (with Todos Geller) and a brief association with a somewhat eccentric Chicago patroness of the arts, but in the main his education consisted of going out and drawing what he saw. Following the advice of a friendly art director, he made one hundred sketches a day, emphasizing the bare elements of action and form, without regard for detail or finish, and during this apprenticeship period regularly produced two to three thousand drawings a month. (Some years later, Groth recounts, he thanked that art director for the advice only to be told, with incredulous laughter, that the advisor hadn't expected to be taken seriously.)

In 1933, he was exhibiting his "Speed Line Drawings" at a Grant Park outdoor art show when Arnold Gingrich happened by. "They looked like what they were called," Gingrich later wrote, "quick sketches done in a variety of colored inks, with a lot of fast-flowing lines." Having just launched a new magazine, *Esquire*, Gingrich was in desperate need of an artist to fill out its innovative color format, and "Speed Line Drawings" sounded just the thing. The sketches on display were depression/ashcan in substance—soup kitchens, bread lines, hobos, striking workers—but executed with a sense of humor which suggested to the bemused publisher "those improbable collaborators, Daumier and Disney." He thus hired the twenty five-year-old unknown and Groth responded by providing that maiden issue of *Esquire* with seventeen pages of monotypes, aquatints, drypoint etchings, and drawings. So dominant was his graphic influence, Gingrich gave him the title of art director, though Groth would never have any responsibility for layout. In fact, the canny proprietor immediately recognized Groth's unique strength as a graphic journalist and over the next three years would send him on assignment to Mexico (where his portrayals of a degraded peasantry and a corrupt government got the magazine banned), London (where he spent time studying the English graphic arts), Russia (where his socially conscious work was warmly received), and Germany (where his anti-Nazi sentiments became so fierce that he would ultimately come to be regarded as a "Red" in his own country).

Leaving *Esquire* in 1936, Groth moved to New York City where he freelanced as a sports cartoonist and editorial illustrator for such left-leaning journals as the *New Republic* and the *Nation* while studying oil painting with George Grosz, among others, at the Art Students League on West 57th Street. In 1939 he mounted his first exhibit of oils, "Impressions of War and Peace," and was hired by Heywood Broun as art director of his *Connecticut Nutmeg*. This latter venture was a *success d'estime* but a financial flop, and it folded with Broun's death in late 1939, shortly before a fire destroyed Groth's studio in 1940. This loss and the clamor of creditors left him in bad financial straits. Editor Fred Sparks, in 1941, responded by offering him the job of art director at *Parade* magazine, but this time he was expected to fill that function in fact as well as name and thus was obliged to give up his painting. Then in 1944 he went to Europe as a war correspondent for the *Chicago Sun-Times* and *Parade*. He was present for some of the great closing battles of that conflict. He documented this in a 1945 book, *Studio: Europe*, and his subsequent coverage of the Korean and French Indo-Chinese wars in a companion volume, *Studio: Asia*, in 1952. Taken together, these two books not only reveal Groth as a vivid and witty anecdotalist, but demonstrate his peculiar gift for graphically communicating fact, attitude, and action from a distinctly personal point of view.

After the war, Groth was a frequent contributor to all the major magazines as well as a much sought-after illustrator of books. And long before the shallow, splashy successes enjoyed by such pop practitioners as LeRoy Neiman, Groth had built an unrivalled reputation in the relatively ignored field of sports art. The origin of this reputation lay in the

same qualities that made his battlefield sketches as memorable as any done by an American artist since Thomas Nast's Civil War etchings. On a basic technical level there was his sheer dexterity as a penman, his physical ability to capture with a seemingly continuous line the kinetic essence of a split second. But on the more subtle emotional level, he possessed an uncanny knack for investing his sketches with a sense of *imminence*—the way he could portray a squad of soldiers charging out of their foxhole, catching them in an attitude at once brazen and wary as they faced one of those moments of truth that define the experience of war; or a matador doing likewise on the floor of the Plaza de Toros in Pamplona. No hard lines announce, "Here, this is an event"; in Groth's renderings everything is in process.

It is this feeling for pure motion and its consequences—the same sort of feeling his friend Hemingway had for spare prose and its special power—that sets Groth apart as an artist. And while his hallmark is generally held to be the portrayal of violent action—on the fields of battle and sport—this same feeling is appealingly evident in his studies of quieter moments: a Greek soldier in Korea being shaved by a buddy while one of those ubiquitous Asian mutts, itself invested with an almost Dickensian life, looks curiously on; a kimono-clad Japanese maiden under an umbrella in the rain, her body a gently curving "S", eyes demurely lowered, platform-sandaled feet picking their way daintily over the damp pavement; two race track touts caught in confidential conversation, side by side at a bar. No finished illustration, of course, can ever wholly match the spontaneity of its original inspiration; but as the *Asia* volume art makes clear in its evocations of Hong Kong street scenes, frowsy harborside barrooms, even a Macao opium den, Groth has frequently succeeded in meeting the formal requirements of

"Pig-sticking in India," a pen-and-ink drawing (© 1970, John Groth. Reprinted by permission.)

composition and design while preserving much of the immediacy of his first impulsive readings.

Asked once whether he considered himself a fine artist or an illustrator, Groth suggested that such distinctions were not all that meaningful, noting that both Rembrandt and Daumier had been called illustrators by their contemporaries. He proposed rather the terms "abstractionist" and "classicist," and though he placed his own work somewhere in between, he confessed to a bias in favor of classicism. "I feel the abstractionists are content with only the skeleton of a painting, and this is done largely for their own benefit and pleasure," he was quoted in a 1958 *American Artist* profile; "I doubt that any abstractionist would in any seriousness claim he was trying to communicate with the viewer. If I fail to communicate . . . I feel the work is a distinct failure."

BIOGRAPHICAL/CRITICAL SOURCES: Current Biography, 1943, Wilson, 1944; *American Artist*, January, 1949, January, 1958; *Coronet*, February, 1960; Arnold Gingrich, introduction, *John Groth's World of Sport*, Winchester Press, 1970; *Something About the Author*, Vol. 21, Gale, 1980; *Contemporary Authors*, Vol. 101, Gale, 1981.

—Sketch by Richard Calhoun

H

HAAS, Robert   1898-

PERSONAL: Born April 16, 1898, in Vienna, Austria; emigrated to London, England, 1938; emigrated to the United States, 1939; son of Daniel (a merchant) and Erna (Pick) Haas; married Maude E. Dabbs (a piano teacher), August 4, 1946; children: Catherine A., Miriam McB. Haas Zeltsman. *Education:* Attended Kunstgewerbeschule (Academy of Fine Arts), 1920-23; took master class in calligraphy at Akademie fur Bildende Kunst (Applied Arts Academy), 1924; received engineering degree from Technische Hochschule (Technical University), 1925; all in Vienna. *Home:* 15 Blenis Pl., Valhalla, N.Y. 10595. *Office and studio:* Ram Press, 48 W. 25th St., New York, N.Y. 10010.

CAREER: Co-founder and owner, Officina Vindobonensis (private press), Vienna, Austria, 1925-38; photographer and teacher of calligraphy in London, England, 1938-39; photographer and teacher of calligraphy and photography at Goddard College, Vermont, and Hidden Villa Ranch, California, 1939-40; founder and owner, Ram Press (private press), New York City, 1941—; teacher of calligraphy, lettering, and typography and head of Typography Department, Cooper Union Art School, New York City, 1954-67. Type designer, 1926-35. Art director of architectural review, *Profil*, 1935-37. News photographer for Austrian newspapers in the 1930s and for *Hartford News*, 1940; staff photographer for *Salzburger Illustrierte*, 1936, and Salzburger Festspiele music festival, 1936-37; also portrait photographer. Teacher of hand-press printing at Yale University, 1970-71; teacher of calligraphy at State University of New York at Purchase, 1977-82, and Continuing Education Department of Westchester Public School System, 1980—. *Military service:* Austrian Army, 1916-18; became first lieutenant; received three decorations.

AWARDS, HONORS: Gold medal for photo-mural in the Austrian Pavilion and Grand Prix for photography, both from Paris World's Fair, 1937; Award of Excellence from American Institute of Graphic Arts, 1945; given honorary title of Berufs-Professor by the President of Austria, 1972.

WRITINGS: Das Drucken auf der Handpresse (textbook of hand-press printing), Technical University of Darmstadt, 1927. Contributor of articles to typography and graphic arts journals in Europe and the United States.

EXHIBITIONS: One-man shows include "Robert Haas: Schrift, Druck, Photographie" (a sixty-year retrospective of calligraphy, typography, painting, and photography) at the Austrian Museum of Applied Art, Vienna, Austria, 1983, and "Painting, Calligraphy, Typography," at Fairleigh

ROBERT HAAS

Dickinson University, Madison, N.J., 1984. Work also exhibited in many group shows in Europe, Asia, and the United States, including annual exhibitions in Vienna, Austria, 1928-37; "Books and Art," Antwerp, Belgium, 1927; Goethe Centenary, Leipzig, Germany, 1932; World's Fair, Paris, France, 1937; and shows in Amsterdam, Netherlands, 1928; Cologne, Germany, 1929; London, England, 1933 and 1934; Tokyo, Japan, 1935; San Francisco, Calif., and Brooklyn, N.Y., both 1985.

WORK IN PROGRESS: A book on calligrapher Rudolph von Larisch; a translation of von Larisch's textbook *Ornamental Writing*.

SIDELIGHTS: Will Ransom, in his *Private Presses and Their Books*, describes the work of private-press printers as "the typographic expression of a personal ideal conceived in freedom and maintained in independence," and Robert Haas, in creating Austria's first firm dedicated to the revival of fine book production on July 11, 1925, met this exacting definition. Haas presided over the Officina Vindobonensis (a name derived from the Latin name of Vienna, *Vindobona*) for thirteen years, until the freedom and independence of his country disappeared in the Nazi takeover of 1938. During his tenure the Viennese studio produced limited editions of twenty hand-press books, published fifteen other volumes, and created layouts of catalogues, posters, and exhibition notes of the Viennese Artists Association. As the only hand press in Austria devoted to the art of the fine press book, the Officina became a gathering place for authors and artists, who came to observe and participate in the work.

In addition to the design and production of beautiful volumes, Haas was commissioned to print deeds and documents for the Austrian Ministry of Public Instruction as well as work for the Vienna Burgtheater, the University of Vienna, the Vienna Philharmonic Society, and many museums. He also printed the death roll of the war victims at the Austrian War Memorial from 1935 to 1937. Bookplates designed and produced by Haas during this time include those for the president of the Vienna Philharmonic, the Viennese Art Gallery, the Salzburg Archdiocese Library, conductor Arturo Toscanini, and many artists and authors. His work was in demand in England and throughout the continent.

Also a photographer of note, Haas served as news photographer for such Austrian papers as *Interessantes Blatt, Wiener Bilder, Die Buhne,* and *Die Pause,* and did portraits of many theatrical personalities, including opera stars Fyodor Chaliapin and Ezio Pinza, playwright Carl Zuckmayer, and performers Sacha Guitry, Werner Krauss, Marlene Dietrich, and Carmen Miranda. He was the official photographer for the Salzburg music festival from 1936 to 1937 and the staff photographer of the *Salzburger Illustrierte* in 1936. His photographs appeared worldwide in such periodicals as *Vogue* and *Harper's* in the United States, *Figaro* and *Vue* in France, *Sphere* and the *London Illustrated News* in Great Britain, and the *Zuricher Illustrierte* in Switzerland. In 1937

Cover of *In Memoriam Gustav Klimt* (© 1926, Robert Haas. Reprinted by permission.)

Egon Schiele **poster** (© 1918, Robert Haas. Reprinted by permission.)

his photographs won both the Grand Prix and the gold medal at the Paris World's Fair, the only work by an Austrian ever to do so.

Printing and photography did not exhaust Haas's energies and talents during his years in Austria; from 1935 to 1937 he served as art director of the architectural review *Profil*, and between 1926 and 1935 he designed no fewer than five different type faces. His Helen Fraktur, a black-letter type face of extraordinary grace and flexibility, was designed for the Monotype Corporation in 1930, and a Futura Black was done for the Bauer Type Foundry in the same year. His other faces—Uncial Grotesk in 1926, Greek Sanserif in 1935, and Officina Uncial, an elegant script-like type with Celtic overtones done in 1932—were created for his own press. In all of his type faces, Haas's design combines sinewy strength and legibility in forms of great beauty and harmony.

Haas's work in typography came to an abrupt halt in 1938. The Nazi party recognized the danger of private presses and the independent thought they represented, and the Officina was forced to close when the Germans occupied Austria. Haas moved to London for a year, teaching photography and producing a photo-mural for the John C. Lewis department store in Oxford. In April, 1939, he succeeded in

obtaining an immigration visa to the United States, where he has been working and teaching ever since.

In 1940 Haas became a news photographer for the *Hartford* (Conn.) *News*, and soon established such a reputation in the field in his new country that he was called upon to teach it. In the decades to follow he taught photography in Vermont, California, Pennsylvania, and New York and worked and exhibited as a free-lance photographer; but the art of typography always held a central place in his life. He taught printing, typography, type design, and calligraphy in many universities in the United States, from 1954 to 1967 at the Cooper Union School of Art, where he became the head of the typography department. In 1941 he founded the Ram Press, its name and logo deriving from his zodiac sign, and was soon called upon for work by the United States Government, the Guggenheim Museum, and the Museum of Modern Art in New York. In 1949 he supervised the printing of the completion of the catalogue for the Frick Collection. Nearly a half-century after its opening, Haas continues actively to direct the Ram Press.

Considering himself semi-retired by the mid-1980s, Haas found the time for a project long dear to him, the translation of a trailblazing text on calligraphy written in 1905 by his master-class teacher Rudolph von Larisch. As the oldest surviving student of von Larisch, who died in 1937, Haas has taken on the responsibility of establishing the text and choosing the illustrations for the pioneer calligrapher's text on ornamental writing, which went through eleven much-revised editions during its author's lifetime. At an age when most artists would be content to rest on their laurels, Haas displays unflagging energies in his work, maintaining a full schedule with his scholarship and his business. The letter press with which he did his early hand work in the United States was sold to Calhoun College of Yale, but the master regrets that it is now gathering dust on display instead of being used, as a press should.

Haas's many contributions to the art of the book were recognized in a 1986 exhibition of his work sponsored by the Austrian Ministry of Education and Art at the Klingspor Museum in Offenbach am Main. Moreover, the Mayor of Vienna presented silver medals of honor to him and to other artists and scholars on the occasion of the opening of an exhibition of turn-of-the-century Viennese arts and crafts at New York City's Museum of Modern Art. Nevertheless, Robert Haas does not consider his work to be finished. As

A bookplate design (© Robert Haas. Reprinted by permission.)

busy as ever, he continues with his mission, "the typographic expression of a personal ideal."

BIOGRAPHICAL/CRITICAL SOURCES: Hanna Egger, *Robert Haas: Druck, Photographie* (title means "Robert Haas: Lettering, Printing, Photography"), Osterreichisches Museum fur Angewandte Kunst, 1983; Renee Weber, *Robert Haas: Printing, Calligraphy, Photography*, Friends of the Library, Fairleigh Dickinson University, 1984.

—*Sketch by Dennis Wepman*

* * *

HESS, Dick
      See HESS, Richard

* * *

HESS, Richard 1934-
      (Dick Hess)

PERSONAL: Born May 27, 1934, in Royal Oak, Mich.; son of Cletus P. (a milkman) and Evelyn (in management; maiden name, Stanley) Hess; married Diana Woodard, February, 1954 (divorced, 1960); married Carol Woodward, June, 1961 (divorced, 1976); children: (first marriage) Mark; (second marriage) Adam, Sarah. *Education:* Attended Michigan State University, 1953-54. *Home and studio:* Southover Farm, Roxbury, Conn. 06783. *Agent:* Milton Newborn, 135 E. 54th St., New York, N.Y. 10022.

CAREER: Art director, J. Walter Thompson (advertising agency), Detroit, Mich., 1955-57; art director, Grant Advertising, Detroit, 1957-58; art group head, N. W. Ayer & Son (advertising agency), Philadelphia, Pa., 1958-61; art group head, Benton & Bowles (advertising agency), New York City, 1962-63; creative director, Van Brunt Advertising, New York City, 1963-65; president, Richard Hess Inc., New York City, 1965-76; partner, Hess & Hess, 1976—. Consultant for Champion International. Instructor at Syracuse University, 1975—, and Cooper Union, New York City.

MEMBER: Alliance Graphique Internationale, American Institute of Graphic Arts (board member, 1970-74), Society of Publication Designers (board member, vice-president, 1970-73).

AWARDS, HONORS: Many medals and awards from Art Directors Clubs around the United States and from American Institute of Graphic Arts, Society of Publication Designers, and Society of Illustrators.

WRITINGS: (Editor) Yvonne and Philippe Halsman, *Halsman Portraits*, McGraw-Hill, 1982; (retold and illustrated) *The Snow Queen* (a Hans Christian Andersen fairy tale), Macmillan, 1985; (with Miriam Muller; also illustrator) *Lou Dorfsman and CBS*, American Showcase, 1986; (with Jo Durden-Smith) *The Illustrator's Workshop: Six Influential Artists*, Graphis Press (Zurich), 1986; (with Durden-Smith) *The Visual Experience*, Graphis Press, 1986; (with Durden-Smith) *The Elders: 1000 Years in the Life of the Republic*, Champion International, 1986.

Contributor to *National Lampoon, Time, New York, Vista, Esquire*, the *New York Times*, and many other periodicals. Contributing editor of *California Magazine*.

"Future Building," an advertising illustration, ca. 1980 (© Richard Hess. Reprinted by permission.)

FILMS: (Producer) *The Elders*, Richard Hess, 1986. Designed many television commercials and film titles.

EXHIBITIONS: Venice Film Festival, Italy, 1961; Louvre Museum, Paris, France, 1970; Venice Biennale, 1976. One-man shows in New York City, Paris, Tokyo, Philadelphia, Detroit, Minneapolis, and Spokane, Wash. Numerous group shows, including Push Pin Studio exhibitions in France, Italy, Brazil, and Japan. Represented in permanent collection of Museum of Modern Art, New York City; National Portrait Gallery, Washington, D.C.; Yale University Library, New Haven, Conn.; Amon Carter Museum, Fort Worth, Tex.; and in a collection in Beijing, People's Republic of China.

WORK IN PROGRESS: Contemporary Writers of the English Language (book of portraits and selection of works); *The Wild Swans* (an illustrated children's book); *The Adventures of Cock Robin* (an illustrated children's book); a multi-game sports project; a U.S. history project.

SIDELIGHTS: Although Richard Hess dropped out of Michigan State University in 1954 after only two years' attendance, the fact that his intended majors were art and psychology seems in retrospect rather instructive. The choice of these two different, yet potentially complementary disciplines signified the coexistence of abilities and aspirations which, in fact, has persisted to this day. Hess left school to pursue a painting career only to end up plotting canvases for the Palmer Company, the Detroit firm that introduced the paint-by-numbers hobby kits of the 1950s. Fortunately he was able to do a few unnumbered canvases

Portrait of Billie Holiday, ca. 1976 (© Richard Hess. Reprinted by permission.)

on the side and won first and third prizes in the 1955 Detroit Art Directors Club Show. This achievement was then parlayed into a job with the J. Walter Thompson advertising agency's local shop. Three years later he moved to Philadelphia and a job with N. W. Ayer, and in 1962 he finally reached Madison Avenue in New York City as a creative director for Benton & Bowles. Then, in 1965, after only ten years in the business, the thirty-one-year-old Hess founded his own design firm.

In a 1966 article in *Print*, Hess modestly suggested that his rapid emergence as a top designer had rather more to do with his ability as a problem solver and his business sense than with his talents as an artist. "Graphic design is only rarely an art form," he told critic John Lahr, "I'm seldom aware when it is. Sometimes I discover later that I've done something that's not only a solution to a problem and handsome, but something that, hopefully, may last. More often you get absorbed and intrigued in problem solving, but there's really no intrinsic value in solving the problem beyond the money you're paid and the communication of an industrial idea." If anything, he insisted, his approach to design deliberately subordinated visual imagery to verbally expressed ideas. "I don't see a design in my mind," he said, "I think of an idea." For him design was, above all, communication, a process that could be disrupted by giving aesthetic considerations too much weight. "Sometimes you come up with a gimmick which you know is going to stop the person, or shock him—the visual pun, symbolism. But if people don't understand it, it's worthless, because the design doesn't communicate." It wasn't that he had been turned into a philistine by the imperatives of the marketplace—he confessed that he would like one day to resume painting and even try his hand at sculpting—it was simply that he was aware of, and able to separate the competing strains in his makeup in the interests of commercial realities.

In 1971, after more than fifteen years as an idea man marshalling and meshing the talents of practicing artists, Hess decided to pick up once more his own long-neglected paint brush. Since one of his firm's clients was the United Nations Association magazine *Vista*, he hired himself to do some illustrations for it. The experience was apparently an enjoyable one, for increasingly thereafter he devoted himself to the comparatively ill-paying field of illustration. In contrast to the analytical, process-oriented point of view adopted by Hess the designer, Hess the painter seemed to value impulse above premeditation. Oddly, considering his sophistication as a problem solver, his favored mode of artistic expression was the so-called "primitive" or "naive" style associated most often with the French artist Henri Rousseau. "The primitive works when my facility is surrendered to the subject matter and I lose myself in it," he remarked apropos of this apparent anomaly in a 1974 profile in *Print*; "Rousseau's *Sleeping Gypsy* is what I want to do the rest of my life. Not copying reality."

Even so, as celebrated American artist/illustrator Edward Sorel noted, Hess's naivete is hardly the product of untutored innocence. First of all, as Sorel pointed out in an appreciation written for *Graphis*, Hess is the master of a technique which produces so clear a surface as to cause "both bumpkin and sophisticate to press their noses against the canvas in order to see if it was really done with brushes." Additionally, there is a deceptive complexity to his paintings, "always something. . . for a second look, some detail one missed the first time around." Finally, Sorel pronounced him "a superb caricaturist. . . [with] an unerring intuition for which facial feature to stress." Such praise, coming from an artist of Sorel's stature, is persuasive indeed. Nor, as a survey of Hess's output over the past decade or so proves, is it unmerited. In addition to the underlying sophistication of his "naive" style, he employs elements of surrealism, satire, and parody, often in combination, to communicate with the same effectiveness as in his designer days. Except that now, the "products" he is promoting are his personal sentiments and beliefs.

Like Sorel and other first-rate satirists, Hess excels at graphic political commentary. Three examples of this have been included in the readily available collection *The Image of America in Caricature and Cartoon*, all of them bona fide modern classics in the genre. "The Great GOP Middle of the Road Show" reduces Richard Nixon's 1968 presidential campaign to the image of a one-ring circus under the strict control of the stern-faced ringmaster, later Attorney General, John Mitchell; "The Peaceable Kingdom" parodies the well-known Edward Hicks painting to characterize the naivete and at times muzzily expressed idealism of George McGovern's 1972 presidential campaign; and "Rosemary's

"Singleness of Purpose," an illustration, ca. 1983 (© Richard Hess. Reprinted by permission.)

Baby" is a wickedly funny reference to President Richard Nixon's Watergate difficulties and his secretary Rosemary Woods's effort to shield her boss from the consequences of a certain famous eighteen-minute silence.

Working in the surrealist vocabulary, Hess exhibits a Daliesque flair for the bizarre. Two striking efforts that lend themselves to thumbnail appreciations are his illustration for an article on chronic insomnia which portrays the sufferer as a figure lying in bed, ordinary in all respects save the head, represented as one large, unlidded eyeball; and a promotional piece for IBM utilizing a visual illusion which recalls the work of M. C. Escher, with two conventionally dressed businessmen figures positioned at right angles to each other on a staircase, one ascending, the other descending, the direction depending upon which figure is regarded as representing the vertical axis. Most of Hess's excursions in this vein, however, are simply too complex and rich in meaning to be easily described. Hess shows similar adeptness in using symbol and parody to make his visual statements. Some of these, like the reproduction of Grant Wood's *American Gothic* couple equipped with gas masks, or the hilarious send up of Delacroix's *Liberty Leading the People* in which the human figures are replaced by laboratory rats, are as direct and accessible as any of his corporate designs. Others show allegorical complexities worthy of a medieval morality play: for example, two men shown trying to sneak aboard the Ark disguised by the skins of the pair of unicorns they have slain in hopes of saving themselves.

Superficially, there is a temptation to divide Hess's career thus far into two distinct phases, that of the objective, idea-oriented designer and that of the subjective, impulse-driven artist. Yet a survey of his work suggests that neither phase has been quite so pure, and that, in 1986 as in 1966, the intelligence and the ability to communicate characteristic of his design work remains a powerful element in his art.

BIOGRAPHICAL/CRITICAL SOURCES: Print, May-June, 1966, May-June, 1974; *Graphis*, Number 178 (1975-76), Number 191 (1977-78); *The Image of America in Caricature and Cartoon*, Amon Carter Museum, 1976; *Who's Who in Graphic Art*, Vol. 2, De Clivo Press, 1982; *Who's Who in America, 1984-85*, Marquis, 1984.

—*Sketch by Richard Calhoun*

* * *

HILL, L(eroy) Draper 1935-

PERSONAL: Born July 1, 1935, in Boston, Mass.; son of Leroy Draper (an investment banker) and Jean (Thompson) Hill; married Sarah Adams, April 22, 1967; children: Jennifer, Jonathan. *Education:* Harvard University, B.A. (magna cum laude), 1957; graduate study at Slade School of Fine Arts, University College, London, 1960-63. *Office: Detroit News*, 615 W. Lafayette Blvd., Detroit, Mich. 48231.

CAREER: Reporter and cartoonist, *Quincy Patriot Ledger*, Quincy, Mass., 1957-60, 1963-64; editorial cartoonist, *Worcester Telegram* and *Evening Gazette*, Worcester, Mass., 1964-71; editorial cartoonist, *Commercial Appeal*, Memphis, Tenn., 1971-76; editorial cartoonist, *Detroit News*, 1976—. Instructor in basic drawing and figure drawing at School of the Worcester Art Museum, 1967-71.

MEMBER: Association of American Editorial Cartoonists (first vice-president, 1974-75; president, 1975-76).

AWARDS, HONORS: Fulbright fellowship, 1960-63; Guggenheim fellowship, 1983-84.

L. DRAPER HILL

An editorial cartoon by **L. Draper Hill** (© 1978, *Detroit News*. Reprinted by permission.)

WRITINGS: The Crane Library, Trustees of Thomas Crane Public Library (Quincy, Mass.), 1962; *Cartoon and Caricature from Hogarth to Hoffnung*, Arts Council of Great Britain, 1962; *Mr. Gillray: The Caricaturist*, Phaidon, 1965; (editor) *Fashionable Contrasts: 100 Caricatures by James Gillray*, Phaidon, 1966; *Illingworth on Target*, Boston Public Library, 1970; (with James Roper) *The Decline and Fall of the Gibbon*, Inadvertent Press, 1974; (author of introduction) *I Feel I Should Warn You*, Preservation Press, 1975; *The Satirical Etchings of James Gillray*, Dover, 1976; (contributor) *Encyclopedia of Collectibles*, Time-Life Books, 1978; *Political Asylum: Editorial Cartoons by Draper Hill*, Art Gallery of Windsor, 1985.

EXHIBITIONS—One-man shows: Casdin Gallery, Worcester, Mass., 1966; Wolf River Society, Memphis, Tenn., 1972, 1973, 1975; Memphis Public Library, 1972-75; Brooks Memorial Art Gallery, Memphis, 1975; Brad Macmillan Gallery, Memphis, 1982; Hayes Presidential Center, Fremont, Ohio, 1982-83; Somerset Mall, Troy, Mich., 1983; Art Gallery of Windsor, Windsor, Ont., 1985. Collective: Amon Carter Museum, Fort Worth, Tex., 1975.

WORK IN PROGRESS: A biography of cartoonist Thomas Nast, supported by a Guggenheim fellowship.

SIDELIGHTS: Draper Hill's enthusiasm for cartooning developed at an early age and expressed itself in his graduation paper which he devoted to nineteenth-century cartooning great Joseph Keppler. A visit in London with the legendary political cartoonist David Low definitively decided him on his subsequent career. Going from small local newspapers to a large metropolitan daily, Hill has earned

An editorial cartoon by L. Draper Hill (© 1985, *Detroit News*. Reprinted by permission.)

high praise from the public and his colleagues alike for the fairness of his views and the subtle point of his editorial cartoons.

In 1975 Hill was cited with Pat Oliphant and Paul Szep as being "among the outstanding penmen publishing in daily newspapers" by Ron Tyler, curator of the show "The Image of America in Caricature and Cartoon"; *The World Encyclopedia of Cartoons* said of Hill, "His caricatures are simple, as are the backgrounds and nonessentials in his handsome, liberal-oriented cartoons." As one of the country's major cartoonists Hill has seen his work often reprinted in major newspapers and national newsmagazines.

Hill is also a scholar in the field of cartooning, with a number of books on the subject to his credit, as well as numerous articles and reviews in such publications as the *New York Times*, the *Detroit News*, *The Dial* and *Target*. He is author of a column, *History Corner*, in the *AAEC Notebook*, the quarterly of the Association of American Editorial Cartoonists, and a contributing editor of *Eighteenth Century Life*. In addition to teaching college courses in drawing, Hill has conducted seminars and given lectures on various topics of artistic and historical interest at colleges and institutions throughout the country. "In the guerilla warfare of the political cartoon," Hill's colleague Duncan Macpherson wrote, "Draper Hill aims at the brain."

BIOGRAPHICAL/CRITICAL SOURCES: Stephen Hess and Milton Kaplan, *The Ungentlemanly Art*, Macmillan, 1968; *The Image of America in Caricature and Cartoon*, Amon Carter Museum, 1975; *Contemporary Authors*, New Revision series, Vol. 12, Gale, 1984; *Getting Angry Six Times a Week*, Beacon, 1979; *The World Encyclopedia of Cartoons*, Chelsea House, 1980; Duncan Macpherson, foreword, and John Silverstein, introduction, *Political Asylum: Editorial Cartoons by Draper Hill*, Art Gallery of Windsor, 1985.

HOGARTH, William   1697-1764

PERSONAL: Born November 10, 1697, in London, England; died October 26, 1764, in London; son of Richard (a classical scholar, schoolmaster, and journalist) and Ann (Gibbon) Hogarth; married Jane Thornhill, March 29, 1729. *Education:* Studied under his father in London; apprenticed to Ellis Gamble, a goldsmith and silver-plate engraver, 1712-20; attended St. Martin's Lane Academy, 1723, and Sir James Thornhill's free drawing academy, 1724. *Religion:* Anglican.

CAREER: Engraver, illustrator, and painter. Began as independent engraver, mostly of heraldic plates and book illustrations, 1720; painter, 1728-64. Among his best-known illustrations are those for Milton's *Paradise Lost*, 1724, Samuel Butler's *Hudibras*, 1726, and Cervantes's *Don Quixote*, 1733. Famous series of paintings and engravings include *A Harlot's Progress*, 1732; *A Rake's Progress*, 1735, original paintings now in the Soane Gallery, London; *Marriage a la Mode*, 1745, original paintings now in the National Gallery, London.

AWARDS, HONORS: Elected governor of St. Bartholemew's Hospital, 1735; appointed Serjeant Painter by King George II, 1757.

WRITINGS: "Britophil," *St. James's Evening Post*, June 7-9, 1737; *Analysis of Beauty*, privately printed, 1753, reprinted as *Artistic and Psychological Analysis of Beauty*, Gloucester Art, 1981.

Illustrator; all privately printed: William King, *Pantheon*, 1710; Aubrey de la Mottroye, *Travels*, 1723; John Milton, *Paradise Lost*, 1724; Lucius Apuleius, *The Golden Ass*, 1724; S. Beaver, *Roman Military Punishment*, 1725; Gautier de Costes de la Calprenede, *Cassandra*, 1725; Samuel Butler,

WILLIAM HOGARTH

Hudibras, 1726; N. Amhurst, *Terrae Filius*, 1726; A. Leveridge, *Songs*, 1727; Ebenezer Forrest, *Five Days Peregrination*, 1732; Moliere, *L'Avare*, 1733; Moliere, *Le Cocu Imaginaire*, 1733; Miguel de Cervantes, *Don Quixote*, 1738; Laurence Sterne, *Tristram Shandy*, 1759.

Collections of prints: *Complete Works of William Hogarth*, London Printing & Publishing Co., 1800; John Nichols, editor, *The Works of William Hogarth*, Baldwin, Cradock & Joy, 1822; *Works of William Hogarth*, privately printed, 1825, reprinted, Marathon, 1978; Arthur M. Hind, editor, *William Hogarth: His Original Engravings and Etchings*, Frederick A. Stokes, 1912, 1972; Sean Shesgreen, editor, *Engravings of William Hogarth*, Dover, 1943; A. Poppe, editor, *Drawings of William Hogarth*, Phaidon, 1948; Joseph Burke and Colin Caldwell, editors, *William Hogarth: The Complete Engravings*, Abrams, 1968; Ronald Paulson, editor, *The Art of Hogarth*, Phaidon, 1975.

Series of engravings: *A Harlot's Progress* (six engravings), 1732; *A Rake's Progress* (eight paintings, engraved by

Hogarth), 1735; *Four Times of Day* (four engravings), 1738; *Marriage a la Mode* (six paintings, engraved by Hogarth), 1745; *Industry and Idleness* (twelve engravings), 1747; *Four Stages of Cruelty* (four engravings), 1751; *Four Prints of an Election* (four engravings), 1758.

SIDELIGHTS: When essayist William Hazlitt included William Hogarth among the subjects of his study of English comic writers fifty years after the artist's death, he reflected the unique reputation Hogarth has had since his own time as a narrative artist. Although a significant portraitist, historical painter, and genre artist, it is Hogarth the "author" of satirical stories in art—series of narrative engravings—that has become fixed in critical history as a major figure not only in the art but in the literature of England.

In such picture series as *A Rake's Progress* or *Marriage a la Mode*, Hogarth foreshadowed the development of the twentieth-century comic strip. From a modern point of view his special merit lies in his clever blending of text and picture

An engraving from *A Rake's Progress* by William Hogarth, 1735

to make a telling point in a single statement. His creations were so clearly different from the conventional illustrations of his time that a new name—cartoon—was coined for them. And, indeed, it is as the father of the modern editorial cartoon that Hogarth is most revered. As stated in "The Graphic Arts: An Overview" in Volume 1 of *CGA:* "William Hogarth . . . is the first artist to whom the term *cartoonist* can be legitimately applied, and he is widely regarded as the founding father of the art. He gave cartooning a function as well as a form: the subject of the cartoonist's pen would henceforth be the state of the world and more specifically, society."

The son of a poor schoolmaster who was often reduced to hack writing to support his family, Hogarth showed little enthusiasm for scholarship and was glad to be apprenticed at the age of fifteen to an engraver, under whom he devoted himself for eight years to cutting armorial devices in silver and gold plate. By 1720, however, his lively imagination had become so impatient with the limitations of repeating the unvaried "monsters of heraldry" that he determined to set himself up in his own business as a copper-plate engraver, illustrating books and doing shop bills, business cards, and theater prints. Engraving scrollwork and stylized griffins had not prepared him for such a career, as he recalled later, and he briefly took life-classes in 1723 to learn "to draw objects something like nature." His impatience with the formal discipline of copying soon brought his studies to an end, however, and except for a brief period the next year at the free school of celebrated historical painter Sir James Thornhill, he learned his art by direct attention to the real life around him.

Beer Street, **an engraving by William Hogarth, 1751**

Hogarth made a meager living as an engraver during the early 1720s, but developed a growing reputation for his lively book illustrations and was soon much in demand. Like his father, whose scholarly writings were ill-rewarded, he was much exploited by the booksellers who used his services and, always morbidly sensitive to injustice, came to yearn for freedom from their control. In 1723 he produced his first major privately-printed work, "Masquerades and Operas," a small print vigorously attacking the popular tastes of the times.

His intimacy with the household of Sir James Thornhill, the first English artist to receive a knighthood for his art, was strained when he eloped with Thornhill's daughter Jane in 1729, but his growing success as a satirical artist soon reconciled his father-in-law. Hogarth's prints attracted a lively market, and the artist purchased a large house in Leicester Fields (now Leicester Square) in London, where he made his home for the rest of his life.

In 1728 Hogarth turned his interests to painting, ever ambitious for the respect accorded to artists who worked in "the grand style," and for the remaining thirty-six years of his life pursued the reputation his father-in-law had won. In this he had little success. Although his work in oil—notably his proto-impressionist piece *The Shrimp Girl*—have won much posthumous admiration for their vitality and animation, in his own time Hogarth was often ridiculed for his work in the medium, and the accounts of his efforts at selling his oil paintings make sorry reading. In 1748 he auctioned off the six original paintings of his immensely popular print-series *Marriage a la Mode* (in elegant frames which cost four guineas each) for a total of 126 pounds—to the only bidder.

If Hogarth never achieved the honor of a knighthood, his long-time dream, his great public popularity earned him some political notice, and in 1757 he was appointed Serjeant Painter to the King—the only national honor he was ever to receive. The position was not an exalted one—its salary was only ten pounds a year (while that of the Rat-Catcher to the King was over forty-eight pounds), and it ranked him with the Master Bricklayer and the Serjeant Plumber—but it carried some prestige and probably brought in some commissions, as well as allowing him to dispose of lucrative contracts for the painting and gilding of the royal palaces and carriages.

Hogarth's ambitious historical oils were never financially successful, but his portraits were appreciated and his love of the stage inspired numerous theatrical paintings which won him great popularity among actors and playwrights. His *Beggar's Opera*, from John Gay's 1728 criminal farce of that name, and his 1746 *Garrick as Richard III*, for which he was paid the largest price to date in England for a painting, were among Hogarth's most popular work in any medium. It was in 1732, however, that he hit upon the form which was to make his name in his own time and define it for posterity. In that year he produced the first of his "modern moral subjects."

Taking his title from John Bunyan's famous allegory *The Pilgrim's Progress,* he issued a series of six engravings under the title *A Harlot's Progress.* Continuing to exploit his taste for both the theater and rough, earthy subjects, he made his first "modern moral subject" as deliberately a dramatic piece as any playwright's. He determined, he reported later,

Finis, or the World's End, **an engraving by William Hogarth, 1764**

"to compose pictures on canvas similar to representations on stage. . . . I have endeavored to treat my subjects as a dramatic writer. My picture was my stage and men and women my actors." His objects, in this as in his later series, were twofold: to entertain with his dramatic narratives and to instruct with the moral message they conveyed. *A Harlot's Progress* is a cautionary tale—developed inexorably from plate to plate—of a country girl's corruption in the wicked city and the terrible price she pays. The tale was captivating to a wide public and earned its artist over twelve hundred pounds in subscriptions, freeing him from dependence on dealers for the rest of his life.

Although Hogarth profited hugely from his sales, he was infuriated by the free use of his work made by others. Booksellers openly made cheap copies of his prints and returned the original prints to him unsold. Determined to protect himself and his fellow-artists from this piracy, he made an eloquent appeal to Parliament for an act securing the rights of artists to their own work, and withheld his second series—the eight engravings he called *A Rake's Progress*—until he saw the act pass in June of 1735. "Hogarth's Act," as it has come to be called, is the forerunner of the modern British copyright law.

Other "pictur'd morals" followed *A Harlot's Progress* for many years—colorful, robust engravings of high and low life, teeming with character and movement. *A Rake's Progress* shows us how dissolution brings Tom Rakewell to ruin and madness. The high drama of *Marriage a la Mode* narrates in six scenes the deterioration of a "fashionable" marriage through the vices and weaknesses of its high-born partners. *Industry and Idleness* (1747), Hogarth's longest series, contrasts in twelve parts the diligent apprentice (who marries the boss's daughter and becomes Lord Mayor of London) and the lazy Tom Idle (who is duly hanged). The fate of Tom Nero, the protagonist of the 1751 *Four Stages of Cruelty*, is more awful yet: from torturing a dog in the first print he moves by swift stages to the table of a medical class, his cadaver being calmly dissected and a dog munching greedily on his heart. The eighteenth century had little use for subtlety, and Hogarth was pre-eminently a man of his age.

No more concerned with elegance of composition than with delicacy of theme, Hogarth filled every inch of his canvases and copper plates with life and action. His kaleidoscopic backgrounds are cluttered with emblematic detail. Kenneth Clark, in his *Civilization*, voiced a common complaint when he wrote, "His pictures are always such a muddle. He seems entirely without the sense of space which one finds even in mediocre Dutch painters." But it is not his pictorial, so much as his narrative and thematic, gifts that have immortalized William Hogarth. By presenting in sequential form exaggerated, simplistic statements without the distortions of a caricaturist, he created a fusion of the cartoon (in the modern sense) and what he himself considered "High Art." If he established a genre which was to lead, by one path, to Picasso's *Guernica*, it is no less true that, by another, as Maurice Horn has observed in *The World Encyclopedia of Comics*, "His drawings can be acknowledged as the first direct forerunners of the comic strip."

Hogarth's last years were spent in controversy and some bitterness. He was repeatedly disappointed by the failure of his paintings to sell at a good—or sometimes at any—price, and he became embroiled in legal and personal conflicts. His one effort at political cartooning, "The Times" (1762), an attack on William Pitt, excited so violent and abusive a public response that he withdrew into partial retirement. Ultimately he was always an isolated figure in art, neither a historical painter nor a cartoonist. As English painter John Constable concluded in the century after Hogarth's death, "Hogarth has no school." His posterity has proved to be that of the quill rather than that of the palette; his keen critical observations of his society and the dramatic form in which he presented them moved essayist Charles Lamb to call Hogarth "perhaps next to Shakespeare the most inventive genius which this island has produced."

BIOGRAPHICAL/CRITICAL SOURCES: John Nichols, *Biographical Anecdotes of William Hogarth*, privately printed, 1781; Georg Christoph Lichtenberg, *Ausfurliche Erklarung der Hogarthischen Kupferstiche*, 1794-1816, translation by Arthur S. Wensinger published as *Hogarth on High Life*, Wesleyan University Press, 1970; William Hazlitt, "William Hogarth," in *Lectures on the English Comic Writers*, M. Carey, 1819, reprinted, Russell, 1969; Charles Lamb, "On the Genius and Character of William Hogarth," *The Reflector*, 1811, reprinted in *Complete Works and Letters*, Modern Library, 1935; Austin Dobson, *Hogarth*, S. Low, Marston, Searle & Rivington, 1879, reprinted, Heinemann, 1902; Edward Garnett, *Hogarth*, Duckworth, 1910; William Gaunt, *The World of William Hogarth*, Pitman, 1950; Peter Quennell, *Hogarth's Progress*, Viking, 1955; Frederick Antal, *Hogarth: His Place in European Art*, Basic Books, 1962; Ronald Paulson, *Hogarth: His Life, Art, and Times*, Yale University Press, 1971; Derek Jarrett, *The Ingenious Mr. Hogarth*, M. Joseph, 1976; *The World Encyclopedia of Comics*, Chelsea House, 1976; Jack Lindsay, *Hogarth: His Art and His World*, Taplinger, 1979; David Bindman, *Hogarth*, Thames & Hudson, 1985

—*Sketch by Dennis Wepman*

* * *

HULL, Cathy 1946-

PERSONAL: Born November 4, 1946, in New York, N.Y.; daughter of Max H. (a stockbroker) and Magda (Stern) Hull. *Education:* Connecticut College, New London, Conn., B.A., 1968; School of Visual Arts, M.F.A., 1970. *Studio:* 236 East 36th St., New York, N.Y. 10016.

A humorous illustation (© 1984, Cathy Hull. Reprinted by permission.)

CAREER: Free-lance illustrator, 1970—, with clients including Mobil Oil, Pan American Airways, Columbia Broadcasting System, National Broadcasting Co., Random House, Harper & Row, and Doubleday. Instructor at School of Visual Arts, 1983—. Member of School of Visual Arts Alumni Advisory Council.

MEMBER: Society of Illustrators.

AWARDS, HONORS: Text Book Cover Award from Printing Industries of America, 1971; Special Prize, Fourth World Cartoon Gallery, Skopje, Yugoslavia, 1972; Silver Award from Society of Publication Designers, 1974; Certificate of Excellence from American Institute of Graphic Arts, 1974. Member of jury for Sixth World Cartoon Gallery, Skopje, Yugoslavia, 1974, Society of Publication Designers, 1982, and Society of Illustrators Student Exhibition, 1983.

WRITINGS—Illustrator: G. B. Davis, *An Introduction to Electronic Computers*, 2nd edition, McGraw, 1971; G. W. Kisker, *The Disorganized Personality*, 2nd edition, McGraw, 1972.

EXHIBITIONS: Seventeenth National Print Exhibition, Brooklyn Museum, 1970; World Cartoon Gallery, Skopje, Yugoslavia, 1972, 1973, 1974 (one-woman show), and 1975; Frankfurt Art Messe, Frankfurt, West Germany, 1973; "*New York Times* Show," Society of Illustrators, New York City, 1973; International Cartoon Exhibition, Istanbul, Turkey, 1974; International Cartoon Exhibition, Athens, Greece, 1975; "Statue of Liberty Show," Musée Beaubourg, Paris, France, 1977; "Women in Design," Pacific Design Center, Los Angeles, Calif., 1980; Collection of Caricature and Cartoons, Basle, Switzerland, 1980 and 1982; "Women in Design" International Show, Scottsdale Center for the Arts, Scottsdale, Ariz., 1981; "Contemporary Graphics, Design, and Illustration," Maryland Institute, Baltimore, Md., 1981; Contemporary American Graphic Design and Illustration Show, Butler Institute of American Art, Ohio, 1983; American Peace Posters Exhibition (to mark fortieth anniversary of Hiroshima bombing), toured United States, Canada, Japan, Europe, and Russia, 1985.

SIDELIGHTS: Her linear technique is impeccable and she uses vibrant, glowing colors, but Cathy Hull's purpose is not decorative embellishment. Nor, although her rendering of detail is often close to photographic, is she interested in the documentation of commonplace, humdrum reality. Her impressive skills are devoted exclusively to communication in a graphic style she calls "pseudo-surrealistic satire." Actually, there seems nothing particularly "pseudo" about her surrealism—a spare blend of common but incongruous forms and symbols executed on a level of craftsmanship very much in the manner of Belgian painter Rene Magritte—but the satirical element is a highly personal one. Her fondness for the visual pun may echo Saul Steinberg and her social concern mirror that of the "new illustration" school (Jean-Claude Suares, Brad Holland, et al.), but the ideas and attitudes which preoccupy her make her work unique.

A native of New York City, Hull graduated from Connecticut College and the School of Visual Arts. As a free-lance illustrator, she contributes regularly to *Time, New York Times*, and *Penthouse*, and her work has appeared in many other major magazines in the United States and Europe. She is also well-known for her book illustrations, and is an award-winning cartoonist. Although she has done advertising assignments for major commercial accounts like Mobil Oil and Pan American Airlines, Hull's most striking work has been done in the realm of editorial illustration. Her first noteworthy success, in fact, was a commission to illustrate a book entitled *An Introduction to Electronic Computers*, which won awards from the American Institute of Graphic Arts both for cover design and as one of the year's fifty best illustrated books. Analyzing this achievement as well as her

subsequent illustration of *The Disorganized Personality* in the Swiss magazine *Graphis*, critic Alastair Allen was particularly impressed by her conceptual approach to the specialized material with which she had to work. The psychology text posed a particular challenge because its author wished to avoid a negative presentation of mental illness and show instead that personality disorder was not so much a disease as a series of reactive patterns to a misperceived reality. Hull's solution was to use geometric patterns to convey, in abstract, nonliteral terms, the idea of personality as structure which, when coherent, is perceived as "organized" but when incoherent, or "disorganized," loses the symmetry that confers an acceptable, normal identity.

"An illustration, like an article, should be to the point," she told an interviewer in 1977. "Symbols and content should be reduced to a minimum so that nothing is arbitrary, gratuitous, or superfluous." This commitment to minimalism gives her visual vocabulary a surprising universality, particularly when dealing with phenomena of mental aberration and deviancy that so often figure in her work. One form of graphic communication Hull has exploited to good effect is the visual pun. It can be as cleverly simple as the visual metaphor she invented to illustrate an article entitled "When Virtue Becomes a Vice" (a lifelike pair of praying hands as the jaws of an otherwise ordinary vise-clamp) or as ideographically complex as her book illustration for a chapter

Self-portrait of Cathy Hull

headed "Anxiety and Depression" (a building of seven or eight stories tilted precariously up on one corner and only being prevented from toppling over by a feather quill leaning in opposition against it).

Another of Hull's approaches depends upon the deployment of widely recognized symbols to express, in visual short-hand, complicated ideas. Images such as the Mona Lisa, a heart, a window, a worm, and fire appear to be favorites of hers because of the stable meanings they convey and the predictable emotions they evoke (a set of handcuffs, one side open and forming a heart shape, the other side locked shut). Finally there are her socially conscious, issue-oriented op-ed pieces, mixing elements of the first two styles in order to state an issue and imply an opinion (a street person facing away from viewer stands flanked by a possession-laden grocery cart and a shopping bag with the outer facade of a colonial style suburban house; an archery target propped up against the end of a crib in a nursery presided over by a picture of a worried looking Humpty-Dumpty).

Above all, Cathy Hull regards herself as a conceptual artist, relying on her audience to participate in the communication process, to interact, not to be passive bystanders. "I like to show the absurdity in situations, so my style is as real as possible. You have to do a double take. The illustration leads you in, and then it hits. . . There is a willing suspension of disbelief and one accepts familiar objects in unfamiliar situations. Fantasy is recognized as a form of insight."

BIOGRAPHICAL/CRITICAL SOURCES: Graphis, Number 164 (1972-73); *Art Direction*, May, 1977; *Print*, May-June, 1977; *Who's Who in Graphic Art*, Vol. 2, De Clivo Press, 1982; Les Krantz, *American Artists*, Facts on File, 1985; *Upper and Lower Case*, May, 1986.

* * *

HUNTER, (James) Graham

PERSONAL: Born in LaGrange, Ill.; son of William Clarence (in business) and Rebecca A. (Faul) Hunter; married Cornelia Isabel Seward (a church organist and choir director). *Education:* Took correspondence courses from C. N. Landon School of Cartooning and Art Instruction Schools; attended Chicago Art Institute. *Politics:* Republican. *Religion:* Presbyterian. *Home and studio:* Lindenshade, 42 Clovanor Rd., West Orange, N.J. 07052.

CAREER: Mailroom and office worker, Quaker Oats Co., Chicago, Ill., for seven years; free-lance cartoonist, watercolorist, caricaturist, and advertising writer and artist. Drew *Jolly Jingles* (a kid comic strip) for the *Philadelphia Record* and later for the *Chicago Sunday Tribune*; worked with the Philadelphia Public Ledger Syndicate, Associated Editors Syndicate in Chicago, Readers' Syndicate and McClure Syndicate, both in New York City; drew *Sycamore Center* (a cartoon panel) for *Southern Agriculturist and Country People*; drew *Rhubarb Ridge* (a cartoon feature) for Curtis Publishing Co.; did many children's cartoon series for Marvel Comics and other magazines.

AWARDS, HONORS: Distinguished Service Citation from U.S. Treasury Department, 1943, for promoting national war savings program; George Washington Honor Medal from Freedoms Foundation, 1959 and 1962.

WRITINGS: Doin's at Sycamore Center (a cartoon book), 1946. Contributor to cartoon course textbook for Art Instruction Schools, 1960. Contributor of cartoons and illustrations to the *New York Journal-American*, *Chicago Tribune*, and other periodicals.

EXHIBITIONS: Cartoons exhibited at Wayne State University, Detroit, Mich., 1968. Work represented in permanent collections of Federal Bureau of Investigation, Freedoms Foundation at Valley Forge, Pa., and Peter Mayo Editorial Cartoon Collection, the State Historical Society, Columbia, Mo.

WORK IN PROGRESS: Cartoons, writing, advertising art.

SIDELIGHTS: Graham Hunter wrote *CGA:* "Drawing has been a part of my life since I was four years of age, though this talent required training. I suppose I inherited this avocation from my father who drew many crude 'funny pictures,' and always wished there were a school of cartooning which he might have attended.

"When I was fourteen the local newspaper editor printed one of my 'editorial' cartoons. It gave a big boost to my ambitions, until one of the printers took me aside and cautioned me not ever to try to become a professional cartoonist because, he averred, there are so few job openings in this field. But I somehow managed to ignore the warning."

Unlike his father, Hunter did attend a cartooning school (if only through the mails), that of the legendary Charles Nelson Landon who instructed many famous cartoonists, from *Reg'lar Fellers'* Gene Byrnes to Roy Crane, creator of Buzz Sawyer, in the fundamentals of their profession. After a seven-year interval of "business training" (as Hunter calls this period of his life) with a cereal company, and some more advanced instruction from the Chicago Art Institute, the budding artist decided to enter the field of free-lance cartooning on a full-time basis.

His first sale was to the *Philadelphia Record*, which took a children's comic strip called *Jolly Jingles*. The series told impish little fables, as the name suggests, in jingling verse. After the *Record* folded, the strip was transferred to the *Chicago Sunday Tribune* where it ran for seven years.

Hunter created a number of other features, including *Motor Laffs*, *Biceps Bros.*, and *Getting the Business* for the car magazine *Motor*, the cartoon feature *Rhubarb Ridge* for the Curtis Publishing Company, and several children's comic series for Marvel and other comic book companies.

Hunter specializes in what he calls "busy-scene" cartoons. This started with *Sycamore Center*, a feature about the doings in a small American town, in which the artist managed to cram an incredible number of characters and incidents in the space of a half-page. He later used the same technique in a variety of settings (family reunions, winter scenes, etc.), always blocking his composition within a tight frame viewed at a sharp, downward angle. (The technique, though not the style, strongly recalls Dudley Fisher's long-lasting Sunday feature *Right around Home*.)

BIOGRAPHICAL/CRITICAL SOURCES: Who's Who in America, Marquis, 1984; *Who's Who in American Art*, Bowker, 1984.

I-J

IMPIGLIA, Giancarlo 1940-

PERSONAL: Surname is pronounced "Impeelia"; born March 9, 1940, in Rome, Italy; son of Italo and Anna Impiglia; married Nina Frand (a real estate broker), 1975; children: Thomas G. F. *Education:* Attended Italian Center of Cinematography, Rome, Italy, 1957, Academy of Fine Arts, Rome, 1958-62. *Office and studio:* 182 Grand St., New York, N.Y. 10013.

CAREER: Graphic artist, illustrator, and muralist in Rome, Italy, 1963-74, and New York City, 1974—.

EXHIBITIONS—All one-man shows, unless otherwise indicated: Gallery Worth Avenue, Palm Beach, Fla., 1976; Bloomingdale's Art Gallery, New York City, 1980; Kiva Gallery, Scarsdale, N.Y., 1980; Renneth Gallery, West Hampton, N.Y., 1980 and 1981; Rizzoli Gallery, New York City, 1981 and 1982; Rizzoli Gallery, Chicago, Ill., 1981; Pace University, New York City, 1981; Rizzoli Gallery, Costa Mesa, Calif., 1982; Miller Gallery, San Francisco, Calif., 1982; (group show) Central Gallery, Osaka, Japan; Lincoln Center Gallery, New York City, 1982-83; Works II

Top of the City (© 1981, Giancarlo Impiglia. Reprinted by permission.)

Gallery, Southampton, N.Y., 1983, 1984, and 1985; Goldman-Kraft Gallery, Chicago, Ill., 1984; Alex Rosenberg Gallery, New York City, 1984; Carolyn Hill Gallery, New York City, 1985; First Impressions Gallery, Toronto, Canada, 1985.

WORK IN PROGRESS: Preparing for a number of one-man shows in New York City for 1986-87.

SIDELIGHTS: Giancarlo Impiglia wrote *CGA:* "I am essentially a European artist looking at New York, questioning existing artistic and societal values. My work is an example of society's preoccupation with appearance. Costume and posture are epitomized to the exclusion of content, communication, and emotion."

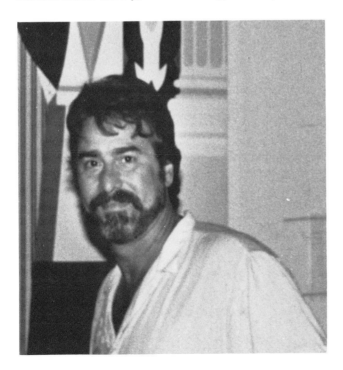

GIANCARLO IMPIGLIA

It is not surprising to learn that one of Giancarlo Impiglia's paintings has appeared on the dust jacket of a book entitled *Understanding Social Psychology*, because social behavior is the dominant motif of his art. He works in the usual media and manipulates form and shape in conventional ways. His paintings are colorful and geometric, and his graphic vocabulary's debt to various trends in twentieth-century art is evident. He might, indeed, be just another one of dozens of capable but derivative artists active on the downtown art scene in New York were it not for the cerebral (as opposed to emotional) quality of his creations—paintings that might be described as a logical post-Picasso development in the field of documentary art (i.e., the art of time, place, and manner).

Born in Rome in 1940, Impiglia received his formal training at the Academy of Fine Arts there. He came to the United States in 1974 to undertake a commission for a mural in the lobby of the American Insurance Company in the heart of lower Manhattan's financial district. The specifications of the commission were to evoke the peculiar aura of the neighborhood, which is the city's oldest, dating back to the seventeenth-century Dutch settlement. The European artist brought a fresh eye to this environment of narrow, twisting, undulating streets stretching from Broadway to the East River. And what seduced that eye was not so much the present reality as the past glory, still decipherable in many of the area's storefronts, architectural details, and accouter-

Night People II (© 1985, Giancarlo Impiglia. Reprinted by permission.)

ments (antique police call boxes, black iron-columned traffic signals, the liveliness of the old Fulton Fish Market before the restoration of the South Street Seaport). The result of his year's devotion to this project was, in Impiglia's own words, "an assemblage of beautiful things that New York is destroying which should be in a museum." To portray the streets he was celebrating in the light he felt they deserved, he retreated in his imagination to the 1920s and '30s, when one might have encountered a well-dressed young matron wheeling an ornate pram, a uniformed cop actually walking a beat, a street vendor selling lemonade for five cents a glass. The production is a colorful, bold, five-by-sixty-foot, five-panel acrylic that humanizes a city without necessarily humanizing its residents (who are presented as well-dressed, faceless mannequins).

The success of this undertaking won him similar mural assignments for public buildings in Manhattan and Brooklyn, but by 1980 he was beginning to take an increasing interest in the occupants of his cityscapes. This was not the interest of a Daumier or (closer in time and spirit) a Peter Arno, artists who documented the low and high life of their respective societies as individual cases; for as Impiglia is inescapably post-Picasso in his aesthetics, so his intellectual outlook has apparently been shaped by the legacy of such social theorists as Marshall McLuhan, Eric Berne, and Erwin Goffman, all of whom have done pioneering work in the field of nonverbal communication. It is Impiglia's impression, as revealed in his paintings, that the more sophisticated a society is, the greater its stress on sending the right signal, striking the right attitude, making the right impression.

As he sees it, no slice of life available for portrayal in this light is richer in material than the American upper-middle class of the twentieth century. Unprecedented levels of wealth, education, and geographical mobility, coupled perhaps with a lingering sense of inferiority toward European culture, have made this influential segment of the U.S. population probably the most image-conscious group in modern history. This "other-awareness" impregnates all aspects of national life, from our foreign policy to our credit cards, and as such provides the keen-eyed Italian immigrant artist with a fertile field for his wit and acuity.

In 1984 at the Rosenberg Gallery Impiglia put together a show of his works entitled "Icons of Respectability." The title is significant, for his figures are indeed "icons"—highly stylized composites of fashion, pose, and mannerism whose decorous attitudes define the very ideal of an upwardly mobile society, as pictured in the pages of glossy, upscale magazines like *Town and Country*, *Vogue*, and *GQ*. "Besides consisting of perfect posture, elegance is shown here to be a matter of deportment—for example, how well one carries a champagne glass, a pair of gloves or a purse," wrote a reviewer in *Art News*. "By reducing facial features to emblems, the artist focuses attention on pose and gesture. And by generalizing his figures through such devices as square jaws, rounded waists and hips and simplified clothing details, he creates rhythmic compositions notable for their linear and planar movement." Even the colors he uses—aristocratic mauves, aquamarines, blue-grays, and salmons—reflect his conviction that style has become the opiate of the elite. There is indeed much to delight the eye in his oversize canvases, put together with humor, liveliness, and an unmistakably Italian sense of design; but beneath

Night People I (© 1984, Giancarlo Impiglia. Reprinted by permission.)

these immediate impressions lurks a disturbing suggestion of hollowness.

BIOGRAPHICAL/CRITICAL SOURCES: New York Times, December 5, 1975, February 15, 1981; *Art News,* September, 1984; Les Krantz, *American Artists,* Facts on File, 1985; *Sun Storm,* September, 1985.

—*Sketch by Richard Calhoun*

*   *   *

JETTER, Frances 1951-

PERSONAL: Born December 20, 1951, in New York, N.Y.; daughter of Joseph Leonard (a clothing cutter) and Rose (a bookkeeper; maiden name, Goldstein) Jetter; married Irving Grunbaum (a graphic designer), July 22, 1973. *Education:* Parsons School of Design, B.F.A., 1972. *Home and studio:* 390 West End Ave., New York, N.Y. 10024.

CAREER: Free-lance illustrator for newspapers, magazines, publishers, and industries, New York City, 1975—. Clients include *New York Times, Time, Nation, Progressive,* Random House, Arista Records, Celanese, and AT&T. Instructor of illustration at School of Visual Arts, 1979—.

MEMBER: Graphic Artists Guild.

AWARDS, HONORS: Awards from Society of Illustrators, 1976 and 1983-86, Society of Newspaper Designers, 1981, Society of Publication Designers, 1981-82 and 1986, and *Communication Arts,* 1984 and 1985; Certificate of Merit from 65th Annual Art Directors Exhibition, 1986; Creativity Award from *Art Direction.*

WRITINGS—All as illustrator: Bernard Malamud, *The Fixer,* Franklin Library, 1978; Elie Wiesel, *The Fifth Son,* Franklin Library, 1982; Steve Heller, editor, *Warheads: Cartoonists Draw the Line,* Penguin, 1983; Nikolai Gogol, *Taras Bulba and Other Tales,* Franklin Library, 1984.

EXHIBITIONS—One-woman show: Davidson Galleries, Seattle, Wash., 1983. Two-person show: New York Art Directors' Club, New York City, 1982.

Group shows: "200 Years of American Illustration," New-York Historical Society, 1976; group show of anti-nuclear work, Sindin Galleries, New York City, 1983; 65th Annual Art Directors Exhibition, New York City, 1986.

SIDELIGHTS: When Frances Jetter begins an illustration, her motivation is as much ethical as aesthetic. Since 1975, when she first became an independent free-lance illustrator

Photograph by Irving Grunbaum. Courtesy of Frances Jetter.

FRANCES JETTER

in New York City, she has employed a highly personal style expressive of her profoundly held social and moral convictions. Jetter never uses her art for decoration; her powerful images are employed in the service of communication, and her illustrations seek always to accomplish the purpose implicit in the etymology of the word: to bring light. She draws her inspiration as much from a grandfather active in union organization in 1915 as from the masters of German Expressionist art with whom she is invariably identified by contemporary critics; whatever her assignment, her work emerges as a personal statement of great emotional force. Whether illustrating a novel or an editorial, doing an album cover or creating an advertisement for a commercial product, her art is unmistakably and identifiably her own.

Jetter never wanted to be anything but an artist. Trained in design and photography, she considered becoming a photographer at one time, but found the ideal medium for her talents in the linocut to which she primarily devotes herself. The stark, dramatic effect that results from cutting directly into linoleum and transferring the image of its inked surface onto paper affords a dynamic expression of the intense feeling that underlies her work. She also does collage and mixed media, which may include watercolor, pastel, acrylic, photographs, or whatever strikes her as appropriate. She has done scratchboard, but she finds it uncongenial and never uses it now. She has also done woodcuts, and is beginning to explore the possibilities of lithography, but it is to linoleum that she remains most devoted. "I love the linocut," she has stated; "I always get that sense of surprise at the finished print which I cannot get with a pen drawing."

She was intrigued, as a child, by the bizarre humor of *Mad* magazine, and recalls the work of German Expressionist artist Kathe Kollwitz as an inspiration of her early youth. Like Kollwitz, Jetter employs stark, simplified forms to achieve raw emotional power in her graphic statements but avoids the extremes of stylization that characterize the German Expressionist movement. Other artists whom she admires include Egon Schiele, Alice Neel, Jose Clemente Orozco, Tomi Ungerer, and Edvard Munch. With all she has some discernible affinity of technique or theme, but she cannot be called a disciple of any. As Charles Goslin wrote of her in *Idea*, "In any evaluation of Jetter's work, we must start with the proposition that it isn't like anyone else's. She is pioneering new artistic and intellectual ground. . . . Like all masters (regardless of age) she has a vision—and hears her own voices."

Above all, Jetter's art is the expression of a keen emotional sensibility and an often angry intelligence. Already in a professional position to chose her clients, she accepts assignments from the *New York Times*, *Nation*, *Time*, and *Progressive* because of the forum these periodicals offer to her ideas. She also works for such book publishers as Franklin Watts, Arbor House, McGraw-Hill, and the Franklin Library. She also illustrates for trade and technical journals and does record-album covers. Basically, however, she considers herself a journalist and prefers to work only on what she considers relevant. Much in demand, she goes with her own feelings and ideas for jobs. She is impatient with art

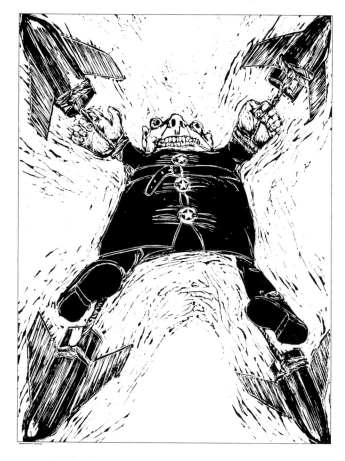

"Evaluating Arms Sales," an illustration for the *New York Times* (© 1980, Frances Jetter. Reprinted by permission.)

An illustration by Frances Jetter for *Taras Bulba* (© 1984, Franklin Library. Reprinted by permission.)

directors who insist on directing her art into their own channels of thought. Although she is given more freedom now than when she was first entering her field, editors still try to make the faces in her work less harsh. This she sternly resists. "When I am told my caricatures are too grotesque, it makes me angry, because that's the way it is, it's all there for anyone to see," she told *Graphis* in 1979. She will work with an editor or an art director, but only to a point. "I've taken out a grimace," she admits, "but if I over-correct a figure, the work loses its edge. I won't pretty-up the art, make it banal. This is something I insist on."

This artistic and intellectual integrity is apparent in every stroke of Jetter's art, and sometimes forces her into paths more somber than she would like. Editors turn to her with regularity when they have an article on the Holocaust to be illustrated. She is beginning to find this topic difficult because she feels that she has no new comment to make on it and because, as she explained to *CGA*, "The horror of the Holocaust is ultimately inexpressible in graphic form." Indeed, she somewhat regrets being typecast primarily as the artist of concentration camps and the nuclear winter. She likes the excitement of breaking through into new material

and has an ironic angle of vision which is seldom permitted to appear in her work. She likes dark humor, she points out, but usually gets subjects that are dark without humor. If a wry smile is evoked by one of her editorial illustrations, it is usually by the wit of her graphic metaphor, as when a U.S. general is shown as a junkie giving himself a fix with a nuclear warhead as his needle in an illustration on the spread of nuclear arms, or a million-dollar pricetag tied to a man's tongue illustrating an article on freedom of speech and the libel laws.

Jetter has promulgated her ideals and technical standards as an influential teacher of illustration at the School of Visual Arts in New York City since 1979. An admiring former student who acknowledges Jetter's influence is *Newsday*'s hard-hitting editorial cartoonist M. G. Lord, who affirmed to *Savvy*, "[Jetter] taught me all about distortion, to say in line what I had in my head. She encouraged me to use black and to treat the drawing as an abstract design rather than just a portrait of a situation."

One of the most significant voices in modern illustration, Frances Jetter has presented a wide public with a body of imagery characterized by sometimes grimly funny, often chilling wit, passion, and intellect. In a series of brilliantly executed visual statements made with uncompromising honesty, she has taken a humane and affirmative position with defiant conviction and immense intellectual vigor, establishing herself in a remarkably short time among the most articulate contemporary thinkers in any medium. As *New York Times* art director and critic Steve Heller wrote in *Graphis* in 1979, Jetter "speaks loudly through her linocuts."

BIOGRAPHICAL/CRITICAL SOURCES: Society of Illustrators Annual, 1976, 1983, 1984, 1985, 1986; *Graphis Annual*, 1976, 1977, 1979, 1980, 1982, 1983, 1984, 1985; *Art Directors Annual*, 1977, 1986; Edward Booth-Clibborn, editor, *200 Years of American Illustration*, Random House, 1977; *Graphis*, January-February, 1979, March-April, 1985; *Idea*, Number 157, 1979; *Upper and Lower Case*, March 1979; *Savvy*, June 1982; *Seattle Times*, June 17, 1983; Edward Booth-Clibborn, editor, *American Illustration 3*, Abrams, 1984.

—*Sketch by Dennis Wepman*

* * *

JOHNSON, Lonni Sue 1950-

PERSONAL: Born April 15, 1950, in Princeton, N.J.; daughter of Edward O. (an electronics engineer) and Margaret (an artist; maiden name, Kennard) Johnson; married Henry John Martin (a composer), December 22, 1980. *Education:* University of Michigan, B.F.A., 1972; attended School of Visual Arts, 1977-78. *Home:* 2109 Broadway, New York, N.Y. 10023.

CAREER: Art instructor, Stuart Country Day School, Princeton, N.J., 1974-76; free-lance artist and illustrator, New York, N.Y., 1976—.

MEMBER: Graphic Artists Guild.

AWARDS, HONORS: Awards include Desi Awards from Graphic Design USA, 1983 and 1985; awards from *Communication Arts*, 1983 and 1984, and Society of Publication

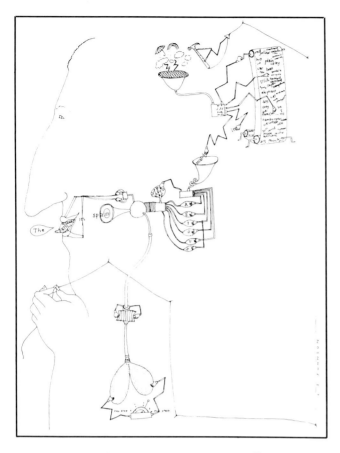

"The Rain in Spain," a humorous illustration (© 1985, L. S. Johnson. Reprinted by permission.)

Designers, 1983; and certificate from *Art Direction*'s Creativity Show, 1984.

WRITINGS—All as illustrator: Judi Barrett, *A Snake Is Totally Tail*, Atheneum, 1983; Marty Asher, *Fifty-Seven Reasons Not to Have a Nuclear War*, Warner, 1984; Barbara Shook Hazen, *Fat Cats, Cousin Scraggs, and the Monster Mice*, Atheneum, 1985; Barrett, *Pickles Have Pimples and Other Silly Statements*, Atheneum, 1986.

Contributor of illustrations to the *New Yorker, New York Times, Time, Fortune, Business Week, Good Housekeeping*, and many other national publications.

EXHIBITIONS: Work represented in the permanent collections of Rockefeller University, Princeton University's Permanent Graphic Collection, Newark Museum, Smithsonian Institution, and other organizations.

SIDELIGHTS: "If environment contributes to the development of an artist," writes critic Steven Heller, "then living in New York City is doubtless the foundation for Lonni Sue Johnson's comicalities; and the cramped urban workspace which she occupied for many years explains her diminutive manner." Certainly this is apparent in her crowded cityscapes and the often exaggerated contrasts in size between the people in her drawings and watercolors and their immediate environments; but this Manhattan state of mind shows up even more cleverly in other ways. An August 1983 *New Yorker* cover, for example, offers a beach scene, viewed

from overhead, in which urban day-trippers have simply transferred the asphalt gridwork of their native environment to the sandy shores of the ocean, replacing the isolating blocks of stone, steel, cement, and glass with parti-colored beach blanket islands, each separate and distinct. It is an effective, yet light-handed evocation of the peculiar anomie of life in the metropolis, as it affects both behavior and art.

Stylistically, Johnson's work expresses a combination of influences. She is a third-generation artist, her grandmother and mother both being painters (the latter studied with Joseph Albers). "My mother," she has said, "was a great teacher; she introduced me to the wonders of Saul Steinberg, who continues to be my ideal, but, more important, she showed me that illustration was as expressive as fine art."

Johnson attended the University of Michigan's School of Architecture and Design, graduating in 1972 with a degree in drawing and printmaking, but no consistent vision about what she wanted to do artistically. Having studied the viola since youth, she continued to do so for several years after college. She also taught art at a private school and painted, mainly for self-amusement. Then in 1976 she made the decision to devote herself seriously to a commercial art career. "My work at that time," she later recalled, "while fun for me, was undirected, self-obsessed and not very saleable."

Seeking direction, Johnson enrolled in the cartooning class taught by R. O. Blechman and Charles Slackman at the School of Visual Arts. This experience provided her with a focus she had heretofore lacked, teaching her not only the comic technique for which the instructors were themselves noted, but also instilling in her the all-too-often elusive realization that to communicate successfully, an illustration must be a symbiosis of art and idea. With these lessons learned, Johnson has since enjoyed excellent success as an editorial and commercial illustrator.

Her work, according to Steven Heller, places her among a group of young artists he calls "the New Humorists," characterized by "rejection of the angry, polemical satire of an earlier generation; a tendency to avoid reliance on surrealist symbology; an introspective, sometimes obsessive search for a personal statement; and, in many cases, a diminutive drawing style." For the majority of this group (Johnson included), he observes, "humor has become an illustrational tool rather than a 'free-standing' or self-motivated art." Thus, to complement an article on the causes and cures of chronic insomnia (*Pan Am Clipper*, November, 1980), Johnson executed a simple line drawing of one of her lilliputians entering his bedroom and finding a large sheep waiting for him on his bed. For an article on the renaissance of the entrepreneurial spirit in the United States she composed a watercolor showing a large dull-colored automobile being steadily abandoned by a stream of passengers for tiny and colorful single-passenger vehicles. In each of these illustrations, Johnson demonstrates the use of humor to underline a key point in the text—i.e., that one's personal attitude can contribute greatly to the severity of one's insomnia, and that many prefer the risks (and challenges) of going it alone to the security (and boredom) of corporate life.

Even when the humor seems to be "free-standing," as in the covers she has done for the *New Yorker* since 1981, it makes the sort of subtle literary point that magazine has made

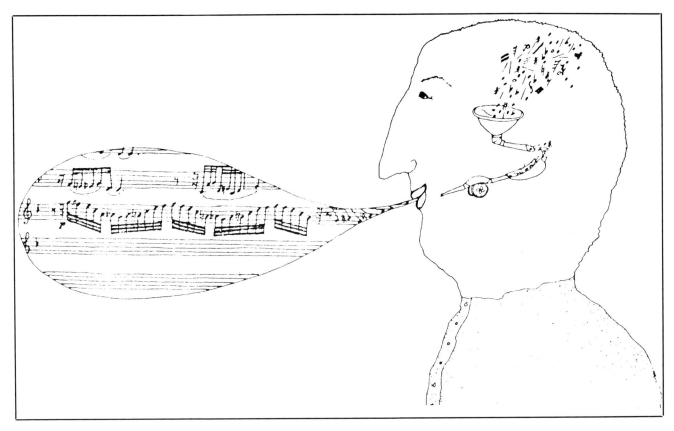

"Music Talks," a humorous illustration (© 1985, L. S. Johnson. Reprinted by permission.)

famous through the art of such giants as Peter Arno, Saul Steinberg, Jean-Jacques Sempe, Ronald Searle, and William Steig. Consider, for example, her March 18, 1985 cover: an artist in her studio with a portion of the city's skyline visible through a large arched window and surrounded by numerous canvases celebrating that view in its various details, in different lights, and under varying conditions of weather, is just beginning work on yet another blank panel. The point, of course, is the infinite variety of the city; but beyond that there is the conviction of the artist that an entire lifetime of painting the same tree, the same mountain, the same face, cannot exhaust its potential for stimulating fresh insights. To be sure, living in the city of New York can more than occasionally be a disgruntling experience to which Johnson

is no more immune than anyone else. But here too, wit comes to her rescue: a winsome watercolor of the sun rising over a submerged Manhattan, identifiable only by the tops of a few bridge spans, the upper stories of several of its most famous skyscrapers, and the head and shoulders of the Statute of Liberty. Four tiny boats peacefully troll these waters, carrying eight people—one of whom, this viewer suspects, is a playfully vengeful Lonni Sue Johnson.

BIOGRAPHICAL/CRITICAL SOURCES: Steven Heller, "The New Humorists," *Print*, January-February, 1984; S. Heller, "Lonni Sue Johnson," *Graphis*, July-August, 1984.

—Sketch by Richard Calhoun

K

KASSOY, Bernard 1914-

PERSONAL: Born October 23, 1914, in New York, N.Y., son of Harry (a custom tailor) and Toby (Drobner) Kassoy; married Hortense (a sculptor; maiden name, Blumenkranz), June 30, 1946; children: Meredith S., Sheila K. Krstevski. *Education:* City College (now City College of City University of New York), B.S.S. (cum laude), 1935, M.S.E., 1936; graduated from Cooper Union Art School, 1937. *Home:* 130 Gale Pl., Bronx, N.Y. 10463. *Studio:* Butternut Hill Studio, R.D. 1, Box 74, Burlington Flats, N.Y. 13315; and 130 Gale Pl., Bronx, N.Y. 10463.

CAREER: Artist, Federal Art Project of the Works Progress Administration (W.P.A.), New York City, 1936; teacher of painting, printmaking, and filmmaking, High School of Music and Art, New York City, 1939-72; instructor in painting, Harriet FeBland Advanced Painters Workshop, New Rochelle, N.Y., 1974—. Artist and sculptor in many media. Adjunct professor of lithography at City College of City University of New York, 1966-67; instructor in lithography at National Academy of Design, 1968. *Military service:* U.S. Army, 1942-46, served as photographer and draftsman in Southeast Asia; became technical sergeant; received two Combat Stars.

MEMBER: International Association of Artists (UNESCO), American Society of Contemporary Artists (vice-president, 1983-85), Pastel Society of America, Contemporary Artists Guild, New York Artists Equity Association (member of board of directors, 1962—).

AWARDS, HONORS: Merit awards from Art Directors Club of New York, 1979, Pastel Society of America, 1981 and 1982, American Society of Contemporary Artists, 1984; Florian Kraner Memorial Award from City College Art Alumni Exhibition, 1985.

WRITINGS: (Illustrator) E. Caplow-Linden and others, *Therapeutic Dance/Movement*, Human Sciences, 1979. Author of quarterly news column "Pallette Scrapings" for *New York Artists Equity Newsletter*, 1980—. Contributor of articles, illustrations, and editorial cartoons to *Teacher News*, 1950-60.

FILMS: (Photographer and editor) *Birdiness*, New York Board of Education, 1957.

EXHIBITIONS—One-man shows: Bronx Council of the Arts, Bronx, N.Y., 1968 and 1969; Caravan House Gallery, New York City, 1975; Ward Nasse Gallery, New York City,

BERNARD KASSOY

1979, 1984, and 1986; (retrospective), Mid-Hudson Art and Science Center, Poughkeepsie, N.Y., 1979; Bronx Museum of Art, Bronx, 1985; and others.

Group shows include those at ART-USA, 1958, National Academy of Design, 1968 and 1975, Bronx Museum of Art, 1971, and International Sculpture Exhibit, Pietrasanta, Italy, 1976; also shows at Lever House, National Design Center, ACA Gallery, New York Community College, and the Hudson River Museum.

Paintings and prints represented in the permanent collections of the Butler Institute of American Art, Slater Memorial Museum, University of Georgia Museum, Ar-

Self-portrait as a young man (© 1946, Bernard Kassoy. Reprinted by permission.)

chives of American Art; also in private collections in the United States, Italy, England, and Ceylon.

WORK IN PROGRESS: A series of oil paintings titled *Survivors*, dealing with victims of the Holocaust.

SIDELIGHTS: Bernard Kassoy's art has ranged over many media during the past half-century, and his restless imagination still continues to explore new forms, themes, and methods. Few contemporary artists display a range as great: he has worked professionally in oil, watercolor, gouache, pastel, charcoal, and pencil, and he has done etching, engraving, lithography, intaglio, woodcuts, and monotypes. He has carved stone and cast in bronze, done portraits and landscapes, editorial cartoons and abstractions, stage design, book illustration, and photography. In all these diverse media his work evinces both technical proficiency and aesthetic sensibility.

After graduating with honors in fine arts from City College in New York, Kassoy went on to take a masters degree and then to further course work at the Cooper Union Art School. He also studied with noted artists John Ferren, Isaac Soyer, and Arthur Osver. In 1936 he went to work for the federal Work Progress Administration (W.P.A.; later known as the Works Projects Administration) in its New York art project. For several years thereafter he contributed prints,

drawings, and oil paintings for the W.P.A. and remains in contact with the few New York artists of that group still active after half a century. This little band of survivors meets from time to time and presents shows of their work in New York.

In 1939 the twenty-five-year-old artist was appointed to teach in New York's high schools, and finished his teaching years at the famed High School of Music and Art, where he taught painting and printmaking and introduced the subject of filmmaking. He remained the school's only instructor of filmmaking until his retirement in 1972. Kassoy has also briefly taught lithography at City College and the National Academy of Design and has taught painting in a private school in Westchester County in New York; however, although he has been a teacher for over four decades, he has always considered himself an artist first.

Always closely associated with the cause of labor, Kassoy worked for many years with the Teachers Union, the forerunner of the United Federation of Teachers, contributing articles as well as spot illustrations and editorial cartoons regularly to its newspaper *Teacher News*. His cartoons, vivid pen-and-ink drawings dramatizing educational issues in the conventional nineteenth-century tradition, ran regularly from 1950 to 1960 and showed a keen sense of visual metaphor. Their lines often went beyond graphic representation of situation and made strong, independent statements. A particular target for Kassoy's indignant barbs was Senator Joseph McCarthy, whose virulent anti-communist investigations during the 1950s terrorized the school system.

Kassoy's social involvement expresses itself in other media as well. Much of his major work in oil is dedicated to powerful statements on social or political issues. During the period of the Vietnam War Kassoy did a series of surrealistic oils opposing the war: such ironically titled paintings as *Three Cheers for the Red, White, and Blue*, showing bloodied soldiers under a flag, or the cartoon-like *We Won the War! Hooray!*, stressing the utter desolation of war, reveal the passionate feeling that inspired them. The more somber canvas *The Complete Defeat of the Enemy Was Announced at Five A.M.*, showing a general making that announcement as victims march dully to their deaths, reveals the artist's acknowledged influence by the sixteenth-century surrealist Hieronymus Bosch. Other themes that have inspired statements on canvas from Kassoy have been civil rights and, in a current series, the Holocaust under the Nazis in World War II.

In striking contrast to these dramatic and stark canvasses, the artist has done a large body of work in pastels and watercolors which reveal a serene spirit and a delicate touch. These lyrical works—mostly landscapes—are light and airy, their pale, luminous colors sensitive and gentle. A series of twenty watercolors entitled *Country Landscapes*, done in the eighties, comprised an exhibition in New York in 1986. These scenes are dynamic in composition and vivid in color, and they show a rhythmic sense and freedom of line which shows the influence of Chinese art on Kassoy. Most were done in New York State and the rest in Pietrasanta, Italy.

Another medium employed by Kassoy is the hand-colored aquatint, "a very tricky method" according to the artist, in which colored inks with different proportions of oil are applied at once to a zinc plate etched to different levels of depth. In 1984, the Ward Nasse Gallery in New York City

An editorial cartoon (© Bernard Kassoy. Reprinted by permission.)

held a show called "Night Fires" of Kassoy's abstract colored-pencil drawings. Although he has worked extensively in abstraction, Kassoy feels that his drawings and prints are never totally non-objective. "There are organic references in the shapes," he points out.

Turning to sculpture, Kassoy has worked in wood, clay, bronze, and stone. His figures include both abstractions and human forms, some of them portraits. All seem to emerge powerfully from their materials and give a profound impression of force and strength. Kassoy and his wife, Hortense Blumenkranz, a prize-winning sculptor, share a large studio in the union-sponsored Amalgamated Houses development, which makes studio space available to its artist-tenants.

Bernard Kassoy's work has a place in many major public and private art collections in this country and abroad. Since it was made in 1957, his film *Birdiness*, which shows a water color painting lesson, has been in circulation by the New York City Board of Education and by the Museum of Modern Art, as part of its "Art for Education" resource archive. After a half-century of widely diverse work, Bernard Kassoy's artistic output remains high. He is busy with many new projects and sees his artistic horizons as constantly expanding. His full and active professional life continues as productive and diversified as ever.

BIOGRAPHICAL/CRITICAL SOURCES: Riverdale Press, October 21, 1971; *Upper Catskill Community Council of the Arts News Report*, fall, 1972; *American Printmakers*, Graphis Group, 1974; *Dictionary of International Biography*, International Publications Service, 1983; *Freeman's Journal*, October 29, 1975; *Who's Who in American Art*, Bowker, 1984; *Who's Who in the East*, Marquis, 1985; Les Krantz, *American Artists*, Facts on File, 1985; *Riverdale Press*, January 16, 1986.

—*Sketch by Dennis Wepman*

* * *

KENT, Jack
    See KENT, John Wellington

* * *

KENT, John Wellington   1920-1985
    (Jack Kent)

OBITUARY NOTICE: Born March 10, 1920, in Burlington, Iowa; died October 18, 1985, in San Antonio, Tex., of leukemia. Cartoonist, comic strip artist, author, and illustrator of over seventy children's books, Jack Kent had no formal art training, but always drew with ease and proficiency. He sold cartoons to *Collier's* and other magazines while still in his teens; in 1950 he created his first and only comic strip, *King Aroo*, for the McClure Syndicate. An intellectual strip in the mold of *Pogo*, it was greatly admired by the critics; in his introduction to the collection of *King Aroo* strips published by Doubleday in 1952, Gilbert Seldes wrote: "Jack Kent brings to the small company of fantasists the primary faculty of being able to create a compact universe that adheres strictly to a logic of its own." The general public, however, did not support the strip, and in 1960 Kent

decided to leave the syndicate (the feature was continued for some time by a small syndicate, Golden Gate Features). After again freelancing cartoons to magazines "from *Humpty Dumpty's* to *Playboy*," as he reported, he turned to writing and illustrating children's books in 1968. Among his early books were *Just Only John, Clotilda*, and *Mr. Elephant's Birthday Party*. A prolific artist and writer, Kent produced up to six books a year. His books were regularly reviewed by many journals as well as by general interest publications such as the *New York Times, Christian Science Monitor*, and *Economist*. Among his more recent books were *Silly Goose, Jim Jimmy James*, and *Joey*; he was working on *The Gorfu*, with publication expected in 1986, at the time of his death. "Surely the captivating books of Jack Kent," Dennis Wepman said in the first volume of *Contemporary Graphic Artists*, "have awakened a taste for the creative imagination—and the creatively imaginative use of language—in many young readers and pre-readers over the last two decades."

BIOGRAPHICAL/CRITICAL SOURCES: Gilbert Seldes, introduction, Jack Kent, *King Aroo*, Doubleday, 1952; *The World Encyclopedia of Comics*, Chelsea House, 1976; *Contemporary Graphic Artists*, Vol. 1, Gale, 1986.

OBITUARY SOURCES: Publishers Weekly, November 8, 1985.

* * *

KIPNISS, Robert   1931-

PERSONAL: Born February 1, 1931, in New York, N.Y.; son of Sam (a commercial artist) and Stella Anita (a commercial artist; maiden name, Blackton) Kipniss; married Jean Elizabeth Prutton, July 6, 1954 (separated, 1982); children: Max, Ivan, Ruby, Benjamin. *Education:* Attended

ROBERT KIPNISS

***Backyard II,* a lithograph** (© 1972, Robert Kipniss. Reprinted by permission.)

Art Students League, New York, N.Y., 1945, and Wittenberg University, 1948-50; University of Iowa, B.A., 1952, M.F.A., 1954. *Home:* Hudson House, Box 7099, Ardsley-on-Hudson, N.Y. 10503. *Studio:* 35 Main St., Tarrytown, N.Y. 10591.

CAREER: Artist and illustrator, 1954—; manager of a book store; postal employee, 1958-63; *Military service:* U.S. Army, 1956-58.

MEMBER: National Academy of Design, Society of American Graphic Artists, Audubon Artists, Boston Printmakers, Print Club of Philadelphia.

AWARDS, HONORS: Ralph Fabri Prize in Lithography, National Academy of Design, 1976; James R. Marsh Memorial Award in Lithography, Audubon Artists, 1978; Charles M. Lea Prize, Print Club of Philadelphia, 1979; award from Charlotte Printmakers, Charlotte, N.C., 1979; Lithography Society of America Prize, Society of American Graphic Artists, 1979; honorary Ph.D., Wittenberg College, 1979; elected member of National Academy of Design, 1980; award, National Academy of Design, 1982; Medal of Honor in Graphics, Audubon Artists, 1983; prizes in lithography

from Print Club of Philadelphia and North Carolina Art Association.

WRITINGS: Karl Lunde, editor, *Robert Kipniss: The Graphic Work* (a collection of prints), Abaris, 1979; (illustrator) *Collected Poems of Emily Dickinson,* Crowell, 1964; (illustrator) *Selected Poems of Rainer Maria Rilke,* Limited Editions Club, 1981.

Portfolios of prints: "Four Seasons," Association of American Artists, 1977; "Interiors and Backyards," Merrill Chase Galleries, 1977; "Selected Poems of Rainer Maria Rilke," privately printed, 1984.

EXHIBITIONS—One-man shows: Creative Gallery, New York City, 1951; Harry Salpeter Gallery, New York City, 1953; The Contemporaries, New York City, 1959, 1960, 1966, 1967; Alan Auslander Gallery, New York City, 1963; Gallery Vendome, Pittsburgh, Pa., 1964; Allen R. Hite Institute, University of Louisville, Louisville, Ky., 1965; FAR Gallery, New York City, 1968, 1970, 1972, 1975; Merrill Chase Galleries, Chicago, Ill., 1972, 1974, 1976; Hartley Gallery, Rensselaerville, New York, 1974; Albion College, Albion, Mich., 1975; Kalamazoo Art Institute, Kalamazoo, Mich., 1975; Centro de Arte Actual, Pereira,

Interior with Chair and Shadow, **a lithograph** (© 1976, Robert Kipniss. Reprinted by permission.)

Columbia, 1975; Museo de Arte Moderno la Tertulia, Cali, Colombia, 1975; Galeria Sandiego, Bogota, Colombia, 1975, 1977; "9" Galeria de Arte, Lima, Peru, 1977; Quadrum Gallery, Marblehead, Mass., 1977; Association of American Artists, New York City, 1977; River Gallery, Irvington-on-Hudson, N.Y., 1977.

Group shows: Butler Art Institute, Youngstown, Ohio, 1953; Massillon Museum, Massillon, Ohio, 1957; Tweed Gallery, Duluth, Minn., 1961; Art in America, New York City, 1961; American Federation of Art Traveling Show, 1963, 1964, 1965; Herron Institute, Indianapolis, Ohio, 1964; Ohio University, Athens, Ohio, 1965; Albright-Knox Gallery, Buffalo, N.Y., 1966; Corcoran Gallery, Washington, D.C., 1966; Museum of Modern Art, New York City, 1966; New York Public Library, New York City, 1967; Westmorland Museum, Pittsburgh, Pa., 1972, 1973, 1974; Whitney Museum of American Art, New York City, 1972; National Academy of Design, New York City, 1974, 1976; International Exhibition of Original Drawings, Museum of Modern Art, Rejeka-Dolac, Yugoslavia, 1976; III Bienial Americana de Artes Graficas, Museo la Tertulia, Cali, Colombia, 1976; and many others.

WORK IN PROGRESS: Preparing a major retrospective, "The Important Prints, 1965-1985," for the Gerhard Wurzer Gallery, Houston, Tex.

SIDELIGHTS: Robert Kipniss has always had an intensely personal approach to art, and, though impeccably rendered, his work reveals as much of his own subjective experience as it does of outside reality. An exhibit fittingly entitled "My Inner Landscapes" prompted the observation that his work was "a projection of inner feelings and moods, and expression of all our internal views." In a wide variety of media, including oil, drypoint, etching, mezzotint, and sculpture, he has produced an increasingly respected and appreciated body of these "inscapes" for three decades, and has earned a reputation as one of the most original and satisfying of modern painters, illustrators, and printmakers.

Although technically well equipped, Kipniss never considered formal education relevant to his artistic experience. "I thought art school was ridiculous," he stated later. "There is nothing anyone can teach. An artist can learn only from his own desires, disappointments, and approximations of fulfillment—and work, lots of work, and the most important, a keen attention to his deepest feelings." He studied at the Art Students League in New York City and Wittenberg University in Ohio, and took a B.A. in literature and an M.F.A. at the University of Iowa while making a scant living managing a book shop. He had little encouragement: his parents, both commercial artists, thought the pursuit of "fine art" a luxury and never reconciled themselves to his choice. But Kipniss was driven, and never felt that he had any real alternative. "One does not choose to be an artist," according to him. "It is an overwhelming inner need that cannot be denied. There is an old saying about such careers. 'If anything can stop you, let it.'" Fortunately, neither poverty nor parental disapproval was able to stop Robert Kipniss.

Kipniss had his first one-man show in 1951, but it was not for a few years more that he was able to consider himself a self-sufficient professional and to trust himself to follow his own direction with assurance. The somewhat rigid and formal character of his early work began to give way to a deeper and freer style in the 1960s. It was of this stage of his

career that the artist has written, "I began working from the imagery within my mind rather than directly from nature. . . . It was only when I began painting what I felt that my work took on the character that it has today." What he has felt and said in his work, though diverse in medium and content, has a remarkable uniformity of spirit. His paintings and prints are consistently representational, yet profoundly suggestive. Always underneath the serene, harmonious surface of his conventional scenes lurks a secret, not painful or violent but mysterious and sometimes sinister. The tranquillity of Kipniss's landscapes, interiors, and still lifes is always fraught with a private weight, and the infinite solitude of the artist glimmers darkly through the peaceful light of his images.

Everyone may read his own message in these eerie scenes. In 1973 a New York reviewer spoke of "the intense terror, the fearful silence of these works," but others may find peace, or relief, or unity in them. Their gentle, luminous colors hold and diffuse the light, reducing all to a misty timelessness. The monumental stillness of his scenes, which the critic found "fearful," vibrates with the ambiguous light of the impressionists. The artist whom Kipniss first calls to mind is an acknowledged favorite of his, the pointillist Georges Seurat, but the dream-like romanticism of Odilon Redon can also be seen as an influence on Kipniss. A third acknowledged favorite, the fifteenth-century German engraver Albrecht Durer, provides the model for elegance of composition and meticulous execution so evident in Kipniss's work.

Kipniss divides his time among the many genres he has mastered, giving four months a year to printmaking and the remaining eight to oil painting. He finds the different media synergistic, each increasing his passion for the others, and he profoundly enjoys the excitement of extending his aesthetic range and insight. He immerses himself in each medium, whether sculpture, engraving, or oil, while he engages in it, and brings into each something of the spirit of the others. Each new technique is an exciting challenge to him, and after thirty years art remains an adventure.

To the painterly sensibility with which he approaches his work in etching, he brings also the literary sprit which inspired his choice of undergraduate major in college. He has done one cover painting for a book—*Collected Poems of Robert Graves*, for Doubleday in 1966—and illustrated two other poetry collections. The first offered the work of Emily Dickinson, a poet to whom Kipniss's artistic sensitivity is acutely responsive; the second represented a particular favorite, the German Rainer Maria Rilke, whose work he illustrated for the prestigious Limited Editions Club in 1984. So acute was his feeling for this poet that he refused to undertake the job unless his choice of translator was accepted, and the publisher consented to his demand.

Kipniss's work has found an increasing audience, both in the United States and abroad. It is represented in such permanent collections as those of the Chicago Art Institute, the Cleveland Museum, the Los Angeles County Museum, the Museo de Arte Moderno of Cali, Colombia, the Yale University Art Gallery, the Whitney Museum in New York, and the Library of Congress, as well as in many private collections. In 1980 his old school, Wittenberg University, recognized his achievement in art with an honorary doctorate of philosophy. The highly personal road which Robert Kipniss has so steadfastly taken has led him to a secure position in both critical and popular esteem.

BIOGRAPHICAL/CRITICAL SOURCES: Time, February 3, 1966; *Art International*, April, 1966; Karl Lunde, "Preface," in *Robert Kipniss: The Graphic Work*, Abaris, 1980; *New York Times*, October 10, 1982; *Who's Who in America, 1984-85*, Marquis, 1984; *Who's Who in American Art*, Bowker, 1984; Les Krantz, *American Artists*, Facts on File, 1985.

—*Sketch by Dennis Wepman*

* * *

KLEINSMITH, Bruce John 1942- (Footsie Nutzle, Futzie Nutzle)

PERSONAL: Born February 21, 1942, in Lakewood, Ohio; son of Adrian R. (in U.S. Army) and Naomi I. (an assistant store manager; maiden name, Firth) Kleinsmith; married Laura Warner (an accountant), December 3, 1976; children: Adrian David. *Education:* Attended Ohio State University, 1960-62, and Cleveland Institute of Art, 1962-63; "primarily self-taught." *Studio:* "Top secret." *Agent:* Self-represented as Futzie Nutzle, P.O. Box 325, Aromas, Calif. 95004.

CAREER: Cartoonist, illustrator, and artist. Has worked in such jobs as "stock clerk, men's clothing sales, casino employee, gallery and museum administrator, show coordinator, [and] publicity manager." Editor and partner, *Balloon Newspaper*, Santa Cruz, Calif., 1968-72; feature cartoonist under pen-name Futzie (sometimes Footsie) Nutzle, contributing to magazines and newspapers, including *Sundaz Independent* and *Santa Cruz Express*, 1973-76, *Rolling Stone*, 1975-80, *Real Paper*, 1978-79, *Sierra Club Magazine*, 1983-84, and *San Francisco Bay Guardian*, 1983—. Lecturer at many colleges in California.

MEMBER: Eagles.

AWARDS, HONORS: Pushcart Prize from *Quarry West*, 1978; College Journalism Award, 1981, artist in residence, Victor Valley College, Apple Valley, Calif. 1983.

WRITINGS—Books of cartoons, under name Futzie Nutzle: *Box of Nothing*, Nothing, Ltd., 1980; *The Modern Loafer*, Thames & Hudson, 1981; *Futzie Nutzle*, Jazz Press, 1983; (contributor) *Not Bad for Left-Handed*, privately printed, no date.

Illustrator: Brent D. Peterson, *Speak Easy: An Introduction to Public Speaking*, Brigham Young University Press.

FILMS: Documentation for films by Spaceco, Oakland, Calif., 1968—, and Eric Mathes, Santa Cruz, Calif., 1975—; interview with Jack Wheeler.

EXHIBITIONS—One-man shows: David Gallery, Houston, Tex., 1971; Hundred Acres, New York City, 1972; Cedar Street Gallery, Santa Cruz, Calif., 1979; Santa Barbara Museum of Art, Santa Barbara, Calif., 1980; Artvarks, San Jose, Calif., 1980; McHenry Library, University of California at Santa Cruz, Santa Cruz, Calif., 1980; Swope Gallery, Venice, Calif., 1980; Gavilan College, Gilroy, Calif., 1981; Park and Wade Gallery, San Francisco, Calif., 1982; San Jose State College, San Jose, Calif., 1984; University of California at Santa Cruz, 1984; Les Anges, Santa Monica, Calif., 1986.

Self-portrait of "Futzie Nutzle," oil on canvas (© 1984, Nutzle. Reprinted by permission.)

Work exhibited in group shows, including first Monterey Pop Festival, Monterey, Calif., 1967; Moore Gallery, San Francisco, Calif., 1969; Whitney Museum, New York City, 1970; San Francisco Art Gallery, San Francisco, Calif., 1971; Otagawa Gallery, Hiroshima, Japan, 1972; Modesto Junior College, Modesto, Calif., 1972; University of California at Santa Cruz, Santa Cruz, Calif., 1973; Contemporary Graphics, Santa Barbara, Calif., 1975; Nathan Hart, San Francisco, Calif., 1983; San Jose State College, San Jose, Calif., 1984; University of California at Santa Cruz, 1984.

Work represented in permanent collections of the Museum of Modern Art and Whitney Museum of American Art in New York City.

WORK IN PROGRESS: A video entitled *American Epiphany*, with painter Phillip C. Hefferton; *Corporate Rebel*, a book of drawings; *Bay of Familiarity*, a book of drawings on poems by George Fuller.

SIDELIGHTS: Under the facetious nom de plume of Futzie Nutzle, Bruce John Kleinsmith has produced a serious and impressive body of work for both the alternative and the mainstream art market since he began his career over two decades ago. As Futzie (and sometimes "Footsie") Nutzle he has contributed cartoons and illustrations to a wide variety of periodicals, ranging from the *West Bay Dadaist* and various "mail art" productions to *Mainliner* and *Sundancer* airline magazines and many other national newspapers and magazines. He has done posters and book illustrations, designed a soap-box derby trophy, created a calendar, and done symphony orchestra program covers. From 1968 to 1972 he edited and drew for *The Balloon Newspaper*, a venture he partnered in Santa Cruz, California. For five years he drew a feature regularly for *Rolling Stone* magazine and has had regular features in the Boston *Real*

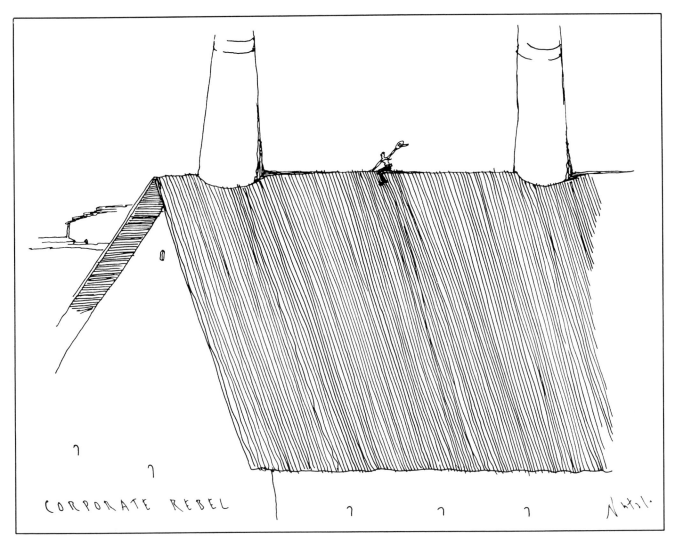

CORPORATE REBEL

A humorous drawing, ca. 1980 (© Nutzle. Reprinted by permission.)

Paper, Sierra Club Magazine, and *San Francisco Bay Guardian.*

Although Nutzle has attended art schools in Ohio and California, he describes himself pointedly as "self-taught," and his highly personal graphic style shows no evidence of the conventional training of the academic artist. The only influence he acknowledges is from "collaboration with exceptional artists, both known, unknown, alive, deceased, 1962-present." His first published work was done while he was in his teens, his high school newspaper *Red and Black Journal* carried cartoons by him from 1958 to 1960; during the two years he spent at Ohio State University, the school paper *Sundial* provided an outlet for his work. Since the late 1960s, Nutzle's cartoons have appeared in hundreds of newspapers and magazines of almost every type. He has appeared widely in small, esoteric papers in California, many of them his own brainchildren, but his national reputation is probably most solidly built on his regular (if "regular" can be used of Futzie Nutzle's art) bimonthly feature in *Rolling Stone* in the late 1970s. It was from this source that most of his 1981 collection, *The Modern Loafer,* was taken.

Within the highly evolved subculture of "alternative" or "Newave" art, however, the idiosyncratic and often deliberately obscure drawings that have appeared over the past twenty years in self-produced publications—often small one-time editions rather than true periodicals—represent Nutzle's major and most important work, and it is to these rare and ephemeral printings, depending on private sales for their meager support, that art critics must turn for material. *The Balloon Newspaper,* which Nutzle established with Spinny Walker and henry humble [sic] in 1968 (the masthead of this shoestring operation lists Nutzle, Walker, humble, and "various chicks as secretaries" as the entire staff) was typical of the genre. Published irregularly ("when Futzie feels like putting it out," as *Esquire* phrased it in 1974) at ten cents an issue and sold to a tiny cult following of fans, it was never a substantial commercial venture, and issues of it are now earnestly sought after by such institutions as New York's Museum of Modern Art.

Like most of the work of the "Newave," Nutzle's sparely drawn, profoundly evocative cartoons sometimes contain oblique social commentary, as when he depicts "The Filthy

A humorous drawing, ca. 1980 (© Nutzle. Reprinted by permission.)

Rich" as a house literally bulging with the detritus of an over-indulged consumer society. Often simple visual puns or literal depictions of cliches and collocations are all the content there is to be found in his cartoons: "Toilet Training" shows a man with a whip training a toilet as a lion tamer trains his animal; "Different Brands of Humor" shows cows with "Ha," "Haw," "Ho," etc., burned into their flanks; "Missile Beach" has missiles instead of muscles at the waterfront. But much of Nutzle's work contains deeper statements: an untitled drawing of a headless man discarding a series of masks, for example, or a bemused figure considering a series of impossibly fenced off areas, captioned "The Freedom of Choice," or the haunting sketch of an artist who has mounted to and entered his own canvas, labeled "Escape Artist."

Nutzle is a deliberate naif whose deceptively simple, seemingly crude style conceals great control and masterful design. Like the nineteenth-century artist-poet Edward Lear of the *Nonsense Songs and Stories* and the *Nonsense Botany*, whose work Nutzle's often resembles, the California artist occupies a shadow land between the conscious and the subconscious, the rational and the mad. It is perhaps the

combination of Lear-like naivete with a contemporary sensibility that produces the most powerful effects in Nutzle's work. He speaks to the turned-on generation—indeed narcotics have been a frequent motif in his work, as in "Snowshoe," which depicts a shoe with a straw in one of its eyes angled to draw up "snow" (cocaine)—but he speaks with a subliminal vocabulary which is intelligible to all. His recent drawings have moved into an even more interpretative style, and his cartooning has now become secondary to oil paintings and drawings.

It is unlikely that Futzie Nutzle will ever be popular in the mass market, and it does not appear that he has ever had any serious ambition to be. It is in fact a testimony to the extent of the cultural revolution of the past three decades that his audience is as great and as diverse as it is. Nutzle's defiant, anarchic spirit, which would at one time have branded him hopelessly as an outsider, has made him something of a lion within the very establishment which he derides so forcefully. Along with the avant-garde galleries of the West Coast, New York's prestigious Museum of Modern Art and Whitney Museum of American Art have purchased prints of his work and established files on him in their archives. He has received commissions from the *New York Times Magazine* and been collected by a mainstream publisher.

Popular cartoonist Bernard Kliban has written, "Nutzle the artist produces works of surgical precision, like lenses which allow us to peek at his neurons and synapses." The artist is unwilling to make a statement about his own work. "I would prefer to think that the work makes statements about me," he says. But in 1980 he added, "So far the work has survived the absurdity of the name and it seems the name has survived the absurdity of the work." Since "absurdity" is most often what Futzie Nutzle's work is all about, we may accept the comment as a quite proper estimate of success.

BIOGRAPHICAL/CRITICAL SOURCES: Eye Magazine, 1967; *San Francisco Chronicle,* January 4, 1972; *Esquire,* August, 1974; *Santa Barbara News Press,* September 23, 1974; *Quest,* February, 1979, June, 1979; *Santa Cruz Sentinel,* October 12, 1980, May 2, 1982; *Monterey Life,* August, 1980; *Publisher's Weekly,* June 5, 1981; *Ampersand,* May, 1982; *Columbia Dispatch Magazine,* December 26, 1982; *San Jose Mercury,* May 13, 1983; *Who's Who in America 1984-85,* Marquis, 1984; *Who's Who in American Art,* Bowker, 1984; Les Krantz, *American Artists,* Facts on File, 1985.

—*Sketch by Dennis Calhoun*

* * *

KRIG, B. B.
   See KRIGSTEIN, Bernard

* * *

KRIGSTEIN, Bernard   1919-
   (B. B. Krig)

PERSONAL: Born March 22, 1919, in New York, N.Y.; son of Selick (a civil engineer and manufacturer) and Rose (Bloom) Krigstein; married Natalie Horvitz (a poet and writer), September 8, 1940; children: Cora Zaboly. *Education:* Brooklyn College, B.A., 1940. *Home:* 140-21 Burden Crescent, Jamaica, N.Y. 11435. *Office and studio:* 4. W. 18th St., New York, N.Y. 10011.

CAREER: Comic book illustrator, MLJ Comics, New York City, late 1930s; free-lance artist and illustrator, 1939—; teacher of life-drawing and painting and copyist at Metropolitan Museum of Art, Works Progress Administration (WPA), New York City, 1940-41; comic book illustrator, sometimes under name B. B. Krig, for publishers, including Novelty, Fawcett, Pine, National, Orbit, Hillman, Marvel, and Ziff-Davis, late 1940s; comic book illustrator, Dell, New York City, 1947-52; comic book illustrator, EC Comics, New York City, 1953-57; book illustrator for publishers, including Knopf, Putnam, Doubleday, Looking Glass Library, and Farrar, Straus, New York City, 1958-62; painting teacher, High School of Art and Design, New York City, 1962-81; painting teacher, New York Technical College, New York City, early 1980s. *Military service:* U.S. Army, 1943-45, served at Division Headquarters for 28th Infantry Division; became sergeant technician.

BERNARD KRIGSTEIN

MEMBER: American Society of Contemporary Artists (member, board of directors), Pastel Society of America (former member, board of directors), Allied Artists, Federation of Modern Painters and Sculptors (vice-president), Society of Comic Book Illustrators (founder and president), Audubon Artists, WPA Artists, Painters and Sculptors of New Jersey (former member, executive board).

AWARDS, HONORS: Many awards for oil paintings and pastels, including first prize for graphics from Brooklyn Society of Artists, 1949; Jersey City Museum Award for oil painting, 1972; honorable mention for watercolor from Audubon Artists, 1975; Grumbacher Gold Medal for oil painting from Allied Artists of America, 1981; Ralph Mayer Award for oil painting from American Society of Contemporary Artists, 1981; President's Award for oil painting from Painters and Sculptors of New Jersey, 1982; 40th Anniversary Award for oil painting from Audubon Artists, 1982; Bachman Award for Landscape from Pastel Society of America, 1984; Lee Loeb Memorial Award for oil painting from Allied Artists of America, 1985; Bocour and Robert Simmons Awards from American Society of Contemporary Artists.

WRITINGS—All as illustrator: E. S. Lampman, *Rusty's Space Ship,* Doubleday, 1957; Lloyd Anderson, *Border Hawk August Bondi,* Covenant Books/Farrar, Straus, 1958; Ann Colver, *Borrowed Treasure,* Knopf, 1958; Louis De-Wohl, *St. Helena and the True Cross,* Farrar, Straus, 1958, H. G. Evarts, *Jedadiah Smith, Trail Blazer of the West,* Westerners/Putnam, 1958; Frieda Clark Hyman, *Jubal and*

1865: The War Is Over, **a painting** (© 1965, B. Krigstein. Reprinted by permission.)

the Prophet, Covenant/Farrar, Straus, 1958; Sylvia Rothschild, *The Life and Times of I. L. Peretz,* Covenant/Farrar, Straus, 1959; F. W. Rowland, *Eo of the Caves,* Walck, 1959; Anderson, *The Flagship Hope,* Covenant/Farrar, Straus, 1960; Harry Cogswell, *Find a Career in Advertising,* Putnam, 1960; Diane diPrima, editor, *Various Fables from Various Places,* Capricorn/Putnam, 1960; Frank R. Stockton, *Buccaneers and Pirates of Our Coasts,* Looking Glass Library, 1960; Arnold Lazarus and Robert Freier, editors, *Adventures in Modern Literature,* Harcourt, Brace, 1962.

EXHIBITIONS—One-man shows: Graduation Award Show, Brooklyn College, Brooklyn, N.Y., 1940; Harry Salpeter Gallery, New York City, 1964 and 1967; Harbor Gallery, Cold Spring Harbor, N.Y., 1966, 1973, and 1978; Fashion Institute of Technology, New York City, 1970; Adirondack Center Museum, Elizabethtown, N.Y., 1979; Grace Gallery, New York City Technical College, 1982.

Group shows in New York City include those at Society of Illustrators, 1963 and 1964; American Watercolor Society, 1965, 1968, and 1972; National Academy of Design, 1974 and 1980; "New York City WPA Art," Parsons School of Design, 1977; "The Artist and the Fable," Pratt Graphics Center Traveling Exhibition, 1982-84; Audubon Artists at National Arts Club, 1986. Work also exhibited in shows by Silvermine Guild, American Society of Contemporary Artists, Allied Artists of America, Federation of Modern Painters and Sculptors, Pastel Society of America.

SIDELIGHTS: When Bernard Krigstein left Brooklyn College with an art degree in 1940, he received the honor of a graduation award show and set out for a career as a painter. He has never ceased to see himself as a serious artist and has established a solid reputation in the art world with his illustrations and his gallery work in oils, casein, pastels, and watercolors, exhibiting widely and winning many prestigious awards. Along the way, and quite by chance, he was to achieve a collateral career in comic-book art which, in the special world of that genre, was to make him the object of a virtual cult. His two worlds seldom touch, and he easily supports his two separate reputations—as a respected "serious artist and as a legendary comic-book innovator. In fact, he has never been less than "serious" in any part of his career in art, and a thread of fierce artistic integrity runs through and unifies both elements.

His first professional assignments, done before World War II, were hack work for MLJ Comics. After copying the old masters at the Metropolitan Museum and teaching adults to draw and paint for the WPA Art Project in 1940, Krigstein did super-hero comics and began to glimpse the artistic possibilities in the field. Returning from military service, he explored these possibilities in greater depth, doing westerns, romances, science fiction, and jungle, crime, and horror stories (often as "B. B. Krig") for such publishers as Novelty, Fawcett, Pines, National, Hillman, and Atlas in the late 1940s and early 1950s. In 1953, Harvey Kurtzman invited him to join EC Comics, then the leader in the field. It was at EC that Krigstein did the work that established him as a master and a pioneer in modern comic art.

Krigstein was the last major addition to the famous staff of artists at EC. He was also, as Joe Brancatelli has written in *The World Encyclopedia of Comics,* "the most artistically talented—and the hardest to handle from the conformity standpoint." Bringing into the comics field the trained sensibilities of the fine artist, along with a restless, innovative mind, he was a maverick from the beginning, and often came into more-or-less amicable conflict with the editors and publisher at EC, fighting for his own aesthetic position and altering the work presented to him for illustration to suit his own artistic vision. Krigstein describes "The Catacombs," a 1954 EC *Vault of Horror* story, as his "first exciting experience in really splitting up panels. . . the first time I tried to change the pre-lettered text." In it he redistributed the material in the script supplied to him, making six panels of the original one-panel splash page. The effect was cinematic—and revolutionary; and, like most revolutionary ideas, was not accepted easily. It was not until years later, in a 1982 reprint of the story, that critic Bill Mason could confidently state, "There can be no doubt that 'The Catacombs' fulfilled Krigstein's stated ambition to raise comic book art to the level of Goya."

His next story for EC, "Master Race," went further, introducing so many innovative motion-picture elements that the publisher was reluctant to risk running it, and it wasn't until the next year that it was printed as the cover feature of a new series called *Impact.* The effect of motion and what the artist describes as the "richer dramatic feeling" his new arrangement of panels and highly original angle of

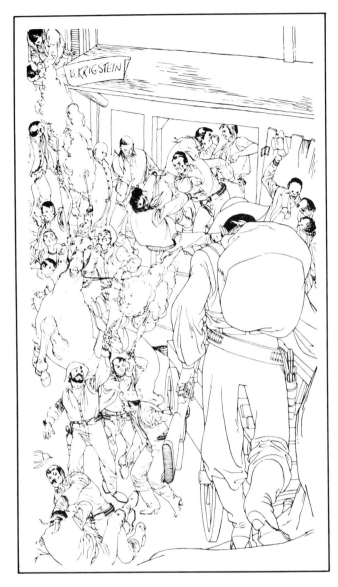

A western scene, ca. 1952 (© Bernard Krigstein. Reprinted by permission.)

vision produced were stunning. Probably the most famous of his works in comic fiction, this haunting story of psychological terror and revenge remains an unforgettable graphic achievement and prompted Douglas Menville to write in the 1971 reprint of *Vault of Horror* that Krigstein's "precise and delicate style and bold, fresh approach to layout often raised the comic book to the level of fine graphic art."

The new creative avenues that Krigstein opened up for comics were not to be much traveled, and when public protest of the horror comics began to bring the industry down in the mid-1950s, he directed his attention to commercial illustration. In a few years he illustrated some thirteen books and did covers for fifteen more, including the entire six-volume series of Joyce Cary's novels for Grosset's Universal Library. He also did eleven record jackets. In illustrations as in comics, Krigstein always followed his own artistic convictions, even when it meant fighting for them, and his defiant independence so impressed novelist Richard Condon, for whose best-selling *Manchurian Candidate* Krig-

stein did the cover art, that he included him by name as a character in one of his later novels.

In 1962 and 1963 Krigstein began teaching and dropped out of comic book and cartooning work. He felt that he had learned a great deal and was grateful for what it had given him; if he had brought a painterly sophistication and depth to the medium, he had taken from it a deeper understanding of the possibilities of narrative rhythm and a contemporary sense of movement. But his first commitment had always been to painting and since he felt that he had had to struggle to do what he felt was right in comics, it was with no regret that he left the field and returned to painting full-time, free at last of editorial constraint and restraint.

For some years Krigstein devoted himself primarily to landscapes and spent much of his time painting directly from nature in the Adirondacks, until, as he reports, he "reached the stage where [he felt he had] captured an aspect of this pristine and rugged land, the brilliant skies, the forever changing and mysterious mountains." Lately he has turned more toward figures, and his love of music has led him to use musical themes, including jazz and classical musicians, in his work.

After his years in the public world of comic-book art, Krigstein is reconciled to the relative obscurity of "fine" art. He considers the work to be an end in itself, and he has enough confidence in his own to let it speak for itself. His artistic ideal has always been integration and synthesis, although his career has often been characterized by conflict with those in authority. Through it all, as comic-book artist, illustrator, and painter, he has always obeyed the dictates of his own aesthetic. He looks back now on the many turnings of his life in art with the satisfaction of knowing that he has had no other master.

BIOGRAPHICAL/CRITICAL SOURCES: Bhob Stewart, "B. Krigstein: An Evaluation and Defense," *The EC World Press,* Number 4, 1954; Bhob Stewart and John Benson, *Talk with B. Krigstein,* John Benson, 1963; Ron Barlow and Bhob Stewart, editors, *The EC Horror Library of the 1950's,* Nostalgia Press, 1971; *Graphis,* Number 159, 1972; Larry Bails and Hames Ware, *The Who's Who of American Comic Art,* Larry Bails, 1974; *Squa Tront Number 6, Special Issue: Bernard Krigstein,* 1975; *The World Encyclopedia of Comics,* Chelsea House, 1976; Michael Barrier and Martin Williams, *A Smithsonian Book of Comic-Book Comics,* Smithsonian Institution Press/Harry N. Abrams, 1981; John Carlin and Sheena Wagstaff, *The Comic Art Show,* Whitney Museum of American Art/Fantagraphics, 1983; *Who's Who in American Art,* Bowker, 1984; Les Krantz, *American Artists,* Facts on File, 1985.

—Sketch by Dennis Wepman

* * *

KURTZMAN, Harvey 1924-

PERSONAL: Born October 3, 1924, in New York, N.Y.: son of David (a jeweler) and Edith Sherman (Perkes) Kurtzman; married Adele Hasan, September 7, 1948; children: Meredith, Peter, Elizabeth, Cornelia. *Education:* Attended Cooper Union Art School, 1944-45. *Home:* Mount Vernon,

Self-portrait of Harvey Kurtzman (© Harvey Kurtzman. Reprinted by permission.)

N.Y. *Office*—Cartoon Department, *Playboy*, 747 Third Ave., New York, N.Y. 10017.

CAREER: Free-lance comic book artist for such publishers as Ace/Periodical House, Quality, Aviation Press, Timely, Feature Publications, and Toby Press, 1939-50; artist for comic strip *Silver Linings, New York Herald Tribune*, New York, N.Y., 1948; staff artist, writer, and editor of *Two-Fisted Tales, Frontline Combat, Three-Dimensional E.C. Classics, Mad*, and other magazines, E C Comics, New York City, 1950-56; editor and artist for *Trump* (magazine), HMH Publishing Co., Chicago, Ill., 1957; founder, editor, and cartoonist for *Humbug* (magazine), Humbug Publishing Co., New York City, 1957-58; editor and cartoonist for *Favorite Westerns of Filmdom*, Central Publishing Co., 1960; editor and cartoonist for *Help!*, General Promotions Co., 1960-65; writer and editor of *Little Annie Fanny* comic feature, *Playboy*, 1962—. Cartoon editor for a number of periodicals, including *Esquire*, 1970, *American Health* and *Vanity Fair*, both 1982. Instructor in satirical cartooning at School of Visual Arts, New York City, 1972—. *Military service:* U.S. Army, 1942-44.

MEMBER: "Not a joiner."

AWARDS, HONORS: Best Humorist Award, *Yale Record*, Yale University, 1960; Shazam Award, Academy of Comic Book Arts, 1972; annual *Playboy* editorial award, silver anniversary, 1978; many other awards.

WRITINGS—Original books: (Author of introduction) Roger Price, *In One Head and Out the Other*, Ballantine,

1956; *Harvey Kurtzman's Jungle Book*, Ballantine, 1959; *Who Said That?*, Fawcett, 1962; *Harvey Kurtzman's Fun and Games*, Gold Medal, 1965; *Beat It, Kid. . . You Can't Vote*, Fawcett, 1967; (introduction "Sideword") Chuck Alverson, editor, *Wonder Wart Hog, Captain Crud, and Other Super Stuff*, Fawcett/Gold Medal, 1967; (with Will Elder) *Goodman Beaver* edited by Denis Kitchen, Kitchen Sink Press, 1984.

Reprints of magazine and comic-book material: *The Mad Reader*, Ballantine, 1954; *Mad Strikes Back*, Ballantine, 1955; *Inside Mad*, Ballantine, 1955; *Utterly Mad*, Ballantine, 1956; *The Humbug Digest*, Ballantine, 1957; *The Brothers Mad*, Ballantine, 1958; *Mad for Keeps*, Crown, 1958; *Bedside Mad*, Signet, 1959; *Son of Mad*, Signet, 1959; *Fast-Acting Help!*, Gold Medal, 1961; *Second Help!-ing*, Gold Medal, 1962; *Executive Comic Book*, MacFadden, 1962; *Esquire's Book of Humor*, Esquire, Inc./Harper, 1964; *Playboy's Little Annie Fanny*, Playboy Press, 1966; *The Ridiculously Expensive Mad*, World Publishing, 1969; *Kurtzman Komix*, Kitchen Sink Enterprises, 1976.

Editor: *Two-Fisted Tales* Numbers 18-35, Fables Publishing Co., 1950-53; *Frontline Combat* Numbers 1-15, Tiny Tot Comics, Inc., 1951-54; *Mad* Numbers 1-28, Educational Comics, Inc. 1952-56; *Three-Dimensional E.C. Classics* number 1, I.C. Publishing Co., spring, 1954; *Trump* numbers 1-2, HMH Publishing Co., 1957; *Humbug* numbers 1-11, 1957-58; *Favorite Westerns of Filmdom* numbers 1-2, Central Publishing Co., 1960; *Help!* numbers 1-26, General Promotions Co., 1960-65; *Nuts!* numbers 1-2, Byron Preiss/Bantam, 1985.

FILMS: (Screenplay; with Len Korobkin) *Mad Monster Party?*, Embassy Pictures, 1967; (directed; with Phil Kimmelman) "Nellie", "Count Off", and "Boat", one-minute animated cartoons for *Sesame Street*, Phil Kimmelman & Associates, 1972.

EXHIBITIONS: Frequently exhibited during the 1960s and 1970s at the Brooklyn Museum of Art, Brooklyn, N.Y.; Whitney Museum, New York City; Lincoln Center for the Performing Arts, New York City; Museum of Cartoon Art, Port Chester, N.Y.; and others.

WORK IN PROGRESS: Continuation of the series *Nuts!* published by Bantam Books; further collections of *Little Annie Fanny* published by *Playboy*.

SIDELIGHTS: Probably no cartoonist of this century has had more impact on our culture than Harvey Kurtzman. Described by art critic P. M. Garriock in 1978 as "a major innovator who has influenced at least two generations of comic book artists," Kurtzman has set his unmistakable stamp not only on the art of the comic book but, more importantly, on the thought, style, and speech of America.

Kurtzman's love of comics goes back as far as he can remember, and his life has been dedicated to the genre with a single-mindedness that amounts to a religious vocation. At the age of seven he was drawing a daily comic strip, *Ikey and Mikey*, in chalk on the sidewalks of Clinton Avenue in the Bronx. "In high school," he recalls, "when everyone else was taking notes, I'd be scribbling cartoons. I got approval that way." He was fifteen when he made his first comic-book sale—a "Buffalo Bob" contest cartoon for *Tip Top Comics* number 6, in 1939—and he has been gaining approval by scribbling cartoons ever since.

"Hey Look!," a comic page (© 1948, Harvey Kurtzman. Reprinted by permission.)

Even during Kurtzman's two-year army stint, 1942-43, he kept cartooning, and after his discharge he returned to it full time. For six years he drew and sold whatever the publishers wanted, in whatever style they wanted it. He did mystery and romance, fantasy and horror, adventure and humor. A thoroughly all-round professional, he commanded any form and any theme, and at the same time evolved a personal style of his own. From 1946 to 1949, he produced ninety-seven *Hey Look!* pages—self-contained gag strips of six to eleven panels—for Timely publications. Still much admired, these features have been widely reprinted since. For a time, he did a Sunday comic strip, *Silver Linings*, which appeared irregularly (March 7 and 14, April 4 and 25; May 9 and 23, and June 6, 13, and 20, 1948) for the *New York Herald Tribune*. By 1949 he was well enough known to be called on to do a sixteen-page giveaway comic book for the Communication Materials Center at Columbia University on the dangers of venereal disease. *Lucky Fights It Through: The Story of That Ignorant Ignorant Cowboy*, drawn in a style as sober as its subject and as masterful as that of Milton Caniff, was printed by Bill Gaines's E C Comics, and the next year Kurtzman joined the staff of that prospering publishing house.

Kurtzman quickly became a headliner for E C's "New Trend" comics, writing, drawing, and editing horror, science fiction, adventure, and war stories. To all of them he brought a new sensibility and a new depth. *Two-Fisted Tales*, of which he produced numbers 18-35 from 1950 to 1953, and *Frontline Combat*, of which he did numbers 1-15 from 1951-54, were the first war comics to articulate a clear anti-war message. Literate, mature, often moving, they bluntly de-glamorized war. The benchmark of Kurtzman's art was a concern for truth. Other adventure and war strips, he observed later, "showed an idealized world without real life. It bothered me to see the stuff they were handing out to kids." His dramatic layouts employed cinematic techniques that greatly heightened the impact of his artfully crafted plots. As cartoonist and writer Les Daniels has written, these effective comics "played an important part in educating a new generation about mankind's oldest curse."

In 1950 Kurtzman created the comic book that was to revolutionize not only the industry but the thought and speech of the nation: *Mad*. As he describes its inspiration in the editorial "Mad Mumblings" in the first issue, "We were tired of the war, ragged from the science fiction, weary of the horror. Then it hit us! Why not a comic book! Not a serious comic book . . . but a *comic* comic book!" *Mad* number 1, fully entitled *Tales Calculated to Drive You Mad*, dated October-November, 1950, though it appeared in August, was a bombshell whose reverberations have not ceased yet. The exuberant irreverence of its parodies struck exactly the right note for a disillusioned post-war generation impatient with the phoniness of the consumer culture it lived in. A year before novelist J. D. Salinger's Holden Caulfield gave a somber literary voice to the generation's obsession with authenticity, Kurtzman's gap-toothed cretinous invention Alfred E. Neuman, later the symbol of *Mad*, was expressing it hilariously.

With his staff of artists—principally Wally Wood, Jack Davis, John Severin, and Bill Elder—Kurtzman made fun of every aspect of American society. He satirized newspapers and magazines, movies and television, advertising and,

above all, the comic books themselves. Nothing was sacred to the *Mad*men: Little Orphan Melvin, Superduperman, Mickey Rodent, Darnold Duck, and Captain Marbles spoofed our most beloved comic-strip characters without mercy, and the public loved it. Its wild, anarchic humor and angry contempt for hypocrisy gave a voice to the young and supported their suspicion, as a *New York Times* article pointed out in 1977, that "there was something wrong, phony and funny about a world of bomb shelters, brinkmanship, and toothpaste smiles." It was not written for children, though children took it to their hearts and classrooms as their very own; Ernie Kovacs used to read it over dinner at the 21 Club in New York. "The original *Mad*," states Kurtzman, "had no particular market. I wrote to please H.K." That he pleased people of all ages is proved by the range of fans it had. Underground cartoonist Robert Crumb has written: "*Mad* was a revelation. Nothing I read anywhere else suggested there was any absurdity in the culture," and feminist Gloria Steinem, who worked for Kurtzman for a time, states, "There was a spirit of satire and irreverence in *Mad* that was very important, and it was the only place you could find it in the 50s." Acknowledging the "severe satire" of college humor magazines as his own major influence, Kurtzman sees *Mad* as having, in its turn, influenced the creation of such present-day sources of humor as the *National Lampoon* and *Saturday Night Live*.

After a dispute with Gaines in 1956 over editorial control, Kurtzman left E C and joined Hugh Hefner, whose *Playboy* financed a new, more ambitious humor magazine, *Trump*, for him in 1957. "A move upward," according to Kurtzman, *Trump* was an artistic success, but Hefner couldn't sustain it financially. It lasted only two issues; a public used to paying twenty-five cents for *Mad* would not pay fifty cents for *Trump*, however superior its humor or lavish its production.

After the failure of that noble experiment, Kurtzman organized his own company to produce *Humbug*, a fifteen cent black-and-white comic magazine. He and his artists, now including Al Jaffee, put their own money into it, but were unable to keep it afloat for more than eleven issues despite its low price and high standards. When William Gaines offered to take it over, Kurtzman, still determined to be his own man, refused, and the brave venture sank, like *Trump*, with no survivors.

With the partnership of publisher Jim Warren, Kurtzman and his loyal band of artists made one further try, a modest venture called *Help!*, in 1960. At thirty-five cents, *Help!* lasted twenty-six issues, to September, 1965, and showcased many artists later famous in underground comics. Among artists whose first public appearances were in the pages of *Help!* were Jay Lynch, Gilbert Shelton, Robert Crumb, and Skip Williamson.

Since 1962, Kurtzman has been writing an adventure-humor strip, drawn by Will Elder, for *Playboy*. *Little Annie Fanny*, described by *Mad* writer Frank Jacobs as "the most exquisitely rendered comic parody of all time," is drawn in full color and lavishly printed, about three times a year, in *Playboy*. Its heroine is a female adaptation of Kurtzman's earlier character Goodman Beaver, who first appeared in *Kurtzman's Jungle Book* in 1959. Beaver was a winsome naif out of Candide by Li'l Abner who passed endlessly through corruption undefiled; his voluptuous female counterpart Annie, whose inspiration is Harold Gray's Little Orphan of the same first name, similarly retains an almost incandescent

A page from *The Jungle Book* (© 1959, Harvey Kurtzman. Reprinted by permission.)

ingenuousness unscathed through a succession of gross encounters with brutes, lechers, and assorted scoundrels. As cutting as ever, Kurtzman's satire ranges over political, literary, artistic, and social targets including the Peace Corps, James Bond, the Beatles, Madison Avenue, and television.

Although still associated in the public mind with *Mad*, he is today, thirty years after leaving that magazine, as active and productive as ever, and his influence on humor and popular art remains great and pervasive. Called by National Cartoonist Society foreign-affairs chairman David Pascal "the father of the modern comic strip in Europe," he has had as profound an impact overseas as he has in the United States; and the American underground comics owe him both the name of their movement and much of its early inspiration and support. He has been, according to British comics-critic Denis Gifford, "a sort of patron saint" to the field.

When not teaching his popular cartooning course at the School of Visual Arts, Kurtzman continues to produce comic art. His latest venture, *Nuts!*, is a magazine in book form with a new comic strip about teenage girls by Kurtzman and Sarah Downs. It is as new as *Mad* was in the 1950s, and as unmistakably a Kurtzman creation. Kurtzman

has rarely compromised his work, and his artistic integrity has been responsible for one of the most distinctive and distinguished bodies of work in the history of American humor.

BIOGRAPHICAL/CRITICAL SOURCES: "Now Comics Have Gone Mad," *Pageant*, June, 1954; Rolf Malcolm, "The Little World of Harvey Kurtzman," *Playboy*, December, 1957; J. M. Flagler, "The *Mad* Miracle," *Look*, March 19, 1968; Les Daniels, *Comix: A History of Comic Books in America*, Outerbridge & Dienstfrey, 1971; James Boni, "Citizen Gaines," *National Lampoon*, October, 1971; Frank Jacobs, *The Mad World of William M. Gaines*, Lyle Stuart, 1972; Mark James Estren, *A History of the Underground Comics*, Straight Arrow Books, 1974; *The World Encyclopedia of Comics*, Chelsea House, 1976; Tony Hiss and Jeff Lewis, "The 'Mad' Generation," *New York Times Magazine*, July 31, 1977; Hubert H. Crawford, *Crawford Encyclopedia of Comic Books*, Jonathan David, 1978; Denis Gifford, *The International Book of Comics*, Crown, 1984; David Hinckley, "This Guy Went from Mad to Nuts," *New York Daily News*, July 25, 1985.

—Sketch by Dennis Wepman

L

LANGTON, John 1939-

PERSONAL: Born February 14, 1939, in New York, N.Y.; son of Frank (a restaurateur and bar owner) and Muriel (Arbuckle) Langton; married Anne Marie Whelan, June 27, 1959; children: John, Michael. *Education:* Graduated from School of Visual Arts, 1957, also attended, 1960-61. *Home:* 90 Belmont Blvd., Elmont, N.Y. 11003. *Office: New York Post*, Art Department, 210 South St., New York, N.Y. 10013.

CAREER: Free-lance gag cartoonist for magazines, New York, N.Y., 1958-65; staff artist, *New York Post*, 1965—. Creator and artist on a number of syndicated features, including *Quick Quiz*, distributed by General Features Syndicate, 1967-68; *Think You Know Sports?, Think You Know TV?*, and *Think You Know Movies?*, distributed by Compulog Syndicate, 1980-82, and by Cartoonists and Writers Syndicate, 1982-84. Humorous artist and writer for such periodicals as *Cracked* and *Sick*, 1965-85; comic book artist for Western Publications, 1970-72. Free-lance cover artist for crossword puzzle magazines, 1968-82; founding artist and designer, Hang-Ups by Langton, 1984—.

MEMBER: National Cartoonists Society.

SIDELIGHTS: John Langton's beginnings in art were uninspiring, but they laid the foundation and provided the discipline which were to support him throughout his career. His first job in the field was as a draughtsman for a firm of marine engineers, and the precision and control of the work he did there never left him. But he had loved the comics since he was a child, and never wavered from his determination to escape the narrow confines of mechanical drawing. The only ambition he ever had, he reports, was to be a cartoonist, and he began submitting gag cartoons to magazines before he graduated from the School of Visual Arts in New York in 1957. He sold cartoons—generally to "girlie" magazines, he reports—from his late teens and continued until more professionally demanding and rewarding projects came to assume more of his time.

Langton acknowledges the training he received from the School of Visual Arts, and particularly the influence of Jerry Robinson, a prominent comic book and comic strip artist who drew *Batman* for many years and created both Robin and the Joker for that strip. Robinson, who was Langton's instructor at the School of Visual Arts, for a time employed the younger artist privately as an assistant. Other artists whose influence on his graphic style Langton recognizes include Mort Drucker and Jack Davis, whose work in the 1960s and 1970s has much in common with Langton's and who worked for many of the same outlets. From 1965, for example, Langton drew, and sometimes wrote, parodies and

Self-portrait of John Langton (© John Langton. Reprinted by permission.)

other humorous features for such magazines as *Cracked* and *Sick* and from 1970 he did comic book art, drawing complete Bugs Bunny, Yosemite Sam, and Tweety and Sylvester stories for Western Publications. From 1968 to 1982, Langton also did two or three covers a month for G. and D. Publications' crossword puzzle magazines *Harle Crosswords, Quickie Crosswords, Speedy Crosswords*, and others.

A regular staff artist for the *New York Post* since 1965, Langton does a wide variety of work including illustration, sports drawing, and political cartoons. His gift for caricature was demonstrated in 1967 when he developed an independent trivia-quiz feature, *Quick Quiz*, distributed by General Features Syndicate until the syndicate's demise in 1969. The feature experienced a multiple rebirth as three quiz features: *Think You Know Sports?, Think You Know Movies?*, and *Think You Know TV?* These were all syndicated by Compulog from 1980 to 1982 and picked up, when that syndicate went out of business, by Cartoonists and Writers Syndicate, which distributed them until 1984.

Think You Know...Movies? **Panel by John Langton** (© 1983, Cartoonists & Writers Syndicate. Reprinted by permission.)

Think You Know...Sports? **Panel by John Langton** (© 1984, Cartoonists & Writers Syndicate. Reprinted by permission.)

Since 1970, Langton has worked widely as a free-lance producer of clip art (spot illustrations for nonexclusive use in advertising and promotional literature). His line art has been used by many large firms and has been distributed by such syndicates as Dynamic Graphics, in Peoria, Ill.; S.C.W., Inc., in Chatsworth, Cal.; Harry Volk Art Studio, in Pleasantville, N.J.; and Metro New Media, in New York City. North American Precis Syndicate, which specializes in "featurettes," has also handled his work for several years and distributed it to periodicals and business publications throughout the country.

In 1984 Langton and a partner established their own firm, Hang-Ups by Langton, which produces wall plaques with his graphics printed on masonite. Other products of his firm include T-shirts silk-screened with Langton graphics, and decorated clocks. In these products, as in his newspaper and clip-art work, he does only line drawing, usually using a number 0 brush. He rarely uses a pen except for lettering and signing his name. His preference for black-and-white, rather than wash, is appropriate to the meticulous, controlled nature of his work.

Langton regrets the passing of what he considers "the heyday of newspaper art," when such heroes of his as sports cartoonist and illustrator Willard Mullins had the space to perfect and display their art. As the newspaper space available to cartoons diminishes and the art is reduced to ever-smaller dimensions when it does appear, Langton sees a decline in the standards of the field. As markets disappear and the space that remains progressively diminishes, he has had to seek out, or create, new outlets for his inventive mind and skilled brush. In art for newspapers and magazines, brochures, and now wall plaques, T-shirts, and clocks, John Langton's clean, economical line and witty, affectionate messages may be seen around the country.

BIOGRAPHICAL/CRITICAL SOURCES: Cartoonist Profiles, June, 1978, September, 1980; Charles Green and Mort Walker, compilers, *The National Cartoonists Society Album*, Museum of Cartoon Art, 1980.

* * *

LANIGAN, Jack
    See LANIGAN, John Patrick

* * *

LANIGAN, John Patrick 1922-
    (Jack Lanigan)

PERSONAL: Born October 8, 1922, in Chicago, Ill.; son of Thomas P. and Bertha (Gunderson) Lanigan; married Emily

JOHN PATRICK LANIGAN

Caltabino, April 19, 1961. *Education:* Attended Art Institute of Chicago, 1946-49, Longwood Academy, Chicago, Ill., 1947-49, Art Students League, New York City, 1949-50. *Home:* 105 Summer St., New Bedford, Mass. 02740. *Office:* Standard-Times, 555 Pleasant St., New Bedford, Mass. 02742.

CAREER: Self-employed painter and sculptor, 1949-64; staff cartoonist, *Standard-Times,* New Bedford, Mass., 1964—. *Military service:* U.S. Navy, 1941-45, served with amphibious forces in the Pacific, was with atom bomb-testing unit at Eniwetok Atoll; U.S. Navy, 1952-55, served in Korea.

AWARDS, HONORS: Best Foreign Cartoonist Award from International Salon of Humor, Bordighera, Italy, 1969.

An editorial cartoon by Jack Lanigan (© *Standard-Times.* Reprinted by permission.)

EXHIBITIONS: Salon of Humor, Bordighera, Italy, 1969; U.S. Embassy, London, England, 1971; First International Cartoon Exhibition, Athens, Greece, 1975. Represented in permanent collection of Syracuse University.

SIDELIGHTS: No sooner had Jack Lanigan, fresh from three years of classes at the Art Institute of Chicago (and four years of World War II service before that), embarked upon a career of painting and sculpture than he was recalled to serve in Korea with the Navy. Demobilized for the second time, he freelanced variously as an illustrator and cartoonist in the course of the 1950s, before landing the job of editorial cartoonist on the New Bedford *Standard-Times.* If, as another editorial cartoonist, Tom Engelhardt, has asserted, the position is tantamount to "a marriage between newspaper and cartoonist," the marriage between Lanigan and the *Standard-Times* must have been made in heaven, for it has lasted since 1964.

Working up his ideas often late into the night, Lanigan usually submits two roughs a day to his editors; he then finishes his cartoons at the office. Drawn in a straight pen-and-ink, no-nonsense style, his drawings appear with the briefest of captions. In one cartoon, captioned "Debt Valley Daze," a grizzled Ronald Reagan on horseback surveys a corner of "Boot Hill" Cemetery where the tombstones mark some of the most egregious financial failures which occurred during his Presidency, including "Continental Illinois," "International Harvester," and "Dome Petroleum." In another drawing, a peg-legged buccaneer with a treasure map marked "U.S. Treasury" under his arm and a sword labeled "General Dynamics" in his hand simply proclaims, "I'm back!"

Lanigan's cartoons display a strong left-of-center position, with frequent literary or artistic connotations, which have made them favorites with Europeans. The artist won the best foreign cartoonist award at the twenty-second Salon of Humor in Bordighera, Italy, and he was among the American cartoonists represented in a 1975 exhibition in Athens marking the first anniversary of the return of democracy to Greece. Lanigan's work was hailed there for keeping the military junta under fire all throughout the preceding period of military dictatorship.

BIOGRAPHICAL/CRITICAL SOURCES: "City Cartoonist Honored," *Standard-Times,* September 8, 1969; Syd Hoff, *Editorial and Political Cartooning,* Stravon, 1976; *Who's Who in the East,* Marquis, 1979; *Best Editorial Cartoons of the Year,* Pelican, 1979.

* * *

LOCHER, Dick
    See LOCHER, Richard Earl

* * *

LOCHER, Richard Earl   1929-
    (Dick Locher)

PERSONAL: Surname is pronounced "*Lo*ker"; born June 4, 1929, in Dubuque, Iowa; son of Joseph John (a dentist) and Lucille (a musician; maiden name, Jungk) Locher; married Mary Therese Cosgrove, June 15, 1957; children: Stephen Robert, John Joseph, Jana Lynn. *Education:* Attended Loras College, 1948, and University of Iowa; Chicago Academy of

RICHARD EARL LOCHER

Fine Arts, B.F.A., 1951; attended Art Center of Los Angeles, 1954. *Office:* Chicago Tribune, Room 3200, 435 N. Michigan Ave., Chicago, Ill. 60611. *Agent:* Dominick Abel Literary Agency, 498 West End Ave., New York, N.Y. 10024.

CAREER: Assistant artist and writer for comic strip *Buck Rogers*, 1950-53; illustrator, Feldkamp Malloy Art Studio, Chicago, Ill., 1953-57; assistant artist and writer for comic strip *Dick Tracy*, 1957-62; art director in sales promotion, Hansen Co., Chicago, 1962-68; president, Novamark Corp. (sales promotion studio), 1969-76; editorial cartoonist, *Chicago Tribune*, 1973—, with cartoons distributed nationally by Tribune/New York Daily News Syndicate (now Tribune Media Services), 1973—. Artist for comic strips *Dick Tracy* and *Clout St.*, 1983—. Painter and sculptor, 1960—. Art teacher in local high schools and colleges. Trustee of Illinois Benedictine College. *Military service:* U.S. Air Force, 1952-53, served as test pilot; held permanent rank of captain; U.S. Air Force Reserves, 1953-64, worked in aircraft design.

MEMBER: National Cartoonists Society, Association of American Editorial Cartoonists (vice-president).

AWARDS, HONORS: Dragonslayer Award, U.S. Industrial Council, 1976, 1977, 1978, 1980, 1981, 1982; runner-up, Award for Best Cartoon on Foreign Affairs, Overseas Press Club, 1978; Special Citation for Distinguished Journalism, Scripps-Howard Foundation, 1978; Gold Award, Health Journalism, 1979, 1980, 1981, 1982, 1984; Sigma Delta Chi Journalism Award, 1983; John Fischetti Award, 1983; Award for Best Cartoon on Foreign Affairs, Overseas Press Club, 1983 and 1984; Pulitzer Prize in cartooning, 1983.

WRITINGS—Collections of editorial cartoons: *Dick Locher Draws Fire*, Chicago Tribune Press, 1980; *Send in the Clowns*, Chicago Tribune Press, 1982; *Flying Can Be Fun*, Pelican, 1985. Contributor to *Best Editorial Cartoons of the Year*, Charles Brooks, editor, Pelican, 1975—. Also contributor of articles and drawings to many magazines in the United States and abroad, including *U.S. News and World Report*, *Forbes*, *Playboy*, and *National Review*.

EXHIBITIONS: Traveling *Dick Tracy* Exhibit, (on permanent tour).

SIDELIGHTS: Dick Locher is that great rarity among cartoonists, a man whose name and work are widely recognized in several distinct fields of art. A nationally syndicated editorial cartoonist and winner of many awards since 1973, he has also drawn three popular comic strips, *Buck Rogers*, *Dick Tracy*, and *Clout St.*, designed characters for McDonald's hamburgers, drawn advertisements for Coca Cola, Beech Aircraft, John Deere, Cessna Aircraft, U.S. Steel, and the New Jersey Turnpike Association. His paintings and sculptures are now in galleries and collections all over the world, including those of Gerald Ford, Walter Cronkite, Henry Kissinger, the White House, and the Kremlin.

Locher's love of the comics, his first field of work in cartooning, goes back to his grade-school days, when his comics-fan father used to read him the Sunday funnies every week. "He'd read *Dick Tracy* first," Locher recalls, "because that was on the front page of the comic section of the *Chicago Tribune*. Dad would linger over the page, looking for the little intricacies that Chester Gould was very good at including in the strip. . . . Needless to say, all this rubbed off on me. I remember him saying one time, 'If you can grow up and be like Chester Gould or like James Montgomery Flagg who painted the 'I Want You!' recruiting poster, you'll really be something!" In 1950 Locher got his first job on the path toward really being something when the twenty-one-year-old cartoonist "lucked into" assisting Rick Yager on the comic strip *Buck Rogers*. For three years he penciled, did a little inking, and helped with the writing of that strip for Yager.

In 1957, after a stint with a commercial art studio in Chicago, Locher had the opportunity he had dreamed of since childhood: he became an assistant on *Dick Tracy* for his hero Chester Gould. From 1957 to 1962 he worked with Gould on the story line, inked the characters and lettering of the daily and Sunday strips, and colored the Sundays of *Tracy*. It was Chester Gould who later led Locher into his career as an editorial cartoonist. He called Locher in 1972 to inform him that Joe Parrish, the *Chicago Tribune*'s political cartoonist, had reached the mandatory retirement age of sixty-five and that the newspaper was looking for a replacement for him. Locher had always been interested in editorial cartooning and had tried his hand at it for his own amusement, so he was able to round up a dozen samples to submit to the *Tribune*. The editor liked what he saw and gave Locher a three-month trial assignment. On January, 1973, Locher was hired as a full-time editorial cartoonist, and in the years since then he has won virtually every award the profession offers, including its highest, the Pulitzer Prize, in 1983.

Locher's broad, humorous style of drawing and the keen wit of his commentary have a wide popular appeal, and his

An editorial cartoon by Dick Locher (© 1985, *Chicago Tribune.* Reprinted by permission.)

cartoons bring him letters from all over the world, agreeing with or disputing his views. "Comments come," the artist reports, "from unknown people, farmers, business men, senators, representatives, presidents, and kids." Distributed nationally by the Tribune/New York Daily News Syndicate (now Tribune Media Services) since he started with the *Tribune,* he is seen daily in hundreds of newspapers. One reason for the broad base of his audience is the generous sympathy he expresses in his work. He takes on government and big business in a good-humored way, genially emphasizing the absurdity of much of public life and drolly deflating the pompous. He takes his philosophy from Pulitzer prize-winning cartoonist J. N. "Ding" Darling: "You can let just as much hot air out of a balloon with a needle as you can with an ax."

Nevertheless, often the points Locher makes are serious ones, and he pulls no punches in expressing them. A 1976 cartoon shows a gun-bearing thug assuring another as they leave a beaten victim in an alley, "Don't worry! Cruel and unusual punishment applies to *us* if we're caught! Not to our victims!" In that same year he took on the gun lobby, showing a crazed assassin pointing a pistol from the back of a patriotic crowd while sitting on the shoulders of a lobbyist. Another target of Locher's wit has been Interior Secretary James Watt; in a 1981 cartoon Locher shows Smokey the

Bear demanding of an indifferent President Reagan, "Is it going to be the environment or Watt?" and Reagan replying "What?" More typical of the good-natured style of Locher's editorial cartoons, however, is his famous 1981 drawing of President and Mrs. Carter in the classic pose of Grant Wood's painting *American Gothic,* labeled "Just Plains folks."

Expressing once again his bemused attitude toward government, Locher joined forces with famed editorial cartoonist Jeff McNelly in 1983 to do a comic strip making fun of city politics. *Clout St.,* which debuted in February, 1983, and was immediately distributed by the Tribune Syndicate, is set in an unnamed big city and centers on the corruption and stupidity of its government. The spokesperson for the cartoonists involved is an anarchic bag lady who lives in a shopping bag and attacks everything the city does. McNelly soon left the strip, which is now signed "Tribs and Locher." Locher draws it, and "Tribs" represents the *Tribune* team who share its authorship: Managing Editor Dick Ciccone, Editor Jim Squires, and Locher.

A month after the beginning of *Clout St.,* Locher's work load was increased by yet another major job. The death of Rick Fletcher, one of the two men who took over the comic strip *Dick Tracy* when its creator Chester Gould retired in

1977, left an opening which Locher was asked to fill, and with a seemingly insatiable capacity for work he accepted. Since then he has been drawing *Clout St.* and *Dick Tracy* as well as doing six editorial cartoons every week for the *Chicago Tribune*. The crisp, controlled style of *Tracy*, in striking contrast to the looser, more spontaneous-appearing style of *Clout St.* and the editorial cartoons, maintains Gould's clean, balanced style without being a slavish imitation of it. Locher states that he is trying to emulate Gould: "The use of blacks, the balance, the perspective, and the depth that he would put into a panel, was just unbeatable," he states. Fortunately, Locher's son John had just finished art school when Locher took over the strip, and the two have been working together on every aspect of it.

The restless mind of Dick Locher seems to have no limits; with two syndicated comic strips and a nationally admired editorial feature to keep going, he ranges over the entire field of graphic art for new challenges. In 1971 he patented a game, "Poker Face," which permits its players to play poker without cards. Smuggled aboard the Apollo 15 spacecraft by the astronauts, it was the first game to circle the moon. During all of his busy career, while drawing cartoons, doing comic strips, designing advertising, and inventing games, he has been seriously working in "fine art" since the early 1960s. His oils and bronze sculpture, done in vivid, illustrational style, have won praise from critics and collectors around the world and been eagerly sought by both private and public collections. Locher has suggested a formula for success: $E^3 = MC$, which he explains, "Education, excellence, and energy equal maturity and contentment." His own prodigious output bear witness to the rewards of his education, excellence, and energy.

BIOGRAPHICAL/CRITICAL SOURCES: Cartoonist Profiles, December, 1971, December, 1984; *National Cartoonists Society Album,* 1980; *Who's Who in America 1984-85,* Marquis, 1984; *Contemporary Authors,* New Revision Series, Vol. 16, Gale, 1986.

—*Sketch by Dennis Wepman*

* * *

LORD, M(ary) G(race) 1955-

PERSONAL: Born November 18, 1955, in La Jolla, Calif.; daughter of Charles Carroll (an aeronautical engineer) and Mary (Pfister) Lord; married Glenn Horowitz (a rare book and manuscript dealer), May 19, 1985. *Education:* Yale University, B.A. (cum laude), 1977. *Home:* 23 E. 10th St., New York, N.Y. 10003. *Office:* Newsday, 235 Pinelawn Rd., Melville, N.Y. 11747. *Agent:* Liz Darhansoff, 1220 Park Ave., New York, N.Y. 10028.

CAREER: Reporting intern, *Wall Street Journal,* New York City, 1976; staff artist, *Chicago Tribune,* Chicago, Ill., 1977-78; editorial cartoonist, *Newsday,* Melville, N.Y., 1978—. Cartoons distributed nationally by Los Angeles Times Syndicate, 1984—; regular contributor of illustrations to the *nation.* Radio commentator for National Public Radio.

MEMBER: National Cartoonists Society, Association of American Editorial Cartoonists, National Book Critics Circle.

Self-portrait of M. G. Lord, specially drawn for *Contemporary Graphic Artists* (© 1986, M. G. Lord.)

AWARDS, HONORS: Selected for the "Esquire Register" ("The Best of the New Generation Men and Women Under Forty Who Are Changing America"), *Esquire,* 1984.

WRITINGS: Mean Sheets: Political Cartoons by M. G. Lord (a collection of editorial cartoons with commentary), Little, Brown, 1982; (illustrator) Judy Bachrach and Claudia de Monte, *The Height Report: A Tall Woman's Handbook,* Andrews & McMeel, 1983; (contributor) Carew Papritz, editor, *100 Watts: The James Watt Memorial Cartoon Album,* Khyber Press, 1983; Steven Heller, *Warheads,* Penguin, 1983; *ReaganComics,* Khyber Press, 1984.

EXHIBITIONS: One-woman show of editorial cartoons, Museum of Cartoon Art, Rye Brook, N.Y., 1985.

WORK IN PROGRESS: A collection of syndicated editorial cartoons.

SIDELIGHTS: M. G. Lord says of her employment, "Editors contracted to buy Kate Greenaway and ended up with George Grosz." One of the most penetrating and acerbic of the new generation of political cartoonists, she directs her barbed wit fearlessly at many of the most revered of modern institutions and in a remarkably short period of time has made herself a force to be reckoned with in American journalism. Her brief apprenticeship as a reporter and staff artist on two other newspapers brought her to the attention of a major metropolitan newspaper two years after her graduation from Yale in 1977. She has been acquiring a national reputation at Long Island's *Newsday* ever since.

Lord was cut out to be an editorial cartoonist from before her birth. She reports that her mother was reading the mordant English satirist Evelyn Waugh during her pregnancy and that the infant M. G. "emerged from the womb quoting Dorothy Parker out of the side of [her] mouth." Her earliest drawings were cynical. "I was born jaded," she concludes. Never one to follow the crowd, she rebelled early against "all those blond, sun-tanned California types," and her independent spirit won her their awed respect. In a society where the bland lead the bland, Lord was a compelling presence. She was elected president of her high school class and made the editor in chief of the school newspaper. Her career as a political cartoonist may not have been clearly indicated yet, but a future commenting caustically on the scene around her was already inevitable.

While at Yale University, she served a summer internship with the *Wall Street Journal*. "That newspaper's abortive experiment in editorial caricature," as she described the experience, gave her a preview of the life of a journalist, but it was classes with Pulitzer prize-winning cartoonists Bill Mauldin, creator of World War II's Willy and Joe, and *Doonesbury* artist Garry Trudeau that really directed her into the field. Both remain her friends and fans. Trudeau observed of her work that it displays "a wonderful seditiousness that hasn't been seen since the days of Watergate. . . . M. G. Lord takes no prisoners." Mauldin, who wrote the foreword to her 1982 collection of cartoons *Mean Sheets*, disclaims all credit for her success. "She really did everything herself," he recalls. "[She] was two jumps ahead of me."

Life in the real world did not begin so easily for the aggressive young firebrand, however. She began as a "staff artist" at the *Chicago Tribune*, which, she explains, meant that for her ten-month stint there she made coffee for the

editorial cartoonists. At last a fund-raising cartoon she had done caught the eye of someone with the Long Island, New York, newspaper *Newsday*, and she was offered a job illustrating articles, with an occasional shot at political cartooning. After six months of "probation," the twenty-three-year-old Lord became *Newsday*'s regular editorial cartoonist. In 1984 the Los Angeles Times Syndicate began national distribution of her cartoons.

Lord's technical control of her medium has grown steadily in the eight years since she assumed her position with the Long Island paper. "*Newsday* let me be bad," she states candidly, "and for a year I was." As her powers of graphic invention have increased, her assurance has increased with them, and she now feels confident of the authority of her work. Her style is decisive and unequivocal, although she admits to a limited palette. She has what she calls "a generic extraterrestrial," for example, and any face with a beard and a turban will do for Ayatollah Khomeini. Detail is not important to her; indeed, she acknowledges a lively distaste for overdrawn work. "I'm not big on verisimilitude," she says. "I like to keep my sketches loose, and I'd be more minimal if my editors permitted." In keeping with the looseness and freedom of her line, Lord employs strong, simple compositions using tone flat as a design element rather than to model form. The forceful sweep of her graphic style owes something to the editorial illustrations of Frances Jetter, whose work appears in the *New York Times* and the *Nation* and with whom Lord took summer classes a few years ago. "[Jetter] taught me all about distortion, to say

An editorial cartoon by M. G. Lord (© 1985, *Newsday*. Reprinted by permission.)

in line what I had in my head," she says. "She encouraged me to use black, and to treat the drawing as an abstract design, rather than as a portrait of a situation." Other artists whose stylistic influence Lord acknowledges are *Punch* cartoonist Arnold Roth and "the most anarchic pen in modern caricature," Ralph Steadman.

Like most editorial cartoonists, Lord views her editors as the enemy, although she admits to respecting her deputy editorial-page editor Jay Lynn, who is the first to review her sketches. She feels that she is allowed complete editorial freedom except to disagree with the policy of her paper. If a cartoon is rejected by *Newsday*, she simply sends it off to her syndicate and starts work on another. She is never at a loss for a subject. Among her favorite topics in the past eight years have been television, crime in New York, environmental issues (she produced some stinging comments on Interior Secretary James Watt) and racism in South Africa. President Reagan—"old iguana neck," as she calls him—is an irresistible target, both graphically and politically, and she confesses to missing Richard Nixon—"God's greatest gift to editorial cartoonists"—dreadfully. She presented President Jimmy Carter, on the other hand, as poignant rather than ridiculous. Soviet leader Leonid Brezhnev was a joy to draw, but she complains that his successor Mikhail Gorbachev is dull: "He looks like someone's next-door neighbor from Syosset," she states.

One of the few women in her exacting field, M. G. Lord has never taken advantage of that fact. "I guess if I pandered to the 'woman' angle, my work could be in a lot more newspapers, and maybe the women's magazines," she reported to *Savvy*, "but I can't comfortably be exploitative of it. Because in the long run the constraints of being categorized far outweigh the advantages." Inevitably, however, her sympathies—as a liberal if not as a woman—do tend to favor women's rights. A boss in one of her cartoons is shown gallantly reassuring a woman worker, "It's not sex discrimination, dear. Your salaries are different because your jobs are different. You're a cleaning lady and he's a sanitation engineer." No less severe on her own sex, however, she shows two matrons commenting on a display of judges' robes on women, "These new styles are scandalous."

A diligent and dedicated commentator on her world, M. G. Lord devotes most of her time to her work. She reads the *Los Angeles Times, New York Times, Newsweek, Time, Washington Post,* and, of course, her own paper, and keeps up on current literature and the arts. The cultural richness of her background is apparent in her literate jabs. Less obvious, however, is the care with which she plans and draws her loose, seemingly spontaneous creations. She describes the originals as looking like topographical maps, with little mountains of correction fluid (a product for which she has unstinting praise). The final result of this painstaking labor appears to be the unchecked effusion of a moment.

Lord finds current cartoonists generally unoriginal but blames it on the editors. "The marketplace doesn't encourage originality," she states. "Editors buy junk by clones of Jeff MacNelly." Another complaint she has about editors is their timidity; they are so worried about offending people in the community, she says, that they would rather compromise than risk trouble.

M. G. Lord began her career as an impassioned campaigner, fighting the good fight and ready if necessary to offend rather than back down. In fact, she frankly rejoiced in her image as a merciless assailant. "I like drawing vicious pictures of people," she stated unabashedly to *Ms.* magazine in 1983. However, her belligerence probably made her more friends than enemies, and the sensitivity lying close beneath the bellicose surface was not hard to discover. Now, at thirty, Lord claims to have become mellower. If this means that she is softer on moral issues that outrage her, it has not been noticeable to her fans.

Sometimes frustrated by the limitations of space available to her, Lord never fails to contain her point succinctly in her daily panel. Her personal identity as an artist and as a concerned citizen have become increasingly clear with time as, in Steven Heller's words, "She has instilled in the form a personal vision and a distinct graphic personality." Never one to shrink from criticism, which she describes as "water off the back of a very morally committed duck," she has given her public no reason to expect her to do so. This "smart, tough, funny, and original" cartoonist, as colleague Jules Feiffer calls her, has lost none of her cutting edge since passing the landmark age of thirty.

BIOGRAPHICAL/CRITICAL SOURCES: National Cartoonists Society Album, 1980; Bill Mauldin, "Foreword," in M. G. Lord, *Mean Sheets*, Little, Brown, 1982; Helen Rosengreen Freedman, "The Outraged Pen of M. G. Lord," *Savvy*, June, 1982; Ralph Cornelis, "Comic Relief: Three Political Cartoonists," *Ms.*, January, 1983; Steven Heller, "The New Humorists," *Print*, January/February, 1984; "Esquire 1984 Register," *Esquire*, December, 1984

—*Sketch by Dennis Wepman*

* * *

LUQUE VERA, Nazario 1944-
(Nazario)

PERSONAL: Born January 3, 1944, in Castilleja del Campo, Spain; son of Braulio (an independent farmer) and Maria Luisa (Vera) Luque. *Education:* Graduated from Teacher's College, Seville, Spain, 1964. *Home:* Plaza Real, 12, 08002 Barcelona, Spain. *Agent:* Josep Maria Berenguer, Plaza de las Beatas, 3, 08003 Barcelona, Spain; Josep Toutain, Selecciones Illustradas, Diagonal 325, 08009 Barcelona, Spain; Bernd Metz, S.I. International, 43 E. 19th St., New York, N.Y. 10003.

CAREER: Primary school teacher, 1964-73; free-lance cartoonist, 1973—. *Military service:* Spanish Army, 1963-65, served in infantry; became sergeant.

WRITINGS—All books of comics; all under name Nazario: *La pirana divina*, "underground" publication, 1974; *San Reprimonio y las piranas*, Rock Comic, Barcelona, 1976; *Nazario. Historietas. Obra completa 1975-1980*, (title means *Nazario: Comics: Complete Work 1975-1980*), La Cupula, Barcelona, 1981; *Anarcoma*, La Cupula, Barcelona, 1983; Catalan Communications, New York, 1984.

Contributor to *El Vibora* (magazine).

WORK IN PROGRESS: Anarcoma 2, a comics series to be

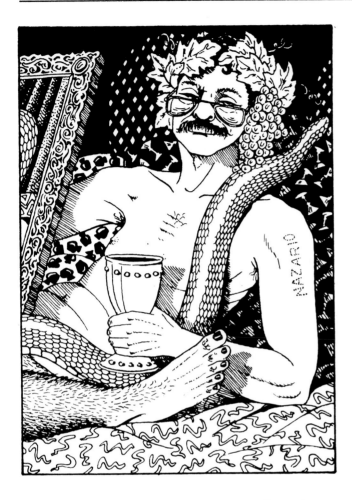

Self-portrait of Nazario Luque Vera as Bacchus (© Nazario Luque Vera. Reprinted by permission.)

have apparently decorative elements serve a narrative function, and a stylistic insertion of caricatural elements in dramatic situations.

"My comics (since I am my own scriptwriter) are born written," Nazario states. "I like realistic stories about scabrous characters and milieus (homosexuals, transvestites, dandies, etc.), told in a minute and baroque form. I study expressions, movements, and gestures. The locales have to be appropriate to each situation and each character, with great attention given to details. I draw in black-and-white with the pen, and later add colors. Being self-taught, I have difficulties keeping the proper perspective and anatomical proportions, although I delight in foreshortening, down- and up-shots."

In his work *Salome* (1981), published in the magazine *El Vibora*, Nazario succeeded in endowing the famous biblical story with a singular lyricism, both in its narrative structure and in its graphic depictions, transforming his very expressive limitations into the facets of an authentic personal style in which the imaginative use of color burned bright.

It is, however, with *Anarcoma* (which first appeared in the pages of *El Vibora* in 1979-80) that Nazario best defines himself, in a production that extends to date to two long narratives and several short stories. As Maurice Horn notes in *Sex in the Comics*, "Firmly set amid the gay underlife of Barcelona, with its hero a transvestite private eye, *Anarcoma* shows just how far the comics have traveled." In counterpoint to *Salome*, which was a distillation of the Nazario "look," *Anarcoma* is less a stylistic exercise than a statement of position. With this series, Nazario appropriates many of the themes of heterosexual comics (and the heterosexual world), and ironically twists and amplifies them to absurdity. The author's brutally provoking attitude reclaims realism for the gay universe, a realism adapted to the mindset of that universe. Through his lead character, a transvestite, and the seedy characters who surround him, Nazario converts the elements of violence, blood, crime, and sadism into so many dream-motifs. Despite his fantastic connotations, the protagonist of *Anarcoma* reveals himself as a living and corrosive character, the extravagant mirror of a world in disintegration.

At any rate *Anarcoma* becomes, perhaps in spite of its own intentions, less savage and cruel than it first appears. In the first place the characters live and assault one another within the closed boundaries of a peripheral milieu whose extremism unavoidably distances the reader. In addition, the plot and its multiple vagaries seem to parody the very universe they purport to mirror, thus sending up even the most blood-curdling sequences with a humorous wink in the direction of the reader. Finally, Nazario's graphic style—midway between rigidity and pointillism and further embellished by the artist's use of color—ends up smoothing out the series of savage acts depicted in his tales with its ironically lush and ornamental look. All this contributes to make *Anarcoma* a highly personal as well as a morally ambiguous work.

published in installments in *El Vibora* before publication in book form; *Mujeres Raras* ("Freakish Women"), an anthology volume reprinting diverse stories published in *El Vibora*.

EXHIBITIONS: "El original y la reproduccion," Galeria Brossoli, Barcelona, 1981.

SIDELIGHTS: Nazario received his initial artistic inspiration from the American magazine *Mad*, and later from American underground comics. He encountered hardships as he tried to have his works published during the last years of dictator Francisco Franco's regime. What immediately distinguished Nazario's production was the ferocity with which he treated sexual themes, including those aspects considered most socially heterodox. He has applied the violence of his narratives and descriptions to traditions of the Catholic church, but mostly to daily life in society's most marginal and dispossessed precincts. Progressively evolving from his underground influences, Nazario's current esthetic individuality shows a tendency towards graphic minuteness, a wish to encompass all of reality through extremely detailed panels, an intelligent use of varied angles of vision, theatrical and scenographic treatment of compositions, a concern to

BIOGRAPHICAL/CRITICAL SOURCES: Javier Coma, editor, *Historia de los Comics*, Toutain, Barcelona, 1983; *Comics Journal*, October, 1984; Maurice Horn, *Sex in the Comics*, Chelsea House, 1985.

A panel from *Salome* (© 1983, Nazario Luque Vera. Reprinted by permission.)

M

ROBERT R. MALONE

MALONE, Robert R.   1933-

PERSONAL: Born August 8, 1933, in McColl, S.C.; son of Robert Roy (a department store manager) and Anne (Matthews) Malone; married Cynthia Enid Taylor, February 26, 1956; children: Brendan Trevor. *Education:* University of North Carolina, B.A., 1955; University of Chicago, M.F.A., 1958; post-graduate work at University of Iowa, 1959. *Home and studio:* 600 Chapman St., Edwardsville, Ill. 62025. *Agent:* Merida Galleries, 2007 Frankfort Ave., Louisville, Ky. 40206.

CAREER: Art instructor, Union University, Jackson, Tenn., 1959-60; art instructor, Lambuth College, Jackson, 1959-61; assistant professor, 1961-67, associate professor of art, 1967-68, Wesleyan College, Macon, Ga.; associate professor of art, West Virginia University, Morgantown, W.Va., 1968-70; head of printmaking program, 1970—, associate professor, 1970-75, professor of art, 1975—, Southern Illinois University, Edwardsville, Ill. Visiting artist at many universities.

AWARDS, HONORS: Over thirty purchase awards nationwide. Named University Research Scholar by Southern Illinois University, 1975-76 and 1984-85.

EXHIBITIONS: Over thirty one-man shows, including those at University of Wisconsin, Madison, Wis., 1968; Contemporary Art Center, Oklahoma City, Okla., 1968; De Cinque Gallery of Fine Art, Hollywood, Fla., 1968 and 1971; Gallery Illien, Atlanta, Ga., 1969; C. M. Russell Museum, Great Falls, N.D., 1973; Illinois State Museum, Springfield, Ill., 1974; Sheldon Swope Art Gallery, Terre Haute, Ind., 1979; Elliot Smith Gallery, St. Louis, Mo., 1985; Merida Galleries, Louisville, Ky., 1985; and Prairie House, Springfield, 1985.

Work exhibited in over two-hundred-fifty group shows, including "15th National Print Exhibition," Brooklyn Museum, Brooklyn, N.Y., 1966; "Graphics '68: Recent American Prints," University of Kentucky, Lexington, Ky., 1968; "Biennale Internationale de L'Estampe," Musee d'Art Moderne, Paris, France, 1970; "Five Contemporary Printmakers," Northern Arizona University, Flagstaff, Ariz., 1974; "Art Expo '79," Basel, Switzerland, 1979; "Showcase 1983," Art Center Association, Louisville, Ky., 1983; St. Louis Arts Festival, St. Louis, Mo., 1985; "Currents 29: Drawing in St. Louis," St. Louis Art Museum, 1985.

Work represented in permanent collections of Smithsonian Institution, U.S. Information Agency, Baltimore Museum of Art, California Palace of the Legion of Honor, Indianapolis Museum of Art, Library of Congress, New York Public Library, Philadelphia Museum of Art, Ringling Museum of Art, Illinois State Museum, Cleveland Museum of Art, Art Institute of Chicago, and many others.

WORK IN PROGRESS: A series of humorous prints with art and artists as its theme, funded by Southern Illinois University's office of research and projects; a re-examination of large-scale group portraits for the 1980s.

SIDELIGHTS: Although his style has changed a good deal over the years and influences as varied as the Renaissance and Baroque masters, Paul Gauguin and Henri de Toulouse-Lautrec, the Surrealists, and the Pop movement of the 1960s and '70s have contributed to his artistic evolution, Robert Malone's primary interest has always been the human figure. However, in his recent drawings, prints, and paintings, he has pushed beyond the limitations imposed by so specific a focus in such a way as to proclaim the expressive potential of a minimalist approach. Using only human figures in sparsely detailed to empty environments, the play of light and shadow, and idiosyncratic spatial arrangements, he finds it possible to create art that is at once didactic in

"Undirected Activity," a charcoal drawing in the collection of the artist (© 1984, Robert R. Malone. Reprinted by permission.)

intent and participatory in impact. He achieves these effects by fusing a disciplined technique in the construction of his curiously alienated crowd scenes and a philosopher's concern with its underlying social dynamics.

Malone is clearly a meticulous draftsman, exhibiting a fine line honed by years of development, and he understands well the uses of light. He is also a skilled photographer, a talent which figures importantly in his work as he uses his camera for research. But his photo-based work, according to critic John Paul Wolf, "is more personal and emotional than photographically correct," a quality that sets him apart from his "photorealist" colleagues. The mechanics of assembling one of his groupings involves selecting from among hundreds of candid snaps a number of figures whose attitudes, postures, and senses of movement especially appeal to him. These become the basis for a series of small-scale sketches in which the artist experiments with various arrangements. When an acceptable scheme has been worked out, he begins working up the much larger finished piece in whatever medium (charcoal, oil, or print) he has selected. "The figures often contrast size, shape, age, sex, attire, and movement," the artist told *CGA*; "I enjoy juxtaposing

athletes, political types, children, musicians, photographers and ordinary people. There is usually a element of humor in the work. The various figures never look at one another and they often appear to be moving right into one another with total indifference."

Eccentric as it sounds, however, this technique cannot fully explain the cumulative effect Malone's work produces. Its peculiar impact, in fact, goes back to the philosophical notion that provided the artist his original inspiration: the concept of separate realities. By snatching different individuals out of widely varying contexts and transplanting them, complete with their individual time-space auras (represented by their seeming obliviousness to one another), Malone states an eternal verity in a fresh way. Whether it is called egoism, alienation, isolation, or individuality, Malone's graphic presentation of the phenomenon allows the viewer to draw his own conclusions. Is man's essentially unitary nature a tragedy or a comedy, a curse or a blessing? A jury might well be hung on the evidence provided by Malone, who perhaps tips off his personal uncertainty by making occasional appearances (in one instance standing on his head) in his crowds. Wherever one comes down, ultimately, on the philosophical issues involved, there is an undeniable sense of fun in Malone's odd-lot groupings—the same sort of fun one associates with a hard-to-pin-down day in early spring when people unwittingly express their personalities by the way they dress: the deep-dyed, mistrustful pessimists in furs, mufflers and gloves; the impractically optimistic wearing tee-shirts and shorts—each inhabiting his or her own personal reality.

BIOGRAPHICAL/CRITICAL SOURCES: Howard Derrickson, "Malone Finally Gets St. Louis Exhibit," *St. Louis Globe-Democrat*, January 19-20, 1985; John Paul Wolf, "Memorable Canvases in Elliot Smith Gallery Show," *West End World*, February 7, 1985; Diane Heilenman, "Reviews," *Louisville Courier-Journal*, March 10, 1985; Les Krantz, *American Artists*, Facts on File, 1985; *Drawing in St. Louis* (exhibition catalogue), St. Louis Art Museum, 1985.

* * *

MARGULIES, Jimmy 1951-

PERSONAL: Surname rhymes with "Hercules"; born October 8, 1951, in New York, N.Y.; son of Henry N. (a graphic designer) and Miriam (a fashion illustrator; maiden name, Horowitz) Margulies; married Martha Golub, May 21, 1978; children: Elana, David. *Education:* Carnegie-Mellon University, B.F.A., 1973. *Religion:* Jewish. *Home:* Houston, Tex. *Office:* Houston Post, 4747 Southwest Freeway, Houston, Tex. 77001. *Syndicate:* United Feature Syndicate, 200 Part Ave., New York, N.Y. 10166.

CAREER: Cartoonist, Rothco Cartoons, 1973-85; artist, CETA, New York, 1978-80; cartoonist, *Journal Newspapers, Army Times*, Springfield Va., 1980-84; editorial cartoonist, *Houston Post*, 1984—. Work distributed nationally by United Feature Syndicate, 1985—.

MEMBER: Association of American Editorial Cartoonists.

AWARDS, HONORS: George Washington Honor Medal, Freedoms Foundation at Valley Forge, 1980 and 1981; George Washington Honor Certificate, Freedoms Founda-

JIMMY MARGULIES

tion, 1982; second place, National Newspaper Association, 1982; second place, Virginia Press Association, 1982; first and third places, National Newspaper Association, 1983; third place, Virginia Press Association, 1983; first place, Maryland-D.C.-Delaware Press Association, 1983; second place, National Newspaper Association, 1984; first place, Virginia Press Association, 1984; second place, Maryland-D.C.-Delaware Press Association, 1984; second place, editorial cartoons, International Salon of Cartoons, Montreal Pavillion of Humor, Montreal, Canada, 1985; Western Hemisphere Award from Population Institute, Washington, D.C., 1985; Global Media Award, Population Institute, 1985.

WRITINGS—Contributor: Charles Brooks, editor, *Best Editorial Cartoons of the Year*, Pelican, 1977-85; Carew Papritz, editor, *100 Watts: The James Watt Memorial Cartoon Collection*, Khyber Press, 1983; *ReaganComics*, Khyber Press, 1984.

Author of "American Drawing Board" column for *Target: The Political Cartoon Quarterly*, spring, 1983—.

WORK IN PROGRESS: Scheduled for publication in the 1986 edition of *Best Editorial Cartoons of the Year*.

SIDELIGHTS: Editorial cartoonists use different methods to make their points: some employ pathos, others melodrama. Jimmy Margulies uses humor as his weapon. "I feel as though the reader will remember more what's funny than what he thinks is politically correct," he explains. "In this way, humor reaches out to people who may not agree with you."

The choice of editorial cartooning as a means to "reach out to people" with his political ideas came naturally to Jimmy Margulies, the articulate son of two artists, who has drawn since he was a child. Growing up during the revolutionary 1960s and 1970s, he became acutely aware of social issues as a student, and while studying graphic design at Carnegie-Mellon University in Pittsburgh he turned inevitably to the medium as a combination of his interests in art and politics and an expression of his distinctively wry humor.

In his early twenties, Margulies launched his career with Rothco Cartoons, which he describes as "a means of getting exposure but unfortunately not much money." In the next few years his work was to appear in the *New York Post, Boston Herald-American, U.S. News and World Report, Newsday,* and many other national periodicals. In June, 1975, he won the National Cartoonists Association-Johnson Wax contest with a humorous drawing for Shout stain remover (a crowd of Israelites shouting "Author! Author!" at Moses as he carries the tablets down Mount Sinai), and at the end of that year worked with *New York Times* editorial cartoonist Ranan Lurie in his studio in Greenwich, Conn. In 1978 Margulies began contributing political cartoons regularly to Suburban Features, a division of Newspaper Enterprise Association (N.E.A.) distributed to two hundred fifty papers. Work at the *Bergen Record* in New Jersey, *Army Times,* and the Virginia and Maryland *Journals* extended and deepened his experience from 1980 to 1984.

His witty political observations won Margulies the post of editorial cartoonist with the *Houston Post* in 1984, although that newspaper was seeking someone with a more conservative political philosophy than the irreverent young cartoonist. "My humor allowed me to get the job," the artist modestly states, but he has held it with growing national popularity ever since.

An editorial cartoon by Jimmy Margulies (© 1984, *Houston Post.* Reprinted by permission.)

An editorial cartoon by Jimmy Margulies (© 1985, *Houston Post*-United Feature Syndicate. Reprinted by permission of United Feature Syndicate.)

The *Post* has allowed Margulies a free hand with his commentary, even when his cartoons express ideas opposed to the paper's opinions, and this is one of the features he most values in his position. Editor Lynn Ashby "went so far as to tell me that if they printed an editorial supporting Reagan, and I called the President a horse's ass in a cartoon printed right next to it, that was okay with him," Margulies reports. His stinging criticisms of the present administration, published by his generally moderate-conservative newspaper, have repeatedly proved the truth of his assertion. He shows his editor from one to a handful of rough sketches every day, and reports that he almost never fails to score with at least one.

Margulies' national reputation has grown steadily since his appointment to the *Post*, and his work has been included in every issue of Charles Brooks's *Best Editorial Cartoons of the Year* since 1977. Among his favorite targets have been U.S. Interior Secretary Watt and President Reagan. Three of his cartoons appeared in *100 Watts: The James Watt Memorial Cartoon Collection* in 1983 (along with his sketch of Watt on the back cover), and he was featured the next year in the same publisher's *ReaganComics*. In both of these collections, his contributions have been among the most cutting, and among the wittiest.

Although he stresses the humorous aspect of his work, Margulies is as hard-hitting as his more solemn colleagues. When he shows James Watt trampling the shrubbery on his way into the Department of the Interior or depicts a submarine-launched missile next to President Reagan and asks "Which dangerous warhead is it possible to recall?" he makes his point as powerfully as if he were writing a stinging editorial. Indeed, as he points out, for him "a cartoon is a graphic editorial." The fun he pokes at corruption and pollution takes a broad and jocular form sometimes bordering on slapstick, but it does not conceal the genuine indignation that underlies his graphic metaphors.

If Margulies has become increasingly well-known through his national syndication for comments on national and international issues, he has not abandoned his local scene, to which he feels a primary responsibility. "A lot of cartoonists feel that local subjects are unglamorous and small-time," he says, ". . . [but] a lot of readers will respond best to the local stuff. It affects them more directly; I've always gotten my strongest response from readers that way, and I do at least one or two local ones a week."

Aware that an editorial cartoonist must remain in close contact with what is happening at all levels, Margulies begins his day early (he usually arrives at his office around 8:30), mails out prints of that day's cartoon to his syndicate clients, and devotes the rest of the morning to reading the *New York Times, Houston Post*, and its local competitor, the *Chronicle*. At night he never misses the television news because, as he explains, "TV supplies so may important visual images." In addition to the news, Margulies stays abreast of events in his own profession. Since its first issues, *Target: The Political Cartoon Quarterly*, the only journal devoted to the field, has carried trade news by Margulies, and since its seventh issue, in spring, 1983, he has been writing a regular column for it. "The American Drawing Board" reports such trade news as job changes, libel suits, and exhibitions.

Among the most newsworthy items he has had to report in recent years was his own trip to the People's Republic of China in November, 1985. The trip was a prize he won from the Population Institute, which voted him their Global Media Award in that year as "the best cartoonist in the Western Hemisphere concerning population control." The 1984 cartoon which took the prize showed Uncle Sam smugly and proudly handing out cigars among representatives of other countries distributing material for population control.

Margulies draws in a bold, free style fitting to the freewheeling humor of his cartoons. His strong, dynamic compositions have ample areas of solid black and powerful, emphatic contrasts, and his characters all have the giant noses and loose features of traditional gag-cartoon figures, clearly one of the cartoonist's major stylistic influences. Another influence which he freely acknowledges is that of Mike Peters, whose spirit is very much akin to Margulies's. "His irreverent, off-the-wall humor really turns me on," Margulies admits.

For all the spontaneity and freedom of Margulies' line and slapdash air of his images, however, there is great internal control in his technique which can be seen from year to year growing crisper and more assured. A careful, methodical worker, Margulies draws with great deliberation and discipline. He reports: "I do a fairly tight drawing with pencil on tracing paper. Then I tape a piece of bristol board over it on my light table to do the finished drawing. Occasionally I'll use a Uniball micro ballpoint pen for finer lines. All of my lettering is drawn with felt-tip pens of one sort or another."

The results of this controlled workmanship are often scathing assaults on what Margulies finds wrong in the world as he sees it. The cartoons are always direct and to the point; Margulies never uses obscure symbols or belabors abstract, theoretical points. "Something too ideological simply turns me off," he says. "I prefer to reflect the inherent ridiculousness of a particular situation." Margulies has shown himself able again and again to find that ridiculousness in a wide range of situations. Even such emotion-laden topics as the racism of the Moral Majority can suggest something funny to him. Although his cartoons are often prompted by outrage, their impact is balanced and their effect increased by the artist's sure eye for the absurd.

BIOGRAPHICAL/CRITICAL SOURCES: National Cartoonists Society Album, Museum of Cartoon Art, 1980; Jerome Weeks, "Margulies—The Houston Post," Cartoonist Profiles, June, 1985; Houston Post Magazine, October 27, 1985.

—Sketch by Dennis Wepman

*   *   *

MARTIN, Don (Edward) 1931-

PERSONAL: Born May 18, 1931, in Passaic, N.J.; son of Wilbur Lawrence (a school-supply salesman) and Helen Henrietta (Husselrath) Martin; married Rosemary Troet-schal, December 14, 1956 (divorced January, 1976); married Norma Haimes (a librarian, sculptress, and writer), August 23, 1979; children: (first marriage) Max. Education: Attended Newark School of Fine and Industrial Art, 1948-51; Pennsylvania Academy of Fine Arts, Philadelphia, Pa., 1952. Politics: Democrat. Religion: "Wasp." Home: Miami, Fla. Studio: P.O. Box 1330, Miami, Fla. 33243.

CAREER: Free-lance commercial illustrator, paste-up artist, and cartoonist, creating record album covers, advertising magazine art, magazine spots, and greeting card art, 1955—; cartoonist, Mad (a magazine), New York, N.Y., 1957—. Set designer and collaborator in choreography for comic ballet Heads Up, New World Festival of the Arts, Miami, Fla., 1982.

MEMBER: Graphic Artists Guild, National Cartoonists Society, Cartoonists Association, Authors Guild.

AWARDS, HONORS: Ignatz Award from Orlando Comicon, 1980; Special Features Awards from National Cartoonists Society, 1982 and 1983.

WRITINGS—All original collections of gag cartoons and cartoon stories except as noted: (With E. Solomon Rosenblum) Don Martin Steps Out, New American Library, 1962; (with Rosenblum) Don Martin Bounces Back, New American Library, 1963; (with Rosenblum) Don Martin Drops Thirteen Stories, New American Library, 1965; (with Dick DeBartolo, Phil Hahn, and Jack Hanrahan) The Mad Adventures of Captain Klutz, edited by Nick Meglin, New American Library, 1967; (with DeBartolo) Mad's Don Martin Cooks Up More Tales, New American Library, 1969; (with DeBartolo) Mad's Don Martin Comes On Strong, edited by Meglin, New American Library, 1971; Mad's Don Martin Carries On, edited by Meglin, Warner, 1973; The Completely Mad Don Martin (reprints from Mad), Warner, 1974; (with DeBartolo) Don Martin Steps Further Out, edited by Meglin, Warner, 1975; Don Martin Forges Ahead, edited by Meglin, Warner, 1977; (with DeBartolo, Edwing, Jacobs, and John Gibbons) Mad's Don Martin Digs Deeper, edited by Meglin, Warner, 1979; Don Martin Grinds Ahead. Warner, 1981; Captain Klutz II, edited by Meglin, Warner, 1983; Don Martin Sails Ahead, Warner, 1986.

WORK IN PROGRESS: Compiling collections of original gag cartoons and cartoon stories for publication in Don Martin Collection and Captain Klutz, the Triumphant; a children's book, The Biggest Pie-Eating Contest in the World.

SIDELIGHTS: Few cartoonists have become as thoroughly identified with a single periodical as Don Martin has with Mad magazine, and few have developed styles so distinctively original and personal as his. Its outrageously slapstick and often violent nature have earned Martin the proud sobriquet of "Mad's maddest artist," along with the undying devotion of millions of gleeful young readers.

A childhood in a peaceful, pastoral setting in New Jersey seems an unlikely background for the outlandish humor of Martin's cartoon stories, but the artist grew up in the rural town of Brookside, among the trees and gentle streams outside of Paterson. Although it has become a suburb of that city now, it was still wooded countryside when Martin left it to go to school in Newark in 1948.

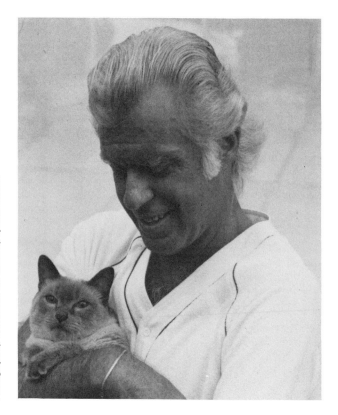

DON MARTIN

During his idyllic childhood, Martin drew continuously, though with no clear ambition to make a career of it at first. As the son of a school-supply salesman, he always had an unlimited supply of pads, pens, pencils, and erasers around, and his mother always encouraged him by proudly saving his drawings. Sketching was, from his earliest days, as natural and spontaneous an action as walking or speaking. He kept an illustrated diary and at age twelve with a friend produced a newspaper, all hand-done and seen only by its two creators. His pleasure in reading the comics in the newspapers at first led to no very clear ambitions to enter the field himself.

Among his favorite cartoons were *Krazy Kat, Bringing Up Father, Polly and Her Pals,* and *Toonerville Folks,* but few evidences of these early tastes can be noted in his own work. The first cartoon characters he can remember deliberately copying were Mickey Mouse and the Big Bad Wolf, which he duplicated at the age of five, but he was to grow thoroughly out of any tendency to imitativeness, and no trace of Disney can be found in *Mad*'s maddest artist today.

Perhaps more significant to the style that was to emerge was an early taste for animated cartoons, especially the Warner Brothers cartoons featuring the Road Runner and Sylvester the Cat, whom he considers "the funniest cartoon character." Among his live motion-picture favorites he numbers the Three Stooges and Laurel and Hardy. The robust and cheerful mayhem of these childhood tastes can be clearly seen in the artist's later cartoons.

Martin's artistic education was conventional and substantial. His three years at the Newark School of Fine and Industrial Art and his year at the Pennsylvania Academy of Fine Arts

in Philadelphia prepared him to realize his early ambitions of becoming a magazine illustrator or a serious painter. He submitted his work to the *Saturday Evening Post* and *Collier's* while he studied, but he never sold a single drawing.

Still, he was not discouraged. He stayed in school and painted, and when he graduated he worked at art-related jobs and waited for a break. He did window displays and sold picture frames, and in 1955 moved to New York where he got a job doing paste-ups. Determined to make a living at art, he returned to the humorous drawings he had done as a child and began selling them free-lance. He placed drawings with magazines as spot illustrations and advertising art, but not gag cartoons. "They were very flat, design-type drawings that I did with a crowquill pen, using very thin lines," he reports. "They were humorous, and I had some success with them." His taste for jazz (which is still the background music in his studio) led him to offer some work to record companies for album covers, and some of his cover art for Miles Davis, Stan Getz, and Sonny Stitt records is still being used, although he sold the art outright for fifty dollars and receives no payment for it now.

His work from 1955 to 1957 ranged over the entire spectrum of commercial art: in addition to album covers and spot illustrations, he did fantasy art for such science-fiction magazines as *Galaxy* and *Fantasy and Science Fiction,* he sold work to greeting-card companies, and he did advertising flyers. For a time he worked for a commercial art studio in downtown Manhattan, on Canal Street. His boss there, Bill Levison, liked his work and recognized its special, zany quality. *Mad* magazine had recently opened its office on Lafayette Street, a few blocks away from Canal, and one day in 1957 Levison selflessly suggested that Martin visit them on his lunch hour and show them his portfolio. The rest is art history.

Martin knew and liked *Mad,* which was just changing from a comic-book format to that of a magazine. The editor, Albert B. Feldstein, couldn't find a place for Martin's work in the new magazine, but he liked it enough to ask the shy young artist to try an illustrated article in the broad parodic

"Moses on the Mount," a humorous drawing (© 1981, Don Martin. Reprinted by permission.)

A humorous drawing (© 1985, Don Martin. Reprinted by permission.)

style of *Mad*. Martin did a humorous piece on etiquette and a take-off on Norman Vincent Peale's inspirational writing, and Feldstein bought them. But he did not feel that he could run them as they were, since he found the art too tight and fussy, so he asked Martin to loosen it up. Martin complied—so much so, he reports now, that "you could barely see the lines." Feldstein was appalled and said it was unusable. Desperately, Martin asked for a third chance at it, and in one all-night session developed the style he uses today. "That's what I want," Feldstein exclaimed when he saw Martin's work, and that's what *Mad* has been giving a delighted public ever since.

The first issue of *Mad* in a magazine format carried Martin's work, and he has been an integral part of the publication's image ever since. He has had a drawing in every issue since the first in 1957 except one, a recent number which omitted his cartoon by mistake. From the beginning Martin has been one of *Mad*'s best known and loved artists. "He's always pulled the most mail," *Mad* editor Nick Meglin reports. "He's still the most popular."

Martin's first book, done in association with *Mad*, was *Don Martin Steps Out*, in 1962. In it, Al Feldstein explained Martin's appeal in an introductory note: "[Martin's] five or ten million loyal fans . . . love him because his style is unique, because his outlook on life is especially appropriate to our times, because his sequences have the same outrageous physical impact as the old silent-movie greats—Charlie Chaplin, Buster Keaton, the Keystone Kops. But mainly, they love him because he is funny."

The influence of the silent clowns of the movies—along with Red Skelton and the Three Stooges—is obvious in the action of Martin's cartoons, and many of his characters' physical idiosyncrasies can be traced to cinematic prototypes as well. The delicately extended little finger of even his biggest louts recalls Oliver Hardy's poised pinky; the giant feet out to the sides of the bodies clearly draws on Charlie Chaplin's peculiar stance; but nothing in real life can possibly account for the massively prognathous jaws, the huge mouths, the eyes so close that they meet in the middle of their faces and sometimes change places, or the toes that turn up or down as though hinged to their feet. Among the comic artists whose influence Martin acknowledges in his graphic style may be numbered Saul Steinberg and the *Saturday Evening Post* cartoonists of the 1940s. Something of the wildness of John Gallagher, the precision of Tom Henderson, and the abso-

lute freedom of Virgil Partch can be detected in Don Martin's work.

The thirteen paperback books of original gag cartoons and cartoon stories and the one collection of reprints from *Mad* which Martin published between 1963 and 1986 sold over seven million copies in the United States and have been published all over Europe and South America in a dozen languages. Their popularity worldwide attests to the universal appeal of the unfettered spirit of their madcap art. Such preposterous characters as the devious, unshaven little Fester Bestertester and the gigantic, pinheaded oaf Karbunkle who accompanies him in his adventures, the eternally inept superhero Captain Klutz, and the irresistibly named psychiatrist Dr. Fruitcake P. Fonebone have all entered the shared vocabulary of the international community of youth.

To his far-ranging work in cartoons, advertising art, magazine illustration, record-album covers, book covers, billboard art, greeting-card art, and T-shirt design, Don Martin added an unexpected contribution to the ballet in 1982 in his home city of Miami, Florida. Wally Lord, the artistic director of Miami's Fusion Dance Company, called on Martin to collaborate with him on a comic ballet for the New World Festival of the Arts. *Heads Up* premiered in June, 1982, to generally good reviews, and added a new feather to Martin's already heavily feathered cap.

Martin works very deliberately to produce the effect of fluid grace and spontaneity for which he is so much admired. Every drawing is the end result of many carefully worked-out steps and represents far more labor than the zany appearance suggests. The artist begins with a rough pencil or ink sketch on cheap bond, which he sends for the editor's approval. When he has an okay, he redraws it on better paper with a blue Col-Erase pencil, goes over it with a black felt-tip pen, and traces the draft to Strathmore four-ply bristol board over a light box. The finished drawing is executed with a soft pencil, inked with either a Gillott pen point, if he feels a need for a fine, flexible line, or a Hunt Bowl point, and then filled in with a Speedball point. He puts in shadows with colored ink (sepia mixed with blue or siena) and goes over this with a watercolor wash. All of this careful, methodical labor produces the fine, free, swinging line that appears the effusion of a moment and has sustained Martin's reputation as *Mad*'s maddest artist. The method in his madness is no secret among his admiring colleagues.

One Tuesday Morning, a humor page by Don Martin (©
1972, EC Publications. Reprinted by permission.)

Don Martin has never pretended to make a philosophical
point in his art. Although *Mad* sometimes refers to itself as a
journal of satire, he is no satirist and has no message to
deliver. "The purpose of my cartoons," he states unequivo-
cally, "has simply been to be comical, both visually and in
content. I have never intended any social or political
commentary and have only wanted to be funny—the sillier
the better. The anatomical distortions are the way they are
because they strike me as funny. . . I try to amuse myself
with my cartoons and fortunately they amuse other people
as well." Martin's level of amusement is basic; he goes over
no one's head, and excludes no one, and he would be the last
to claim to appeal to, or to possess, a sophisticated taste.
"It's a silly sense of humor," he confesses. "I love Laurel
and Hardy's slapstick and nonsense. Doors slamming in
people's faces are fun. Pies in the face are fun." Fortunately
for Don Martin and *Mad*, millions of readers all over the
world agree with him.

*BIOGRAPHICAL/CRITICAL SOURCES: The World En-
cyclopedia of Cartoons*, Chelsea House, 1980; *Contemporary
Authors*, Vol. 101, Gale, 1981; *Cartoonists Profiles*. December, 1981, and March, 1982; *Who's Who in America 1984-
85*, Marquis, 1984; *Men of Achievement*, Cambridge (England), 1983; Jay Boyar, "The Real Don Martin," *Orlando
Sentinel*, May 12, 1985.

—*Sketch by Dennis Wepman*

McCLOUD, Scott
See McLEOD, Scott Willard

* * *

McLAREN, Norman 1914-1987

PERSONAL: Born April 11, 1914, in Stirling, Scotland;
immigrated to New York, N.Y., 1939; immigrated to Canada,
c. 1941; became citizen; died of a heart attack, January 27,
1987, near Montreal, Canada; son of William (in house
decorating business) and Jean (Smith) McLaren. *Education:*
Attended Glasgow School of Art, Glasgow, Scotland, 1931-36.
Office: National Film Board, Box 6100, Montreal, Quebec,
Canada H3C 3H5.

CAREER: Animation and documentary director, General
Post Office (G.P.O.) Film Unit, London, England, 1937-39;
animation director and producer in New York City, 1939-41;
filmmaker and director, National Film Board of Canada,
Montreal, Quebec, Canada, 1941-84. Taught visual aids
techniques on assignment for UNESCO in China, 1949-50,
and India, 1953-54.

MEMBER: ASIFA, Canadian Music Composers Association.

AWARDS, HONORS: More than three hundred awards for
films, including first prize in art category from International
Film Festival, Venice, Italy, 1950, for *Begone Dull Care;*
Academy Award for Best Documentary Short from Academy

Photograph by National Film Board of Canada. Courtesy of Norman McLaren.

NORMAN McLAREN

A frame from *Pas de Deux* **by Norman McLaren** (© 1968, National Film Board of Canada. Reprinted by permission.)

of Motion Picture Arts and Sciences, 1952, for *Neighbours;* Grand Prix ("Palme d'Or") from International Film Festival, Cannes, France, and first prize from British Film Academy, both 1955, for *Blinkity-Blank;* first prize in experimental and avant-garde category from International Film Festival, Venice, 1957, for *A Chairy Tale;* Bronze Peacock from New Delhi International Film Festival, New Delhi, India, 1965, for *Canon; Pas de Deux* named Outstanding Film of the Year by London Film Festival, London, England, 1968.

Recipient of first Royal Canadian Academy of Arts Medal, 1963, Canada Council Medal, 1966, Medal of Service of the Order of Canada, 1968, Outstanding Achievement Award of the Public Service of Canada, 1971, Molson Prize from Canada Council, 1971, Order of Canada, 1973, Prix Albert-Tessier from Government of Quebec, 1982.

Honorary LL.D. from McMaster University, 1966, and Brock University, 1969; honorary Ph.D. from University of Montreal, 1971, and York University, 1972.

WRITINGS: (Illustrator) *Six Musical Forms* (album of drawings with text by Marthe Blackburn and musical score

and recording by Maurice Blackburn), Jeunesses Musicales du Canada, 1967; *The Drawings of Norman McLaren* (collection), Tundra Books, 1975; *McLaren* (photographic brochure), National Film Board of Canada. Also creator of two portfolios of serigraphs for Graphic Guild (Montreal).

FILMS—Student work using experimental techniques: *Seven till Five,* 1934; *Camera Makes Whoopee,* 1935; *Colour Cocktail,* 1935.

Independent films: (Director) *Hell Unltd.,* 1936; (cameraman) *Defense of Madrid,* 1936.

Director: *Book Bargain,* G.P.O. Film Unit, 1937; *News for the Navy,* G.P.O. Film Unit, 1938; *Love on the Wing* (animated), G.P.O. Film Unit, 1939; *The Obedient Flame,* Film Centre (London), 1939.

Experimental films made independently for the Guggenheim Museum: *Dots,* 1939; *Loops,* 1940; *Scherzo,* 1940; *Stars and Stripes,* 1940; *Boogie-Doodle,* 1941.

Animated or experimental films, unless otherwise indicated; all for the National Film Board of Canada: *Mail Early for Chirstmas,* 1941; *V for Victory,* 1942; *Five for Four,* 1942; *Hen-Hop,* 1942; *Dollar Dance,* 1943; *Keep Your Mouth Shut,* 1944; *C'est l'aviron,* 1944; *Alouette,* 1944; *La-haut sur ces montagnes,* 1945; *A Little Phantasy,* 1946; *Hoppity-Pop,* 1946; *Fiddle-de-dee,* 1947; *La poulette grise,* 1947; *A Phantasy,* 1948; *Begone Dull Care,* 1948.

Around Is Around (stereoscopic), 1950-51; *Now Is the Time* (stereoscopic), 1951-52; *Neighbours* (human figures), 1952; *Two Bagatelles* (human figures), 1952; *Blinkity-Blank,* 1955; *Rhythmetic,* 1956; *A Chairy Tale,* 1957; *Le Merle,* 1958; *Short and Suite,* 1950; *Serenal,* 1959; *Mail Early for Christmas,* 1959; *Lines Vertical,* 1960; *Opening Speech* (human figure), 1960; *New York Light-board,* 1961; *New York Light-board Record,* 1961; *Lines Horizontal,* 1962; *Canon* (human figures), 1964; *Mosaic,* 1965; *Pas de Deux* (human figures), 1967; *Spheres,* 1969; *Synchrony,* 1971; *Ballet Adagio,* 1972; *Pinscreen* (documentary), 1973; *Animated Motions, Paris 1 to 5,* 1976-78; *Narcissus* (ballet), 1983.

Also made a short feature for television for National Broadcasting Co., Inc. (NBC-TV), 1939. McLaren is subject of *The Eye Hears, the Ear Sees* by British Broadcasting Corp. (BBC-TV), 1970.

EXHIBITIONS—All one-man shows unless otherwise indicated: Art Gallery of Toronto (drawings), 1964; (group show) Isaac's Gallery, Toronto, 1964; Annecy Film Festival, Annecy, France (drawings and paintings), 1965; Montreal International Film Festival (drawings and paintings), 1967, show subsequently traveled to Poland, Czechoslovakia, Belgium, and other European countries; Guggenheim Museum, New York City (graphic works), 1969-70; Philadelphia Museum of Art, Philadelphia, Pa. (drawings, paintings, and films), 1973.

Drawings in permanent collection of National Gallery of Canada, Ottawa. Did four luminous polaroid rotating "sculptures" for the Canadian Pavilion at the 1967 Montreal World's Fair.

Film retrospectives: Annecy Animation Film Festival, Annecy, France, 1965; Montreal International Film Festival, 1967; Guggenheim Museum, New York City, 1967-70; and many others in England, Scotland, Canada, the United States, Europe, Japan, and South America.

WORK IN PROGRESS: "Stereoscopic drawings and paintings, straight painting."

SIDELIGHTS: Norman McLaren's was an art of understatement, of simplicity, almost of denial—denial of needless flourishes, superfluous detail, and wasted motion. He reduced the art of animation to its innermost core. "The animated as

A frame from *Ballet Adagio* by Norman McLaren (© 1972, National Film Board of Canada. Reprinted by permission.)

against the actuality film lends itself with peculiar aptness to this stripped-down approach," he once declared at a UNESCO conference "for not only can the background trivia be left out, but the characters themselves can be simplified, stylized, and generalized in such a way as to strengthen and clarify the meaning of the action. Simple matchstick or pictographic figures may behave so vividly, humorously, tragically, or in any other way that, as the film progresses, they may become enriched, complicated characters in the minds of the audience, though at any one moment they remain extremely simple on the surface of the screen." Yet so luminous was the artist's treatment of these simplified elements that his films display a gaiety, an optimism, a cheerfulness that belies the austerity of his means. With McLaren less was indeed more.

Animation had been a fascination with McLaren from his earliest years. As early as 1933, while a student at the Glasgow Art School, he had used the process. He was influenced by the works of Emile Cohl, Georges Melies, Alexandre Alexeieff, and Oskar Fischinger. McLaren was already experimenting with direct drawing on film when he became familiar with the work of New Zealander Len Nye, the acknowledged pioneer in this technique. "Although I did not work in close proximity to Len Nye when at the G.P.O. Film Unit," he later stated, "and although I started direct drawing on film independently of him, his films have always put me in a state of dithering delight and therefore should be counted as a formative influence." At the G.P.O. Film Unit McLaren also worked with John Grierson, the famed documentary filmmaker. It was in New York City, however, that McLaren made his first abstract camera-less films, *Loops, Dots, Scherzo,* and most notably *Stars and Stripes,* all on commission from the Guggenheim Museum. To fit some of his abstract motion patterns, the artist painted percussive musical rhythms directly on the sound-track area of thirty-five millimeter film with pen-and-ink.

A decisive turn in McLaren's life and fortunes came in 1941, when Grierson, who had just been appointed Canadian film commissioner one year earlier, asked his former colleague to create an animation unit at the National Film Board of Canada. It was in Canada then that McLaren perfected his "direct sound" technique which he later explained in these terms: "I draw a lot of little lines on the sound-track area of the . . . film. . . . The number of strokes to the inch controls the pitch of the note; the more, the higher the pitch; the fewer, the lower is the pitch. The size of the stroke controls the loudness. . . . The tone quality, which is the most difficult element to control, is made by the shape of the strokes." Apart from this direct way of making a sound track, McLaren evolved another method to synthesize music, by photographing striated cards, frame by frame, on the sound-track area of the film, using an animation camera. The music for the film *Neighbours* was made in this way, and *Synchrony* demonstrates the method clearly. It is this close union between the patterns on the sound track and the motion created on the film frames that gives McLaren's animation much of its charm and spontaneity.

Existing music was very often McLaren's inspiration for the visuals. His greatest contributions in this field were his successful attempts to paint, draw, and animate visual correlatives to musical forms on film. In the delightful *Canon,* a much-loved and much-awarded film, he used three kinds of animation to illustrate his point. Also in this vein there is *Pas de Deux,* an analysis, at once scientific and lyrical, of the motions and patterns created by two dancers.

These films, which in many ways sum up McLaren's art, had been preceded by his experimental and witty transpositions of French-Canadian folk songs to animation. These animated shorts rightly put the Canadian Film Board on the map and McLaren's name in the first rank of world animators. Done in the 1940s, they played many variations on simple melodies such as *C'est l'aviron, La-haut sur ces montagnes,* and *La poulette grise.* As Ralph Stephenson judiciously noted, "This group of films tends to have a slow mysterious rhythm, . . .the music soft and gentle, all combining to give a mood of muted tranquility." After a ten-year interval the artist came back to this source, animating in 1959 *Le Merle* ("The Blackbird") with his usual flair, using simple paper cut-outs, superimposed on pastel-drawn traveling backgrounds.

Perhaps the one technique for which McLaren has become best known is that of pixilation (or pixillation). It is a technique for animating real people, by shooting their actions not continuously as in a live-action movie, but intermittently and frame-by-frame, so that the end result resembles the crisp stacatto of early animation more than the smooth flow of modern cinematography. "Pililation," the noted animator and author Kit Laybourne avers, "is trick-film at its trickiest"; and its most striking illustration can be seen in the Oscar-winning *Neighbours.* The film starts with a neighbors' quarrel and ends up in genocide and annihilation, without once losing its off-beat sense of humor. McLaren also pioneered in many unusual animation methods; of all the experimental animators, he was perhaps the most scientifically visionary.

McLaren was an inspiration for two generations of experimental and avant-garde animators far beyond Canada's borders. If his best films are, in Stephenson's words, "great works of art," they should not, however, obscure the artist's achievements in other creative fields; let us not forget that McLaren was an award-winning artist, whose serigraphs and drawings are much admired. In a time of almost relentless specialization he was one of the few creators who remain faithful to the humanistic and universalist ideals of the Renaissance artists.

BIOGRAPHICAL/CRITICAL SOURCES: John Halas and Roger Manvell, *The Technique of Film Animation,* Hastings House, 1968; *The International Encyclopedia of Film,* Crown, 1972; Ralph Stephenson, *The Animated Film,* A. S. Barnes, 1973; Maynard Collins, *Norman McLaren,* Canadian Film Institute (Ottawa), 1976; Robert Russett and Cecile Starr, editors, *Experimental Animation: An Illustrated Anthology,* Van Nostrand, 1976; Kit Laybourne, *The Animation Book* Crown, 1979; *The World Encyclopedia of Cartoons,* Chelsea House, 1980; Thomas H. Hoffer, *Animation: A Reference Guide,* Greenwood Press, 1981; Susan Rubin, *Animation: The Art and the Industry,* Prentice-Hall, 1984.

OBITUARY SOURCES: Variety, February 4, 1987.

—Sketch by Maurice Horn

* * *

McLEOD, Scott Willard 1960-
(Scott McCloud)

PERSONAL: Born June 10, 1960, in Boston, Mass.; son of Willard Wise (an inventor and engineer) and Patricia Beatrice (Calneck) McLeod. *Education:* Syracuse University, B.A. (magna cum laude), 1982. *Office:* P.O. Box 698, Tarrytown, N.Y. 10591.

Self-portrait of Scott McLeod ("Scott McCloud"), drawn specially for *Comtemporary Graphic Artists* **(© 1985, Scott McCloud.)**

CAREER: Production department, D.C. Comics, New York City, 1982-83; free-lance comic book artist and writer, 1983—; free-lance journalist and reviewer, 1985—.

AWARDS, HONORS: Russ Manning Promising Newcomer Award, San Diego Comic Convention, 1985; Jack Kirby Comics Industry Award, for best new series of 1984, 1985, for *Zot!*.

WRITINGS—All comic books, written and illustrated under name Scott McCloud: *Zot!*, Numbers 1-10, Eclipse Comics, 1984-85; *Destroy!* (a comic book parody), Eclipse Comics, 1986.

EXHIBITIONS: Four murals displayed at Symphony Hall, Boston, Mass., 1978.

WORK IN PROGRESS: Design work; return of *Zot!*, scheduled for late 1986.

SIDELIGHTS: Scott McCloud is best noted for the creation of *Zot!*, an experimental and highly innovative comic book which, despite its short run (1984-85), attracted wide critical notice, though not great popular success. Zot was an hyperactive teenager who lived in a weirdly futuristic society of multicolored buildings, ray-guns, flying cars, and ubiquitous robots. In the company of another teenager named

Jenny and her obstreperous brother Butch, he started on his long quest for the key to the Doorway at the Edge of the Universe, which involved him in highly imaginative adventures.

In the course of the series the author displayed an exuberant playfulness and a tongue-in-cheek inventiveness that did not go long unnoticed. "McCloud deals in themes and inventions completely his own," Will Jacobs and Gerard Jones wrote in *The Comic Book Heroes*; "There is, for example, the mad artist Arthur Dekker, who, developing a hatred of life after a bout with cancer and a tragic love affair, becomes obsessed with the inorganic decorativeness of Art Deco, transforms himself into an image of the Chrysler Building, and assaults the world with Deco robots and weapons." There were also arrays upon arrays of colorfully attired warrior-robots, a weird variety of teleportation devices, not to mention any number of Kafka-esque transmogrifications (Butch, for instance, got himself turned into a sententious ape).

The individuality of McCloud's themes and compositions may have baffled the majority of comic book readers, although critics responded very favorably to *Zot!* and heaped kudos upon its creator. This could not have come as a great surprise to the twenty-two-year-old artist, who had graduated magna cum laude only a few years earlier, and as a high school student had painted four murals for the Boston Pops orchestra's opening night. ("I was seventeen at

A page from *Zot!* **(© 1984, Scott McCloud.)**

the time," McCloud now says, "so they were pretty wretched.") Nor are McCloud's innovations confined to the artistic field: his penchant for technology, so apparent in his writings, also affected the production of his color comic books, the last six issues of which were laser-scanned.

"I have a voracious interest in all creative uses of media, especially in music," McCloud told *CGA*, "and I try to discover the patterns that run through all forms of expression, in the hope of putting my own art in perspective. I expect to work in a number of different fields in the coming years, but right now comics are getting all my attention." The artist's continued contributions to the field of comics include a satirical comic book published in a black-and-white magazine format, *Destroy!*, as well as the planned revival of *Zot!* in a slightly altered format.

BIOGRAPHICAL/CRITICAL SOURCES: Comics Interview, Numbers 18 and 19, 1985; Will Jacobs and Gerard Jones, *The Comic Book Heroes*, Crown, 1985; Jeff Rovin, *Encyclopedia of Superheroes*, Facts on File, 1985.

* * *

MELGAR, Fabian 1932-

PERSONAL: Born January 3, 1932, in New York, N.Y.; son of Fabian (a furrier) and Josefa (Montaner) Melgar; married Dorothy Mary Allgeier (in data processing), January 11, 1958; children: Michael, Thomas, Tod. *Education:* Attended School of Visual Arts, New York, N.Y., 1956-57. *Home:* 4 Clover Drive, Smithtown, N.Y. 11787. *Office:* 148 W. 23rd St., New York, N.Y. 10011.

CAREER: Penciler, Star Comics, New York City, 1951; art director, West, Weir, Bartel, New York, N.Y., 1962-64; creative director, Friend-Reiss Advertising, New York, 1964-68; president, creative director, Fabian Melgar Advertising, 1968-70; owner, president, Fabian Melgar Studio (design and photography), New York, N.Y. 1970-82; creative director and partner, Melgar Nordlinger, Inc., 1982—. *Military service:* U.S. Air Force, 1952-56, served as technical illustrator.

MEMBER: American Institute of Graphic Artists, Graphic Artists Guild.

AWARDS, HONORS: Since 1967 has received many awards in all areas of graphic design, including five *CA* awards for excellence, seven merit awards for design, art direction, and photography in packaging and logo design, all from *Communication Arts*, 1967 and 1984; three gold awards, nine merit awards in design, art direction, and photography in packaging and advertising from New York Art Directors' Club, 1983; seven gold Clio awards, seven excellence awards for design, art direction, photography, and copy in packaging and brochures, 1983, 1984; seven first place, four second place, and sixteen Andy awards for design, art direction, photography, copy, and illustration in packaging, advertising, posters, and brochures, all from Advertising Club of New York, 1983 and 1984; nine merit awards for design, art direction, and photography in packaging and advertising, One Club, New York; eleven creativity awards for design, art direction, photography, and illustration in packaging and brochures, all from *Art Direction*; merit award for illustration from Society of Illustrators; nineteen Desi awards for

FABIAN MELGAR

design, art direction, photography, copy, and illustration in packaging, advertising, brochures, and posters, all from *Graphics U.S.A.*

WORK IN PROGRESS: Representational painting in acrylics "with view towards exhibiting and selling."

SIDELIGHTS: Ever since his mother showed him the most efficient way to color a picture for school when he was nine years old, Fabian Melgar has wanted to be an artist. Her technique for "staying within the lines" won young Melgar such praise for his crayon-coloring in elementary school that his path in life was set. Four decades and over one hundred national design awards later, he has no reason to regret the decision. Today he is one of the most widely honored graphic designers working in New York City.

The professional prizes awarded to Melgar since the late 1960s cover the widest possible range. In addition to the rare honor of a gold award for package design from the New York Art Directors Club, Melgar's numerous prizes include thirty-six awards for graphic design, thirty-five for art direction, twenty for photography, eight for copy, and six for illustration. They represent honors for work in packaging, advertising, and brochure, poster, and logo design. Few designers in America have been honored for so varied an array of services. "I have no specialty," Melgar states. "I do everything in the creative field. I love to do the whole package."

A comic-book page for *Star Comics, ca. 1952* (©
Fabian Melgar. Reprinted by permission.)

sales of two million dollars to sales of more than twelve
million dollars a year.

The versatility Melgar displays in the multiple services he
offers his clients came from an extraordinary apprenticeship
in the field. He was first attracted to the comic-book field.
At sixteen he met an artist drawing *Green Hornet* who urged
him to get professional training; still in his teens, Melgar
went to the School of Visual Arts to study under Burne
Hogarth. He soon ran out of money, however, and found his
way to Star Comics, a small New York publisher who gave
him a chance to try his skills. Here he thought he had a
future: beginning as a penciler, the nineteen-year-old hopeful
soon progressed to inking his own pencil sketches and doing
his own lettering. In 1952, after six months with Star, he
went into the U.S. Air Force (where he did report covers
and technical illustrations), and when he got out in 1956 he
found that Star had folded. The comic-book industry had
collapsed, and with it his prospects for a career.

He returned to the School of Visual Arts to study illustration for a year, but during that time he received his most
intensive training outside the classroom. Needing money to
live, he applied to the State Unemployment Office for work,
and a sympathetic and insightful employee there took him in
her charge. (Her memorable name, Mrs. Miracle, seems to
Melgar a perfect one for the role she played in his career.)
Recognizing both his talents and his professional needs,
Mrs. Miracle sent him from one job to another in advertising to expose him to every aspect of the field. He had eleven
jobs in rapid succession, working for small and large art
studios, printing houses, and advertising agencies, until he
had made such personal contacts and received such on-the-
job training and experience in advertising that he was ready
for anything the industry might demand of him. That
strenuous year equipped him in a way that no formal
education could have, and he has never ceased being grateful
for the employment counselor who put him through it.

Firms for which he has done more or less the whole package
include such widely divergent companies as Pfizer Chemi-
cals, Hoffman LaRoche vitamins, Brinks, Cititrust banks,
Foster Grant sunglasses, Bally shoes, Konica cameras,
MGM and Columbia Pictures movie studios, and Holland-
American cruise lines, but the largest percentage of his
clients have been audio-equipment companies like Fisher,
Philips, Columbia, Magnavox, TDK, Pioneer, Ohm, and
Deutsche Gramaphone. His single principal client is Levolor
venetian blinds.

A striking example of Melgar's doing the whole package
occurred in 1982, when he participated in a sales campaign
which has been called "one of the most remarkable marketing successes of recent years." Working with Zelco Industries of Mount Vernon, New York, he helped in the design of
a small, high-intensity portable reading lamp intended to be
attached to a book. Then he organized the entire advertising
campaign. He created the name, "The Itty Bitty Book
Light," designed the book-like package, helped develop the
advertising slogan, planned the trade-show displays, developed the counter cards, and created the ads. Working
closely with his partner Mildred Nordlinger and his client,
Melgar took a small suburban flashlight manufacturer from

An illustration by Fabian Melgar for Levolor blinds (©
1985, Levolor-Lorentzen. Reprinted by permission.)

For eight years Melgar did advertising art and served as art director on the staffs of various New York advertising agencies before he opened his own in 1968. Since then he has alternated between free-lance and agency work, working simultaneously as creative director and partner with Melgar Nordlinger, Inc., and as a free-lance graphic artist. In 1985 he broadened his creative horizons by beginning to paint in acrylics. The discipline of a highly successful career in graphic art (to say nothing of his early efforts in comic books) has given him great proficiency in representational painting, and he looks forward to exhibiting and selling his work. In the meantime, he continues to provide the commercial-art market with anything and everything it requires, and his enthusiasm for the many faces of his work remains undiminished. "[I] love all aspects of advertising," he wrote to *CGA*, "and cannot specialize. I believe in warm, people-to-people advertising." The seemingly unlimited output of his multi-faceted talent lends eloquent support to his statement.

BIOGRAPHICAL/CRITICAL SOURCES: Who's Who in Advertising, Redfield Publishing, 1972.

—*Sketch by Dennis Wepman*

* * *

MODI, Rohit 1943-

PERSONAL: Name is pronounced "Roe-hit Mo-dee"; born January 20, 1943, in Ahmedabad, Gujarat, India; son of Ramanlal Chuninlal (a railroad engineer) and Samuben (Ramanlal) Modi; married Rochelle Emilie Beckler (professional name, Shelley Beckler; a graphic designer), July 14, 1984; children: Shaun Zander. *Education:* Attended National Design Institute, Ahmedabad, India, 1964-66; Maharaja Sayajirao University; Baroda, India, B.A., 1965; Atlanta College of Art, B.F.A., 1968. *Home:* 470 Second Ave., New York, N.Y. 10016. *Office:* Modi & Beckler Design, 271 Madison Ave., New York, N.Y. 10016.

CAREER: Senior visualiser, Mass Communication and Marketing Private, Ltd., Bombay, India, 1966-68; art director, Advertising & Sales Promotion Co., New Delhi, India, 1968-69; design director, Siegel & Gale, New York City, 1971-73; graphic designer, Vignelli Associates, New York City, 1974-76; partner, Modi & Beckler Design, New York City, 1980—.

AWARDS, HONORS: Second prize (with Bob Gill), Bloomingdale/Air India poster competition "for a graphic design which interprets and reflects India—The Ultimate Fantasy," New York, 1978; third prize, Bloomingdale/Air India poster competition, 1978; Special Citation, City of New York Human Resources Administration Agency for Child Development, New York, 1983; invited to compete for design of desk calendar, UNICEF, 1978; Desi for "excellence in the creation of a graphic design and its execution for a publication cover," Graphic Design, U.S.A., 1983; invited to compete for design of 1986 greeting card, UNICEF, 1984; Desi "for excellence in the creation of a graphic design and its execution for a logo," Graphic Design, U.S.A., 1984; STA Design Award, Society of Typographic Arts, Chicago, for a logo for the International Year of the Child, in "Twenty-Five Years of Logo Design," 1985.

EXHIBITIONS: One-man show, "Graphic Design of Rohit Modi," American Cultural Center, U.S. Information Ser-

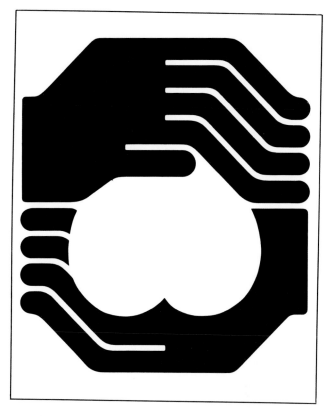

A design for the Frank Spencer Heart Foundation (© 1984, Modi & Beckler Design. Reprinted by permission.)

vice, Bombay, India, 1974; multi-media show, "Environment: Noise, People, and Architecture," Bombay, India, 1977.

SIDELIGHTS: "Every company needs to communicate, to achieve a corporate identity, to tell at a glance about its products, services, and progressive aims," Rohit Modi states. "The designer must find the exact graphic representation for all this. It's like cramming that many vitamins into a tiny pill." The Indian-born graphic designer has employed his talents on a wide variety of such challenges, in his native country and in the United States, for the last two decades. Since 1980, he and his wife Shelley Beckler have directed a busy and growing agency on New York's Madison Avenue.

Modi's education in India provided him with a solid foundation in western graphic design at one of the most distinguished schools of art in his country before he came to do graduate work in the United States. Although India has rich native resources of indigenous design, as revealed in its internationally admired folk arts, Modi reports that the businesses of the nation do not exploit them and the advanced schools in India teach only borrowed western concepts, a heritage of the British Raj which he regrets. "India accepts western technology," he says, "but should develop its own identity in graphic design."

A specialist in the graphic design of logos and publication material such as posters, magazines, and brochures, Modi held several high posts in the field in Bombay and New Delhi before locating in the United States. His exhibition of graphic design at the American Cultural Center sponsored

A design for the Institute for the Advancement of Health (© 1983, Modi & Beckler Design. Reprinted by permission.)

by the U.S. Information Service in Bombay was widely reviewed in 1974. The *Financial Express* of Bombay referred to his "brilliant ideas" and the *Economic Times* described his "clean, uncluttered lines" as "both simple and effective." Among his most highly regarded trademarks in India were that of the State of Gujarat Fertilizer Company, the letter "G" incorporating a leaf, and that of the Baroda Dairy, a white milk bottle forming the staff of the letter "B" in the center of a "D." A special favorite of the artist is his logo for the All-India Mental Retardations Foundation, a broken spiral in a stylized human head.

Work in India with noted designers Armin Hoffman and Charles Eames convinced Modi that the United States offered wider scope for his talents, and in 1969 he came to New York. In his frequent visits to his native land he has kept in touch with developments in his field there, and in 1977 he produced a well-received multi-media show sponsored by the School of Architecture in Ahmedabad. In "Environment: Noise, People, and Architecture" he attempted to present the relationship among these three elements of urban life by means of photographs, posters, and recorded sound. "Art has gone beyond the canvas," he stated at that time. "Exploration of other media is very exciting."

After advanced study in Georgia, Modi came to New York, the center of graphic design in the United States, and had no trouble getting work. He accepted a position as design director for prominent New York firm Siegel & Gale, where he spent two years before joining industrial designer Massimo Vignelli. In 1980 he and graphic designer Shelley Beckler formed Modi & Beckler Design, and four years later the partners became partners in marriage as well. Their work has been done together ever since, with almost all their accounts mutual ones.

The firm, which employs two other artists, has been responsible for some of the most striking and successful graphic design of this decade, and their advertising art has won several awards. Graphic Design, U.S.A. has twice awarded them its coveted Desi "for excellence in the creation of a graphic design and its execution": in 1983 for the publication cover of Volunteer Lawyers for the Arts' booklet *Fear of Filing*, and the next year for the logo of the Frank Spencer Heart and Research Foundation, used in New Delhi, India, by the Escort Heart Institute. This particularly admired design has the form of a heart nestled in two caring hands and has been widely applauded in both the United States and India. The firm has also received the STA Design Award from the Society of Typographic Arts for its ingenious and amusing design for the International Year of the Child, featured in the society's "Twenty-Five Years of Logo Design" in Chicago in 1985.

Modi & Beckler is as aggressive as any design firm, but places a high value on artistic and moral integrity and refuses any account of which the owners do not personally approve. When asked to design a dealership magazine for a well-known cigarette company a few years back, for example, they declined the offer although they estimate it cost them fifteen to twenty thousand dollars. The couple feels strongly about the dangers of smoking and decided that they "would not feel comfortable working on a cigarette account." On their brochure they declare, "Modi & Beckler offers creative design solutions. Because they investigate every aspect of a product. And take pains to understand a client's goals. . . . M&B won't just take any assignment. You can't further a client's goals if you don't believe in them." An examination of their client list bears this out; although they have many major industrial firms such as Pfizer Pharmaceuticals and International Paper, public service agencies predominate. Modi notes, "I enjoy the sort of work that stresses the social and cultural aspects."

Modi has found no obstacle in his foreign birth and education, although he is one of the few Indian graphic designers in the city. The simple, archetypal themes of his work are universal and no cultural interferences occur in his development of it. His approach to the Roman alphabet from the outside may even work to his advantage, as it gives him an objectivity toward its pure abstract form that cultural familiarity might hinder in a native. In India he had made use of the elegant forms of his own native Devanagari alphabet to convey messages beyond the words, and he was easily able to transfer that ability to his new country. Like all educated Indians, he has been fluent in English since early childhood.

Rohit Modi has produced memorable designs on two continents because he has been able to span the two cultures comfortably. He adapts the cultural symbols of his market to the form of his work, marrying East and West into a harmonious amalgam when appropriate. Typical of his conceptual approach is his design of a logo for the Ashoka Hotels: a graceful Indian arch forming the initial letters of the company's name. It is this effort to communicate as much information as possible in a form both striking and aesthetically pleasing that characterizes the work of Modi & Beckler Design and accounts for their increasing reputation in this fiercely competitive field.

BIOGRAPHICAL/CRITICAL SOURCES: Times of India, (Bombay), May, 1973; *American Reporter* (Bombay), July 11, 1973; *New York Post,* April 25, 1978; Wylie Davis, *AIGA: American Institute of Graphic Arts Journal of Graphic Design,* April, 1983; *Overseas Times,* (Jersey City, N.J.), October 21, 1983; *SPAN* (U.S. Information Service Journal) (New Delhi, India), December, 1983.

—*Sketch by Dennis Wepman*

* * *

MOORES, Dick
See MOORES, Richard Arnold

* * *

MOORES, Richard Arnold   1909-1986
(Dick Moores)

OBITUARY NOTICE: Born December 12, 1909, in Lincoln, Neb.; died April 22, 1986, in Asheville, N.C. Cartoonist and illustrator Dick Moores was best known for his successful continuation of the newspaper strip *Gasoline Alley,* following the death of its creator, Frank King, in 1969. In the early 1930s Moores had been assistant to Chester Gould on his famous police strip, *Dick Tracy,* before creating his own detective strip, *Jim Hardy,* in 1936 (it did not succeed in this format and was turned into a Western, *Windy and Paddles,* that lasted till 1942). For the next fourteen years Moores worked for the Disney organization, assisting Floyd Gottfredson and Frank Reilly on *Mickey Mouse* and other Disney strips, drawing the *Uncle Remus* Sunday feature, and doing much of the artwork for the merchandising of Disney products. In 1956 he took the job of assistant on the *Gasoline Alley* feature, finally receiving credit in 1963. Moores revamped the strip following King's death, and his treatment of storyline, drawing, and development of such beloved characters as Uncle Walt, Skeezix, and Clovia won him much praise from fans and critics alike. His work on the strip earned him the National Cartoonists Society's Reuben Award in 1975, as well as many other honors. Moores continued to work on the feature almost until his death, outlining the stories, penciling the action, and inking the faces, before sending them on to his assistant to finish. According to the *New York Times, Gasoline Alley* at the time of Moores's death was appearing in 180 daily newspapers and 125 Sunday newspaper comic sections.

OBITUARY AND OTHER SOURCES: Contemporary Authors, Vol. 69-72, Gale, 1978; *The World Encyclopedia of Cartoons,* Chelsea House, 1980; *New York Times,* April 23, 1986.

* * *

MORENO, Pepe   1954-

PERSONAL: First name is pronounced "Pe-*pe*"; born March 11, 1954, in Valencia, Spain; immigrated to the United States, 1977; son of Saturnino and Carmen C. (Biot) Moreno. *Education:* Attended School of Engineering in Valencia, Spain, 1970-73. *Politics:* "Common sense." *Studio:* 10 Bleecker St., New York, N.Y. 10012.

Photograph by Paul Blanca. Courtesy of Pepe Moreno.

PEPE MORENO

CAREER: Designer, Publipress (advertising company), Valencia, Spain, 1971-73; disc jockey and free-lance comic artist in Spain, 1975-77; free-lance comic artist and illustrator in the United States, 1977—. Free-lance advertising and comic artist in Ceuta, Spanish North Africa, 1974-75. Publisher and editor of *Nart,* an underground magazine, 1978-79. *Military service:* Spanish Army, 1974-75, served in cartography unit in North Africa; became sergeant.

AWARDS, HONORS: First prize in poster design competitions in Ceuta, Spanish North Africa, 1974 and 1975.

WRITINGS—All books of comics: *Rebel,* Albin Michel (France), 1985, Catalan Communications, 1986; *Zeppelin,* Albin Michel, 1985, Catalan Communications, 1986; *Joe's Air Force,* Albin Michel, 1986; *Gene Kong,* Albin Michel, 1986.

Contributor of comic stories to magazines, including *SOS* and *Star* in Spain, *Blitz* in Italy, *Creepy, Eerie, Vampirella, Epic Illustrated, Heavy Metal,* and *Savage Tales* in the United States.

WORK IN PROGRESS: U.S. edition of *Gene Kong* to be published by Catalan Communications in 1987; toy and production designs for *Tiger Sharks* animated television cartoon, produced by Rankin-Bass; computer graphics for motion picture and television animation; forming an electronic studio with computer artist Mike Saenz; contributing to a computer-generated magazine.

SIDELIGHTS: "As far as I can remember," Pepe Moreno wrote *CGA,* "I always drew or painted. My well-intentioned

An illustration from *Joe's Air Force* (© 1985, Pepe Moreno. Reprinted by permission.)

father wanted me to get the education he never had; I found myself studying electronics and engineering. I drew during classes and after classes; I wasn't a bad engineering student, however, and passed the courses, but what I really wanted to do was to go to art school. (Looking back on it now I am glad I never did.) My dad was making many sacrifices to keep my brother and me in school, so I got myself a job and went to school at night. It did not work out. I never passed the finals, and one year before graduation I quit. My father took it hard, but my mother wasn't too surprised; she had bought me art supplies and supported me all along."

The job Moreno held at an advertising agency while still going to school did not hold him long either. He left it after two years to devote himself to his first love, comics. "I remember buying comics almost from infancy. I drew comics of my own; the skills I learned at the ad agency helped me give form to my ideas," he states. He worked first for *SOS,* a local horror magazine, and then for the publishing house Editorial Valenciana; in addition he became a contributor to *Star,* the first acknowledged underground comic book in Spain.

In 1974 the budding artist was drafted into the army and served in North Africa. He was assigned to a cartography unit on the strength of his drawing abilities and thus had access to an unlimited supply of art materials. He kept drawing and won two poster sign competitions, but felt miserable in the army. "I was in jail or on punishment duty most of the time," he recalls. After being discharged from the army he found a job as a local disc jockey, but never gave up his dream of drawing comics. He did work for the Italian comic magazine *Blitz* and the compensation he received enabled him in 1977 to buy an airplane ticket for the United States.

No sooner had Moreno reached New York than he found work with both Warren Publishing Company (as a valued contributor to their line of comics magazines, *Creepy, Eerie,* and *Vampirella*) and DC Comics (which he promptly left after refusing to draw *Superman*). With the money he earned he traveled the United States and learned English; settling in San Francisco, he published the short-lived underground magazine *Nart* with the help of a few friends. He was one the first contributors to *Epic Illustrated* when it appeared in the late 1970s, writing and drawing many comic stories for the magazine. He also started his acclaimed series *Generation Zero* there. At the same time he also worked for *Epic*'s competitor, *Heavy Metal.* Both magazines were New York-based, prompting Moreno's return to the city where he has been living since 1982.

What makes Moreno especially attractive to an American audience is his skillful blending of European styles with American themes. His treatment of the topics of rebellion, violence, and chaos is not too dissimilar from that of another popular European cartoonist, the Italian Tanino Liberatore; they share an accent on somewhat gruesome humor and careful social distancing. Of particular interest are Moreno's cleverly laid-out pages in which a seemingly conventional arrangement of panels in geometrical order contrasts sharply with the anarchistic goings-on and the hyper-kinetic convulsions of the images. This is nowhere as apparent as in *Rebel,* the author's loving homage to (and sophisticated spoof of) the mythic stature of the late film idol James Dean; his story is set in an oppressive society of the near-future.

A page from *Rebel* (© 1986, Pepe Moreno. Reprinted by permission.)

Moreno has now turned to so-called graphic novels, long self-contained stories told in comic strip form, which allow their authors more freedom in content as well as in form than do the conventional comic-book stories. Three of these novels appeared in the short span of eighteen months and earned their author critical kudos as well as a loyal and growing audience. This in turn has brought offers for more and better-paid work; in addition, Moreno, an ardent electronics buff, is now able to experiment with computer animation and with computer-generated comics.

Will fame and money spoil Pepe Moreno? "I visited my parents in Spain recently," he drily comments. "My father claimed he never doubted I would make a success of myself as an artist; my mother just kept laughing."

BIOGRAPHICAL/CRITICAL SOURCES: Pure Entertainment, fall, 1983; *Zona 84* (Barcelona, Spain), Number 14, 1985.

* * *

MOSLEY, Zack (Terrell) 1906-

PERSONAL: Born December 12, 1906, in Hickory, Indian Territory (now Oklahoma); son of Zack Taylor (a merchant) and Irah Corinna (Aycock) Mosley; married Marie Gale, 1931 (divorced, 1944); married Betty Sue Adcock (an art assistant and secretary), May 31, 1945; children: Jill Mosley

Self-portrait of Zack Mosley (© Zack Mosley. Reprinted by permission.)

Sandow. *Education:* Attended Chicago Academy of Fine Arts, 1926-27; studied anatomical drawing at Art Institute of Chicago, 1927-28. *Home:* 262 S.E. Edgewood Dr., Stuart, Fla. 33494.

CAREER: Assistant comic strip artist on *Buck Rogers* and *Skyroads* strips, John Dille Syndicate, Chicago, Ill., 1929-33; comic strip artist and writer for *On the Wing* strip (renamed *Smilin' Jack*, December 31, 1933), Chicago Tribune-New York News Syndicate, 1933-73. *Wartime service:* Civil Air Patrol (later U.S. Air Force Auxiliary), 1942-43, flew anti-submarine patrols; Florida Wing Commander, 1944-46; became colonel; awarded U.S.A.F. Air Medal; inducted into Civil Air Patrol Auxiliary, U.S. Air Force Hall of Honor, September 18, 1976.

MEMBER: Aircraft Owners and Pilots Association (AOPA), American Aviation Historical Society, Aviation-Space Writers Association, Civil Air Patrol (now Auxiliary U.S.A.F.), OX-5 Pioneer Aviation Club, Quiet Birdmen Flying Fraternity, Silver Wings Society, Long Island Early Fliers Club, National Cartoonists Society, Benevolent and Protective Order of Elks.

AWARDS, HONORS: Twenty-Year Public Information Officer Award from Civil Air Patrol Auxiliary, U.S.A.F., 1962; Sharples Award from Aviation Owners and Pilots Association "for promoting aviation for forty years through [a] nationally syndicated comic strip *Smilin' Jack*," 1974.

WRITINGS: Smilin' Jack (original comic books), 1940-45, 1947; Dell; *Smilin' Jack* (quarterly comic books), Numbers 1-8, Dell, 1948-49. *Superbooks of Comics* (reprints from comic books).

Books, all reprints of *Smilin' Jack* comic strips: *The Hot Rock Glide* (reprint of a 1938-39 episode), Gulf Stream Printing Co., Stuart, Fla., 1979; *De-Icers Galore* (reprint of a 1941 episode with other material from 1934, 1935, 1936, 1938, 1940, 1941, and 1942), Gulf Stream Printing Co., 1980.

Autobiography: *Brave Coward Zack*, Valkyrie Press, St. Petersburg, Fla., 1976.

FILMS: Adventures of Smilin' Jack, a thirteen-episode serial produced by Universal Productions (based on Mosley's character and comic strip), 1943.

WORK IN PROGRESS: An independent producer is negotiating a Smilin' Jack feature-length film, *Smilin' Jack, Pioneer Aviator*, for 1986. Further collections of comic-strip reprints are under consideration.

SIDELIGHTS: Zack Mosley vowed at the age of eleven that "someday [he] would fly aeroplanes and draw 'funny papers' about them," and for four decades he did just that. A pioneer aviator and the creator of the best-known and most durable of all aviation comic strips, Mosley entertained two generations of boys with his *Smilin' Jack*, which he wrote and drew from 1933 to 1973. During the heyday of the adventure strip, *Smilin' Jack*'s dashing eponymous hero was probably as well known as any pilot, real or fictional, in the air. A blend of cliff-hanging adventure, voluptuous pulchritude, and solid, dependable aeronautical information gave Mosley's strip a loyal audience estimated at twenty-five million during the 1930s and 1940s.

Born in Indian Territory the year before it was admitted to the Union as the state of Oklahoma, Mosley saw his first airplane—made of "wire, wood, and rags. . . tied and glued together," he later reported—at the age of seven, and even though it crash-landed he caught the flying bug from it. Four years later an army "Jenny" made a forced landing near his hometown, and the boy was hooked for life. Already a comics addict who copied the *Katzenjammer Kids* and *Mutt and Jeff* from the newspapers, he sketched the plane carefully, and never let a day go by after that without drawing something. At the age of twenty, after saving five hundred dollars from a year's work as a soda jerk, he went to Chicago to study art.

For three years Mosley studied at the Chicago Academy of Fine Arts and the Art Institute of Chicago, financing his lessons by working in a restaurant. At last in 1929 he and his roommate, cartoonist Russell Keaton, landed jobs with the John Dille Syndicate, assisting Dick Calkins on *Skyroads* and *Buck Rogers*. For twenty dollars a week (later munificently raised to twenty-five dollars), Mosley lettered and drew parts of *Skyroads* dailies and *Buck Rogers* dailies and Sundays with Keaton, working an average of fifty-sixty hours a week. "The one who did the most work on Mondays," he reports, "was the one with the least hangover." As Mosley's part in the production increased, Dille consented to allow him to sign the strips he drew, and he occasionally wrote an episode of *Skyroads*.

Aviation was a popular subject in the early 1930s, and the newspapers were full of stories of heroic pilots flying dangerous missions and performing daring air rescues. In 1933, Mosley's old friend and fellow Oklahoman Chester Gould, who had just begun doing *Dick Tracy* for the Chicago Tribune-New York News Syndicate, suggested that Mosley try his hand at an aviation strip of his own. Syndicate founder Joseph Medill Patterson, himself a flying-buff, knew the general interest in the subject and signed Mosley to do a Sunday strip called *On the Wing*, which debuted October 1, 1933.

On the Wing, a semi-humorous saga of three scared student-pilots, had a bumpy flight for fourteen weeks before Patterson mysteriously telegraphed Mosley to change its name to *Smilin' Jack*. There was no character in it named Jack, but its hero Mack Martin quietly assumed the new identity in mid-flight on December 31, 1933, and went on unprotestingly smilin' for the next forty years. Mosley reports that he never received a single letter about the unannounced name-change—an evidence either that no one cared or that no one was reading the strip.

It was obvious that people were reading the strip, though, as its market grew to three hundred major newspapers in the United States, Canada, and Latin America during the 1930s, 1940s, and 1950s. *Smilin' Jack* also became one of the most prominent comic-book titles during those years, and in the early 1940s Whitman Publishing Co. of Racine, Wisconsin, issued a series of anonymous hard-covered novelizations of stories taken from the strip, such as *Smilin' Jack and the Daredevil Girl Pilot* (1942), subtitled "Based on the famous comic strip by Zack Mosley" and with "illustrations adapted from the newspaper strip." Two of Mosley's best assistants on the strip were Boody Rogers, from 1936 to 1942, and his brother Bob, an Air Force pilot, from 1944 into the 1950s.

Another medium to feature the ubiquitous pilot was the motion pictures, and in 1943 Universal Productions made a thirteen-episode serial called *The Adventures of Smilin' Jack*. It had Tom Brown in the title role, and its cast included Sidney Toler, Rose Hobart, Edgar Barrier, and Turhan Bey. A cliff-hanger like the comic strip, it showed its hero repeatedly but narrowly foiling a sinister oriental espionage ring in World War II.

Always timely, Mosley's strip had several elements that accounted for its continued popularity. First of all, it never lost the slangy, breezy humor of *On the Wing*, and the wisecracks of its characters captured the vocabulary and cadence of adolescent bravado perfectly. A second element contributing to its success was Mosley's gift for suspense and pacing. After a rather fumbling start, the strip soon became one of the most tightly plotted and exciting adventure strips in the field with a nice blend of soap-opera romance and desperate derring-do. On June 15, 1936, Mosley added a daily strip, and hardly a day in the next thirty-seven years passed without the hero out on some limb. He thwarted vicious villains and (sometimes) escaped the wiles of lustful ladies in episode after episode, and it was a rare kid who, once he started reading the strip, could give it up.

A montage of caricatures (© 1928, Zack Mosley. Reprinted by permission.)

Cover of *Brave Coward Zack* (© 1979, Zack Mosley-
United Media Services. Reprinted by permission.)

Perhaps more important even than humor, action, and
suspense in the appeal of *Smilin' Jack* over the years,
however, were two things: its characters and its facts about
flying. The *dramatis personae* of Mosley's strip were as
motley a gang of characters as ever came out of central
casting. Like his friend Chester Gould, Mosley pitted a
clean-cut (but far more dashing and devil-may-care) hero
against an endless assortment of memorable grotesques:
Limehouse and the Head, the Claw and the Eye, Snake-bite
and Baron Bloodsoe. In 1941, the fat, smirking Toemain the
Great, evil double-agent and all-around miscreant, met his
deserved end as gruesomely as any of Dick Tracy's adversar-
ies, devoured by the very piranhas he had nurtured to fatten
on Jack's flesh. And no less distinctive were the strip's
heroes: the over-sexed Downwind Jaxon, whose face was so
irresistibly handsome that the artist never dared to let us
gaze upon it ("I couldn't come up with a face," Mosley
explains. "When he appeared faceless,. . . hundreds of
letters came in. Because of reader curiosity I never did draw
a full face for Downwind"); Fatstuff, Jack's South Sea
Island sidekick, who was so fat that buttons kept popping off
his shirt into the waiting mouth of a weird, featherless
chicken; and the girls, the stylized-sexy "li'l de-icers" who
were so hot they melted the ice off the wings of planes.
Nothing really racy, ever—just suggestive enough to titillate
the youngsters who turned to *Smilin' Jack* with their
breakfast cereal every morning.

They could do it in good conscience, because there was
always something educational in Smilin' Jack. The planes
were always labeled and technically correct, and for years
his toppers "Smilin' Jack's Flyin' Facts" and "Smilin' Jack's
Aero-Astro Answers" gave them both historical data and
the latest details on aviation. Mosley always kept up with the
field because he was personally active in it. He began, as
nervous as his own Mack Martin, to take lessons with
Keaton in 1932 and received his license in 1936. From then
on, everything he said about planes came from experience.
He helped found the Civil Air Patrol (later the U.S.A.F.
Auxiliary) a week before the United States entered World
War II, and flew over three hundred hours of anti-
submarine patrol; he won the Air Medal and owned nine
planes of his own. Mosley has flown over a million miles in
the United States, Canada, South America, and Europe.
Always closely identified with the Air Force, Mosley has
created squadron insignia for the U.S.A.F. Auxiliary and
many Army, Navy, and Marine units.

By the 1970s, aviation had lost much of its glamor and it
was time to bring the strip down. "The big public doesn't
have a romantic interest in flying any more," Mosley
explained, and television entertainment had led to a general
decline in adventure strips. On April 1, 1973, the old
barnstormer, gray-haired by then but still smilin', hung up
his goggles. Mosley, now "semi-retired," still keeps busy
selling his books and old original drawings. He also is
negotiating a film version of *Smilin' Jack*.

Mosley's art is sometimes dismissed as crude, but it had an
obviously deliberate simplicity which was often stylish in its
naivete, and always dramatically effective. The appeal of the
stylized drawing in *Smilin' Jack* is demonstrated by the
longevity of the strip, which outlived all other aviation strips
and most adventure strips of any kind.

BIOGRAPHICAL/CRITICAL SOURCES: Martin
Sheridan, *Comics and Their Creators: Life Stories of Ameri-
can Cartoonists*, Luna Press, 1971; Coulton Waugh, *The
Comics*, Macmillan, 1947; Stephen Becker, *Comic Art in
America*, Simon & Schuster, 1959; Zack Mosley, "Smilin'
Jack and Zack," *AOPA Pilot*, December, 1964; Richard
Reitberger and Wolfgang Fuchs, *Comics: Anatomy of a Mass
Medium*, Little, Brown, 1971; Herb Galewitz, *Great Comics
of the Chicago Tribune*, Crown, 1972; "Stuart Cartoonist
Mosley Will Retire 'Smilin' Jack,' " *Stuart News*, February
25, 1973; Ron Goulart, "Paper Airplanes," *Nostalgia Illus-
trated*, December, 1974; Jerry Robinson, *The Comics: An
Illustrated History of Comic Strip Art*, Putnam, 1974; Ron
Goulart, *The Adventurous Decade: Comic Strips in the
Thirties*, Arlington House, 1975; Zack Mosley, *Brave
Coward Zack*, Valkyrie Press, St. Petersburg, Fla., 1976;
Bob Swift, "Smilin' Jack Lives On," *Miami Herald*, August
17, 1979; *National Cartoonists Society Album*, 1980; John
Platero, "Old Barnstormer Smilin' Jack Just Doesn't Fit
Into Space Age," *Miami News*, May 7, 1981; Donald Phelps,
"Wild Blue Yonder," *Nemo*, June, 1984; T. W. Black, "The
Devil-May-Care Life of Smilin' Zack Mosley," *Miami
Herald*, December 12, 1984; *Who's Who in America
1984-85*, Marquis, 1984.

—Sketch by Dennis Wepman

N

NAKAZAWA, Keiji 1939-

PERSONAL: Born March 10, 1939, in Hiroshima, Japan; son of Harumi (a painter) and Kimiyo Nakazawa; married Misayo Yamane, 1966; children: Keiko. *Education:* Graduated from Eba Middle School, Hiroshima, Japan, 1954. *Home:* 2-6-5 Nishibori, Niiza City, Saitama Prefecture, Japan.

CAREER: Professional cartoonist, 1961—.

AWARDS, HONORS: Japan Journalism Conference Special Award, 1975; Original Story Award at Czechoslovakia's Karlovy Vary Film Festival, 1977.

WRITINGS: Kuroi Ame ni Utarete (title means *Struck by Black Rain*), Domie Shobo, 1971; *Hadashi no Gen* (title means *Barefoot Gen*) Yubunsha, 1975; *Nakazawa Keiji Senshu Zengokan* (title means *The Collected Works of Keiji Nakazawa in Five Volumes*), Bunminsha, 1975; *Yukari no Ki no Shitade* (title means *Under the Eucalyptus Tree*), Yubunsha, 1981; *Itsuka Mita Aozora* (title means *The Blue Sky I Once Saw*), Yubunsha, 1981.

FILMS: Live-action films include *Hadashi no Gen*, 1976, 1978, and 1979; feature animation includes *Hadashi no Gen*, 1982, and *Kuroi Ame ni Utarete*, 1984.

SIDELIGHTS: Japan's Keiji Nakazawa is one of his country's and the world's most effective spokesmen for peace. Although in Japan he has never achieved the wealth and fame of many of his more commercial colleagues, his works have been published in magazines and books, and made into three live-action films, two animated features, and an opera. Moreover, he is one of the best known cartoonists outside of Japan. His books have been translated into English, French, and Swedish.

The main theme in Nakazawa's comics, and the driving force in his life, is the atomic bombing of Hiroshima and the need to prevent nuclear war. On August 6, 1945, at 8:15 AM, first-grader Nakazawa was on his way to school when the atomic bomb fell on the city of Hiroshima. Nakazawa, shielded by a concrete wall, survived, but over one-hundred thousand others in the city were incinerated or later died of radiation sickness, disease, or starvation. Among the casualties were his father, sister, and brother.

Nakazawa's father had been a painter of wooden clogs, who also did traditional-style Japanese paintings. The young Keiji also showed artistic talent, but his interest lay mostly in comics and cartoons. After the war, like many Japanese children, he found them a source of spiritual support, and

KEIJI NAKAZAWA

avidly read the new, lengthy story comics that were then being created by Osamu Tezuka and others. In the third year of middle school, Nakazawa submitted a short work of his own to *Manga Shonen* ("Boys Comic"), which was published. On graduation, he began working as a sign painter in Hiroshima, and drew comics on the side, and finally, at the age of twenty-two resolved to become a professional.

Moving to Tokyo, where nearly all the publishers and artists were concentrated, he first worked as assistant to Daiji Kazumine, and then to the well-known Naoki Tsuji. He continued drawing his own comics on his free time. His first success was a one-year serial sold to *Shonen Gaho* ("Boys Pictorial"), called *Spark 1*. In 1966 he married Misayo Yamane, also of Hiroshima, and finally became an independent cartoonist, but in the same year his mother died. Convinced that her death was linked to the radiation she had received during the bombing, he then resolved to

A page from *Gen of Hiroshima* (© 1980, Keiji Nakazawa. Reprinted by permission.)

dedicate his life to informing people of the horror of Hiroshima and war through his comics.

Subsequently, nearly all of Nakazawa's works have dealt with this theme in the long, novelistic Japanese story-comic format; to date, over fifty paperback and hardback volumes of his work have been published. The most successful of these stories, *Hadashi no Gen*, or *Barefoot Gen*, over two thousand pages long, began in 1973 and was only completed in 1986. Like the best of Nakazawa's works, it is highly autobiographical. Starring little Gen, Nakazawa's alter ego, it is a story of human triumph over suffering, and depicts the destruction of Hiroshima, radiation sickness, the struggle for food, and the persecution suffered later by the survivors. Although written originally for children, it never glosses over the horrors of destruction; nor is it simplistic in its allocation of blame for the tragedy. Responsibility is parcelled out equally to all, including the Japanese militarists of the time. Despite a melodramatic art style, the knowledge on the part of readers that Nakazawa personally experienced the story gives it an impact rarely present in the comic medium. It is for this reason, perhaps, that *Hadashi no Gen* has been made into three live-action films, an animated feature, and an opera. It is also a reason Nakazawa is one of the best known Japanese comic artists overseas. In 1976 Project Gen, a group of American and Japanese volunteers, was formed to translate *Hadashi no Gen* into English, and largely as a result of its efforts, *Gen* is today available, not only in English, but French, German, Esperanto, and Swedish. Another strictly autobiographical short work, *Ore wa Mita*, or *I Saw It*, was also published in the United States in conventional comic book format.

Nakazawa continues his work in animation and comics despite poor health, and his message is still the same. As he stated in his introduction to the U.S. edition of *I Saw It*, "Never have I felt more strongly than I do now that the human race must transcend its ideological differences to stop the arms race. . . . It saddens me that, for all our scientific progress, we human beings remain forever caught in old ways of thinking. . . . We must oppose war and militarism; we must work to eliminate nuclear weapons."

BIOGRAPHICAL/CRITICAL SOURCES: The World Encyclopedia of Cartoons, Chelsea House, 1980; Frederik Schodt, *Manga! Manga! The World of Japanese Comics*, Kodansha International, 1983.

* * *

NAZARIO
See LUQUE VERA, Nazario

* * *

NOVAK, Emil, Jr. 1958-
(Emil)

PERSONAL: Given name is pronounced "A-mul"; born January 25, 1958, in Trenton, N.J.; son of Emil J. (a bookstore owner) and Liz J. (Rizzo) Novak; married Sharon Zamojski (a secretary), October 28, 1980; children: Emil Jacob. *Education:* Self-taught. *Religion:* Roman Catholic. *Home:* 94 Danebrock, Snyder, N.Y. 14226.

CAREER: Manager, Queen City Book Store (a comic-book store), Buffalo, N.Y., 1975—; inker, Americomics, Longwood, Fla., 1985—.

WORK IN PROGRESS: A comic book, to be titled *Skull and Crossbones*, publication expected in 1986.

SIDELIGHTS: Emil Novak has had a life-long love affair with the comics and has been the manager of a shop that sells them since he was seventeen years old. The Queen City Book Shop in Buffalo, New York, one of the largest comic-book shops in the northwest part of the state, is on a major boulevard near the State University of New York at Buffalo, and is always full of young comic-book fans talking comics and exchanging ideas, so Novak is never out of touch with the field at the readership level. Since 1985 he has been professionally connected with comic books at the creative level as well. In that year he joined the staff of Americomics as one of their regular comic-book inkers.

Americomics, of Longwood, Florida, is an independent publisher of comic books producing color comics, black-and-white comics, and black-and-white magazines. Among the trademarked characters of Americomics inked by Novak are Captain Paragon, Nightveil, Stardust, Commando D, Scarlet Scorpion, Atoman, the Vardax Prime, and the Sentinels of Justice. Americomics' series include *Black Diamond, Starmasters, Femforce, Fun Comics, Ms. Victory, Power Plays*, and a growing list of others.

The characters in this gallery of superheroes are all larger, stronger, and more beautiful than life and are drawn and inked to scale. The Sentinels of Justice, a team of superpowered saviors of mankind like Marvel Comics' Fantastic Four, comprise one human and two guest stars from other planets, who spend their time alternately slugging crooks and thwarting extraterrestrial invaders. Under Captain Paragon they sometimes join forces with the sexy Ms.

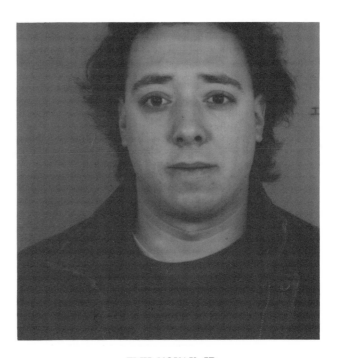

EMIL NOVAK, JR.

The Red Scull by Matt Wagner, inked by Emil Novak, 1985

Victory and her incredibly voluptuous Femforce. All the females at Americomics—including Stardust, a Sentinel of Justice from the planet Rur—are sensual, and all the males muscular.

All of this virility and pulchritude requires the services of an expert inker to fill out the sketched roughs of the penciler, and here Novak provides his specialized skills. When a luscious female crimefighter stops a green Vardaxian or a brawny hero defeats the evil Chromo and knocks out his minions with a single "Krak!," the rounded bosom, menacing Vardax horn, and bulging muscle are the work of Novak's steady hand. In the creative team that produces a comic book, the inker occupies the central position, performing his special work after the writer and penciler have laid the story out and then passing it on to the letterer and colorist to finish. The success of the finished product depends on the harmonious and efficient functioning of the entire team, and also on the skill of each individual specialist

that composes it. Americomics publisher and editor Bill Black credits Emil Novak with "a first-rate job on the inks."

The epic adventures of Americomics have been perfectly suited to Novak's tastes and talents. He acknowledges the influence of the sensational Republic Studio movie serials and the characters in the comic strips of the thirties, forties, and fifties, along with the lurid pulp magazines and adventure books of those years. He is currently working on a comic feature of his own called *Skull and Crossbones*, done in the style of those early favorites.

* * *

NUTZLE, Footsie
　See KLEINSMITH, Bruce John

* * *

NUTZLE, Futzie
　See KLEINSMITH, Bruce John

O

ODOM, Mel 1950-

PERSONAL: Born September 2, 1950, in Richmond, Va.; son of William Joseph (a postal employee and tobacco grower) and Ethel (Hendrick) Odom. *Education:* Virginia Commonwealth University, B.F.A., 1972; graduate work at Leeds Polytechnic Institute of Art and Design, Leeds, England, 1973. *Home:* 252 W. 76th St., B-1, New York, N.Y. 10023.

CAREER: Free-lance magazine, book, and record-album illustrator, New York City, 1975—.

MEMBER: Graphic Artists Guild.

AWARDS, HONORS: Playboy Magazine Illustrator of the Year, 1980; silver award, Society of Illustrators, 1980, gold award, 1981; cover for *Exit to Eden* cited as "best recent book jacket art," *Saturday Review,* 1985.

WRITINGS—Books of drawings and paintings: *First Eyes* (a career-summary book), Genko-Sha Publishing, Japan, 1982; *Dreamer,* Penguin, 1984.

EXHIBITIONS—Group shows: Cooper-Hewitt Museum, New York City, 1979; Society of Illustrators annual show, New York City, 1976-82.

WORK IN PROGRESS: Working on two large oil paintings commissioned by a New York restaurant; collecting drawings and paintings for a new book; studying the techniques of lithography for a series of prints; doing a series of illustrations for Oscar Wilde's *The Picture of Dorian Gray.*

SIDELIGHTS: Mel Odom is an illustrator whose work stands at that shadow-line between commercial and gallery art. In the first ten years after he began his professional career his restless brush explored virtually every area of commercial art: he did magazine illustrations, book jackets, greeting cards, and album covers; he drew poster art, dressed department store windows, created masks, and designed a mural. But in all of his wide-ranging work, his highly personal vision remained clearly visible. Indeed, his childhood crayon drawings—winged elves drawn at the age of six and reproduced in his first book in 1982—already revealed the singular imagination and something of the technical control that characterize his mature work.

The need to project his inner sense of the world in graphic form revealed itself early to Odom, who reports that at four he was "making pictures" on supermarket shopping bags and at ten made the decision to take art lessons after school. At fourteen he made his first sale—a collage called "Happy House," sold for the munificent sum of forty dollars to a

Photograph by Mark Trezza. Courtesy of Mel Odom.

MEL ODOM

wealthy family in Greenville, North Carolina. Portrait commissions soon followed. Before he finished high school, it was clear to Odom what path his life must take. He pursued formal art studies through a bachelor of fine arts degree in illustration at Virginia Commonwealth University and a year's study at Leeds Polytechnic Institute of Art and Design in England. He stayed on in London for six months studying music before he had to return home to Richmond, Virginia. There for nine more months he waited on tables and drew, but the gestation period finally came to an end

"Jennifer," an illustration used for a greeting card (© 1979, Mel Odom. Reprinted by permission.)

with a commission that brought him to New York City in October, 1975. He has remained there as a professional artist with a growing reputation ever since.

During his first decade in New York, Odom did displays for such department stores as Saks Fifth Avenue, Henri Bendel, and Lord & Taylor, and his work was used by Paper Moon Graphics for greeting cards, but his name became best known to the general public for his stylish magazine covers and illustrations. His work appeared frequently in *Playboy*, as well as *Viva, Rolling Stone, Oui, Manhattan Catalogue*, and *Time*. He also produced several album covers for CBS Records, and, since 1980, book covers for many publishers, including Godine, Random House, New American Library, Arbor House, and Time-Life Books. He did eight covers for Penguin Books, including six for the novels of Australian Nobel laureate Patrick White.

In 1979 he did the cartoons for a mural executed in oil, acrylic, and airbrush for the Zoo, a Los Angeles restaurant. The eight by thirty-one-foot painting, dominated by rich tones of blue and green, is a lush and dreamy panorama of animals in nature, but a nature peculiar to the artist's imagination. In 1982 he created his first and only poster, "Spring," for Davis-Blue Artworks in California. After

months of work on it, he was not inspired to continue the planned series because of the difficulties of working with people at such a distance; moreover, he felt that this delicate and sensitive study of a young woman standing among pale flowers was not graphically strong enough for a poster and that its colors were perhaps too subdued for the genre.

Although the precise and subtly colored art of Mel Odom appears in reproduction to have been done in acrylic or airbrush, it is in fact the product of gouache, pencil, and liquid dyes only. The artist reports that the drawings in his second book, *Dreamer*, were done with Winsor-Newton gouache, Venus pencils, and either Luma or Peerless liquid dyes.

Not surprisingly, considering the meticulous detail in which he works, Odom usually draws in the actual size in which his drawings are reproduced. Most of the pictures in *Dreamer* were originally done in dimensions no greater than eight-and-one-half by eleven-and-one-quarter inches; some were drawn as small as three-and-one-quarter by five-and-one-quarter inches. He is happy to discover that his work can be enlarged or reduced without significant loss. The cover art for Richard Adams's *Maia*, done for New American Library in 1986, was blown up to considerably larger size to the general satisfaction of all concerned.

Odom is currently working on two large oil paintings commissioned by the fashionable New York restaurant Sign of the Dove. As his studies in fashion illustration never allowed him time for oil, he is now devoting himself with characteristic thoroughness to a study of that medium, and the sensual, larger-than-life angels that are emerging from his palette satisfy both his client and himself that oils are appropriate to his style. The greater range that this work is giving him may also lead him back to portraiture.

Odom plans to assemble enough of his painstakingly done work for a one-man show. He hopes also to improve his technical control of silk screen and lithographic reproduction so that he can continue selling prints of his works without losing control of the originals. Furthermore, the adventurous spirit of the artist is fascinated by the challenge of acquiring a new skill and a new channel of expression.

Whether in oil or acrylic, pencil or gouache; whether done as private work, to illustrate a story, or to advertise shirts for the *Playboy Guide*, Mel Odom's work is invariably and unmistakably his own. Even his portraits of such public figures as President Ronald Reagan, British Prime Minister Margaret Thatcher, and Iran's Ayatollah Khomeini for *Time*, although scrupulously representational, are infused with subtle elements of the artist's personal sensibility. Jim Mullen, editor of *Manhattan Catalogue*, has written that the Reagan piece may be viewed "as a realistic portrait or an incredibly sophisticated caricature. . . . Your interpretation will be based on what you feel."

Odom's figures are poised, serenely self-contained in static compositions of almost unearthly perfection, their mysterious, expressionless faces hermetic and faintly sinister. As Bill Franklin wrote in 1985, Odom's "contemporary icons are caught flashfrozen in time, utterly assured and nearly unmovable." An elusive eroticism pervades nearly all his work; even the curious 1978 painting *Smoke*, depicting a somewhat overblown gardenia puffing on a cigarette against a cool blue latticework background, is subtly suggestive. But

Detail of an illustration (© 1980, Mel Odom. Reprinted by permission.)

which he will not treat: although a loyal Virginian, for example, he will not advertise cigarette-smoking (except for gardenias) because he does not approve of it. Ultimately, he approaches his work reverently, as a total expression of his life and a sacrament. "I always do my work for myself," he says. "I draw for personal reasons. My work keeps me sane. If it did not," he continues, "it would be just a profession, rather than a dedication—and a passion."

This passion for perfection—which inspired his signature/ logo of a perfect circle—accounts for his growing reputation in the art community. He has been called "a powerful artist on the verge of general public acclaim," and his work is already in collections from Japan to New York, including those of Erte, the master of art deco, in Paris, rock star Elton John in Los Angeles, and Playboy, Inc. Odom sees himself as on the threshold of his career.

BIOGRAPHICAL/CRITICAL SOURCES: Kerig Pope, Jim Mullen, and Hiroko Tanaka, "First Eyes: The World of Mel Odom," introduction to *First Eyes*, Genko-Sha Publishing, 1982; Edmund White, "Introduction," Mel Odom, *Dreamer*, Penguin, 1984; *Gentleman's Quarterly*, October, 1984; Ray Bradbury, "Mel Odom," in *The Art of Playboy*, Alfred van der Marck, 1985; Freeman Gunter, "Mel Odom: Masculine Intuition," *Mandate*, March, 1985; *Pennsylvania Gazette*, April, 1985; "Judging a Book by Its Cover", *Saturday Review*, July/August, 1985; Bill Franklin, "Mel Odom," *In Style*, December, 1985; Claire Williams, "Les Reveurs Innocents: La Merveilleuse Histoire de Mel Odom," *Scope-RTL* (Belgium), 1985.

—Sketch by Dennis Wepman

* * *

if there is something slightly perverse in his subjects, there is never anything lurid. His sensuality is clean, pure, with an almost edenic innocence. Among the symbols for our times which preoccupy Odom is the Barbie doll, which he calls "an American icon" and to which he devoted a series of paintings reproduced in his two books.

It is perhaps Odom's blend of classic severity with a certain fin-de-siecle decadence that gives his work its uniquely haunting quality. Science-fiction writer Ray Bradbury has written of Odom's art that it is "right out of Roman and Greek mythology," but there is something of the Celtic Twilight in it, too. Odom acknowledges the early influence of turn-of-the-century British illustrator Aubrey Beardsley, whose sinuous strength and elegance of line may be seen in Odom's graphic style; but the luminous colors and the mysterious, private character of his figures is distinctively his own. He is consecrated to a cult of beauty; his subjects may elude the rational mind, but they never fail to ravish the eye. "Whatever I may draw," Odom states in a kind of artistic credo, "the most important thing to me is that the people who see my work think of it as beautiful."

Odom works in the early hours of the morning so that he can be free of all distraction and put himself wholly at the service of his art. Although he works for others, illustrating more or less to order, he transcends the conventional image of the commercial artist. He is always true to his own artistic integrity and to his own private aesthetic. There are subjects

OPPER, F(rederick) B(urr)   1857-1937

PERSONAL: Born January 2, 1857, in Madison, Wis.; died August 28 (some sources say August 27), 1937, in New Rochelle, N.Y.; son of Lewis (a craftsman) and Aurelia (Burr) Opper; married Nellie Barnett, 1882; children: Lawrence, Sophia. *Education:* Left school at fourteen; self-taught.

CAREER: Cartoonist, *Madison Gazette*, Madison, Wis., 1871-77; staff artist, *Wild Oats* (a magazine), New York City, 1877-78; news correspondent, cartoonist, and staff artist, *Leslie's Magazine*, New York City, 1878-81; political and humor cartoonist, *Puck* (a magazine), New York City, 1881-1899; political cartoonist and comic strip artist, Hearst newspaper chain, 1899-1932, drawing comic features, including *Happy Hooligan*, 1900-32, *Our Antediluvian Ancestors*, 1900-03, *Alphonse and Gaston*, 1902-10s, *And Her Name Was Maud!*, 1904-10s and 1926-32; drew *Howson Lott*, 1905-10s; *Mr. Dubb*, 1919-21, *On the Farm*, 1921-23, *Mr. Dough and Mr. Dubb*, 1925-27.

WRITINGS—All self-illustrated; all books of cartoons, unless otherwise indicated: *A Museum of Wonders* (juvenile), Routledge, 1884; *Puck's Opper Book*, Keppler & Schwartzmann, 1888; *The Folks in Funnyville*, H. R. Russell, 1900; *Willie and His Papa, and the Rest of the Family*, Grosset, 1901; *Alphonse and Gaston*, Stokes, 1902;

A typical *Alphonse and Gaston* pose by F. B. Opper, ca. 1905

Our Antediluvian Ancestors, Stokes, 1902; *Happy Hooligan*, Stokes, 1902; *John, Jonathan, and Mr. Opper*, Grant Richards (London), 1903; *Happy Hooligan's Travels*, Stokes, 1905; *Maud*, Stokes, 1905; *Happy Hooligan Home Again!*, Stokes, 1907; *Maud the Matchless*, Stokes, 1907; *Happy Hooligan 1904-05*, Hyperion Press, 1977.

Illustrator: Emma A. Opper, *Slate and Pencil People*, White, Stokes & Allen, 1885; Edgar Wilson Nye, *Bill Nye's History of the United States*, Thompson & Thomas, 1894; Finley Peter Dunne, *Mr. Dooley's Philosophy*, H. R. Russell, 1900; George Vere Hobart, *Dinkelspiel, His Gonversationings*, New Amsterdam Book Co., 1900; Eugene Field, *The Complete Tribune Primer*, Mutual Book Co., 1901; *Mother Goose* (a retelling of familiar fairy tales), Lippincott, 1916; *Aesop's Fables* (an illustrated version of familiar fables), Lippincott, 1916; Marion Kinnaird, *The Story of Happy Hooligan*, McLoughlin, 1932.

Contributor of cartoons and illustrations to *New York Journal, Harper's Magazine, Scribner's, St. Nicholas*, and other periodicals.

SIDELIGHTS: The son of an Austrian immigrant who came to the United States in the mid-nineteenth century, Frederick Burr Opper began his long and successful cartooning career at the age of fourteen on his hometown newspaper, the *Madison Gazette*. The confines of Wisconsin

A *Happy Hooligan* Sunday page by F. B. Opper, 1906

proved too constricting for the ambitious youngster, and he was soon mailing out cartoons to every major and not-so-major national publication. After successful sales to *Scribner's*, *St. Nicholas*, *Century*, and other magazines, Opper decided to move east and found a position as staff artist on the humor publication *Wild Oats*, continuing to free-lance for other magazines at the same time. The 1880s saw his work appear in *Harper's Magazine*, *Leslie's Magazine* (where for more than three years he served as cartoonist, illustrator, and even news correspondent), and especially in *Puck* where his cartoons and continuing series established him as one of the preeminent cartooning talents of his time.

It was in the pages of *Puck* that he created in 1881 one of the forerunners of the American comic strip, *Streets of New York*, in which he humorously described all the mishaps, contretemps, alarums, and excursions that were already besetting the denizens of Manhattan. The series ran intermittently until 1886, when Opper developed *The Age of Handbooks*, his irresistible parody of the self-improvement manuals that had become all the rage at this time. In this series Opper detailed the vexations befalling the readers of such probable and near-probable how-to books as "How to Become a Perfect Portrait Painter in Two Hours," "How to Avoid the Perils and Pitfalls of a Great City," "The Young Housekeeper's Infallible Cookbook," "The Graceful Guide to Dancing," and "The Handbook of High-Toned Etiquette." Other humorous series followed, including *The Suburban Resident* (1889), one of the first satiric swipes at the sterility and uniformity of suburban life.

It wasn't long before that redoubtable recruiter of cartooning talent, William Randolph Hearst, noticed Opper's work and brought him (or bought him) over in 1899 as the main political cartoonist for his chain of daily newspapers. He soon became one of the most feared pen artists of the era of presidents William McKinley and Theodore Roosevelt. His depiction of McKinley as a puppet in the hands of a bloated Wall Street tycoon was one of the most savage attacks perpetrated against an American president since the time of Thomas Nast (whose work Opper greatly admired). Nor was he more lenient toward McKinley's vice-president, Theodore Roosevelt ("Little Teddie") whom he portrayed as a circus-show cowboy, although the cartoonist's criticism changed to admiration when "Teddie" as president decided finally to take on "the Trusts." As Alan Gowans noted in his study *The Unchanging Arts*, "What Opper castigates is not a wicked man like Nast's Andrew Johnson, or a fool like Nast's Horace Greeley, but the abstract symbol of a government controlled by vested economic interests."

Opper's editorial cartoons were often organized in comic-strip form, sometimes running for considerable periods of time under their own titles, like *Mr. Trusty*, *The Cruise of the Piffle*, and the well-known parodies *Willie and Poppa* and *Willie and Teddie*. Whatever the merits of these political series (and they are considerable) their importance pales in comparison to the cartoonist's achievements in the related field of comic strips. Opper had been a keen observer of the development of the medium—a logical extension of the earlier humorous series—in the pages of Hearst's newspapers where, alongside his own work, such pioneers of the form as R. F. Outcault, Rudolph Dirks, and James Swinnerton were displaying their creations. Opper entered the field in the early months of the twentieth century with a master stroke: *Happy Hooligan*, created on March 26, 1900. A

bedraggled little Irish tramp with a lunar face and a tin-can for a hat, Happy was a hapless innocent who fell victim to his generous impulses; his various doings (as his adventures were initially called) were always half-baked attempts at winning sympathy from ungrateful strangers and correcting wrongs that almost invariably landed him in jail. Despite all these mishaps Happy remained true to his name and smiled through every misfortune. In Happy we can already recognize the figure of the beaten-down but indomitable "little man" epitomized later in films by Charlie Chaplin; and like Chaplin's tramp, Happy, in the end wins the girl, the pert Suzanne whom he courts under the very nose of her disapproving father.

Other characters soon came to populate the strip: Gloomy Gus, Happy's long-lost brother, whose luck and lugubrious mien were in sharp contrast to his sibling's unbounded optimism and fathomless misfortune; another brother posing as an English lord, the bespatted and waistcoated Montmorency; his pet dog Flip; and a host of other Happy relatives. Beginning in 1910 Happy's adventures turned into long narratives often set in exotic lands, with the hero and his cohorts falling into the most unlikely situations. *Happy Hooligan* was Opper's most enduring creation, lasting till 1932, when the artist's failing eyesight forced him to abandon the feature. "Stylistically," Coulton Waugh said of *Happy Hooligan*, "this is a handsome strip. Opper's 'doodle' for a head was a very special; one can pick it out of the old newspapers at a glance. . . . It is a round head with an enormous upper lip, two lines bounding this from nose to mouth corners. With this convention Opper carved a career. These heads were expressive: a little changing of the two lip lines and one had pathos, anger or joy; and they were funny, always."

The success of *Happy Hooligan* prompted Opper to venture further into the comic strip field. In 1902 he created *Alphonse and Gaston*, a weekly half-page feature about two ludicrously polite French gentlemen, later joined by their Parisian friend Leon. Attired in nineteenth-century dandy clothes they went through every kind of contretemps and mishap without once losing their good manners. Their constant scraping and bowing were part of the strip's charm, as were their repeated exchanges of courtesy—"After you, my dear Alphonse," "No, after *you*, my dear Gaston"—in the face of even deadly peril. These phrases have now passed into the language; in the early part of this century they helped form in no small measure the idea many Americans had of Frenchmen.

Like *Happy Hooligan*, *Alphonse and Gaston* enjoyed tremendous popular success, and Opper could have continued indefinitely with their adventures, had he not tired of the limitations imposed upon him by the basic situation. Their appearance became rarer and rarer after 1905, and they practically faded from view in the 1920s. The two main characters left their names as the legacy for overpoliteness; in this respect Opper emerged as a creator of types in a way that recalls Mark Twain.

Another Opper creation that has withstood the test of time is Maud, the unforgiving, unredeemable mule with the devastating kick. She first appeared as an occasional relief for the much better-known Happy and Alphonse and Gaston as early as 1904. An old, bespectacled, bewhiskered farmer named Si had bought her for ten dollars and as he

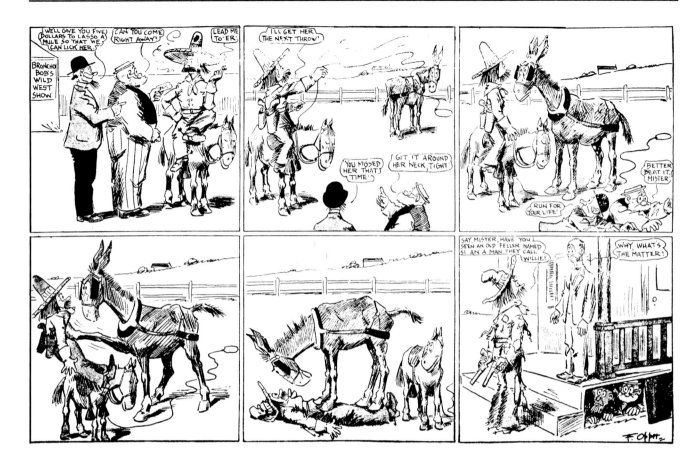

A *Maud* Sunday page by F. B. Opper, 1912

was showing off his acquisition to his wife Mirandy, the mule exhibited the first of what was to become an endless series of kicks, catapulting her master clear to the other side of his field. This turned into a weekly ritual, and the feature became firmly established as *And Her Name Was Maud!*, with the mule demonstrating her propulsive skills on farmhands, debt collectors, visiting relatives, and undesirable vagabonds alike; her supreme prowess, however, was reserved for the hapless Si whose schemes to rid himself of the terrible mule by means fair and foul always ended in a cataclysmic kick. "*And Her Name Was Maud*," Stephen Becker wrote, "was an endless variation on an ancient and explosive theme. . . and the plot varied only in nonessentials." Maud herself was temporarily dropped from Opper's gallery of characters in the mid-1910s, but the feature was revived in 1926 and ran as the companion strip to *Happy Hooligan* until both were dropped in 1932.

Opper often featured all of his characters together in his Sunday pages, having them run in and out of the action as the situation required. He also tried his hand at yet other comic-strip creations, most of them short-lived, such as *Howson Lott* (a variation on the theme of the suburban resident), *Mr. Dubb* (about still another helpless little man), and *Our Antediluvian Ancestors*, a very funny series about a family of prehistoric cavemen which is an obvious forerunner of television's *Flintstones*.

Opper's comic talents made him a favorite of humorous writers whose works he often illustrated, from Bill Nye's

comic *History of the United States* to Finley Peter Dunne's *Mr. Dooley's Philosophy* to Mark Twain's short stories. The cartoonist also did a very funny version of the fables of Aesop, for which his caricatural style was ideally suited. However, Opper's many achievements as an illustrator are far surpassed by his contributions to the art of the cartoon and, above all, to the nascent medium of the comics. Older than most of the early comic strip pioneers (Rudolph Dirks, James Swinnerton, etc.), he brought his considerable experience as a magazine cartoonist to the new medium. His role was that of catalyst and consolidator. In his many creations Opper summed up the possibilities of the form and brought to it many stylistic and narrative innovations, such as week-to-week continuity. His influence on latter generations of comic strip artists was therefore considerable.

Opper has often been described by those who knew him as a dour and cold man, insensitive to his family and derisive with his colleagues. Despite popular success and critical acclaim (he was known as "the dean of American cartoonists"), he was not a happy man and only found consolation from his misanthropy in his work. His forced retirement in 1932 and his subsequent (but vain) efforts at re-establishing his position soured him further on the human race. He died of a heart condition at his home in New Rochelle, New York, in August, 1937.

MEDIA ADAPTATIONS: Happy Hooligan (a series of animated shorts based on Opper's comic strip creation), International Film Service, 1917-19.

An editorial cartoon by F. B. Opper, 1922

BIOGRAPHICAL/CRITICAL SOURCES: Coulton Waugh, *The Comics*, Macmillan, 1947; *Dictionary of American Biography*, Supplement 2, Scribners, 1958; Stephen Becker, *Comic Art in America*, Simon & Schuster, 1959; *Who Was Who in America*, Vol. 1, Marquis, 1968; Pierre Couperie and Maurice Horn, *A History of the Comic Strip*, Crown, 1968; Alan Gowans, *The Unchanging Arts*, Lippincott, 1970; *Who Was Who among North American Authors*, Omnigraphics, 1976; *The World Encyclopedia of Comics*, Chelsea House, 1976; *Authors in the News*, Vol. 1, Gale, 1976; *The World Encyclopedia of Cartoons*, Chelsea House, 1980.

—Sketch by Maurice Horn

* * *

ORLIN, Richard   1947-

PERSONAL: Born October 27, 1947, in the Bronx, N.Y.; son of Louis (a post office employee) and Judith (Saportin) Orlin; married Arlene Grollman, August 15, 1971 (died, February, 1981); married Lindsay Gough (in foreign service), March 17, 1985. *Education:* Attended School of Visual Arts, 1978; Parsons School of Design, 1979. *Home and studio:* 2550 Olinville Ave., Bronx, N.Y. 10467.

CAREER: Account supervisor, Credit Clearing House (a collection agency), Harrison, N.Y., 1971-82; free-lance cartoonist, 1982—. *Military service:* U.S. Air Force, 1967.

MEMBER: Cartoonists Association, Graphic Artists Guild.

AWARDS, HONORS: Charles M. Schulz Award from the Scripps Howard Foundation, 1985.

WRITINGS: Contributor of cartoons to *Good Housekeeping, Better Homes and Gardens, New Yorker, National Lampoon, National Enquirer, TV Guide, Wall Street Journal,* and other publications.

WORK IN PROGRESS: "Self-syndicating a daily panel called *Doubletakes.*"

SIDELIGHTS: Richard Orlin, whose professional motto is "Quality humorous illustration with a different point of view," came into his calling by a circuitous route. While he admits to doodling at school instead of listening to his teachers, he never thought of art as a career until relatively late in life. He first tried his hand at cartooning soon after his marriage in 1971, but his efforts went largely unrewarded. "Several magazines sent me small checks to encourage me to stop submitting," he now says wryly. Changing course, he then took a job as a field collector for a finance company which he now regards as "great preparation for free-lance cartooning full-time—lots of rejection."

Orlin credits his first wife's insistence for his returning to the art field. In order to improve his draftsmanship he took courses at the Parsons School and the School of Visual Arts in New York City. One of the guest speakers at both schools was cartoonist Sam Gross who encouraged Orlin to go into professional cartooning. Gross's advice, coupled with Orlin's wife's death and his first sales to major markets such as *Good Housekeeping* and *Better Homes and Gardens*, prompted him to take up the risks (and rewards) of the free-lance cartoonist's life in 1982. "I gave myself one year," says Orlin about his decision; much to his surprise, he managed to surpass the financial goals he had set for himself even before the year was out.

Now an established cartoonist, with frequent contributions to such publications the *National Lampoon, TV Guide, Wall Street Journal,* and others, and with such corporate and institutional clients as Mobil Oil, the American Medical Association, and Consumers Union, Orlin sees the rewards of successful freelancing in more than monetary terms. "The biggest joy is having control of my life," he declares. "I enjoy setting my own boundaries and trying to exceed

Self-portrait of Richard Orlin (© 1985, Richard Orlin. Reprinted by permission.)

A humor cartoon (© 1984, Richard Orlin. Reprinted by permission.)

them." He usually puts aside one day in the week for developing gag ideas, and devotes the rest of the week to drawing and writing. An intense self-starter, he spends much time looking for new markets and cultivating old ones. His advice to beginning cartoonists is never to forget that "an artist is primarily a businessman with a product to sell."

Orlin admits to being "still mostly self-taught, and my cartoons probably look it." His line is simple and slightly grotesque, not unlike that of his mentor, Sam Gross. His ideas are often zany take-offs on well-worn cliches and conventions: A man comes to the end of the rainbow only to find an empty pot, while a leprechaun informs him that the gold has been moved to a Money Market account; in another instance a wishing well comes with a limited warranty. Orlin's cartoon panel, *Doubletakes*, which he syndicates himself, exhibits the same off-beat, yet unobtrusive humor that has become the artist's hallmark.

BIOGRAPHICAL/CRITICAL SOURCES: "Close Up: Richard Orlin," *Artist's Market*, Writer's Digest Books, 1985; Richard Orlin, "Working Well Is the Best Revenge," *Draw Magazine*, spring, 1985.

* * *

OSRIN, Ray(mond Harold) 1928-

PERSONAL: Surname is pronounced "Ozrin"; born October 5, 1928, in Brooklyn, N.Y.; son of Elkan (a jeweler) and Amelia (Boll) Osrin; divorced, 1977; married Stephanie Hearshen, 1981; children: (first marriage) Joanne, Caren, Glenn. *Education:* Attended Art Students League of New York, 1945-47. *Politics:* Independent conservative. *Religion:* Jewish. *Office:* Cleveland Plain Dealer, 1801 Superior Ave., Cleveland, Ohio 44114.

CAREER: Free-lance comic book illustrator, 1945-57; television animator, W. R. Smith, Inc., 1957-58; staff artist, *Pittsburgh Press*, 1958-63; staff artist, 1963-66, political cartoonist, 1966—, *Cleveland Plain Dealer*, Cleveland, Ohio.

MEMBER: Association of American Editorial Cartoonists.

AWARDS, HONORS: Freedoms Foundation, 1966 and 1967; National Headliners Award, 1971; International Salon of Cartoons, Montreal, Canada, 1975; Award for Excellence

in Journalism, Cleveland Press Club, 1978 and 1982; Sigma Delta Chi Distinguished Service Award, 1983; honorable mention, Fischetti Memorial Award, 1986.

WRITINGS: The Wizard of Osrin (collection of editorial cartoons), Plain Dealer Publishing Co., 1972.

FILMS: The Wizard of Osrin (a television montage), WKYC, Cleveland, 1972.

EXHIBITIONS: Caine Park Arts Festival, Cleveland Heights, Ohio, 1978-83. Represented in the permanent collection of the Lyndon B. Johnson Library, Austin, Tex.

SIDELIGHTS: After graduating from the High School of Industrial Art in New York City and while attending classes at the Art Students League, Ray Osrin worked a dozen years as a free-lance inker and illustrator for various comic book publishers. Many of these drawings show the influence of the great comic strip artists of the period, such as Milton Caniff, Burne Hogarth, and Frank Robbins, particularly in his background settings and the physical presence of his characters. Of special interest are comic books like the classic *Sheena, Queen of the Jungle, Jungle Comics*, and *Wings*, for Fiction House, "The Black Condor" in *Crack Comics*, and the perennial *Archie*.

When, in 1957, he decided to change artistic careers, Osrin moved to Pittsburgh, where he worked as a full-time animator for W. R. Smith Co. When Smith went out of business in 1958, Victor Free of the *Pittsburgh Press* hired him as staff artist, doing layouts and occasional cartoons. It was not until he went to the *Cleveland Plain Dealer*,

Self-portrait of Ray Osrin (© 1986, Ray Osrin. Reprinted by permission.)

An editorial cartoon for the *Cleveland Plain Dealer* (© 1985, Ray Osrin. Reprinted by permission.)

however, that he was offered the best opportunity to rise up the ladder. Although his title was still staff artist, Osrin, whose humor and graphic talent caught the attention of his editors, was soon given editorial page assignments, including one cartoon a week. Upon Edward D. Kuekes's retirement in February, 1966, Osrin was promoted to principal political cartoonist.

"It was tough going at first," declared Osrin in a *Cartoonist Profiles* article. "I really didn't feel qualified and at times, this got me down . . . Gradually I seemed to get in the right groove of thinking. But when I look back on some of my early efforts, I don't think I was hitting the ball." If at first he borrowed technique and subject matter from fellow cartoonists (for instance, Bill Mauldin, Paul Conrad, and Don Wright), he quickly acquired a caricatural style and a punchy brevity and directness of his own.

Over the last twenty years at the *Plain Dealer*, Ray Osrin has satirized presidents and their administrations from Johnson to Reagan, but his most trenchant barbs were aimed at Watergate and President Nixon. In one 1974 cartoon, under the heading "History," Abraham Lincoln sits next to an uneasy Richard Nixon (dressed in an ill-fitting suit, with holes at the knees) and asks him, "They called me 'Honest Abe.' What did they call you?" Politicians of every stripe and their shenanigans are, of course, fair game for Osrin's bite, whether it is Ed Meese the "thoroughly unqualified" candidate for Attorney General or the blanket rejection of officeholders by the man who tells his wife, "I'd give my eye teeth for a little taxation without representation."

In the field of foreign affairs, Osrin is outraged by the Russian attack on a Korean airliner (winning the victorious fighter pilot a "Marxmanship" medal), by Arab and Irish Republican Army terrorists and their ilk, and by the treatment of the Soviet dissidents Yelena and Andrei Sakharov. At home, he pokes fun at merger mania, increased telephone rates, sales of Saturday-night specials, President Ronald Reagan's hopes for a balanced budget, General Westmoreland's surrender to CBS. Cleveland and Ohio, too, are not immune, as in his cartoon of a highway over which a sign reads, "Leaving Ohio—Last chance to dump your hazardous wastes." Often, Osrin enjoys a bit of grim humor. On March 12, 1985, he drew a Soviet general crying at Soviet President Chernenko's funeral and on whose armband is written "Watch this space"; the very next day, Osrin published a cartoon of the Kremlin where two voices can be heard: "Are you ready for this. . . ?" "What?" "Gorbachev just called in sick."

In all his work, Ray Osrin shows that he has not only the eye of a fine caricaturist, but also the sharpness of a very perceptive observer of the political and social scene. Nevertheless, after almost thirty years at the drawing board, he looks forward to retiring and enjoying life's simple pleasures. This explains perhaps the lassitude that peeks through his advice to would-be cartoonists: "I would advise any young person to go into other work—McDonald's franchise, shoe store, plumbing, auto mechanic, carpenter, etc. But not law."

BIOGRAPHICAL/CRITICAL SOURCES: Cartoonist Profiles, March, 1976; *The World Encyclopedia of Cartoons*, Chelsea House, 1980; *Who's Who in America 1984-85*, Marquis, 1984.

—Sketch by Pierre Horn

P

PARK, W(illiam) B(ryan) 1936-

PERSONAL: Born June 12, 1936, in Sanford, Fla.; son of Charles Lanier, Sr. (a physician) and Geneva (Whitehead) Park; married Eva Kratzert (director of a Presbyterian Weekday School), December 28, 1961; children: Bryan, Christopher, Anne-Marie. *Education:* University of Florida, B.A., 1959; graduate study at School of Visual Arts, 1960-61, Rollins College, 1967 and 1977, Loch Haven Art Center, 1979, and Maitland Art Center, 1982. *Studio:* 110 Park Ave. S., Winter Park, Fla. 32789.

CAREER: Staff artist, McGraw-Hill Publishing Co., New York, N.Y., 1960-61; assistant art director, Tucker Wayne Advertising, Atlanta, Ga., 1961-63; owner, manager, and creative director, Park-Art Studio, Winter Park, Fla., 1963—. Free-lance writer and illustrator, 1968—. Creator of *Off the Leash* daily cartoon panel, syndicated by United Feature Syndicate, 1985—. Instructor at University of Central Florida, 1982-84; lecturer at colleges and institutions throughout Florida. *Military service:* U.S. Army Reserve, 1959-67.

MEMBER: Authors Guild of the Authors League of America, Cartoonists Association, Society of Illustrators.

AWARDS, HONORS: Hatch Merit Award from New England Art Directors Club, 1985; Chicago Book Clinic Award from Chicago Book Clinic, 1985.

WRITINGS—Juveniles, all self-illustrated: *The Pig in the Floppy Black Hat*, Putnam, 1973; *Jonathan's Friends*, Putnam, 1977; *Charlie-Bob's Fan*, Harcourt, 1981; *Bakery Business*, Little, Brown, 1983; *The Costume Party*, Little, Brown, 1983; *Who's Sick!*, Houghton, 1983.
Illustrator: William Kottmeyer and Audrey Claus, *Basic Goals in Spelling*, McGraw, 1972; R. N. Peck, *King of Kazoo*, Knopf, 1976; Peck, *Basket Case*, Doubleday, 1979; *Junior Great Books*, Great Books Foundation, 1984.

Contributor of stories, articles, and illustrations to national magazines, including *Smithsonian*, *Publisher's Weekly*, *Saturday Review*, *Intellectual Digest*, *New Yorker*, *Look*, *Fortune*, *Time*, *Reader's Digest*, and *TV Guide*.

EXHIBITIONS: One-man show at University of Central Florida, 1979. Work also represented in shows at the Time Building, 1977, Society of Illustrators, 1984, and Master Eagle Gallery, 1985, all in New York City, and in Switzerland, 1976 and 1986, and Japan, 1978 and 1986.

SIDELIGHTS: Few top flight graphic artists have enjoyed success in as many different formats as W. B. Park. He has covered air shows for *Flying* and horse and auto races for

"I told you we shouldn't have brought him."

A panel from *Off the Leash* by W. B. Park (© 1985, United Feature Syndicate. Reprinted by permission.)

Sports Illustrated as a journalist; done editorial illustrations for the *New York Times*, *Fortune*, and *Smithsonian*; worked on such prestige commercial advertising accounts as IBM, Westinghouse, and Marathon Oil; cartooned for the *New Yorker*; created a syndicated comic feature about people and their pets entitled *Off the Leash*; and written and/or illustrated several volumes of juvenile literature. It is this refusal to specialize, more than a signature style, that sets Park apart from his contemporaries. A student of design, Park's initial foundation was broader than that of the typical communication arts or fine arts graduate, but that alone does not explain his wide-ranging interests. By temperament he is a seeker with certain insights about society which he wishes to share with his fellows. "One of the goals of my work," he has said, "is to open up and encourage communication between people." And his own career seems a very mirror of the struggle which has has produced this desire for communication: the conflicting impulses of control and freedom in contemporary society.

A humorous illustration (© 1985, W. B. Park. Reprinted by permission.)

Just a few weeks after his college graduation Park decided to take a trip to Cuba, where Castro had just come to power, in order to spend some time recording in words and pictures the flavor of the post-revolutionary environment. The resulting illustrated article was enthusiastically received by the *Orlando Sentinel.* Buoyed by the discovery that he could make a living with his pen, Park moved to New York and a job as a staff artist with McGraw-Hill. His work there was not particularly challenging, but the opportunity to live in the city, he later recalled, was an education in itself—figuratively, with its dozens of museums and galleries, and literally, as a night student at the School of Visual Arts. Nonetheless, when the chance came to better himself professionally in 1961, he moved to Atlanta to take the position of assistant art director with an agency there. In 1963, that agency cut back and the junior art director found himself out of a job. At this point, he confronted the dilemma that would hereafter preoccupy him as an artist and as a thinker; and he opted for freedom rather than conventional security. On the theory that he stood the best chance of doing what he liked to do and the least chance of being laid off if he worked for himself, he returned to the Orlando area to found Park-Art Studio and try to make a living off local accounts.

By 1968 he had achieved enough commercial success to begin doing some independent creative work. His initial

essays in this direction were a series of illustrated fables—little moral parables in which he addressed himself to such quintessentially 1960s themes as peace, preservation of the environment, and, of course, the constant struggle between convention and (in the vernacular of the times) "letting it all hang out." It was while trying to interest the art director of *Holiday* magazine in one of these that he was offered instead the job of illustrating an article entitled "Chutzpah, Israeli Style." Told the work had to be done by ten the following morning, Park spent the night hurriedly completing the assignment in his hotel room, and it turned out to be the break in the New York market he had long been seeking. Soon his editorial work and fables were regularly appearing in such magazines as *Look, Holiday,* and *Intellectual Digest.* With the contraction in the number of mass circulation periodicals during the 1970s much of the market for editorial illustration also evaporated, but by this time Park had gained enough of a reputation as a reporter-illustrator to maintain a share of what remained.

Park also successfully expanded during this period into creating juvenile books. In what amounted to a statement of principle in *Contemporary Authors,* he argued passionately against "hard-eyed realists" who insisted on cutting down the "weeds and wildflowers. . . [to] create a golf green out of childhood," and "sweep the children's books of fun and innocence from the shelves and replace them with serious books about anger and truth and success and justice." His success as an author-illustrator of children's fiction is just another example of his spiritual agility. "In order to be successful," he declares, "I've had to climb back into childhood: I have to look at things the way a child would. I do a similar thing," he adds, "when I work on my *New Yorker* cartoons: it takes a mental leap to see things the way very sophisticated people do."

As befits one whose artistic and intellectual points of departure are so various, Park does not have a set style that is as immediately identifiable as an Edward Sorel, Charles Saxon, or Rowland Wilson. Instead he uses two basic approaches: ink and watercolor for relatively representational imagery for his commercial and editorial assignments and children's books; and ink line and wash impulse drawings for his cartoon and comic strip work. The artistic influences he admits to are, characteristically, intellectual rather than aesthetic, artists like Goya and Daumier "who struck out against the repression of people." Otherwise he refuses to be specific: "One of the things I do when I run up against a blank wall, and everyone does occasionally, is to look at good work. And not just illustration, but photography, sculpture—fine art. It really gets me cranked up." One rather eccentric compositional quirk is his occasional shift of pen from the right to the left hand; but the reason he gives for doing this is once again philosophical rather than technical: "I never know what will happen when I use my left hand. It's kind of interesting to see what develops."

Whatever style he works in, Park's drawings are invariably well-drafted and his sense of color is excellent; but their dominant distinction remains the intelligence and thought that go into them. A cover for the American Bar Association's quarterly *Litigation* devoted to the subject of "Procedure," for example, portrays a suited, briefcase-toting Minotaur standing in a labyrinth. Or his wickedly funny graphic complement to the caption, "Highly sophisticated robots will delight people with their life-like appearance and actions," in a mildly critical article about Walt Disney World in the *St. Petersburg Times*: a mechanical Abe Lincoln entering a men's room. This is, of course, the sort of wit and intellectual breadth that endears him to advertisers and cartoon editors.

Many graphic artists have retreated from high pressure environments like New York, Chicago, and Los Angeles to labor in comfortable obscurity; very few have managed to build national reputations from such narrow bases. That Park has done so owes, obviously, to his talents as an artist; but the qualities that have contributed the most to his success have been above all an independent mind and tenacity of purpose. In this respect, it is worth noting that one of his closest companions during his rise to prominence, as well as the inspiration for his *Off the Leash* comic feature was a free-spirited bulldog named Larry.

BIOGRAPHICAL/CRITICAL SOURCE: Communication Arts, January/February, 1978; *Something about the Author*, Vol. 22, Gale, 1981; *Contemporary Authors*, Vol. 97-100, Gale, 1981; *Print*, November/December, 1985.

—*Sketch by Richard Calhoun*

* * *

PENA, Amado Maurilio, Jr. 1943-

PERSONAL: Surname is pronounced "*Pen*-ya"; born October 1, 1943, in Laredo, Tex.; son of Amado Maurilio (a fireman) and Maria Beldomera (Arambula) Pena; children: Marcos, Jose Luis, Amado Maurilio, III. *Education:* Texas Agricultural and Industrial University, Kingsville, Tex., B.A., 1965, M.A., 1971. *Home:* 11511 Catalonia, Austin, Tex. 78759. *Agent:* El Taller Galleries, 510 East Ave., Austin, Tex. 78701.

CAREER: Free-lance artist in Texas, 1970—. Teacher, Laredo Independent School District, Laredo, Tex., 1965-70; teacher, Texas Agricultural and Industrial University, Kingsville, Tex., 1970-72; teacher, Crystal City Independent School District, Crystal City, Tex., 1972-74; Austin Independent School District, 1974-80. Curator and juror of art, demonstrator, and lecturer.

AWARDS, HONORS: Corpus Christi Art Foundation Award, Corpus Christi, Tex., 1979. Citation Award, Laguna Gloria Art Museum, Austin, Tex., 1982; Award of Recognition, City of Austin, 1983.

*EXHIBITIONS—*All one-man shows: Dos Patos Art Gallery, Corpus Christi, Tex., 1969 and 1970; Texas Agricultural and Industrial University, Kingsville, Tex., 1969 and 1970; Estudio Rios, Mission, Tex., 1971-73; New Mexico Highlands University, 1973; TSVM Architects and Associates, Austin, Tex., 1975; Washington State University, 1975; Kerby Lane Galleries, Austin, Tex., 1976, 1977, and 1979; Casa Adobe Gallery, El Paso, Tex., 1979-83.

El Taller, Austin, Tex., 1980-83; Dagan-Bela Gallery, San Antonio, Tex., 1980-83; Gallery 26 East, Tulsa, Okla., 1980-82; Hanging Tree Gallery, Midland, Tex., 1980; Hobar Gallery, Santa Barbara, Calif., 1980-82; Quail Hollow Gallery, Oklahoma City, Okla., 1980; Brush Gallery, Houston, Tex., 1981 and 1982; Ethnios II Gallery, Albuquerque, N.M., 1981; Galeria Elena, Newport Beach, Calif., 1981;

Houshang's Gallery, Dallas, Tex., 1981-85; Inter-American Development Bank, Washington, D.C., 1981; Julia Black Gallery, Taos, N.M., 1981; Kemper Galleries, Colorado Springs, Colo., 1981 and 1982; Lake Gallery, Tahoe City, Calif., 1981-83; Los Llanos Gallery, Santa Fe, N.M., 1981 and 1982; Westwood Gallery, Portland, Ore., 1981 and 1982; White Buffalo Gallery, Wichita, Kans., 1981 and 1982; Adagio Gallery, Palm Springs, Calif., 1982-85; Albatross Gallery, Boulder, Colo., 1982; American West, Chicago, Ill., 1982-85; Byrne-Getz Gallery, Aspen, Colo., 1982, 1983, and 1985; Galeria Capistrano, San Juan Capistrano, Calif., 1982, 1983, and 1985; Gekas-Nicholas, Tucson, Ariz., 1982; Los Arcos Art Gallery, Laredo, Tex., 1982.

Canyon Gallery, Ft. Lauderdale, Fla., 1983 and 1984; El Taller, Santa Fe., N.M., 1983 and 1984; El Taller, Taos, N.M., 1983-85; Graphic Image, Milburne, N.J., 1983 and 1984; Jentra Fine Arts, Freehold, N.J., 1983; Joan Cawley Gallery, Wichita, Kans., 1983; Joy Tash Gallery, Scottsdale, Ariz., 1983-85; Parke Gallery, Vail, Colo., 1983 and 1985; Impressions Gallery, Tucson, Ariz., 1984; Sterling Fine Arts, Laguna Beach, La Brea, San Jose, Calif., 1984; Vis-a-Vis, New Orleans, La., 1984; Squash Blossom, Vail, Colo., 1984; Gallery at Hog Hollow, St. Louis, Mo., 1984; Quintana Gallery, Portland, Ore., 1984; Squash Blossom Gallery, Denver, Colo., 1985; Lincoln Square Gallery, Arlington, Tex., 1985; Andrews Gallery, Albuquerque, N.M., 1985; Museum of Native American Art., Spokane, Wash., 1985; Kauffman Gallery, Houston, Tex., 1985.

SIDELIGHTS: Amado Pena is a painter and printmaker who has identified himself very strongly with both his region and his people, but has not thereby limited himself to the category of regionalist. A Mexican-American with strong cultural and aesthetic links to his Indian ancestry, he employs the American Southwest as his setting and the native American as his model, but his highly distinctive graphic style elevates his work from the plane of local color

AMADO MAURILIO PENA, JR.

and gives it a universal significance. Pena is clearly more preoccupied with concerns of form and line than with anthropologically or topographically correct depictions of character or scene.

Substantially educated in his profession, Pena has taken both a bachelor's and a master's degree in art and taught for fifteen years in the schools of Texas. His technical command of his media is evident in the refinement of his style and his control of color. Proficient with the complex techniques of serigraphy, lithography, and etching, Pena also works in oils and acrylics, and has recently explored the possibilities of mixed media employing oil, acrylic, pencil, ink, pastel, and watercolor. His range extends from murals to small-scale illustrations, although he is perhaps best known for his visually arresting serigraphs.

Pena has been widely employed in civic commissions and has executed many large and small public works. In 1980 his work was used in a commemoration of National Hispanic Heritage Week in Washington, D.C., and in 1982 an oil painting of his was presented to President Reagan by the National Hispanic Youth Institute. Fourteen separate commissions came to him in 1983, the sources including the Americana Museum in El Paso, the Santa Fe Festival of the Arts, the Nuevo Santander Museum in Laredo, the Scottsdale Festival in Arizona, the Laguna Gloria Art Museum in Austin, the Amarillo Art Center, the University of Texas at Austin, the El Paso Pro Musica Season, and the National Chicano Art Exhibit at Eastern Michigan University in Ypsilanti. The years since then have similarly brought Pena a wide range of commissions for public work. Pena's work has found its way into many private and public collections, including those of the Governor of Baja California (Mexico), the Universities of California and Texas, his own alma mater, Texas Agricultural and Industrial University, the Smithsonian Institution in Washington, and the People's Republic of China. A painting by Pena hangs in the presidential palace in Mexico.

Pena draws his themes most obviously from the life and spirit of the Indians of the U.S. Southwest and of Mexico, and his sometimes starkly simple compositions dramatically emphasize their ethnic identity. The elegance of his graphic design borders on Art Nouveau, with its sinuous line and delicate modeling, but the content of his work is too strong ever to allow him to fall into preciosity. His delicate colors are warm and vibrant, their luminosity evoking the sun-drenched desert landscape of the artist's home region, although Pena employs richer colors than the subdued palette of most of the genre artists of his area. Clearly his inspiration has been the folk art of the people he depicts, and their influence is evident in the artist's sense of mass and line.

Pena's subjects are humble, but his work never sinks to bathos or melodrama. Sometimes seeming merely decorative, his work may offer only the pleasure of form and color, his flowing line and massed plane always providing a balanced and pleasing whole. Often, however, his work is more illustrative and his subjects more specific. His Indian figures are often shown in traditional situations of work or domesticity. His *Tejedora* ("Weaver"), for example, shows an old Indian woman at her loom; other pictures show family groups or artisans in wood at their work. Pena has

Artesanas Elegantes, **a serigraph** (© 1985, Amado Pena. Reprinted by permission.)

seemingly not been tempted to follow the model of such noted Mexican muralists as David Alfaro Siqueiros, Jose Clemente Orozco, and Diego Rivera, whose often bombastic murals make strong moral statements, and he never allows himself to be reduced to the pop-anthropology of their more commercial pieces. If there is much in his modeling of faces that recalls Rivera's, there is more of the frankly nostalgic artist and illustrator Miguel Covarrubias, whose sensitive renderings of the native face of the Mexican reveals the same passionate devotion that can be seen in Pena.

If a message exists in the work of Amado Pena, it is not a revolutionary social or political one as in the murals of Siqueiros, Orozco, or Rivera, but rather a gentle reminder, a wistful suggestion, of the continuity and dignity of cultural forms. The hauntingly evocative serigraph *Antepasados* ("Ancestors"), for example, depicts a modern Indian family integrated into a slightly abstract curvilinear unit and set against a Mayan hieroglyph. Although the modern faces are not the same as the antique ones, the message comes through with clarity and eloquence, and the whole stylized arrangement forms both a dramatic statement and an aesthetically satisfying composition. With such pieces, Amado Pena has staked a claim to a well-defined territory for his work, and the sensitivity of his perceptions and the skill of his execution have established him as one of the most original and forceful artists of the Southwest.

BIOGRAPHICAL/CRITICAL SOURCES: Les Krantz, *American Artists*, Facts on File, 1985.

—*Sketch by Dennis Wepman*

* * *

PEREZ CLEMENTE, Manuel 1941- (Sanjulian)

PERSONAL: Born June 30, 1941, in Barcelona, Spain; son of Manuel (in the merchant marine) and Maria (Clemente) Perez; married Maria Isabel Castro Vega, May 21, 1971; children: Manuel, Daniel. *Education:* Attended Escuela Superior de Bellas Artes, Barcelona, 1961-66. *Home:* Pintor J. Miro, 27-29, Zona Terramar, Sitges (Barcelona), Spain. *Agent:* Herbert Spiers, S.I. International, 43 E. 19th St., New York, N.Y. 10003.

CAREER: Movie advertising artist, 1958-62; comic strip artist, Editorial Bruguera, Barcelona, Spain, 1961; comic strip artist, Selecciones Ilustradas, Barcelona, 1962-63; cover, book, and magazine illustrator, 1963—. *Military service:* Spanish Army, 1967-68, served in artillery and as an artist for the army publication *Ciudadela.*

MEMBER: Society of Illustrators (United States).

AWARDS, HONORS: Warren Publishing Co. Award as cover illustrator, New York City, 1973-76; "1984" Award for covers, Barcelona, 1979, 1982; Caran d'Ache award as best international illustrator, Lucca-16, Lucca, Italy, 1984; Premio Area de Juventud, Barcelona, 1985.

WRITINGS: Sanjulian—Ilustradores contemporaneos (anthology), Editorial Norma, Barcelona, 1984.

WORK IN PROGRESS: Illustration work, paintings, and advertising concepts.

SIDELIGHTS: The concept of "narrative figuration" could describe the essential directions of the gigantic illustration *oeuvre* signed Sanjulian (the pseudonym chosen by Manuel Perez Clemente for all of his works). Anatomy, pictorial classicism, epic feeling, along with the compositions that suggest vast horizons, the expressionistic instinct for the right lighting effects, the dramatic symbolism, and the striking angles of vision are the characteristic connotations of Sanjulian's style, and they all merge into what can be termed "the great spectacle of color illustration."

In conjunction with his studies at the Fine Arts School (which extended to graduate courses) and with the knowledge of the great pictorial works of the past, the roots of Sanjulian's brilliant artwork go back to his early works for the comics and for movie advertising; from both activities arose a narrative conception of his task that would later increase the artist's efficacy as an illustrator. We should not forget also how much Sanjulian is indebted in his meticulous perfectionism to one of his teachers at the School of Fine

MANUEL PEREZ CLEMENTE ("Sanjulian")

Arts; it was indeed this teacher, Maestro Sanvicens, who was also a painter, who talked him out of following his father's seafaring profession, and who led him to pursue his art studies.

His association with Josep Toutain's agency, Selecciones Ilustradas, resulted, first, in his abandoning his advertising work, and, later, his work for the comics; Toutain had found out that Sanjulian's comics lacked somewhat in sequential unity, but that, on the other hand, they displayed frequently powerful images. This led Toutain to conclude that the artist's natural medium should be illustration. From there followed Sanjulian's consecration as a noted oil painter and cover illustrator, as international success greeted his works for Scandinavian publishers. Sanjulian recalls that he was asked to supply "spectacular covers," and doubtlessly the fulfillment of this task was to determine his style in the future.

At the beginning of the 1970s Sanjulian added to the influences derived from the classical painters (Velazquez above all, in addition to the pre-Raphaelites) those of illustrators like Norman Rockwell and Frank Frazetta, borrowing from the latter the bold use of color and his conception of the fantastic. These contemporary American artists began to shape his work in 1971 when he entered, through Selecciones Ilustradas, the American market with an assignment for Dell (as a sidebar, his remuneration for this work was spent on an engagement ring for his future wife). From then on Sanjulian has developed an intense work relationship with American publishers, particularly in

An illustration for a western novel (© 1982, Sanjulian. Reprinted by permission.)

the field of covers for paperback novels. To date the artist has worked for Ace, Avon, Ballantine, Bantam, Berkley, Literary Guild, Reader's Digest, Jove Press, Dell, Fawcett, New American Library, Playboy, Scholastic, Harlequin, and Warner (for which he did the famous cover to the paperback edition of Umberto Eco's *The Name of the Rose*). He has also done covers for comic magazines such as *Creepy, Eerie, Vampirella*, and *Heavy Metal.*

In 1983 Sanjulian changed agents, passing from Selecciones Ilustradas to´ Norma, without the slightest break in his prolific career, a career that has its center in the United States, and its impetus in a strong feeling for the spectacular. The artist looks upon his work as that of a specialized painter, whose production is aimed at a multitudinous audience. Among other ambitions, Sanjulian is planning to re-enter the field of film illustration, this time, of course, on an international scale.

BIOGRAPHICAL/CRITICAL SOURCES: Comix Internacional, Number 8, Barcelona, 1981.

* * *

PFLUGH, Gerald J.   1942-
(Jerry Flu)

PERSONAL: Surname is pronounced "flu," hence the artist's nom de plume; born June 22, 1942, in Hoboken, N.J.; son of Theodore J. (an accountant) and Eileen (an insurance broker; maiden name, Burke) Pflugh; married Sue Kraft, July, 1968 (divorced July, 1983); children: Gerald, Jr., Gretchen, Kristine, Jordan. *Education:* University of Bridgeport, B.S., 1964; Yale University, B.F.A. and M.F.A., 1966. *Home:* Anchorage, Alaska. *Office:* P.O. Box 102066, Anchorage, Alaska 99510.

CAREER: Artist and book designer, Harcourt, Brace & World, New York City, 1966-68; free-lance commercial artist and book designer, 1968-70; elementary school teacher, Craig, Alaska, 1970-73; artist, Walt Disney Studio, Burbank, Calif., 1974-75; teacher, Craig, Alaska, 1975-78; editorial cartoonist and staff artist, *Anchorage Times*, Anchorage, Alaska, 1978—, comic strip artist and writer, *Casey's Cabin,* 1978-79, *Casey's Office Gang*, 1979-82, and *Muk 'n Luck*, 1982-84.

MEMBER: National Cartoonists Society.

WRITINGS—Under name, Jerry Flu: *Alaskatoons*, Arctic Circle, 1982. Also author and illustrator of six yearly Christmas story-supplements for *Anchorage Times*, 1979-84.

EXHIBITIONS: Many shows in libraries and banks in Anchorage, Alaska.

WORK IN PROGRESS: Painting in acrylics for local exhibition; developing newspaper features for possible syndication; work scheduled to appear in an anthology of cartoons on the Statue of Liberty edited by Tony Aguillo.

SIDELIGHTS: Jerry Flu's adventurous spirit and restless imagination have taken him from graduate studies in fine arts at Yale University to the frozen wastes of Alaska. After a promising beginning in book design, doing covers, sample

GERALD J. PFLUGH

pages, typography, and page layouts for secondary-school textbooks at Harcourt Brace in New York and book jackets for others on the side, he spent two years as a free-lance artist doing jackets and sample pages for such major publishers as Praeger, McGraw-Hill, Doubleday, and Oxford University Press. During this time he also redesigned the weekly New York newspaper *Manhattan East*. At the age of twenty-eight, he felt the call of wanderlust and made his way to Alaska, where he spent three years teaching in a tiny fishing village accessible only by float plane. As one of three teachers in the elementary school of Craig, on Prince of Wales Island in southeast Alaska, Flu came to know the island's population of four hundred Tlingit and Haida Indians so well that he returned two years later for another three-year stint as a teacher in Craig.

Between these two adventures, however, Flu fulfilled his lifetime fantasy of working for the Walt Disney Studio. Asthmatic as a child, he had spent much of his time in bed reading comics and dreaming of being a cartoonist with Disney. In 1973 he decided to present the Burbank, California, studio with a portfolio and ask for a job, and for the next two years he penciled pages for *Mickey Mouse* comics for foreign publishers (the American publisher was using reprint material at the time) in the same studio as such legendary Disney artists as Floyd Gottfredson, Manuel Gonzales, Mike Arens, and Frank Grundeen, all childhood heroes of his.

After three more years back in the classrooms of Craig, Flu took a position with the *Anchorage Times* in 1978. He has been there ever since as editorial cartoonist and staff artist.

An editorial cartoon by Jerry Flu (© 1986, *Anchorage Times.* Reprinted by permission.)

During that time he has produced many features, both for his newspaper and on his own, and he continues to generate new ideas. In 1982 he did a tourist item, *Alaskatoons,* for the local publisher Arctic Circle, and the far north remained his artistic setting for several other efforts. The *Anchorage Times* has run three daily and Sunday comic strips by Flu: *Casey's Cabin,* the humorous adventures of a rural sourdough living in the Alaskan bush, which ran six times a week from June 19, 1978 to September 1, 1979; *Casey's Office Gang,* taking his hero Casey to Anchorage and showing him in an office job, which ran daily from September 4, 1979, to May 30, 1982, and as a color Sunday page from November 18, 1979, to May 21, 1982; and *Muk 'n Luk,* an "off the wall" humor strip about a Mutt-and-Jeff pair of Alaskans, which ran daily and Sunday from the middle of 1982 to the middle of 1984. In 1984 Flu "dropped the strips to take on a variety of art chores for [his] newsroom, including such things as graphics, illustrations, court room sketches, etc.," but he continues to develop new ideas and usually tries to submit at least one set of samples to the major syndicates each year.

The center of his professional output, however, remains his two regular features with the *Anchorage Times.* His daily editorial cartoon, *Alaska Fever,* began on March 3, 1978, and has appeared six times a week ever since; his Sunday editorial-page features, *Week in Review,* began at the same time and includes about three cartoons relating to some topic of the week. With all of this large output, Flu still finds time to undertake other projects. In 1982 he scripted and drew a twenty-page tabloid-size supplement as an advertising feature for his newspaper. *The Christmas Caper,* a long, well-developed Christmas story about two burglars and their unplanned affirmation of the holiday spirit for a little boy in danger of losing his faith in Santa Claus, shows the influence of Flu's Disney years and his life-long dedication to the comics. Among the favorites he acknowledges as influences and inspirations, he lists *Barney Google*'s Billy DeBeck, *Beetle Bailey*'s Mort Walker, *B.C.*'s Johnny Hart, *Mad*'s Jack Davis and Wallace Wood, *Sam's Strip*'s Jerry Dumas (whose art Flu's much resembles), and "almost everything done at the Disney Studio."

Flu's editorial cartoons generally deal with local concerns and thus do not make a political statement that would be meaningful outside of Alaska. He wrote *CGA,* "In the sixties I was opposed to the war and in favor of civil rights. In the seventies I was opposed to the mushrooming role of government in private lives. Currently I favor the economic policies of the Reagan administration, but oppose the social agenda and military expansionism of the right." He declines

Muk 'n Luk   by Jerry Flu

A *Muk and Luk* daily strip (©1983, Jerry Flu. Reprinted by permission.)

to identify himself with a political philosophy "beyond believing in democracy."

Flu employs the complete range of artist's tools for his cartooning: pen and ink, brush, marker, etc., along with all the usual screens and shading materials. Outside of his newspaper office, he devotes his spare time to painting, preferring acrylics, and is widely shown in local institutions. He describes the themes of his realistically painted images as "a kind of 'pop-surreal.'" The only aspect of art he still considers adding to his life is teaching it at the university level; otherwise his restless, searching, creative spirit has found satisfaction in his many outlets. "I love art," Flu states. "I am grateful to be able to make a living at what I would otherwise do in my spare time." The citizens of Alaska have reason to be grateful, too, for a witty and skilled artist in their midst.

BIOGRAPHICAL/CRITICAL SOURCES: National Cartoonists Society Album, 1980.

—*Sketch by Dennis Wepman*

* * *

PLETCHER, Eldon L(ee) 1922-

PERSONAL: Born September 10, 1922, in Goshen, Ind.; son of Arthur (a farmer) and Dora (Cripe) Pletcher; married Barbara Jeanne (a bookkeeper; maiden name, Jones), January 29, 1948; children: Thomas Lee, Ellen Irene Metzger. *Education:* Attended Chicago Academy of Fine Arts, 1941-42; John Herron Art School, Indianapolis, Ind., 1946-47. *Politics:* Democrat. *Religion:* Presbyterian. *Home:* 331 Tiffany St., Slidell, La. 70461. *Syndicate:* Rothco Cartoons, Yonkers, N.Y.

CAREER: Worked as construction laborer and in factory, 1947-49; editorial cartoonist, *Sioux City Journal*, 1949-66; editorial cartoonist, *Times Picayune/States-Item*, (*Times Picayune* until 1980), New Orleans, La., 1966-84; free-lance

ELDON L. PLETCHER

FIRST THE GOOD NEWS . . .

A panel from *First the Good News...*(© 1983, Eldon L. Pletcher. Distributed by Rothco Cartoons. Reprinted by permission.)

cartoonist, 1984—; artist and writer of syndicated panel, *First the Good News. . .* , 1977—. *Military service:* U.S. Army, 1943-46, served with 301st Combat Engineers in Europe.

MEMBER: Association of American Editorial Cartoonists.

AWARDS, HONORS: Twelve awards from the Freedoms Foundation; Christopher Award, 1955.

WRITINGS—Contributor: *Best Cartoons of the Year* (annual anthology), Pelican, 1972—; Jerry Robinson, editor, *The 1970s: Best Political Cartoons of the Decade*, McGraw-Hill, 1980. Cartoons have been used in a number of school textbooks and encyclopedias.

EXHIBITIONS: In permanent exhibit at Syracuse University, University of Southern Mississippi, Wichita State University, Boston Museum of Art, Harry S. Truman Library, Lyndon R. Johnson Library.

SIDELIGHTS: After military service and a year of art school in Indianapolis, Eldon Pletcher had to work on construction sites around the Midwest, and later at the Fisher Body plant in Kansas City (where he had moved after his marriage) in order to support himself and his bride, while practicing his cartooning skills in his spare time. When he heard that Roy Justus was leaving his position as editorial cartoonist on the *Sioux City Journal* and moving to Minneapolis, Pletcher promptly applied for the job, and got it on the strength of the cartoons he had done for the *Elkhart Truth* in Indiana (his first professional job before he was drafted) and for the Army magazine *Yank*.

In Sioux City Pletcher waded into Iowa politics with such gusto and wielded the pen with such slashing vigor that he was dubbed "Pletch the Wretch," a nickname bestowed upon him by an irate reader and promptly picked up by the

newspaper staff. During his seventeen years of service with the *Journal*, Pletcher steadily acquired a growing constituency as well as a national reputation, and this helped him gain the much coveted editorial cartooning position on the New Orleans *Times-Picayune*, following the retirement in 1966 of Keith Temple.

By his own admission Pletcher devoted the bulk of his *Times-Picayune* cartoons to local and state issues (and Louisiana politics being what they are, he had a field day with the likes of Mayor Moon Landrieu and Governor Edwin Edwards); but he also touched more than once upon national and international questions, and his cartoons on the Watergate affair and the Vietnam war have been much reprinted and anthologized. His drawing style is quiet and simple, but his commentary and captions are often devastating.

In 1984 Pletcher retired from the newspaper's staff. He now draws an occasional editorial cartoon, but devotes most of his time to *First the Good News. . .* , a two-panel feature which he first developed in 1977 on the *Times-Picayune* (where it appeared twice a week) and which he now draws for the Rothco Cartoons Syndicate. The feature presents two contrasting views of a given issue or situation in each of the two panels: one (drawn on a white background) is appropriately sunny, while the other (done on a gray-shaded background) is correspondingly gloomy. For instance, an automobile company executive is seen sitting at his desk, beaming, under the caption: "Safety first" in the first panel; with the same executive looking crestfallen in the second panel, while the caption now proclaims: "Recall second." In another panel an elderly gentleman proudly declares: "I passed the doctor's stress test," but glumly adds: ". . . but went to pieces when I got the bill."

"The younger cartoonists seem to be following a certain pattern," Pletcher once mused. "College, working on a college paper, and then on to a newspaper somewhere. In looking back on things, this would appear to make a great deal more sense than the construction site-auto assembly plant route."

BIOGRAPHICAL/CRITICAL SOURCES: Cartoonist Profiles, December, 1979; Who's Who in America 1984-85, Marquis, 1984; Who's Who in American Journalism, Media Research & Publishing, 1985.

* * *

POJAR, Bretislav 1923-

PERSONAL: Born October 7, 1923, in Susice, Czechoslovakia; son of Ota (a post-office clerk) and Amalie (Valisova) Pojar; married Jaroslava Kosova, 1946; children: Jaroslav, Jiri. Education: Attended grammar school, 1939-42. Home: Trojicka 1, Praha 2, Czechoslovakia.

CAREER: Animator and director, AFIT (special-effects studio), Prague, Czechoslovakia, 1942-45; animator and director, Studio Bratri v triku (animation studio), 1945-51; animator and director, Studio loutkoveho filmu, Prague, (puppet-animation studio), 1951—.

AWARDS, HONORS: More than one hundred awards from film festivals around the world, including Golden Palm at Cannes, 1954, and Main Prize at Oberhausen, 1956, both for A Drop Too Much; Grand Prix at Montevideo, 1956, for Adventure in Golden Bay; Grand Prix at Annecy, 1960, for The Lion and the Song; St. Mark's Lion (first prize) at Venice, 1961, for School for Cats; First Prize from Karlovy Vary, 1963, for The Opening Speech Will Be Delivered; Golden Pelican (first prize), Mamaia, 1966, for Princesses

BRETISLAV POJAR

Are Not to Be Sniffed at; Golden Palm at Cannes, 1973, for Balablok, and 1979, for Boom; Liv Ullman Special Peace Prize, Chicago, 1984, for If. Named Artist of Merit by Government of Czechoslovakia.

FILMS—All puppet and/or cartoon animation, all as director: Pernikova chaloupka (English-language version known as "The Gingerbread House"), 1951; O sklenicku vic ("A Drop Too Much"), 1954; Spejbl na stope ("Spejbl on the Trail"), 1956; Paraplicko ("The Little Umbrella"), 1957; Lev a pisnicka ("The Lion and the Song"), 1959; Bombomanie ("Bombomania"), 1959; Jak zaridit byt ("How to Furnish a Flat"), 1959.

Pulnocni prihoda ("The Midnight Adventure"), 1960; Kocici slovo ("The World of a Cat"), 1960; Malovani pro kocku ("Drawings for Cats"), 1960; Kocici skola ("School for Cats"), 1961; Biliar ("Billiards"), 1961; Uvodni slovo pronese ("The Opening Speech Will Be Delivered"), 1962; Romance, 1963; Ideal, 1964; Potkali se u Kolina ("They Met near Kolin"), 1965; Jak jeli k vode ("How the Bears Went Swimming"), 1965; K princeznam se necucha ("Princesses Are Not to Be Sniffed At"), 1965; Drzte si klobouky ("Hold Your Hats"), 1966; Jak jedli vtipnou kasi ("How They Ate the Porridge of Wisdom"), 1966; Jak sli spat ("And So to Bed"), 1967; Fanfaron, maly klaun ("The Little Clown"), 1968; Ilusologie ("To See or Not to See"), 1969; Co zizala netusila aneb Darwin Antidarwin ("What the Worm Didn't Guess"), 1969.

Co to bouchlo? ("What's That Bang?"), 1970; Psi kusy ("The Dog-Fiddler"), 1970; A nerikej mi Vasiku ("Don't Call Me Vasik"), 1972; Nazdar, kedlubny!, ("Hello Kohlrabi"), 1973; Balablok, 1973; Milovnik zvirat ("The Animal Lover"), 1974; Jablonova panna ("The Apple-Tree Maiden"), 1974; O te velke mlze ("That Great Fog"), 1975; Jak ulovit tygra ("How to Hunt a Tiger"), 1976; O mysich ve staniolu ("Tin-foil Mice"), 1976; Velryba Arbylev ("Arbylev the Whale"), 1976; Proc ma clovek psa ("Why Do We Have Dogs?"), 1979; Bum ("Boom"), 1979; Kdyby ("If"), 1981.

Documentary films; as director: Josef Manes I, 1951; Josef Manes II, 1952; Svatecni den ("Festive Day"), 1956.

Full-length live-action film; as director: Dobrodruzstvi na Zlate ("Adventure in Golden Bay"), 1955.

Producer and director of television films and advertising shorts.

SIDELIGHTS: Live-action cinematography works with reality or a reasonable model thereof, but a film animator must invent his own universe, including characters, settings, and, above all, methods of animation. All actions are very precisely timed and drawn according to a pre-established screenplay; while a live-action director can shoot six or seven times more footage than required, the animation director must make each shot count and must conform to the iron law of twenty-four frames per second (the number of frames that must pass through the animation camera in order to create the illusion of movement). Among the select band of creative animators around the world Bretislav Pojar occupies the front rank, along with very few others.

Pojar started his career at Prague's AFIT studios in 1942, gradually mastering all phases of animation, as a background man, colorist, main animator, and finally director of

A frame from *Boom* (© 1979, Bretislav Pojar. Reprinted by permission.)

both cartoon and puppet films. (Puppet film is a Czech specialty, using costumed, fifteen-jointed puppets.) He soon become a close collaborator to famous puppet-film director Jiri Trnka. After a short period in film documentaries, he came back to puppet-film animation.

Pojar's directorial debut came in 1951 with *The Gingerbread House*, with Trnka as graphic artist on this fairy tale, and the film was faithful to the methods of Pojar's teacher. With the anti-alcoholic morality play *A Drop Too Much* he still worked with Trnka, but his conception was already taking an original turn. This work (which won first prize at the Cannes Film Festival) introduced for the first time dynamic action animation (substituting for lighting effects) to puppet films. Two years later he shot his first live-action film, *Adventure in Golden Bay*, a full-length movie for children; despite the feature's critical and popular success, Pojar came back (this time definitively) to animation. The possibilities in animated films for dramatic shortcuts, artistic stylization, fantastic exaggeration, and gag building enable him to use his fundamental skill—that of encapsulating a profound idea in one sequence, with a feeling for poetry as well as for irony, for reality as well as fantasy. To be sure, all of Pojar's films are by their very nature for young people, but he speaks to

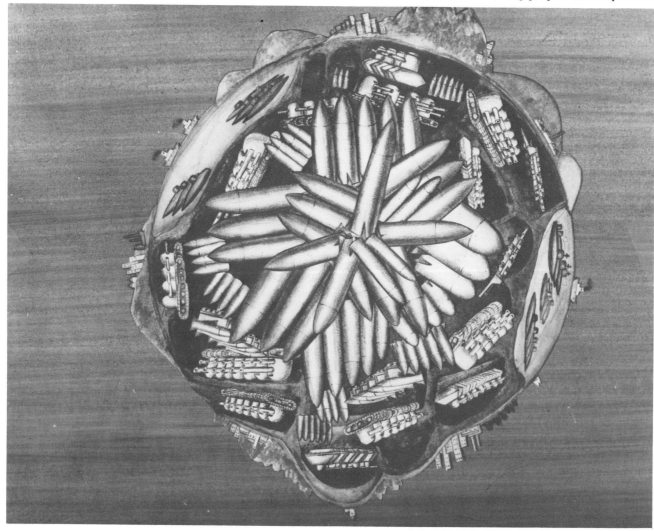

A frame from *If* (© 1981, Bretislav Pojar. Reprinted by permission.)

A frame from *Why Do We Have Dogs?* (© 1979, Bretislav Pojar. Reprinted by permission.)

adults as well as to children, in a lovely, child-like, humorous, but never patronizing way.

The first portent of Pojar's newfound creativity was *The Little Umbrella*, a 1957 film with virtually no storyline, but imbued with great feeling and tenderness. Since 1958 Pojar has worked independently, except for two occasions: he made two animated cartoons with Trnka, *Slava* ("Glory") and *Bombomania*, in 1959 and 1960. The first film dealt with the consumer approach to the arts, the other with people's obsession to build more and more devastating weapons of war; both remain timely to this day.

Pojar's most acclaimed effort came in 1960. *The Lion and the Song* is an expressive puppet film about the immortality of art revealed in a poetic metaphor. In the film a little harlequin plays the harmonica to the animals in the desert, but is silenced when a horrible lion eats him down along with his instrument. Some time later a pilgrim picks up the harmonica from the whitened skeleton of the lion and continues the tune from the point at which the harlequin had stopped. Pojar's talents as a storyteller and an animator are nowhere as apparent as in this film, in which he creates an admirable parable on a too-often trivialized theme.

Other Pojar films made in the 1960s are marked with the same ambitious strivings. In many of them he worked not only as animator but as designer as well; using a variety of materials, he helped improve the blending of graphic and animation inventions. When Pojar judges the theme suitable, he still produces the entire film by himself (as, for instance, with *Boom* and *If*). Nevertheless, when he feels that the subject requires a different graphic approach from his own, he calls on the services of outside designers. Pojar understands fully that film as creative art is most often a collective activity, a team effort in which the director's role is that of an orchestra leader.

If Pojar's adult films can sometimes be filled with a message (except in *The Lion and the Song*), this cannot be said of his children's films, which are playful and charming. In collaboration with designer Miroslav Stepanek he made a trilogy about two mischievous kittens (*The World of a Cat*, *Drawings for Cats*, and *School for Cats*) in 1960 and 1961. In these films Pojar's aim is to fire up children's imaginations with poetry, wit, and playfulness. He needs no story-line, only sketched-out characters, dynamic action sequences, and especially emotion-stirring animation. With two drawn kittens performing tricks with a live mime (Ladislav Fialka), these films create poetry in motion and are very close in excellence and imagination to the distinguished Canadian director Norman McLaren's achievements in the field of children's animation.

In the mid-1960s and early 1970s it can be said without exaggeration that Pojar with his "bear series" and his subsequent films achieved the same artistic stature as McLaren himself, endowing the puppet film with the same limitless possibilities that cartoon animation enjoys. While in the kitten films only the props changed, here the characters themselves underwent fantastic transformations. Thus the little bears, in accordance with the situation, turn into cars, rakes, engines, or garbage cans. These films are beloved by children and adult audiences alike.

During this period, "The Week of Czechoslovak Films" took place in Canada, with one entire evening reserved for Pojar's shorts. After that he was asked to make several advertising shorts for the host country, and present-day Canadian animators learned much from these films. Since the late 1960s Pojar has had a commitment to the National Film Board of Canada for which he has made a number of advertising and educational pictures. He is currently working with Canadian filmmaker Jacques Drouin on a joint film to be called *Romance in the Darkness*, using different kinds of animation techniques.

Pojar's kitten films also brought him to the notice of the United Nations' film and television section and resulted in the director being asked to make a film about the arms race. For a title the artist chose *Boom* because it could be easily understood in a number of languages; the film was animated with cut-out figures against a drawn background. The cartoon won the Golden Palm at Cannes in 1979, making Pojar the only three-time winner of this coveted award (he had been awarded previously for *A Drop Too Much* and *Balablok*) in the entire history of the festival. The great success enjoyed by *Boom* prompted the U.N. to commission a second Pojar film, this time on the economic consequences of the arms race. The result was the 1981 masterpiece about a rainbow-colored dream and a drab-grey reality, *If.*

Pojar's reputation has grown by leaps and bounds during the 1970s, and he is now considered one of the masters of the medium of animation. He is a remarkable example of a versatile filmmaker who approaches his films from two directions simultaneously—that of animator and that of graphic artist. He has not only perfectly mastered both these disciplines, but he is able to achieve their harmonious synthesis. His abundant filmography is remarkable in its consistency and quality and overflows with important works. His visual inventiveness, witty storytelling, and dynamic animation have all contributed to give his films an international flavor and a world-wide public.

BIOGRAPHICAL/CRITICAL SOURCES: Robert Benayoun, *Le dessin anime apres Walt Disney*, J. J. Pauvert (Paris), 1961; Ralph Stephenson, *The Animated Film*, A. S. Barnes, 1973; *The World Encyclopedia of Cartoons*, Chelsea House, 1980.

—*Sketch by Leonid Krizek*

* * *

PRAT, Enric Torres
   See TORRES PRAT, Enric

ALEXANDRU PREISS

PREISS, Alexandru 1952-

PERSONAL: Born October 4, 1952, in Bucharest, Romania; son of Hugo (an economist) and Peppy (Lindenberg) Preiss; married Marlene Kennedy (a graphic designer), May 7, 1983. *Education:* N. Grigorescu Fine Arts Institute, Bucharest, Romania, Bachelor in Decorative Arts, 1976, Certificate in Industrial Design, 1977; Purdue University, M.A., 1981. *Home and studio*: 3007 Courthouse Dr., West Lafayette, Ind. 47906. *Agent:* Cohen Art Enterprises, 663 S. Pearl St., Denver, Colo. 80209.

CAREER: Industrial designer, National Film Co., Bucharest, Romania, 1975-76; industrial designer, Bus Co., Bucharest, 1976-77; graphic designer and fashion photographer, F.C.T.B. Fashion Co., Bucharest, 1977-78; industrial designer, John Deere Co., Moline, Ill., 1979-81; assistant professor of art and design, Purdue University, West Lafayette, Ind., 1981—.

MEMBER: Industrial Designers Society of America, American Institute of Graphic Arts.

AWARDS, HONORS: Art League Award of Excellence, Lafayette, Ind., 1982; Award of Excellence in illustration, Indiana Art Directors Club, 1983 and 1984; Silver Medal, XI Biennial of Graphic Design, Brno, Czechoslovakia, 1984;

***Paradise*, a collage and mixed-media piece** (© 1985, Alexandru Preiss. Reprinted by permission.)

Award of Excellence in trademarks category, from American Corporate Identity, Cincinnati, Ohio, 1986. Named Outstanding Young Man of America, 1984.

EXHIBITIONS: Dalles Gallery, Bucharest, Romania, 1976 and 1977; Kalinderu Gallery, Bucharest, 1976; National Theatre Gallery, Bucharest, 1977; (one-man photographic show) Creative Arts Gallery, Purdue University, 1980; Contemporary Arts Center, Cincinnati, Ohio, 1981; (one-man show) Ralph Beelke Gallery, Purdue University, 1982; Waxenberg Galleries, Denver, Colo., 1982; Cohen Gallery, Denver, 1982 and 1985; Smithsonian Institution Traveling Exhibition, 1982; Owensboro Museum of Fine Art, Owensboro, Ky., 1982; New Orleans Art Association, New Orleans, La., 1982; Gallery II, Charlottesville, Va., 1983; University of North Dakota, Grand Forks, N.D., 1983; WPA Gallery, Chicago, Ill., 1983; Pleiades Gallery, New York City, 1983; International Exhibition of Illustration and Editorial Art, Brno, Czechoslovakia, 1984; (one-man show) Second Street Gallery, Charlottesville, Va., 1984; Stewart Center Gallery, Purdue University, 1985 and 1986; La Grange National Exhibition, La Grange, Ga., 1985.

WORK IN PROGRESS: Collage using wallpaper as media.

SIDELIGHTS: "The main motivation of my work is self-discovery and the ability to convey a message," Alexandru

Preiss wrote *CGA*. "The more I draw, the more I see things that can be explored. Color is a very strong element throughout my work, but the style of drawing and the media which I use have changed. I began by using color pencils and pastels almost exclusively; now I use much more mixed media: transfer images, tempera, collage. The technique varies according to the intended message: color, texture, and drawing all convey subtle meanings. My inspiration derives from the social structure in which we live. The drawings are my interpretation of what I see happening all around us: inter-relationships between individuals and the complex relationships between the individual and the whole of society."

While there is a strong element of realism in Preiss's work, it is subordinated to a sense of foreboding and anxious expectation, heightened by the symbol-laden objects the artist uses in his work. In the 1985 collage titled *Paradise*, for example, the three human characters who occupy the center of the stage peer apprehensively into the sky for some clues to their condition. In *The Supper*, three characters again (two of whom have masks for faces) enact a strange ritual in a room rendered even more ominous by the distortions of perspective that transform into an otherworldly, alien space. There is much in Preiss's oeuvre that recalls the work of such fantastic post-modernist artists as the Italian Giorgio Morandi.

With his qualities of strangeness and incantation, it is not surprising that Preiss chose to illustrate Mikhail Bulgakov's black allegory *The Master and Margareta*, a modern reinterpretation of the Doctor Faust legend. The artist did not disappoint, and his stark, cruel—and at the same time farcical—images perfectly reflect the dark mood and the ambiguous meaning of the author's disturbing fable. (This version remains as yet unpublished.)

BIOGRAPHICAL/CRITICAL SOURCES: Lafayette Leader, July 29, 1982, September 2, 1982; *Indianapolis News*, August 28, 1982; Les Krantz, *American Artists*, Facts on File, 1985.

* * *

PYLE, Howard   1853-1911

PERSONAL: Born March 5, 1853, in Wilmington, Del.; died November 9, 1911, in Florence, Italy; son of William (owner of a leather business) and Margaret Churchman (Painter) Pyle; married Anne Poole (a singer), April 12, 1881. *Education:* Attended private schools, art school in Philadelphia for three years, and Art Students League in New York. *Religion:* Quaker. *Home:* Wilmington, Del.

CAREER: Author, artist, painter, teacher of illustration, and writer of children's stories: employed as an illustrator for *Scribner's Monthly*; taught illustration at Drexel Institute of Arts and Sciences in Philadelphia, 1894-1900, later establishing his own art school in Wilmington. *Member:* National Institute of Arts and Letters, Associate National Academy, National Academy, Century Club (New York), Franklin Inn Club (Philadelphia).

WRITINGS—All self-illustrated, except as noted: *The Merry Adventures of Robin Hood of Great Renown, in Nottinghamshire*, Scribner, 1883, reissued, Dover, 1968 [other editions illustrated by Lawrence Beall Smith, Grosset & Dunlap, 1952; Paul Busch, Whitman, 1955; Benvenuti, Golden Press, 1962; Jo Polseno, Grosset & Dunlap, 1965; Don Irwin, Childrens Press, 1968]; *Otto of the Silver Hand*, Scribner, 1883, reissued, F. Watts, 1971; *Pepper and Salt; or, Seasoning for Young Folk*, Harper, 1886, reissued, Dover, 1967; *The Wonder Clock; or, Four and Twenty Marvellous Tales, Being One for Each Hour of the Day* (with verses by sister, Katherine Pyle), Harper, 1888, reissued, Dover, 1965; *The Rose of Paradise*, Harper, 1888; *Men of Iron*, Harper, 1891, reissued, Scholastic Book Services, 1968 [another edition illustrated by Clark B. Fitzgerald, Webster, 1949]; *Book of Pirates*, Harper, 1891, later published as *Howard Pyle's Book of Pirates*, edited by Merle Johnson, Harper, 1921, reprinted, Harper, 1965; *A Modern Aladdin; or, The Wonderful Adventures of Oliver Munier*, Harper, 1892; *The Story of Jack Ballister's Fortunes*, Century, 1895; *Twilight Land*, Harper, 1895, reprinted, Dover, 1968; *The Garden behind the Moon: A Real Story of the Moon Angel*, Scribner, 1895; *The Price of Blood: An Extravaganza of New York Life in 1807*, R. G. Badger, 1899.

The Story of King Arthur and His Knights, Scribner, 1903, reissued as *The Book of King Arthur*, Childrens Press, 1969, Scribner, 1984, [another edition illustrated by Sergio Leone, Grosset & Dunlap, 1965]; *The Story of the Champions of the*

"The Lady Guinevere," an illustration by Howard Pyle for *St. Nicholas,* 1903

Round Table, Scribner, 1905, reprinted, Scribner, 1968; *Stolen Treasure* (stories), Harper, 1907; (with Winthrop Packard, Molly Elliot Seawell, and others) *Strange Stories of the Revolution*, Harper, 1907; *The Story of Sir Launcelot and His Companions*, Scribner, 1907, reprinted, Scribner, 1985; (with J. H. Upshur, Paul Hull, Reginald Gourlay, and others) *Adventures of Pirates and Sea-Rovers*, Harper, 1908; *The Ruby of Kishmoor*, Harper, 1908, reprinted, C. F. Braun, 1965; *The Story of the Grail and the Passing of Arthur*, Scribner, 1910, reprinted, Scribner, 1985.

Other Writings: *Within the Capes*, Scribner, 1885; (with others) *School and Playground* (stories), D. Lothrop, 1891; (editor) Alexandre Olivier Exquemelin, *The Buccaneers and Marooners of America*, Macmillan, 1891, reprinted, Gryphon Books, 1971; *The Divinity of Labor* (address), J. Rogers, 1898; *Rejected of Men: A Story of Today*, Harper, 1903; (contributor) William Dean Howells, editor, *Shapes That Haunt the Dusk*, Harper, 1907; (contributor) Katherine N. Birdsall and George Haven Putnam, editors, *The Book of Laughter*, Knickerbocker Press, 1911; *King Stork* (illustrated by Trina Schart Hyman), Little, Brown, 1973.

Illustrator: *Yankee Doodle: An Old Friend in a New Dress*, Dodd, 1881; Alfred Lord Tennyson, *Lady of Shalott*, Dodd, 1881; Charles Carleton Coffin, *Old Times in the Colonies*, Harper, 1881; Rossiter Johnson, *Phaeton Rogers*, Scribner,

1881; William Makepeace Thackery, *The Chronicle of the Drum*, Scribner, 1882; Helen Campbell, *Under Green Apple Boughs*, Fords, Howard, 1882; Will Carlton, *Farm Ballads*, Harper, 1882; James Baldwin, *Story of Siegfried*, 1882; C. C. Coffin, *Building the Nation: Events in the History of the United States from the Revolution to the Beginning of the War between the States*, Harper, 1883; Horace E. Scudder, *A History of the United States of America Preceded by a Narrative of the Discovery and Settlement of North America and of the Events Which Led to the Independence of the Thirteen English Colonies for the Use of Schools and Academies*, Sheldon, 1884; Oliver Wendell Holmes, *Illustrated Poems*, Houghton, 1885; Francis S. Drake, *Indian History for Young Folks*, Harper, 1885; Diedrich Knickerbocker (pseudonym of Washington Irving), *A History of New York*, two volumes, Grolier Club, 1886; Thomas Wentworth Higginson, *A Larger History of the United States of America*, Harper, 1886; Will Carlton, *City Ballads*, Harper, 1886; James Baldwin, *Story of the Golden Age*, Scribner, 1887, illustrations reprinted in *Odysseus, the Hero of Ithaca* by Mary E. Burt, Scribner, 1898; Thomas Buchanan Read, *The Closing Scene*, Lippincott, 1887; Elbridge S. Brooks, *Storied Holidays: A Cycle of Historic Red-Letter Days*, D. Lothrop, 1887; Edmund Clarence Stedman, *The Star Bearer*, D. Lothrop, 1888; Wallace Bruce, *Old Homestead Poems*, Harper, 1888.

Lafcadio Hearn, *Youma: The Story of a West Indian Slave*, Harper, 1890; Harold Frederic, *In the Valley*, Scribner, 1890; John Greenleaf Whittier, *The Captain's Well*, New York Ledger, 1890; James Lane Allen, *Flute and Violin, and Other Kentucky Tales and Romances*, Harper, 1891; Oliver Wendell Holmes, *One Hoss Shay, with its Companion Poems*, Houghton, 1892; Holmes, *Poetical Works of Oliver Wendell Holmes*, two volumes, Houghton, 1892; Holmes, *Dorothy Q., Together with A Ballad of the Boston Tea Party and Grandmother's Story of the Bunker Hill Battle*, Houghton, 1893; Holmes, *Autocrat of the Breakfast Table*, two volumes,

"Uncle Bear and the Great Red Fox," an illustration for *Harper's Young People*, 1887

Houghton, 1893; John Flavel Mines, *A Tour around New York* [and] *My Summer Acre*, Harper, 1893; C. C. Coffin, *Abraham Lincoln*, Harper, 1893; Mary E. Wilkens, *Giles Corey*, Harper, 1893; Thomas A. Janvier, *In Old New York*, Harper, 1894.

W. D. Howells, *Stops of Various Quills*, Harper, 1895; E. S. Brooks, *Great Men's Shoes*, Putnam, 1895; E. S. Brooks, *The True Story of George Washington*, D. Lothrop, 1895; A. Conan Doyle, *The Parasite: A Story*, Harper, 1895; Robert Louis Stevenson, *The Novels and Tales of Robert Louis Stevenson*, three volumes, Scribner, 1895; Harriet Beecher Stowe, *Writings of Harriet Beecher Stowe*, two volumes, Riverside Press, 1896; Silas Weir Mitchell, *Hugh Wynne, Free Quaker*, Century, 1896; T. N. Page, *In Ole Virginia*, Scribner, 1896; Henry Van Dyke, *First Christmas Tree*, Scribner, 1897; Woodrow Wilson, *George Washington*, Harper, 1897; Francis Parkman, *Works of Francis Parkman*, three volumes, Little, Brown, 1897-98; Henry Cabot Lodge, *Story of the Revolution*, Scribner, 1898; Ernest Ingersoll, *The Book of Oceans*, Century, 1898; Mary E. Wilkens, *Silence, and Other Stories*, Harper, 1898; Margaret Deland, *Old Chester Tales*, Harper, 1899; Paul Leicester Ford, *Janice Meredith, A Story of the American Revolution*, two volumes, Dodd, 1899.

Mary Johnston, *To Have and to Hold*, Houghton, 1900; Edwin Markham, *The Man with the Hoe, and Other Poems*, Doubleday, 1900, illustrations reprinted in *Modern Pen Drawings European and American*, edited by Charles Holmes, The Studio, 1901; John Lothrop Motley, *Works of John Lothrop Motley*, Harper, 1900; Nathaniel Hawthorne, *Complete Writings of Nathaniel Hawthorne*, Houghton, 1900; Maud Wilder Goodwin, *Sir Christopher: A Romance of a Maryland Manor in 1644*, Little, Brown, 1901; Robert Neilson, *Captain Renshaw; or, The Maid of Cheapside: A Romance of Elizabethan London*, L. C. Page, 1901, illustrations reprinted in *A History of American Art*, by Sadakichi Hartman, L. C. Page, 1901; Woodrow Wilson, *A History of the American People*, five volumes, Harper, 1902, reprinted with additional illustrations, Harper, 1918; *Harper's Encyclopedia of United States History*, ten volumes, Harper, 1902; James Russell Lowell, *The Poetical Works of James Russell Lowell*, five volumes, Riverside Press, 1904; Wilbur F. Gordy, *A History of the United States*, Scribner, 1904.

Justus Miles Forman, *The Island of Enchantment*, Harper, 1905; J. B. Cabell, *The Line of Love*, Harper, 1905; John Greenleaf Whittier, *Snow Bound: A Winter Idyl*, Houghton, 1906; J. B. Cabell, *Gallantry: An Eighteenth Century Dizain*, Harper, 1907; Henry Peterson, *Dulcibel: A Tale of Old Salem*, Winston, 1907; J. B. Cabell, *Chivalry*, Harper, 1909; L. E. Chittenden, *Lincoln and the Sleeping Sentinel*, Harper, 1909; Margaret Sutton Briscoe, John Kendrick Bangs, and others, *Harper's Book of Little Plays*, Harper, 1910; William Makepeace Thackeray, *The Works of William Makepeace Thackeray*, edited by Lady Ritchie, Harper, 1910; William Gilmore Beymer, *On Hazardous Service: Scouts and Spies of the North and South*, Harper, 1912; Don Seitz, *The Buccaneers*, Harper, 1912; Fanny E. Coe, *Founders of Our Country*, American Book Co., 1912; J. B. Cabell, *The Soul of Melicent*, F. Stokes, 1913; W. H. W. Bicknell, *Etchings*, Bibliophile Society, 1913; Margaret Deland, *Around Old Chester*, Harper, 1915; W. F. Gordy, *Stories of Later American History*, Scribner, 1915; Mark Twain (pseudonym of Samuel Longhorne Clemens), *Saint Joan of Arc*, Harper,

An illustration for *St. Nicholas*, 1903

1919; Francis J. Dowd, editor, *Book of the American Spirit*, Harper, 1923; Henry Gilbert, *Robin Hood*, Parents' Magazine Press, 1964.

Contributor of illustrations and writings to various periodicals and newspapers, including *Chicago Tribune, Collier's Weekly, Cosmopolitan, Harper's Monthly, Harper's Young People, Ladies' Home Journal, St. Nicholas,* and *Scribner's.*

ADAPTATIONS—Movies: *The Black Shield of Falworth*, adaptation of *Men of Iron*, starring Tony Curtis and Janet Leigh, Universal Pictures, 1954.

Plays: Sophie L. Goldsmith, *Wonder Clock Plays*, Harper, 1925; Mary T. Pyle, *Robin Hood Plays Matchmaker* (one-act), Dramatists Play Service, 1939; M. T. Pyle, *The Apple of Contentment* (one-act), Dramatists Play Service, 1939; M. T. Pyle, *Three Strangers Come to Sherwood* (one-act), Dramatists Play Service, 1942.

Recordings: "Tales of King Arthur and His Knights," read by Ian Richardson, Caedmon, 1975.

SIDELIGHTS: Although his name is not nearly so familiar today as that of Thomas Nast, Howard Pyle is nonetheless widely regarded as a far more important figure in the development of American illustration. No popular images such as Nast's Uncle Sam or the Republican Party's

elephant are associated with his name, nor did he embroil himself, as Nast did, in the political controversies of his day; but during the course of a thirty-three-year career, his influence in the fields of book and periodical illustration was immense. In common with Nast, he regarded illustration as more than mere decoration or embellishment; but where the latter used his pen as a weapon of persuasion, Pyle used his as a tool for the widest possible dissemination of truth and beauty. "If the word 'illustration' be etymologically defined," he once wrote of his metier, "how proud should [the artist] be of having brought his light into darkness; how should he glory at having illuminated the pages of literature with reflected fragments of God's wholesome sunlight as it shines upon the world of created things." Both he and Nast practiced their creeds tirelessly, but Pyle alone preached it. And he did so with a vigor and enthusiasm that influenced a generation of talented young Americans to regard illustration not as a poor foster child of fine art but as a noble calling in its own right.

Pyle was born in Wilmington, Delaware, in 1853, the son of a Quaker businessman and his wife, a lady of strong cultural and artistic convictions. According to one biographer, it was because Mrs. Pyle was thwarted in her own intellectual growth by the demands of nineteenth-century domestic life that she so carefully nurtured these convictions in her son. As he later recalled, the walls of his boyhood home were hung with what "were thought to be good pictures in those days," but even then he reported liking "the pictures in books best of all." Artists whom he particularly liked were M. K. Browne, John Leech, Richard Doyle, and John Tenniel. Then there was the influence of the idyllic setting in which he grew up, a Chesapeake community which had not greatly altered in either appearance or pace since colonial times, and the way in which its quiet beauty inspired him. "I cannot remember," he said, "when I was not drawing." When he proved but an indifferent scholar, it was owing to his mother's insistence that he was permitted to go to Philadelphia to study privately with an academic painter named Van der Weilen.

Notwithstanding this training, Pyle was always expected to join his father's leather business, and might indeed have passed his life as an obscure provincial merchant but for the inspiration he found to write and illustrate an article on the people of a Virginia coastal island visited during an 1875 vacation. Submitting the effort to *Scribner's Monthly*, he received in reply an encouraging letter from one of the magazine's owners urging him to come to New York and try his hand at a career in illustration. In 1876, he left Wilmington with his parents' blessing to do just that. But Pyle found little immediate demand for his drawings, lacking as they were in technical facility.

Being of sober, hardworking Quaker stock, he thus set about mastering the technical details. He studied at night at the Art Students League and made the acquaintance of such noted contemporaries as Edwin A. Abbey, Frederick S. Church, Arthur B. Frost, and Winslow Homer, all of whom liked and encouraged the earnest and clearly talented young man. Another early believer was Mary Mapes Dodge, editor of the children's magazine *St. Nicholas*, whose regular assignments of illustrated fables provided him with a meager subsistence.

His most important connection was that he made with Charles Parsons, art editor of *Harper's Weekly*, a man who employed the best American illustrators of the day. Parsons was from the outset an admirer of Pyle's sense of artistic drama, but he did not regard the young artist as technically proficient enough to produce "finish" quality work. Thus when he bought a drawing from Pyle he would have it redrawn by a staff artist. By all accounts this arrangement rankled the young artist and he redoubled his efforts to produce work that would meet Parsons's demanding standards. These efforts were rewarded in 1878 when after six weeks labor he completed a piece titled "A Wreck in the Offing." He took it to Parsons with a nickel in his pocket and the desperate hope that the editor would find it worth fifteen dollars. An impressed Parsons not only bought it, but paid the artist seventy-five dollars and put it, as Pyle had drawn it, in the March 9, 1878 *Weekly* as a double page spread.

This first success—a life station crew being alerted to a ship about to founder—exemplified the qualities that would come to distinguish Pyle even among his ablest contemporaries: a palpable feeling of action, the ability to portray drama and mood in purely visual terms, the complex narrative quality that flows from his portrayal of a single arrested moment, and his faithfulness to the smallest detail. With the publication of this drawing, Pyle's career was launched and only two years later was so firmly established that he was able to return to his beloved Wilmington, where he would live and work for the next three decades.

Although he achieved his initial success as a contributor of illustrations to *Harper's*, Pyle hadn't forgotten his boyhood fascination with book illustration, and in 1883 his illustrated reworking of the Robin Hood legend won acclaim on both sides of the Atlantic by breaking with the morbid sentimentality of prevailing Victorian juvenile illustration and offering in its place bold, lively, robust drawings that took their inspiration from medieval woodcuts and manuscript illumination techniques. A series of books for young audiences followed, some retelling old tales like the Arthurian legend and the lives of famous pirates; others presenting original works of fiction like *Jack Balliser* (an American colonial adventure) and *Men of Iron* (a knighthood and chivalry novel); and still others of moralistic fantasy in prose and verse.

All the books were lavishly illustrated by the author in the suitable manner, from ink line to half-tone, in black-and-white and color; and each separate genre has its admirers among devotees of Pyle's work. Such diverse authors as Woodrow Wilson, Mark Twain, William Dean Howells, and Oliver W. Holmes benefited from his graphic complements to their works, not only because of his skill as an artist but because of his scrupulous attention to detail. This latter trait was particularly evident in his illustrations of American colonial and early Federal settings, down to such minutia, according to biographer Elizabeth Nesbitt, as "the number of buttons on the uniform of an officer of a definite regiment, the colour of the hat worn by General Wolfe at Quebec, and in what battles specific regiments fought."

As much as the example of his illustrations—in nineteen of his own books, dozens of books by others, and two hundred magazine articles, as well as thirty-three hundred separately published pictures—Pyle's influence was spread by his activities as a teacher. In 1894 he created the first course devoted specifically to illustration at Philadelphia's Drexel Institute, and in 1900 founded his own studio-school in

Wilmington, where his specially selected pupils would include future greats N. C. Wyeth, Maxfield Parrish, Frank Schoonover, and Stanley Arthurs, among others. His pedagogical methods were unique, reflecting a personal conviction, based on experience, that the best illustration was the result of emotional involvement rather than mastery of technique.

Of his own early training, Pyle said, "The imagination was not trained. We followed hard and fast rules on the theory that pictures were made by technical knowledge. I could draw—anyone could learn to do that, but. . . execution alone, no matter how skilful, cannot make a picture the world cares for." He called his technique "mental projection" and advised his students: "Throw your heart into a picture and jump in after it." In his own application, this required occasional dashes to the door of his studio to clear his lungs of the smoke conjured up by his imagination while working on a battle scene, or actually sharing the sense of shuddering cold while depicting Washington's soldiers at Valley Forge.

Without underrating, as he himself often did, Pyle's technical proficiency—although self-taught, he was master of almost every illustrational genre then known—his most striking strength was the sense of credibility he managed to infuse into his pictures. He did not invariably do this, of course, and his failures slipped occasionally into melodrama or cloying sentimentality, but at its best his work still suggests how vital the graphic arts were to pre-film and

An illustration for *Otto of the Silver Hand*, 1883

television mass audiences. His 1901 painting *The Battle of Bunker Hill*, for example, employs all the artifices and achieves all the effects associated with his best work. Reproduced in half-tone black-and-white, the picture shows various citizens watching the distant action of the Revolutionary War battle in Boston from the roofs of hillside homes across the Bay. The scene's focal point is a family group comprised of a man whose arm is encircling his wife's waist while two young children, a boy and a girl, kneel close beside. Seen from behind, they symbolize the unity and determination of the Republic whose birth labors they are so anxiously following. Pyle's point of view, characteristically, is not that of combatant; his object is to portray the Revolution as fought more than a century earlier for him and his contemporaries, and as such the painting is more a recollection of the civic ideals upon which the nation was founded than an attempt to recreate a distinct moment of military history.

In 1909, two years before his death, Pyle wrote in the pages of *Harper's Weekly*, "I foresaw the time when illustrating would be a very important part of art life in this country. I never lost confidence in my early judgment, and am glad that I have lived to see American illustrating a dignified and major factor in our national art evolution." Modest as always, Pyle forebore mentioning the role he and his work played in this evolution; but it was his determination to forge a purely American art form by eschewing European traditions that made him one of the new world's most respected artists abroad. Vincent Van Gogh is said to have mentioned his work with great admiration, and England's William Morris, scornful as he was of American art, frankly praised Pyle's gifts as an innovator in book illustration and design. Unlike the German-born Nast who was a frustrated historical painter in the "grand manner," Pyle was an illustrator who rendered American scenes in an American style and never felt compelled to call what he did by any term more elevated than "pictures." He died while on a European tour in 1911 and was buried, ironically, in Florence, one of Europe's greatest art centers.

BIOGRAPHICAL/CRITICAL SOURCES: Frank Schoonover, "Howard Pyle," *Art and Progress*, October, 1915; C. D. Abbott, "Howard Pyle," *Dictionary of American Biography*, Vol. VIII; Henry Pitz, "Howard Pyle, Father of American Illustration," *American Artist*, December, 1951; Schoonover, "The Howard Pyle Tradition," *American Artist*, November, 1964; Pitz, "The Brandywine Tradition," *American Artist*, December, 1966; Elizabeth Nesbitt, *Howard Pyle*, Walck, 1966; *Something About the Author*, Vol. 16, Gale, 1979; Howard P. Brokaw, "Howard Pyle and the Art of Illustration," in D. K. S. Hyland and H. P. Brokaw, *Howard Pyle and the Wyeths: Four Generations of American Imagination*, Memphis Brooks Museum of Art, 1983.

—Sketch by Richard Calhoun

Q - R

QUAGMIRE, Joshua 1952-

PERSONAL: Surname is pronounced to rhyme with "flat tire"; born in 1952 in Peoria, Ill. *Education:* Self-educated in art. *Politics:* "I vote for whoever bugs me the least with their telephone campaigns." *Religion:* "#@%$&*** Religion ..!!!" *Home:* Hollywood, Calif. *Office:* J.Q. Enterprises, P.O. Box 2221, Hollywood, Calif. 90078.

CAREER: Worked as carpenter, janitor, and automobile mechanic in "various places"; electrician for General Telephone; free-lance graphic artist, 1972—. *Military service:* U.S. Marine Corps, 1972-76.

MEMBER: Cartoon Art Professional Society, "Stinky Al's Bowling and Softball Team (third base)."

WRITINGS—All comic books: *Army Surplus Komikz* (series featuring Cutey Bunny), J. Q. Enterprises and Eclipse Comics, 1982—; *Fantasy Book* (series featuring Nasty Naughty Nazi Ninja Nudnik Elves), Fantasy Book Enterprises, 1985—.

Contributor to books, including *The Chocolate Moose Book* and *Beep Beep Books*, and such magazines as *Uncle Jam*, *Car-Toons*, and other humor, comic, and cartoon publications.

FILMS: "Worked on some Saturday morning TV. . . but just as soon not mention what shows. . . . It's all garbage."

WORK IN PROGRESS: More Cutey Bunny *Komikz*, the *I Love Bunny Rabbits Cook Book*; more *Nasty Naughty Nazi Ninja Nudnik Elves* strips; *Uncle Quag's Guide to How to Make Enemies and Alienate People*.

SIDELIGHTS: In the highly idiosyncratic and diverse world of "alternative" comics, few artists have a more recognizable creative identity than Joshua Quagmire, and few maintain a more private personal image. Although he frequently appears in his own comics, it is a running joke in them that his face never appears, and, as can be seen in the "Personal" section of his *CGA* entry, he volunteers little about his life and background, preferring to let his work speak for him.

A more-or-less self-taught graphic artist (he mentions once taking a life-drawing class, but evidently never went through the usual academic preparation for a career as a commercial artist), Quagmire made his first sale in 1972, and has been "doing ads, brochures, book layout, story illustration, an' like that," largely uncredited, off and on since then. In over ten years, he reports, he only got one piece of mail about his commercial work, and that was a lawsuit notice. But

nothing came of it. "One of the advantages of bein' poor as a beggar," he points out, "it's not financially feasible to sue you."

The anonymity of his commercial art has done nothing to dim the luster of his reputation among comic-book fans, however. Since the early 1980s his creation Cutey Bunny has come to be a true cult figure, recognized by comics buffs and professionals as a significant development in the history of the field, and as one of its most unlikely. Cutey Bunny, also known as Kelly O'Hare, is a rabbit (technically a hare, Quagmire insists), who is also a funny, voluptuous, black superheroine—as unpromising a combination of features as any in the comics. She came into being in 1980 when Quagmire happened to sketch a rabbit in a Wonder Woman costume, for no particular reason; he named the character Wunner Bunny. Soon, however, this random creation developed into a far more complex character than a mere spoof of

A page from *The Nasty Naughty Nazi Ninja Nudnik Elves*
(© 1986, Joshua Quagmire. Reprinted by permission.)

The Cutey Bunny and Silver Fox characters (© 1986, Joshua Quagmire. Reprinted by permission.)

funny animals, superheroes, and women. A naive sexpot, she shares her innocent sensuality with Little Annie Fanny, created by Harvey Kurtzman and Will Elder, (and her long ears and fluffy tail with Playboy bunnies). The artist himself reports that she derived in part from Preston Blair's Red Hot Riding Hood (in the Tex Avery animated cartoon of that name) and from Grim Natwick's Betty Boop.

Other influences Quagmire recognizes range widely and bear witness to the breadth of his graphic literacy. Besides Avery, he notes animator Bob Clampett. Other comic-strip artists he acknowledges include Walt Kelly, echoes of whose classic strip *Pogo* may be heard in some of his dialogue; Al Capp, whose Candide-like Li'l Abner may have been one of Cutey's prototypes; adventure-strip pioneer Roy Crane; Will Eisner; *Asterix* creators Rene Goscinny and Albert Uderzo; Japanese cartoonists Osamu Tezuka, Reiji Matsumoto, and Akira Toriyama; and, "perhaps more than anyone else," Harvey Kurtzman, whose name he writes in all capitals and follows with two exclamation marks. Less obviously, he has been influenced by movie comics as well, and singles out Laurel and Hardy, Charlie Chaplin, and W. C. Fields, observing astutely that "a great many techniques of comedy and pantomime can be transposed from one medium to another." From Fields he also takes a world outlook: "The paranoids are out to get me!"

In Quagmire's stories Cutey (sometimes "Q.T.") Bunny, her feline sidekick Fatty Tubbins, and an improbable cast of

supporting characters become involved in torturously complex plots, half humorous adventure and half parody. The supporting actors include Kelly's winsome little sister Taffy (possibly to be a spinoff for a children's comic with Fatty Tubbins, the artist reveals); Vicky Feldhyser, alias Ashtoreth, a sexy lesbian fox (a real fox); Grandma Phooby, Fatty's landlady who may or may not be a human being; Chumley Knickenbocher, an archaeologist with an affected manner of speaking who employed Kelly O'Hare before she discovered her superpowers and became Cutey Bunny; and other assorted figures, human, animal, and uncommitted. Cameo parts are played by "President Ronnie" (an occasional good-natured swipe at national politics) and the artist himself, glimpsed fleetingly behind a drawing-table or just off camera. As a back-up feature, a complex subplot runs through the series; it involves Al and Al, Space Gophers, Inc., characters who originated before Cutey Bunny. The two indistinguishable gophers are part of a space-age shipping company whose board of directors are also all named Al.

Another thread of the interconnected story directs its parody at sorcery and at war adventure comics and displays Quagmire's exuberant humor at its most anarchic. He combines martial arts, World War II, middle-earth fantasy, and wild antic slapstick in "The Nasty Naughty Nazi Ninja Nudnik Elves." Unrelated as such an adventure seems, it is all tied together with the rest of the story, which Quagmire intends as a single, complex saga for which he offhandedly suggests the title "The History of the Universe part 37-b, or something like that." He has grown increasingly extemporaneous in his plotting as the opus has developed. As he explains to *CGA:* "In the past I've tightly laid and plotted my stories before starting on the finished artwork, though there's plenty of room for improvisation along the line. Now I'm experimenting just doing the stories a page or two at a time to see where they take me. . . . It keeps me from getting bored since I don't have any idea what's going to happen either."

Quagmire's artistic choices are not prompted by commercial considerations. Although he casts wistful eyes at the financial rewards of wide national distribution and merchandising of his characters, he has made his decision deliberately to follow his own creative path. He knows that funny animals, female heroes, blacks, and parody in general are not as salable as "teen hero teams, Star Wars clones, [and] mystical gobbledygoop garbage," but says, "I had to make the decision to do something I liked or something I thought would sell." Cutey Bunny, he reports, sells "just enough for us to get by."

A lover of his profession more than a seeker of success, Quagmire studs his work with comic-strip and comic-book allusions, past and present; but if his jokes are sometimes inside ones, there are many who share them. His homage to Harvey Kurtzman perhaps comes through most in his *Mad-*style self-depreciation and pose of illiteracy. (The letterhead of Joshua Quagmire Enterprises identifies his firm's services as "Cheepo hackwork an' fumble finger paste-ups our specialty. . . Also neet letterin an gude spellun.")

But a deeper-rooted reverence for the medium lies in his use of it to return to laughter. Comic-book pioneer C. C. Beck, co-creator of *Captain Marvel* (itself slyly lampooned in Cutey Bunny), wrote to Quagmire, "I'm glad to see that

A splash page from "Gopher Wars" (© 1983, Joshua Quagmire. Reprinted by permission.)

someone is having fun in the comic book business," and Disney artist and author Carl Barks wrote, "The comic book field is overloaded with gore and sorcerers and sadists from space. There should be a need for Cutey Bunny who spills laughs instead of intestines." *Army Surplus Komikz* may never be as popular as the "teen hero teams" it satirizes, but the abundant wit and riotous inventiveness of its irreverent humor have established it securely among comics-lovers. It is, in the words of *Comics Buyer's Guide* critic Don Thompson, "one of the funniest of the all-too-few funny comic books being published."

BIOGRAPHICAL/CRITICAL SOURCES: Program, Santa Monica Graphic Arts Festival, October 9, 1983; Diana Schutz, "What's Up, Doc? An Interview with Joshua Quagmire," *Telegraph Wire,* Number 14, April-May, 1984; Don Thompson, "Reviews," *Comic Buyer's Guide*, February 14, 1980.

—*Sketch by Dennis Wepman*

* * *

QUINE, E.
 See DOBBINS, James Joseph

* * *

RANEY, Ken   1953-

PERSONAL: Surname pronounced "rainy"; born December 30, 1953, in Ellsworth, Kan.; son of Kenneth W. (in furniture refinishing) and Shirley (in furniture restoration; maiden name, Turner) Raney; married Deborah Teeter, August 11, 1974; children: Tarl Adam, Tobi Anne, Trey Andrew. *Education:* Attended Butler County Community College, 1971-73, and Kansas State University, 1973-74. *Religion:* Christian. *Home and studio:* 435 S. Ridge, Box 1500, Hesston, Kan. 67062.

CAREER: Free-lance illustrator, 1973—; drafting supervisor, Allard, Inc. (an engineering firm), Ellsworth, Kan., 1980-83; designer, Ellsworth Printing, Ellsworth, 1983-84; technical illustrator, Excel Industries, Hesston, Kan., 1984—. Member of Hesston School Board, 1983-84.

AWARDS, HONORS: Outstanding Artistic Achievement Award from Small Press Writers and Artists Organization, 1982; SPWAO Award of Excellence for artist in fantasy field from Small Press Writers and Artists Organization, 1983; Award of Excellence from Wichita Advertising Club, 1983, for stationery design, 1984 and 1985, for illustration; winner in Kansas Artist Postcard Series, 1985.

EXHIBITIONS: One-man show at Butler County Community College, 1985. Work also exhibited in South Western Bell Cover Art Traveling Show, 1983, and three-man graphic arts exhibition at Hesston College, 1986.

WORK IN PROGRESS: A series of drawings titled "Five Ages of Aviation"; "Black Powder Rendezvous" series; a series on Kansas bootmakers for the magazine *KS.*

SIDELIGHTS: "Creativity is evidence that we are made in the image of God, the Creator," Ken Raney wrote. "That

Self-portrait of Ken Raney (© 1984, Ken Raney. Reprinted by permission.)

sentence sums up my philosophy of art. There has only been one truly creative being—God. Man only 'creates' in response to his environment and his experience. Good art is the end result of two things: creativity and craftsmanship."

The two qualities that he so stresses are certainly obvious in Raney's illustration work. His pen-and-ink drawings are tightly controlled and subtly detailed, with a play of light never garish or glaring, but subdued and dreamy, modulated almost like musical harmony. To borrow again from musical terminology, there is a "misterioso" quality present in his compositions: the contrast between the dark, shadowy figures in the foreground and the half-perceived details in the background leaves an ambiguous space in the middle-ground palpitating alternately in light and darkness. The effect is achieved with careful craftsmanship. "I always ink in the darkest values first," he told his interviewer in *Draw* magazine. "When this is done I have my darkest value plus my lightest (the white paper). . . . Then it is just a matter of adding the middle values."

This lyrical mood can be seen in a piece such as "Morning Melody," in which a young pianist approaches her keyboard with intense concentration. The scene, almost eerily quiet, is lit only through a narrow vertical tier of window-panes in

"In the Barn Window," an illustration (© 1985, Ken Raney. Reprinted by permission.)

the upper left corner of the drawing. The themes of reflective repose and quiet expectancy are also apparent in "Reading," the seemingly serene depiction of a woman lost in her book in the middle of a room engulfed by approaching darkness. Working from a large reference file of photographs which he shoots himself, Raney meticulously works over his drawings until they satisfy his artistic vision.

His works in pen-and-ink, watercolor, pencil, and colored pencil are quiet and understated, displaying a great range of tonal values, but they basically reflect the same approach to life and the world (a young ballerina intently lacing her dancing shoe, harvesters enjoying a moment of rest after their labors). Raney's illustrations have been contributed to small-press publications and regional and national corporations and organizations; their artistic excellence and general attractiveness seem bound to bring the work of the young artist to the attention of an ever wider audience.

BIOGRAPHICAL/CRITICAL SOURCES: "The Drawings of Ken Raney," *Draw*, winter, 1985.

* * *

**REITHERMAN, Wolfgang   1910(?)-1985
(Woolie Reitherman)**

OBITUARY NOTICE: Born ca. 1910; died May 22, 1985, in a car crash in Burbank, Calif. Woolie Reitherman joined

"At the Steam Show," an illustration (© 1985, Ken Raney. Reprinted by permission.

Walt Disney's company in 1933, during the great expansion of the studio. Working successively as an assistant animator, animator, director, and producer, he was one the "Nine Old Men," so dubbed because they spent their entire career with the Disney organization. He animated the character of Goofy in some of the *Mickey Mouse* shorts, then went on to feature animation. His first credit was on *Snow White and the Seven Dwarfs* (he did the mirror sequence). Then came *Pinocchio* (on which he was animation director), *Fantasia* (in which he supervised the animation of the "Rite of Spring" sequence), *Dumbo*, *Bambi*, and every feature-length animated film done at the studio. After Walt Disney's death in 1966 he became producer of the studio's animated features: he brought *Robin Hood* to completion, and oversaw the smooth operation of *The Rescuers* and *The Aristocats*, among others. In 1968 he won an Oscar for *Winnie the Pooh and the Blustery Day*, a charming half-hour featurette. Unlike many of his fellow animators Reitherman was less interested in character than in entertainment and in communicating with the audience (generally through gags and caricature). As he once declared, "The art of animation lends itself least to real people, and most to caricatures and illusions of a person."

BIOGRAPHICAL/CRITICAL SOURCES: Christopher Finch, *The Art of Walt Disney*, Abrams, 1973; Frank Thomas and Ollie Johnston, *Disney Animation: The Illusion of Life*, Abbeville, 1981.

OBITUARY SOURCES: New York Times, May 27, 1985.

* * *

REITHERMAN, Woolie
See REITHERMAN, Wolfgang

* * *

RIFAS, Leonard   1951-

PERSONAL: Surname is pronounced "wry-fuss"; born April 16, 1951, in Washington, D.C.; son of Bertram E. and Bernice (Richter) Rifas. *Education:* University of California at Berkeley, B.A., 1973; San Francisco State University, teaching certificate, 1986. *Office:* P.O. Box 45831, Seattle, Wash. 98145-0831.

CAREER: Founder and owner, EduComics, 1976—, publishing comic books and distributing foreign comic books in the United States; editor, Kitchen Sink (comic-book company), Princeton, Wis. 1978-79. Artist, writer, and lecturer.

MEMBER: Interhelp, Progressive Space Forum, Planet Drum.

WRITINGS—All comic books or series: "Quoz," self-published, 1969; "Gimme 50¢," Head Imports, 1972; "An Army of Principles," self-published, 1976; *All-Atomic Comics*, EduComics-Last Gasp, 1976-80; *Corporate Crime Comics*, Kitchen Sink, 1978-79; *Food First Comics*, Institute for Food and Development Policy, 1982.

Contributor of articles on topics in the field of comics.

WORK IN PROGRESS: Collecting material for a history of the cold war as reflected in American comic books.

SIDELIGHTS: Leonard Rifas grew up in the San Francisco suburb of San Mateo, and thus was exposed early to the free-

wheeling intellectual currents that pulsed in and out of that area in the late 1960s. He read voraciously; his interests tend toward what he refers to as "entertaining" subjects—"ecocide, militarism, disinformation, and so on." In 1967, at the beginning of the underground comics movement, Rifas read works by Robert Crumb and Trina Robbins in the *East Village Other*, and immediately began trying to draw his own. As he says, "I loved the experimental, anything-goes, welcome-aboard attitude of the underground comix movement". Two years later, in 1969, Rifas self-published his first "comic book," an experimental twelve-page work called "Quoz." In 1972, in his third year of studying for a bachelor's degree in philosophy at Berkeley, his second comic, "Gimme 50¢," was published by Head Imports, with a color cover and thirty-two pages.

After graduation Rifas began to concentrate on comics as an educational medium. In 1976, the year of the nation's Bicentennial, he drew and self-published *An Army of Principles*, an informative work about the history and philosophy of the American Revolution. In the same year, he formed his own publishing company, appropriately titled EduComics. Of its unofficial charter, he states, "Art should communicate meaning, broaden the horizons of perception, enrich the experience of the viewer (and the bank account of the artist), and preserve the peak moments of human awareness. The reason that I draw these educational comics instead is that it gives me an excuse to read a lot. Also, I think it's important that somebody be doing this."

Self-portrait of Leonard Rifas, drawn specially for *Contemporary Graphic Artists* (© 1986, Leonard Rifas.)

Two panels from *All Atomic Comics* (© 1976, Leonard Rifas. Reprinted by permission.)

In conjunction with forming EduComics, Rifas drew and edited what has subsequently proven to be his biggest commercial success so far—*All Atomic Comics*. As an entertaining, informative series on the dangers of nuclear power, this struck a chord with the incipient anti-nuclear movement, and went on to sell fifty thousand copies. It appeared in three different German translations. In 1978 and 1979 Rifas also worked as an editor at Denis Kitchen's comic-book publishing firm, Kitchen Sink, in Wisconsin. While working there, and some time afterwards, he published several more educational comics under the EduComics imprint, such as *Mama Dramas* (1978)—the only comic edited, written, and drawn by mothers about motherhood—, and *Energy Comics* (1980).

Early on Rifas established a pattern of soliciting teams of artists to collaborate on an educational theme, while usually contributing the plot and the artwork to at least one story himself. His company has been a pioneer in the introduction of foreign comics and foreign artists to the United States. EduComics has distributed comics imported from Canada, Australia, Nicaragua, Malaysia, China, and South Africa, and reprints of comics from Britain, Japan, and Mexico.

Rifas was the first American publisher to put out an English-language translation of a Japanese comic book in an American format. Because Rifas was moved by the autobiographical comics of Keiji Nakazawa, a survivor of the atom-bombing of Hiroshima, EduComics in 1980 released two issues of *Gen of Hiroshima* (part of a long, epic comic called *Barefoot Gen*). When these two publications achieved critical success despite their limited distribution, Rifas followed this up by releasing a short, American-style comic, *I Saw It*, also by Nakazawa, and also on the theme of the horrors of atomic warfare. In addition to his comic-book activities, Rifas finds time to write articles on such subjects as censorship of comics, war comics, comics in Malaysia, and even underground comics in the Soviet Union.

BIOGRAPHICAL/CRITICAL SOURCES: Comics Journal, August, 1984.

*   *   *

ROMERO, Enrique
 See BADIA ROMERO, Enrique

ROYO (NAVARRO), Luis (Fernando) 1954-

PERSONAL: Born May 20, 1954, in Olalla, Spain; son of Teofilo (a metalworker) and Asuncion (a doorkeeper; maiden name, Navarro); married Pilar San Martin Fontecha (an office worker), in the 1970s; children: Romulo. *Education:* Studied architectural draftsmanship at Escuela de Maestria Industrial, and design and painting at Escuela de Artes Aplicadas y Oficios Artisticos, both Zaragoza, Spain; graduated, 1974. *Home:* Tomas Higuera, 23, 3° D, Zaragoza, Spain. *Agent:* Rafael Martinez, Agencia Norma, Ali Bey, 11, 08010 Barcelona, Spain.

CAREER: Designer for various art studios in Zaragoza, Spain, 1970-79; painter, 1972-78; comic strip artist, 1978—; illustrator and cover artist, 1983—. *Military service:* Spanish Army, 1973-75.

WRITINGS: Contributor of stories and series of comics to magazines in Spain and the United States, including "O'Clock," 1981, and "Color Linea," 1982, both for *Heavy Metal*; *Metalicos y miserables*, 1982, for *Comix Internacional*; *Circulus*, 1982, and *Sataka*, 1983-84, both for *Rambla*.

Also artist for covers of magazines *Heavy Metal* and *National Lampoon* and of books published by Bantam, Berkley, and Tor.

EXHIBITIONS—One-man shows of his paintings: Escuela de Artes Aplicadas, Teruel; Facultad de Filosofia y Letras, Zaragoza; Centro de Lectura, Reus; Galeria Xiris, Zaragoza; all 1977.

Group shows include painting exhibitions in galleries throughout Spain, 1972-76; "Bustrofedon" comics exhibition, Salon de la Bande Dessinee, Angouleme, France, 1980.

WORK IN PROGRESS: Book covers for American and British publishers.

SIDELIGHTS: Luis Royo's style has progressed, from his first and parallel creations in the fields of painting and comics, towards illustration. The artist has explained this process in his own words: "On the one hand I first devoted myself to painting, that is to the picture in itself, with paintings as social statements; and on the other hand I spent hours composing, arranging, and coloring drawings, with no other aim than to effectively and functionally convey the designer's ideas. The simpler, more spontaneous statements made in the comics, their wide-open windows, attracted me; but, seen from the inside, and once you have mastered the required skills, their repetitiveness can become a danger and a burden." In illustration Royo has found a more rewarding creative activity: "Depending only on its visual impact, with no other objectives than the image itself and its effect on the viewer, it keeps the mind clear of so much cerebral clutter, and it is in harmony with the times, which require messages that make their point rapidly (the viewer doesn't have much time to digest them, in the midst of so many other communication media that demand his attention).

"Illustration is to me the most attractive of all the areas in which I work. Even from the viewpoint of style, in quotation marks, I can go through hyper-realism, expressionism, surrealism, futurism, etc., up to total informalism; and, what is more, I can mix all these distinct styles all together. In a time when the old art forms look too much toward the past

and therefore revert to an excessive pattern of formalism (like painting and its latest trends, German post-expressionism and "Young Savages," Mediterranean neo-figurativism, etc.), illustration becomes a field that is relatively free amidst movements that are so dependent upon the past."

Luis Royo's short career in the comics began with the work he did for the Zaragozan group "Bustrofedon," which in 1978 published its own magazine, *Zeta Comic*. Since 1981 he has become a professional in the field, with a number of fantasy tales to his credit, in a style that hovers between abstraction and surrealism. The artist's masterful use of bursts of color, his personal feeling for character, ambience, and composition, and his drawings that are very close to being illustrations, all already announce the direction Royo's career was going to take. In Spain he has realized three successive series of comics: *Metalicos y miserables* for the magazine *Comix Internacional*, *Circulus* and *Sataka* in the magazine *Rambla*. Two of his earlier stories, "O'Clock" and "Color Linea" were published in the American magazine *Heavy Metal* (in November, 1981, and October, 1982, respectively).

In the field of illustration Royo has designed a number of covers for *Heavy Metal* and for *National Lampoon*. He has also done illustration work for such U.S. paperback publishers as Bantam, Berkley, and Tor; of particular note are the twelve covers he designed for Robert Adams's fiction series, *The Horseclans*. In his illustrations Royo allies a futuristic slant with a narrative verve that he learned from the comics; this is the reason why so many publishers call on him to do the covers of their comics magazines.

BIOGRAPHICAL/CRITICAL SOURCES: "Luis Royo," *Rambla* (Barcelona), March, 1984.

* * *

RUNTZ, Vic(tor Alexander) 1922-

PERSONAL: Born July 7, 1922, in Arnprior, Ont., Canada; son of Alexander (a carpenter) and Rose A. (Walters) Runtz; married Aletha Saunders, June 26, 1944; children: Ralph Desmond, Everett Victor Alexander. *Education:* Attended business college, 1939-40, Sir George Williams College of Art, 1946-47, Montreal Artists School, 1948. *Religion:* Baptist. *Home:* 101 Royal Rd., Bangor, Me. 04401.

CAREER: Clerk, Department of Defense, Ottawa, Canada, 1940-41; assistant editor, *Summerside Pioneer*, Summerside, Canada, 1946; editorial cartoonist, *Charlottetown Guardian*, Charlottetown, Canada, 1948-58; editorial cartoonist, *Bangor Daily News*, Bangor, Me., 1958-82; free-lance cartoonist, 1982—. Lecturer and teacher of cartooning and drawing. Trustee of Harris Memorial Gallery and Library, Charlottetown, in the 1950s. *Military service:* Royal Canadian Navy, 1941-45, became petty officer.

MEMBER: Association of American Editorial Cartoonists (vice-president, 1975); Canadian Cartoonists Association (co-founder), Maritime Art Association (former president), Eastern Maine Camera Club (vice-president), Bangor Sketch Club (director).

AWARDS, HONORS: Ten awards from Freedoms Foundation at Valley Forge; Grenville Clark Editorial Page Award, 1961 and 1966; Highway Safety Award, 1968 and 1972.

VIC RUNTZ

WRITINGS: (Contributor) Jerry Robinson, editor, *The 1970s: Best Political Cartoons of the Decade*, McGraw, 1981; *Here Today: Twenty-Five Years of Cartoons*, University of Maine/Bangor Daily News, 1984. Also contributor to *Best Editorial Cartoons of the Year* (Charles Brooks, editor). Editor of Canadian Cartoonists Association's journal in the late 1940s.

EXHIBITIONS—One-man shows: Bangor Public Library, 1968; University of Maine, 1984.

SIDELIGHTS: When Vic Runtz retired in 1982 from the post of editorial cartoonist with the *Bangor Daily News*, he brought to an end a career of nearly three-and-a-half decades of perceptive and witty graphic commentary. The Canadian-born cartoonist reports that he dreamed of becoming a comic-strip artist as a child, and while still in his teens struck up a correspondence with another young hopeful named Mort Walker, who went on the create *Beetle Bailey* and *Hi and Lois*. Runtz, however, traveled a different route. A sensitivity to social and political issues was to draw him into editorial cartooning early in his career. His first job, in fact, was in government, with the Canadian national Department of Defense in Ottawa, and a stint in the Royal Canadian Navy provided him with many subjects. As he points out, "There is always cartoon material where there are gripes." The navy also gave him a chance to develop his graphic skills in several service newspapers.

While stationed ashore in Halifax, the capital of Nova Scotia, however, Runtz's interest in political cartooning became clearly focused through a friendship with the *Halifax Chronicle-Herald*'s veteran cartoonist Bob Chambers. Runtz was soon selling cartoons to magazines and placed his first political cartoon with the *Montreal Star*, now defunct, Runtz laments, "Alas, with so many other great journals." In 1948 he received his first regular job as an editorial cartoonist, with the *Charlottetown Guardian* in the capital of Prince Edward Island. During his ten years with this "small though meritorious paper," Runtz became a thorough professional. He organized a few friends into the Canadian Cartoonists Association—the nation's first group

of its type, before the Association of American Editorial Cartoonists took Canadians to its capacious bosom—and edited its newspaper. It was also in these early years that Runtz developed his distinctive style and tone, as well as his ever-popular mascot/logo, a cheerful little white cat with a polka dot bow tie and a jaunty manner, commenting or reacting ironically from the sidelines.

After a decade at Charlottetown, Runtz crossed the border to the United States, where in 1958 he took the position of editorial cartoonist with the *Bangor Daily News* in Bangor, Maine, a post he was to hold for the next quarter century. From this vantage point he shrewdly observed his new city, state, and country through seven presidential administrations, from Eisenhower to Reagan. Although always a local commentator, very much the voice of Eastern Maine, he never lost sight of the adage "As Maine goes, so goes the nation," and his cartoons showed the larger perspective his adoptive state's role as bellwether confers. His material was always balanced, and he was to win many awards from both liberal groups and such conservative organizations as the Freedoms Foundation at Valley Forge, from which he received ten prizes during his time at the *Daily News*. His work has been exhibited at the University of Maine, and he has lectured there on the history of cartoon art. He has also taught cartooning and drawing in Bangor.

On his retirement, Runtz's long career in Maine was fittingly honored by the publication of a retrospective collection of his cartoons. In 1984 the University of Maine and his newspaper the *Bangor Daily News* jointly published *Here Today* as a record not only of Vic Runtz's work in Bangor but of a quarter-century of American history as reflected by it. The title has a certain irony; Runtz explains in his introduction:"Cartoons like newspapers which carry them are 'here today.' They are destined to wrap tomorrow's fish. Yet looking back we discover that much of yesterday and the yesterdays before remains here today." Marion Flood French called the collection "a superb job" and disputed the implication of the title by stating, "[R]eaders and fans will enjoy this bit of history for a long time to

News Item: CIA director displays poison dart gun which can kill instantly, silently, without trace...

As civilization advances

An editorial cartoon (© 1975, Vic Runtz, *Bangor Daily News*. Reprinted by permission.)

Odd couple

An editorial cartoon (© 1977, Vic Runtz, *Bangor Daily News*. Reprinted by permission.)

come." Its 437 cartoons provide a keen and often wry view of America and the world as seen through the calm, perceptive eye of a Canadian-turned-New Englander.

Runtz's cartoons are never savage, but in his genial way he makes his points clearly enough. His simple drawings are clean and his caricature benign, none of his faces ever grotesque. Runtz never succumbs to the temptation of playing up physical peculiarities in his targets, and while Leonid Brezhnev is recognizable by his jowls, Richard Nixon by his ski-slope nose, and Ronald Reagan by his pompadour, they are never the victims of cheap shots. The effectiveness of Runtz's cartoons lies rather in their content than in their graphic form. His cartoons contain both humor and pathos, irony and fear. His 1975 depiction of a sinister jungle of organized crime and unionism is a frightening one; President Reagan as "the new [air traffic] controller" guiding the airplane of labor support to its destruction, or the specter of Nixon's re-entry into politics terrifying voters on Halloween, is trenchantly funny; and Runtz's comment on the 1972 Christmas bombing of North Vietnam, a rocket streaking through the clear Yuletide sky over a peaceful Oriental village, is deeply moving.

Since his retirement, Runtz has kept his hand and mind active with free-lance work and a return to study. In hopes of indulging a taste for travel, he has begun the study of German, and occupies himself with a "long-time avocation" of photography. Always a voracious reader, he continues to be open to all human experience. "Love to learn any way I can," he reports, "read, travel, meet people." His warm concern for people is evident in his many years of cartooning. The jacket of Runtz's book states, "Vic is an 'old-fashioned' liberal. He believes in the dignity of human beings and the perfectibility of our species." This humane faith shines through his great body of work, illuminating even the darkest of his themes. "[My] efforts as an editorial cartoonist have been hopefully to get people to think (with a touch of humor when possible)," Runtz wrote *CGA*, "and to lift our head out of the sand." Elsewhere he has stated as his credo: "My fervent hope and prayer is that mankind will rouse from apathy and despair and as with one great voice cry out, 'Enough! Enough of this madness! I am going to live.' We cartoonists have a special obligation to add volume to this voice."

BIOGRAPHICAL/CRITICAL SOURCES: John Chase, *Today's Cartoons*, Hauser Press, 1962; Adeline Fixman, *Aim for a Career in Cartooning*, Richards Rosen, 1976; Syd Hoff, *Editorial and Political Cartooning*, Stravon, 1976; *Cartoonist Profiles*, March, 1985; *Who's Who in the East*, Marquis, 1985.

—Sketch by Dennis Wepman

S

SACRISTAN, Vicente Segrelles
See SEGRELLES (SACRISTAN), Vicente

* * *

SALERNO, Steve 1958-

PERSONAL: Born May 25, 1958, in Ticonderoga, N.Y.; son of Joseph Paul (an insurance broker) and Patricia (in billing and sales; maiden name, Helms) Salerno; married Lourdes Sernaque (a graphic designer and painter), February 9, 1985. *Education:* Graduated from Parsons School of Design (with high honors), 1979. *Home:* Branford, Conn. *Studio and office:* Sernaque/Salerno Studio, 80 Kirkham St., Branford, Conn. 06405.

CAREER: Free-lance illustrator in New York and Connecticut, 1979—. Work has appeared in over fifty publications, including books, magazines, and such newspapers as the *New York Times.*

MEMBER: Graphic Artists Guild.

AWARDS, HONORS: Named "Up and Coming Illustrator" by *Art Direction* magazine, 1981.

WRITINGS—Illustrator: Henry David Thoreau, *A Week on the Concord and Merrimac Rivers,* Franklin Library, 1983; Edgar Allan Poe, *Tales of Suspense,* Reader's Digest, 1986.

EXHIBITIONS: Work included in "Ninth International Miniature Print Exhibition," a traveling show at Pratt Manhattan Center Gallery and galleries in eight other states, 1983-84.

WORK IN PROGRESS: A comic strip intended for publication in a magazine; an animated film entitled *Anyone Can Grow Up to Be President,* with artist Martin Kozlowski (project suspended).

SIDELIGHTS: Steve Salerno was born in Ticonderoga, New York, the home of the famous Ticonderoga pencil, which he thinks may account in part for his early inclination to be an artist. It was certainly not early exposure to art that inspired him, as he grew up in a small Vermont town and never saw a museum till he visited New York City at the age of eighteen. The first pictures he remembers seeing as a child were the "American Art" entry in the *Encyclopaedia Britannica,* where the reproductions of work by illustrative artist Winslow Homer made an especially strong impression on him. Other, later favorites were the early surrealist James Ensor and the even earlier European social and comic image

makers Pieter Bruegel, William Hogarth, Honore Daumier, and Francisco Goya. Further inspiration came from the comic strips of such masters as Winsor McCay and George Herriman. In his childhood Salerno was captivated, like most of America's youth, by *Mad* magazine, and especially by its cartoonist Don Martin. But Salerno's work, as he is quick to point out, reflects the style of none of these early favorites. His illustration work is clearly his own.

Salerno's expressive penwork has appeared in over fifty magazines nationwide, including such diverse periodicals as

An illustration for *Prime Time* (© 1986, Steve Salerno. Reprinted by permission.)

An illustration for *Metropolitan Home* (© 1986, Steve Salerno. Reprinted by permission.)

New York, Esquire, Life, Horizon, Psychology Today, Rolling Stone, Gourmet, Forbes, Village Voice, Reader's Digest, and *Scholastic*. He has done illustrations for Oxford University Press, the Franklin Library, and such newspapers as the *Boston Globe* and from 1980 to 1983, the *New York Times*. A familiar figure on the op ed page of the *New York Times*, Salerno made dramatic visual statements, conveying powerful feelings on social and political issues with both grace and wit (he only works occasionally on the page now).

An animated film commenting satirically on the Reagan administration, which Salerno and another artist have been collaborating on, has been shelved for lack of funds, but he feels it remains a possibility. More immediately on his horizon is a humorous comic strip which he is preparing to offer to a magazine. The gag strip is intended for a magazine rather than a newspaper because Salerno is more familiar with the magazine market, having been a magazine illustrator since he finished school. He feels that if the strip is successful he might attempt a newspaper strip for syndication, but at present he prefers to explore the medium in his own way. He is preparing a full year's selection before attempting to market it.

Salerno's work on a humorous comic strip signals a return to his earlier love of sequential art. "I love the characters, plot. . . manipulative use of space and time distorted, [and] the unreality which the audience is forced into accepting," he wrote *CGA*. He recognizes a change in his regular professional work which is in keeping with this reawakened taste. "My illustration work was very figurative, dark, and reflective of [the] influence [of Daumier, Ensor, and Goya]," he wrote, "especially my work for the op ed page of the *New York Times*. Increasingly my illustration work has become

lighter in tone." This represents no regression on the part of the young illustrator, however. When the subject calls for it, he maintains the stark, evocative style for which he has become known. A recent series of crayon drawings he did as illustrations for a Reader's Digest edition of the stories of Edgar Allan Poe, published in 1986, is one of the strongest pieces of work he has done and is, as he describes it, "reminiscent of the darker drawings of [his] earlier career."

BIOGRAPHICAL/CRITICAL SOURCES: Art Direction, February, 1981; Les Krantz, *American Artists*, Facts on File, 1985.

* * *

SANJULIAN
    See PEREZ CLEMENTE, Manuel

* * *

SARGENT, Ben 1948-

PERSONAL: Born November 26, 1948, in Amarillo, Tex.; son of Joseph N. (in newspaper advertising) and Dorothy (Brown) Sargent (in newspaper advertising); married second wife, Diane Holloway (a television critic), September 8, 1984; children: Elizabeth. *Education*: Amarillo College, A.A., 1968; University of Texas at Austin, Bachelor of Journalism, 1970. *Politics*: Democrat. *Religion*: Roman Catholic. *Home*: Austin, Tex. *Office*: *Austin American-Statesman*, 166 E. Riverside Dr., Austin, Tex.

CAREER: Newspaper proof runner, Amarillo, Tex., 1962-68; reporter, Long News Service, Austin, Tex., 1969-71;

BEN SARGENT

reporter, *Corpus Christi Caller-Times*, Corpus Christi, Tex., 1971-72; reporter, *Austin American-Statesman*, Austin, 1971-72; reporter, Long News Service, Austin, 1972-74; syndicated reporter, Austin, United Press International, 1972; editorial cartoonist, *Austin American-Statesman*, 1974—; syndicated cartoonist, United Press Syndicate, 1974—.

MEMBER: Association of American Editorial Cartoonists. American Civil Liberties Union, Texas Women's Political Caucus.

AWARDS, HONORS: Outstanding Communicator Award, Women in Communications, 1981; Media Award, Texas Women's Political Caucus, 1982; Pulitzer Prize for editorial cartooning, 1982; Special Journalism Award, Headliners Club, 1983.

WRITINGS—Collections of political cartoons with text: *Texas Statehouse Blues*, Texas Monthly Press, 1980; *Big Brother Blues: The Editorial Cartoons of Ben Sargent*, Texas Monthly Press, 1984.

Illustrator: Francis Edward Abernethy, *How the Critters Created Texas*, Ellen C. Temple Publishers, 1982.

SIDELIGHTS: Born to a newspaper family with both parents in journalism, Ben Sargent gravitated naturally to the fourth estate, acquiring a familiarity with all aspects of the trade from his earliest days. At twelve he picked up the rudiments of printing, and two years later he began working as a proof runner for the daily newspaper of his hometown of Amarillo, Texas. By the time he entered the University of Texas at Austin to study journalism formally, he had a grounding in the field that only such a background could provide.

Once equipped with a journalism degree from a prestigious school, Sargent became a reporter, and for five years (1970-74) covered the Texas political scene in the state capital of Austin for the *Corpus Christi Caller-Times*, Long News Service, *Austin American-Statesman*, and United Press International. His keen insights into state politics and fierce moral values began to take a graphic form, and by 1974 Sargent's portfolio of political cartoons earned him the post of editorial cartoonist with the *Austin American-Statesman*. Since then a stream of trenchant cartoons has earned him a national reputation and several major awards.

For his sensitive and sympathetic perceptions of women's rights, Women in Communications honored him in 1981 as the "Outstanding Communicator" of the year, and the next year the Texas Women's Political Caucus voted him their Media Award. That same year Sargent received the Pulitzer Prize for editorial cartooning, and in 1983 the Headliners Club gave him its Special Journalism Award.

Sargent's work has twice been collected and published in book form, both times by Texas Monthly Press in Austin. In 1980 his *Texas Statehouse Blues* presented his insights on state politics. Somewhat restricted to Texas figures and issues, the volume had a limited circulation, but was much appreciated in its own state and added to Sargent's stature as a commentator. In 1982, still focusing on his home state, he illustrated a volume of Texas folklore, Francis Edward Abernethy's version of a Texas creation myth *How the Critters Created Texas*, for Ellen C. Temple Publishers in Austin. Sargent's clean, fluid line drawings, occupying more than half of the space in Abernethy's humorous and touching tale, show the range of his art, depending for effect on their harmonious tone and graceful composition rather than on the biting caricature of his editoral cartoons. The warm, affectionate rendering of nature is classic in spirit and perfectly in keeping with the fable-like spirit of the text.

Two years later, Sargent took advantage of the Orwellian theme of 1984 to bring out a second collection of cartoons, this one more ambitious and thematically structured than his first. *Big Brother Blues* presents his recent editorial cartoons on national and international topics in a framework in which George Orwell's Big Brother comments on the world scene, noting the covert authoritarianism and distorted thought in the western world. Seeing through American propaganda as easily as the West sees through that of Russia, he asks rhetorically, "Whose doublethink d'ya buy?" and then scathingly illustrates that of presidential candidates Jimmy Carter, John Anderson, and Ronald Reagan. Perceptively observed, the hypocrisy of many aspects of our government and society is revealed unsparingly in this collection. A ghoulish President Reagan (referred to as "Older Brother") disqualifies one class after another as needy, including "orphaned blind illiterate paraplegic

An editorial cartoon (© 1985, Ben Sargent. Reprinted by permission.)

dwarfs—in Detroit.'' Interior Secretary James Watt visualizes an industrial wasteland as hungrily as another man dreams of a naked woman. The President proposes ''to spend more, take in less, balance the two, make the rich richer and leave everyone happier, all at the same time.'' Sargent observes: ''Just think about the characters that populate the *real* 1984: Little Brother, Older Brother. . . and more doublethink than George Orwell ever imagined.'' Big Brother, the commentator whose remarks run through the collection, is awed at Reagan's ingenuity: ''Why, the old-fashioned doublethink I was familiar with never tried to handle more than two contradictions at one time,'' he admits.

Sargent's technical mastery of his medium belies his lack of formal training in art. His finely etched cross-hatching elegantly balances powerfully placed patches of black in his always attractive compositions. The uncluttered backgrounds—usually totally blank—permit great detail in his focal points, and although his caricature is fundamentally humorous in tone, its moral point emerges with full impact. Sargent pulls no punches. The grotesquerie of his almost movie-monster caricature of South African Premier P.W.

Botha and the vast grossness of his iconic representation of apartheid make his point as clearly as any editorial comment could. Sargent belongs in the sparse ranks of those cartoonists whose styles could never be mistaken for anyone else's. His round bug-eyes and plump sausage-fingered hands are as unmistakably his own as the insignia of any cartoonist in the country working today.

But distinctive as his highly personal graphic style is, Sargent is still first and foremost a journalist, and he has never lost the spirit of the reporter. From his earliest work as a cartoonist, his vigorously liberal statements on public issues have shown an ever-widening range of national and international reference and an increasing depth of moral conviction. His impassioned attacks on social and political injustice at home and abroad disclose a profoundly humanistic spirit and concern, leavened with keen wit and visual acuity.

BIOGRAPHICAL/CRITICAL SOURCES: Who's Who in America 1984-85, Marquis, 1984.

—Sketch by Dennis Wepman

SAUDEK, Kaja
    See SAUDEK, Karel

*   *   *

SAUDEK, Karel   1935-
    (Kaja Saudek)

PERSONAL: Born May 13, 1935, in Prague, Czechoslovakia; son of Gustav (a bank clerk) and Pavla (Kucerova) Saudek; married Hana Woydinkova, 1965; children: Patrik, Berenika. *Education:* Completed grade school. *Home and studio:* Nad Palatou 42, 150 00 Praha 5, Czechoslovakia. *Agent:* Art Centrum, Czechoslovakia.

CAREER: Draftsman-designer, 1954-56; construction worker, 1957-1959; assistant editor and set designer, Barrandov Film Studio, Prague, Czechoslovakia, 1959-68; free-lance cartoonist, illustrator, and painter, 1968—.

AWARDS, HONORS: Second Prize from Molodaya Gvardiya (a publishing house), U.S.S.R., 1970, for graphic design "Siberia 2000."

WRITINGS—All books of comics; all published by Czechoslovak Speleological Society: *Tajemstvi Zlateho Kone* ("Secret of the Golden Horse"), 1979; *Po stopach snezneho muze* ("Picking up the Scent of a Yeti"), 1980; *Trat se ztraci ve tme* ("Railroad Line Vanishes in the Darkness"), 1980; *Lips Tullian*, 1982; *Modra rokle* ("Blue George"), 1984; *Peruansky denik* ("Peruvian Diary"), 1985.

Contributor of comic strips and illustrations to various eastern European periodicals.

FILMS—Live-action features; as art designer: *Kdo chce zabit Jessii?* ("Who Would Kill Jessie?"), 1966; *Ctyri vrazdy staci, drahousku* ("Four Murders Are Enough, Darling"), 1971.

Animated cartoons; as designer: *Sochy* ("Statues"), Slovak Television, 1970s; *Necekane dedictvi* ("Unexpected Inheritance"), Short Film Co., Prague, 1981. Made a number of advertising shorts on Czech television.

EXHIBITIONS—All one-man shows, unless otherwise indicated; all in Czechoslovakia, unless otherwise indicated: Mlada Frotna, Prague, 1969; (group show) Exhibition of Czecholslovak Custom Jewelry, U.S.S.R., 1970; Dum umeni, Brno, 1971; Okresni muzeum, Jilove, 1984; Hall of CSOP, Prague, 1984; Okresni kulturni stredisko, Jicin, 1984; Cinema "Svet," Pardubice, 1985. Several gallery shows of paintings.

WORK IN PROGRESS: More books of comics for Czechoslovak Speleological Society; work for Czechoslovak television; illustrations for various magazines.

SIDELIGHTS: Karel Saudek is a very contradictory person. For example, he is a shy man, but many of his admirers regard Kaja, to use the more familiar form of his name, as almost a playboy. He is known almost exclusively for his comics, but he is in fact a very versatile artist who does literally everything: drawings, magazine illustrations, posters, television commercials, T-shirts, wedding cards, and even key-rings. His popularity is immense in Czechoslovakia, but abroad he is virtually unknown—unlike his brother

Self-portrait of Karel Saudek, drawn specially for *Contemporary Graphic Artists* (© 1986, Kaja Saudek.)

Jan, a photographer whose work is popular world-wide but who is almost unknown in Czechoslovakia.

Saudek has been drawing since age seven; with no formal training in art (nor any higher education), he is truly a self-made man. After grade school he started his career first as an unskilled worker, and later as a set director's assistant in Prague's Barrandov film studios. From creating set decorations for German films being shot at Barrandov, Saudek went on to collaborate on Czech film director M. Macourek's *Who Would Kill Jessie?* This funny science-fiction picture in which three comic characters come alive and hunt down their creator became quite popular both at home and abroad. After leaving Barrandov in the late 1960s, Saudek became a free-lance cartoonist and illustrator, working for a number of youth magazines. His very first comic strip, *Who Would Kill Jessie?*, an adaptation of the movie, was published in a student magazine. One of his most memorable and remarkable creations, *Lips Tullian*, appeared weekly in 1972 in the popular magazine *Mlady svet* ("Young World"). There followed *The Phantom of the Opera Presents. . .* (1973), a unique adaptation of well-known operas in comic-strip form, featuring the likenesses of contemporary Czech pop-singers—sometimes to their displeasure. Some of the operas thus spoofed were *Rigoletto, Carmen,* and *Sarka* (by the Czech composer Z. Fibich).

By 1986 Saudek had published no fewer than forty comic series of lengths varying from five to fifty pages. He has also designed a vast project that will consist of twelve hardbound volumes of comics; parts of it have been published from time to time in various magazines. Saudek has compiled the first two volumes so far (both in color), titled *Muriel and the Angels* and *Muriel and the Orange Death.*

A page from *Railroad Line Vanishes in the Darkness* (© 1980, Kaja Saudek. Reprinted by permission.)

The first volume tells of an angel named Ro who is stranded on Earth in the year 1980; Muriel, a beautiful woman doctor saves his life and subsequently falls in love with him. After many adventures Ro decides to remain with her in the twentieth century. Saudek often depicts his own relatives, friends, and himself in this strip: his brother Jan, for instance, was portrayed as one of the chief villains. Although accepted by a publishing house and subscribed to by many readers, the two books had not yet appeared in print by mid-1986.

Saudek is probably the only Czech artist totally dedicated to comic-strip production on a level comparable with that of foreign artists. He is often said to be parodying American comics, but this is a misreading. Indeed, his style is rooted in American comic art, but he had developed his own distinctive look: his original inspirations and influences have been transcended into a specifically Czech creation. His strips are neither parodies nor mere copies, they are unarguably original productions. He is able to mock his own conventions, both formal and thematic, and then throws the joke off gently, as if winking in complicity to his readers. His fantasy sense and his imagination are immense, his graphic skill admirable, his style recognizable at a glance, his working capacity unbounded. He does everything himself—he is his own penciler, inker, letterer, colorist, and, as often as not, his own writer. In a word, he is unique. There is no cartoonist in Czechoslovakia who comes even close to his level (though there are some who are quite good).

In 1976 and 1977 Saudek published color comic strips in the Polish magazine *Relax*; however, he works best in black-and-white. His line is clear and simple, always at the service of the narrative; and his page layout is highly imaginative. Saudek is willing to draw for everybody, and his graphic output is not confined to his comic strips: he may work with the same enthusiasm for Czech television or for the Gypsy owner of a shooting-gallery. All this requires a great deal of energy—and Saudek is a genuine workaholic, working ten or more hours daily, seven days a week, turning out comics, television titles, record covers, film, theater, and nightclub posters, and more.

Saudek's work with Czech environmentalist groups absorbs a good deal of his time; for them he draws posters, displays, and illustrations. Since 1979 the Czech Speleological Society has published six annuals devoted exclusively to Saudek's comic-strip stories. These are based either on old legends taking place in stalactite caves or on original science-fiction scripts by such Czech writers as Josef Nesvadba. At least half of Saudek's work is somehow linked to science fiction, though his main activity since 1973 has been his work for Czech and Slovak television.

The artist has also done a small number of paintings, perhaps no more than thirty or forty. His pictures are rather large works in oil on canvas, based on drawings. He traces a strong black line that is subsequently shaped either by one color (on a white background) or by several bright colors; some of these pictures resemble, in technique as much as in appearance, colored drawings. One of his favorite subjects is a nude woman posing against a picture backdrop. The pictures are realistic in line, but slightly surrealistic in composition. Many are owned by his relatives and others are snapped up by eager collectors.

—Sketch by Leonid Krizek

SCOTT, Jerry 1955-

PERSONAL: Born May 2, 1955, in Elkhart, Ind.; son of Donald D. (in sales) and Peggy (Williams) Scott; married Leslie Kim Anderson (a registered nurse), February 1, 1975. *Education:* Attended Arizona State University, 1973-74. *Home and studio:* 460 Casa Real Pl., Nipomo, Calif. 93444. *Agent:* United Feature Syndicate, 200 Park Ave., New York, N.Y. 10166.

CAREER: Free-lance graphic artist, 1974-77; artist and author of comic panel *Gumdrop*, 1981—, and comic strip *Nancy*, 1983—, both distributed by United Feature Syndicate.

MEMBER: National Cartoonist Society, NCCHA, Comics Council.

SIDELIGHTS: When twenty-eight-year-old cartoonist Jerry Scott was offered the job of "extending the career of" the classic comic strip *Nancy* in 1983, he accepted the challenge with some hesitation. He had already begun to establish a reputation for his one-line gag panel *Gumdrop*, originated by magazine cartoonist George Crenshaw in March, 1978, and taken over by Scott in January, 1981. Signed simply "Scott," the loosely drawn daily feature taps the inexhaustible comic source of healthy little kids and their bewildered parents, but since Scott took it over he has made it distinctly his own, deliberately giving it what he describes as "an all new look and different premise." It has been distributed nationally by United Feature Syndicate since its origin. Scott also had an original strip under consideration at United when Sid

Self-portrait of Jerry Scott (© Jerry Scott. Reprinted by permission.)

Goldberg, the syndicate's executive editor, suggested his doing *Nancy* instead.

This perennial child strip, one of the last survivors of the golden age of comics, was developed by Ernie Bushmiller as a spinoff of his *Fritzi Ritz*, which he took over from Larry Whittington in 1925. *Nancy* originally featured a lively moppet and her slum-dwelling boyfriend Sluggo (whose lower-class Bronx speech has improved over the years, although his clothes have not). The plump little girl with the red ribbon in her frizzy black hair first appeared as Fritzi's niece in the early thirties, gradually edged her aunt out of the limelight, and finally replaced her as the title character in 1940. When Bushmiller died in 1982, the strip was carried in six hundred newspapers. It was continued by Mark Lasky, whose crisp, economical style duplicated Bushmiller's almost exactly, until Lasky's death the next year. Never a sophisticated strip, *Nancy* remained unflaggingly popular with children, middle-brows, and foreign students of English for many years. Its clean, simple line, uncluttered composition, and good-natured, intellectually undemanding humor, depending largely on sight gags, made it easy to read, and the characters' simplicity was always engaging. "They may be brats," Bushmiller once said of Nancy and Sluggo, "but they don't play with meat choppers. . . . I don't like cruel humor. . . night club humor, where you make fun of somebody. I like a gentle type of humor."

The gentle humor of *Nancy* began to fall out of popular favor during the seventies, and its circulation fell to about five hundred newspapers by the time Scott accepted the assignment. But the youthful cartoonist set himself to reviving the languishing strip. Faithful to Bushmiller's original spirit, he began subtly to modernize *Nancy* without changing the fundamental nature of either its minimal art or its simple, good-natured gags. "It still looks like *Nancy*—simplicity is vital—but the characters move a little more naturally now," Scott has noted. The drawing is bolder and more forceful, employing a darker, heavier line than that of Bushmiller and Lasky, widening the spaces between the spikes of Nancy's hair, increasing the size of her round black button-eyes and rectangular bar of a nose, but leaving Sluggo's shaven head and porcine snout unimproved. More importantly, Scott has given the characters some depth and complexity. "Today," he observes, "(gladly) people are much more aware of subtlety in humor and demand some mid-level emotions, such as disappointment, amusement,

"JUST THINK OF IT AS AN ACUTE CASE OF 'RING AROUND THE COLLAR.'"

A *Gumdrop* panel by Jerry Scott (© 1986, United Feature Syndicate. Reprinted by permission.)

chagrin, etc. . . . . [T]he average six-year-old in 1985 is a lot more aware of the adult world than the average six-year-old was in 1940."

Scott began by doing only the six daily *Nancys* and leaving the Sundays to another artist, but after three months he assumed the full load. By now all former hesitation has left him, and he feels so comfortable with his inherited strip that he sketches it directly on the bristol board and then draws over the penciled gags in india ink. The dynamic new look and the contemporary spirit of both language and characterization with which Scott has infused *Nancy* have paid off handsomely. The fading popularity of the strip has revived significantly and it once more runs in six hundred newspapers worldwide—a greater percentage of the total market than in Bushmiller's last years. The recognition of Nancy and Sluggo have become so great once more that Scott is working with United Media Licensing on several merchan-

A *Nancy* daily strip by Jerry Scott (© 1986, United Feature Syndicate. Reprinted by permission.)

dising projects. "There will be a line of Nancy sleepwear in the stores," Scott reports, "and I've just finished six designs for underwear as well." The pleasure which he takes in the renewal of the tottering comic strip is apparent in his work. "I accept the challenge," he wrote to *CGA*, "and relish the process." It is largely due to this attitude and to the modern spirit which Scott has brought to the work, that *Nancy* has become, in the words of its syndicate, "the funniest strip anywhere about kids the way they *really* are."

BIOGRAPHICAL/CRITICAL SOURCES: Cartoonist Profiles, March, 1986.

*   *   *

SEGRELLES (SACRISTAN), Vicente   1940-

PERSONAL: Born September 9, 1940, in Barcelona, Spain; son of Juan (in sales) and Josefina (Sacristan) Segrelles; married Maria del Rosario Catala, January 1, 1971; children: Alejandra, Barbara. *Education:* Attended Escuela de Artes y Oficios Artisticos, 1954-56. *Home:* General Prim, 36, Cubella, Barcelona, Spain. *Agent:* Rafael Martinez, Agencia Norma, Ali Bey, ll, 08010 Barcelona, Spain.

CAREER: Apprentice, ENASA (a truck manufacturer), Barcelona, 1954-56, draftsman, 1956-61; advertising artist, Barcelona, 1964-70; free-lance illustrator, 1970—; comic strip artist, creator of *The Mercenary*, 1980—. *Military service:* Spanish Army, 1961-63, served in Engineer Corps.

AWARDS, HONORS: Award from Club de los Amigos de la Historieta, Barcelona, 1982, for *The Mercenary.*

WRITINGS—All illustrated popular science books; all published by AFHA, Barcelona, between 1970-1981: *Inventos que conmovieron al mundo* (title means "Inventions That Shook the World"); *Historia universal de las armas* ("World History of Weapons"); *Invenciones y descubrimientos* ("Inventions and Discoveries"); *Historia de los barcos* ("History of Ships"); *Historia de la aviacion* ("History of Aviation").

All books of comics; all published originally by Norma, Barcelona: *El pueblo del fuego sagrado*, 1982, published as *The Cult of the Sacred Fire*, NBM, 1985; *La formula*, 1983, published as *The Formula*, NBM, 1985; *Las pruebas*, 1984, published as *The Trials*, NBM, 1986.

WORK IN PROGRESS: Continuation of the series *The Mercenary*, and works of illustration.

SIDELIGHTS: While apprenticed with the ENASA truck manufacturing company, Vicente Segrelles attended night classes at the School of Arts, where he specialized in advertising art. He rose to the position of project draftsman in ENASA eventually, and at the same time freelanced as an illustrator, with assignments including *The Iliad* and *The Odyssey*. After military service, he devoted himself fully to advertising work, as illustrator and designer. In 1970 he left advertising to freelance as an illustrator, mostly in the field of popular science books (some of which he also wrote) and for magazines, where he gained a solid reputation as a cover artist. In 1980 he became a comic strip artist, with his series *The Mercenary* currently published in fourteen countries, including the United States. At the same time he pursued his career as an illustrator, working for such American publish-

VICENTE SEGRELLES

ers as Tor, Warner, Daw, Bantam, and New American Library.

A characteristic feature of Segrelles's work—and one which applies equally to his illustration work and to his comic strip production—is fantasy. In this field he has a family antecedent in his uncle Jose Segrelles, who was an illustrator of considerable fame in the 1930s and 1940s. Nevertheless, Vicente Segrelles served a fruitful apprenticeship in mechanics' school, and later gained invaluable experience as a project designer. In this capacity he had to familiarize himself with perspective, pen-and-ink drawing, and the use of the airbrush, in order to be able to draw, for instance, a motor engine section from a series of blueprints. Later still his years of working with advertising agencies allowed him to develop his talents as a figurative artist and as a colorist. When in 1980 he started his comic strip series, *The Mercenary*, while already enjoying a deserved reputation as an illustrator and cover artist, he was able to enter this new field, as he said, "through the main door."

Segrelles naturally chose fantasy as the main theme for *The Mercenary*, with some addition of "sword-and-sorcery" and science-fiction elements. Since he is also his own scriptwriter, Segrelles develops his stories in a way that allows him to show his illustrator's gifts to best advantage, composing each panel as a separate picture and maximizing its visual impact through the use of color. The adventures of *The Mercenary* (no name given for the taciturn hero of the series) have been published in the magazine *Cimoc*, and later collected in book form. In the United States Segrelles's creation has been serialized in *Heavy Metal*, with three of the adventures later published in book form. *The Mercenary*'s high graphic quality calls for scripts of equal narrative power, which would take this series out of the beaten path of routine fantasy adventure.

From the outset *The Mercenary* has enjoyed great international success; and the series counts among its admirers the noted Italian filmmaker Federico Fellini who has declared himself fascinated by the pictorial and imaginative density of the images.

BIOGRAPHICAL/CRITICAL SOURCES: Javier Coma, editor, *Historia de los Comics*, Toutain (Barcelona), 1983.

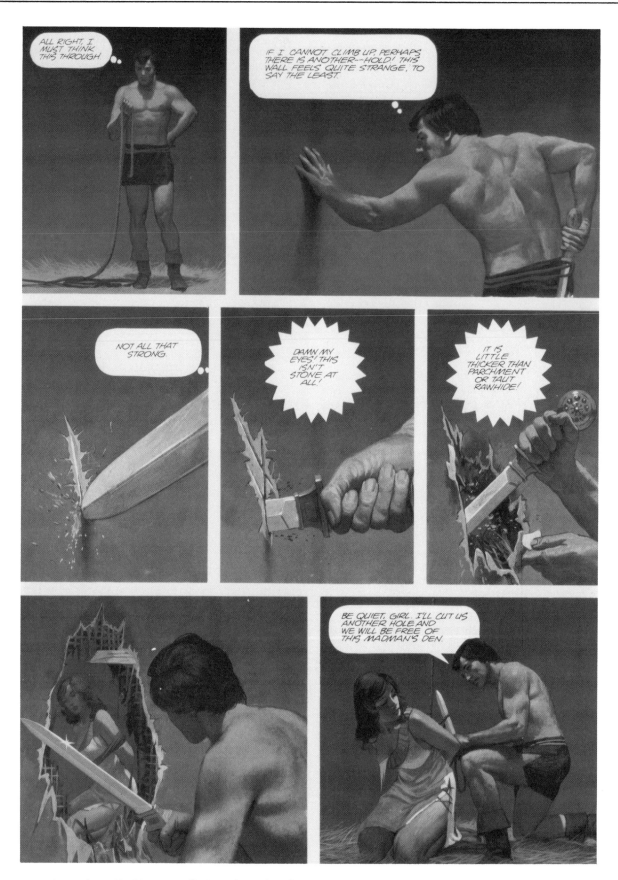

A page from *The Mercenary* (© 1984, Vicente Segrelles. Rights controlled by Norma. Reprinted by permission.)

SITO, Thomas   1956-
(Tom Sito)

PERSONAL: Surname is pronounced "see-toe"; born May 19, 1956, in New York, N.Y.; son of George Victor (a fire fighter) and Regina (Sarama) Sito; married Patricia J. Connolly (an office manager), January 4, 1980. *Education:* School of Visual Arts, B.F.A., 1977; attended Art Students League, New York City, 1978. *Home:* 6551 Densmore Ave., Van Nuys, Calif. 91406. *Office and studio:* Filmation Studios, 18017 Sherman Way, Reseda, Calif. 91335.

CAREER: Animator, R. O. Blechman Films, New York City, 1978; senior animator, Nelvana Ltd., Toronto, Ontario, Canada, 1979-82; animator, Richard Williams Animation (now Welcome Enterprises), Los Angeles, Calif., 1982; animation director, Filmation Studios, Los Angeles, 1983—. Also worked as animator, at Pizzaz Productions (animation studio), London, England, 1984. Instructor of advanced animation at Brandes Art Institute, Los Angeles, 1983—. Member of Judging Committee for Emmy Awards of the National Academy of Television Arts and Sciences, 1984 and 1985.

MEMBER: National Academy of Television Arts and Sciences, Motion Picture Screen Cartoonists Guild, Metropolitan Opera Guild, Metropolitan Museum of Art.

AWARDS, HONORS: "Ruby Slipper" Award from Children's Hall of Fame, for best children's film, 1976, for *Isabella and the Magic Brush*; Emmy Award for best animation from National Academy of Television Arts and Sciences, 1982, for *Ziggy's Gift*.

FILMS—All feature-length animated films: (Assistant animator) *Raggedy Ann and Andy*, Twentieth Century-Fox, 1977; (assistant animator) *Animalympics*, Steve Lissberger Productions, 1980; (senior animator) *The Ring of Power*, Metro Goldwyn Mayer-United Artists (MGM/UA), 1984; (animator) *Starchasers: The Legend of Orin*, Westar-Mihahan, 1985; (storyboard artist) *The Secret of the Sword*, Filmation, 1985; (storyboard artist) *The Further Adventures of Pinocchio*, Filmation, 1986.

TELEVISION—All animated specials: (Animator) *Simple Gifts*, Public Broadcasting System (PBS-TV), 1978; (assistant animator) *Gnomes*, American Broadcasting System (ABC-TV), 1979; (animator) *Easter Fever*, Viacom, 1979; (animator) *Take Me Up to the Ballgame*, Viacom, 1980; (animator) *Ziggy's Gift*, ABC-TV, 1982.

All children's animated programs: (Animator) *Yogi Bear, Superfriends, Godzilla, Laffalympics,* and *Jana of the Jungle,* all Hanna-Barbera, 1978; (storyboard artist) *Q*Bert, Donkey Kong, Rubik, Pitfall,* all Ruby Spears, 1983; (storyboard artist and director) *Fat Albert and the Cosby Kids*, Filmation, 1983-84; (storyboard artist and animator) *He-Man and the Master of the Universe*, Filmation, 1983-85; (director) *Shera, Princess of Power*, Filmation, 1985; (director) *Ghostbusters*, Filmation, 1986—; (storyboard artist) *Robotix*, Marvel Studios, 1985-86.

Animator and designer for many commercial and industrial animated films and children's animated shorts.

WORK IN PROGRESS: Sketching artist on children's show, *Challenge of the Gobots*; developing a newspaper

THOMAS SITO

comic strip for national syndication; doing animation commercial for Kurtz & Friends.

SIDELIGHTS: Tom Sito is among the new breed of up-and-coming animators who are not content, as older generations of animators were, to spend their whole career with the same studio but who flit from one studio to another, and from one city to another, in accordance with available work and opportunity. While still a student at the School of Visual Arts, Sito worked as an assistant animator on the critically acclaimed feature *Raggedy Ann and Andy*. Later he went on to Nelvana Studios in Toronto, Canada, as a senior animator on *The Ring of Power* (originally titled "Rock and Rule"). Among other prestigious productions he has worked on in various capacities are such animated feature films as *Starchasers* and *The Secret of the Sword*, and well-received television animated specials like *Gnomes* and *Ziggy's Gift*. The artist's career seems to have stabilized in California, where he directs such Saturday morning television series as *Shera, Princess of Power* and *Ghostbusters*.

Along with his work on entertainment animation Sito has also made of number of animated commercials for clients, including Nestle's, Sperry-New Holland, and Kellogg's. He has worked on a number of educational films as well, among them the ominous *Protection in the Nuclear Age*, produced for the U.S. Defense Department. Among his other credits are free-lance gag writing for Harvey Kurtzman's *Playboy* comic feature, *Little Annie Fanny*, and teaching intermediate and advanced animation classes. His non-animation projects include the development of a syndicated comic strip feature.

Tom Sito wrote *CGA:* "The field of animation in the United States is currently undergoing great changes, and anyone wishing to make a career in animation must learn to adapt to these changes. The last large studio operations in the United States are either breaking up or in danger of doing so, as producers seek most cost-effective alternatives to traditional

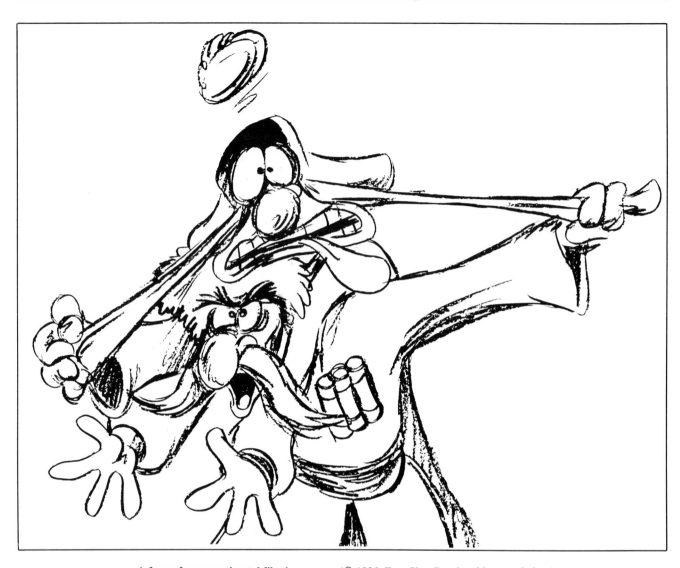

A frame from an animated film-in-progress (© 1986, Tom Sito. Reprinted by permission.)

production methods by moving their operations overseas or by switching to automation. This process, traumatic as it may seem to some, is, after all, the completion of the decentralization process undergone by the Hollywood studios since the late 1950s and early '60s. The future of animation will come to resemble live-action production in its use of entrepreneurial producers assembling small teams of professionals under limited-term contracts.

"As I see it, animators will no longer be able to draw the same character for thirty years or more, but will have to diversify if they want to survive. It has always been a particular problem in animation that, though it is a young medium, the artists involved in it insist on an over-dependence on the work of past artists, most notably that of Walt Disney and Warner Brothers animators. I feel you cannot be an artist by just repeating the work of old masters, you must bring something of *yourself* into your work. Studying your art or your field is not enough, it is only the beginning. You must be a student of the world and bring something original and personal to your art: as for myself I am very deeply influenced by classical music and by history,

which provide to me both a refuge and a wellspring of inspiration and information. These influences permeate all my work, even my most commercial projects."

BIOGRAPHICAL/CRITICAL SOURCES: John Canemaker, *The Animated Raggedy Ann and Andy: An Intimate Look at the Art of Animation—Its History, Techniques and Artists,* Bobbs-Merrill, 1977.

* * *

SITO, Tom
   See SITO, Thomas

* * *

SLACKMAN, Chas B.   1934-

PERSONAL: Born June 10, 1934, in Brooklyn, N.Y.; married Betteanne Terrell (a ballet dancer), December 31, 1963. *Education:* Attended Cooper Union Art School, 1953-55. *Home and studio:* 320 E. 57th St., New York, N.Y. 10022.

CAREER: Free-lance illustrator, 1959—. Instructor, School of Visual Arts, New York City, 1963—. *Military service:* U.S. Army, 1957-59.

MEMBER: American Institute of Graphic Arts, Graphic Artists Guild.

AWARDS, HONORS: Distinctive Merit Awards, *Communication Arts*, 1963, Art Directors Club, New York City, 1965, Society of Publication Designers, 1970; Gold Awards, Art Directors Club, New York City, 1973 and 1976.

WRITINGS—All as illustrator: Elizabeth Janeway, *Angry Kate*, Harper, 1963; Gloria Steinem, *The Beach Book*, Viking, 1963; Shirley Jackson, *Famous Sally*, Harlin Quist, 1966; Leonard Todd, *Trash Can Toys & Games*, Viking, 1974; Judi Barrett, *I Hate to Take a Bath*, Four Winds, 1975; Terry Clifford and Sam Antupit, *Cures*, Macmillan, 1980.

TELEVISION: Animator, "My Christmas" segment of *Simple Gifts*, Public Broadcasting System, 1978.

EXHIBITIONS: Participant in many group shows, including "Anti-War Show," Society of Illustrators, New York City, 1970, and "The Mental Image," American Institute of Graphic Arts, New York City, 1977. Represented in almost all of the annual shows of the Society of Illustrators, American Institute of Graphic Arts, and Society of Publication Designers.

SIDELIGHTS: If one index of an illustrator's competence is the number of top-flight art directors/designers he has worked for, then Chas Slackman ranks as one of the most capable of current practitioners. Among those who have called on him to lend his vision to their magazines over the years have been Herb Lubalin, Milton Glaser, and Richard Hess, a trio by no means easily satisfied. Indeed, each of these designers is noted for his highly literate approach to

An illustration for *New York* (© Chas B. Slackman. Reprinted by permission.)

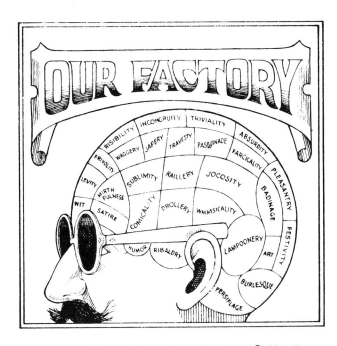

Stylized self-portrait of Chas B. Slackman (© Chas B. Slackman. Reprinted by permission.)

An illustration for *New York* (© 1976, Chas B. Slackman. Reprinted by permission.)

magazine design and dedication to the idea that art and text are interdependent elements of the communications process—which explains precisely why they find Slackman's work so suitable.

Although one of his obvious strengths is draftsmanship, he tends to downplay technical virtuosity. "Good drawing helps, but thought is what counts," he has declared. "What I'm pushing for is a point of view." A man who enjoys reading not only great books but also much of the material he is called upon to illustrate, he claims to have accumulated so large a fund of general information that friends frequently call him with questions. "I sparkle in areas of trivia," he once jokingly told an interviewer, "But if it's really important, call the library." Beyond making him a one-man reference source, his wide reading has provided Slackman with the fund of ideas, facts, and opinions that separates the decorative illustrator from the graphic reporter. Like his

colleagues Brad Holland and Alan Cober, Slackman is by nature an activist who doesn't mind expressing his opinions. He participated in the controversial Society of Illustrators "Anti-War Show" during the Vietnam protest era, has done anti-nuclear design work for SANE and other environmental groups, and was at one time a mainstay of Lubalin's muckraking monthly, *Fact*. But Slackman has a distinctly puckish side as well, based, as one critic put it, on his "realization that the world is perhaps more insane than it cares to acknowledge." In this context, it is perhaps instructive to note that two artists he especially admires are Saul Steinberg and Alexander Calder.

Slackman is also known as a "spot artist" of uncommon talent. "Spot art" describes those small, uncaptioned drawings which often embellish the op-ed pages of newspapers or magazine column heads. At their very best these miniature graphic statements contribute to the over-all design scheme while highlighting the text in such a way as to pique the prospective reader's interest. Steve Heller calls Slackman "the exemplar of contemporary spot drawing," not only because of his "unique engraving style, which has influenced countless illustrators," but also because of his flair for producing drawings that are both intriguing and relevant. Consider the visual riddle he executed to head *New York*'s review of one film: a bespectacled harlequin bearing a suspicious likeness to Woody Allen is shown bursting, jack-in-the-box like, from the end of an unpeeling banana.

A particularly pleasing demonstration of the full range of Slackman's talents—as draftsman, colorist, problem-solver, and wit—is the illustration he did for Shirley Jackson's *Famous Sally*, a sadly neglected work of juvenile literature. There, in a series of full-page color plates as well as text-embellishing "spots," he offers a gentle, funny, and most appropriate visual complement to Miss Jackson's story of how a little girl named Sally set about making her name a household world. In what could (but probably shouldn't) be read as an amusingly sophisticated parody of the "media campaign," Slackman shows Jackson's plucky little heroine tackling and conquering the problem of name recognition in venues as varied and challenging as Tall City, Small City, Soft City, Rose City, Play City, Slow City, and finally Noisy City (where residents "threw pots and pans out of upstairs windows to hear them crash in the street,. . . thirty-seven

An illustration for *Forbes* (© 1982, Chas B. Slackman. Reprinted by permission.)

brass bands played all day long, and eleven times a day the fire sirens blew just for fun").

His representations of each of these environments are so delightfully faithful to the text that one is tempted to consider the book a joint and simultaneous collaboration. The art is in every respect equal to the formidable demands imposed upon it by a storyteller of Jackson's virtuosity. Mirroring the author's own curious blend of classical and modern elements in fiction, Slackman contributes to the project a fineness of line and ornamental sophistication reminiscent of the great Victorian masters as well as the color-sense, visual literacy, and fun associated with the likes of Milton Glaser and Seymour Chwast. *Famous Sally* is, in short, the very model of what an author and an illustrator can accomplish when their talents and intentions are perfectly meshed.

BIOGRAPHICAL/CRITICAL SOURCES: Print, July, 1967, July, 1970, January-February, 1983; *Something About the Author*, Vol. 12, Gale, 1977; *Who's Who in Graphic Art*, Vol. 2, De Clivo Press, 1982.

—*Sketch by Richard Calhoun*

* * *

SMITH, Elwood H. 1941-

PERSONAL: Born May 23, 1941, in Alpena, Mich.; son of Elwood E. (a foundryman) and Virginia P. (Cameron) Smith; married Maggie Pickard (a fine artist and artist's representative), May 11, 1983. *Education:* Attended Chicago Academy of Fine Arts, 1960-62; Institute of Design, Chicago, 1963. *Home and studio:* 2 Locust Grove Rd., Rhinebeck, N.Y. 12572, *Agent:* Maggie Pickard, 2 Locust Grove Rd., Rhinebeck, N.Y. 12572.

CAREER: Art director, Chicago, Ill., for several years in the 1960s; illustrator, 1969—.

*WRITINGS—*Self-illustrated juveniles: *The See & Smell & Taste & Touch Book*, J. Phillip O'Hara, 1972; *A Ball of Yarns*, Harlin Quist, 1979.

Illustrator: Frederick R. Newman, *Zounds! The Kids Guide to Sound Making* (a juvenile), Random House, 1983.

SIDELIGHTS: In an article on "The New Illustration" (*Graphis*, September/October, 1983), critic Jill Bosert placed Elwood Smith among that group of "canny children using sophisticated techniques" who find their inspiration by playing "in the junkyards of consumerism." Like his peers in this movement, Smith's forte is an ironic reworking of the "American Dream" theme developed by the previous generation's most influential commercial and editorial illustrators. And in keeping with Bosert's assertion that "pop culture," as defined by artists like Andy Warhol, Claes Oldenburg, and James Rosenquist, has provided the stimulus for this new departure in illustration, Smith claims the classic (and graphically related) comic strips of George Herriman (*The Dingbat Family/Krazy Kat*) and Billy De Beck (*Barney Google*) as the chief sources of his inspiration.

Born in 1941 and raised in the small Michigan town of Alpena, Smith's youthful diversions were radio comedy

ELWOOD H. SMITH

shows and comic books. Among the latter, his earliest favorites were western adventures and the grisly horror anthologies published by William M. Gaines's E.C. group (especially the work of artist Jack Davis), but it was his discovery of the works of Herriman and De Beck that finally led to his choice of a career. "I read all I could on cartooning," he told a profiler from *Graphis* in 1980, "bought an assortment of pen nibs that the professionals used, and copied from Billy De Beck's *Barney Google* to get a feel for why the pens did what the artist wanted." He studied art formally at the Chicago Academy of Fine Arts

A drawing from the pamphlet "Just Where Is Elwood H. Smith Anyhow?" (© 1984, Elwood H. Smith. Reprinted by permission.)

and at the Institute of Design in Chicago, but his earliest work was done in the non-drawing area of art direction.

After several years of ad agency work, he and two fellow artists founded a studio with the intention of becoming "the Push Pin of the Midwest." In his eagerness to work as an illustrator, he accepted commissions from all quarters and thus was forced to suppress most of his natural instincts in the face of esthetic constraints imposed by the imperatives of the Chicago commercial art scene. "I was unable to draw under those pressures," he admits; "I'm not facile. I don't love drawing—it's something that has to be done. I prefer working with ideas." Moving to New York in 1976 and joining Push Pin Studios in 1979, he was able to establish himself as a successful commercial and editorial illustrator in that city's more open, not to say anarchistic, marketplace by developing the talents and sensibilities that came most naturally to him. His drawing style is strongly reminiscent of De Beck, but his organization of space, eye for graphic detail, and often fantastic, animal-centered scenarios bespeak the profound influence of Herriman. "Sometimes," he told the *Graphis* interviewer, "when I'm blocked, I open my *Krazy Kat* book to see how Herriman breaks up space, the fun he has—and it will free me." Among his peers, he especially admires the work of R. O. Blechman, Saul Steinberg, and Push Pin Studio founder Seymour Chwast—all of whom must be numbered among the most idea-oriented of contemporary illustrators.

A constant doodler, Smith will cover his desk top with caricatures and animal figures, then select those he finds most appealing for inclusion in his sketchbook for possible use and development. When working on commissions, he sketches in pencil on tissue paper, tracing and improving his original until he is satisfied; then he fixes the tissue on a light box, inks a tracing on watercolor paper, and finishes in watercolor. Technically, his works are accomplished; but as befits one who regards himself as a communicator of ideas, Smith makes his chief impression in the realm of substance.

Although his playful sense of humor and deceptively naive cartoon style has great appeal to children—he has written and illustrated two children's books, provided illustrations for a third, and often receives commissions for advertising

art aimed at very young consumers—Smith is nonetheless a shrewd observer of contemporary adult society. Consider the jacket art he supplied for the Beach Boys' "Endless Beach" album (CBS Records), for example. It presents a Google's-eye view of the shore as an ecological disaster area, forcibly occupied by hordes of loud, noisy, messy, inconsiderate, even dangerous human beings against whom the natural denizens (an octopus, a gull, a snake) can only mount individual, guerilla-style actions—although in the background one can see an ocean liner sinking dramatically (and prophetically?) beneath the placid blue surface of the water. Or another piece, "Musical Living," done to illustrate a *Rolling Stone* cover article, in which he portrays the insanity inherent in the technological explosion of home entertainment media—from elaborate stereo systems to walkmans to giant screen projection televisions—by showing a startled householder looking on as his up-to-date total entertainment environment is destroyed by an invasion of frantically boogeying mice. And (to add insult to injury) his own thoroughly co-opted, earphone-wearing cat!

BIOGRAPHICAL/CRITICAL SOURCES: Gertrude Snyder, "Elwood Smith," *Graphis*, July/August, 1980; Jill Bosert, "The New Illustration," *Graphis*, September/October, 1983; John Newcomb, *The Book of Graphic Problem Solving*, Bowker, 1984.

—*Sketch by Richard Calhoun*

* * *

SORAYAMA, Hajime 1947-

PERSONAL: Born February 22, 1947, in Ehime prefecture, on the island of Shikoku, Japan; son of Tadao (a carpenter) and Emiko Sorayama; married Itomi Takahashi; children: Ai, Nami. *Education:* Attended Shikoku Gakuin University; graduated from Chuo Art School, Tokyo. *Religion:* Buddhist. *Home and studio:* 5-7-14 Osaki, Shinagawaku, Tokyo 141, Japan. *Agent:* Ms. Masumi Misaki, 4-12-3 Sendagaya, Shibuya-ku, Tokyo 151.

CAREER: Illustrator, Asahi Tsushin ad agency, Tokyo, Japan, 1969-71; free-lance illustrator, 1971—.

A comic "signature" by Elwood H. Smith (© Elwood H. Smith. Reprinted by permission.)

WRITINGS—Collections: *Sorayama Hajime Sakuhinshu Sexy Robot*, Genkosha, 1983, and *Hajime Sorayama Pin-up*, Graphic-sha, 1984.

FILMS: The Super Art I "Venus Odyssey," Tokuma, 1984; "Sexy and Sexy Robot—Sorayama World," Fuji TV, 1985.

SIDELIGHTS: In the spring of 1978, Sorayama created an illustration for Suntory whiskey in which he depicted a robot sitting on a rock in outer space, holding a bottle of whiskey, accompanied by a robot dog. With the movie *Star Wars* large in the public mind, this light touch of science fiction parody proved extremely popular, and helped launch Sorayama's career as an independent illustrator with a particular knack for drawing robots. Subsequently, Sorayama has illustrated ads for dozens of Japanese firms, and also achieved considerable recognition overseas, with drawings gracing the covers and pages of *Playboy, Heavy Metal, Air Brush*, and other periodicals. He has also illustrated record jackets for RCA, and participated in a Fiat Y10 ad campaign in both Europe and Israel. In Japan, Sorayama's robot illustrations have been in particular demand among large manufacturers, perhaps as a way of "softening" otherwise "hard" products.

Sorayama's illustrations, particularly his depiction of metallic surfaces, often look uncannily real, and are painstakingly executed with pencil, inks, acrylics, and airbrush. His realism is most striking when depicting robot women; in what seems a contradiction, curved metallic surfaces come alive, become sexy. Sorayama is a master at the depiction of reflections.

Not surprisingly, Sorayama's other main theme in illustration is that of the pin-up. Often working from centerfolds in U.S. "skin magazines," he draws women in painstaking detail. Although best known for his robot images, the erotic women that he draws complement their metal sisters: it is the pin-up quality of his female robots beneath their metal skins that is so titillating.

Above all, Sorayama is a craftsman, and the cool, almost detached objectivity of his art seems particularly apt for the age we live in.

BIOGRAPHICAL/CRITICAL SOURCES: Sorayama Hajime Sakuhinshu Sexy Robot, Genkosha, 1983; *Hajime Sorayama Pin-up*, Graphic-sha, 1984; *The Illustration*, Genkosha, 1984.

T

TING
See TINGLEY, Merle R.

* * *

TINGLEY, Merle R. 1921-
(Ting)

PERSONAL: Born July 9, 1921, in Montreal, Canada; son of Hartley Amos (a machinist) and Edna Blanche (Erb) Tingley; married Dorothy Gene Rowe, July 5, 1952; children: Cameron, Graham. *Education:* Attended Valentine School of Commercial Art, Montreal, Canada, 1939. *Home:* 412 Baker St., London, Ont., Canada N6C 1X7. *Office:* *London Free Press*, London, Ont., Canada N6A 4G1.

An editorial cartoon (© 1986, Merle R. Tingley, *London Free Press*. Reprinted by permission.)

CAREER: Draftsman, Walter J. Armstrong (a consulting engineer), Montreal, Canada, 1939; staff artist, Shipping Containers Ltd., Montreal, 1941; editorial cartoonist, *London Free Press*, London, Canada, 1947-86. Illustrator, lecturer, and circuit speaker. Member of advisory board of Storybook Gardens, London's children's park. *Military service:* Canadian Army, 1942-46; enlisted in Signal Corps, became staff cartoonist for Army magazine and newspaper; received Volunteer Service Medal, War Medal, Korea Medal.

MEMBER: National Cartoonist Society, American Association of Editorial Cartoonists, Canadian Cartoonists Club, Canadian Legion, War Correspondents Association, London City Press Club.

AWARDS, HONORS: National Newspaper awards from Toronto Press Club, 1955 and 1976; World Newspaper Forum Award, 1960; award from Cartoons for Peace, 1960; National Headliners Club Award, 1965; award from International Salon of Cartoons, Montreal, Canada, 1967; Western Ontario Newspaper Award (five times).

WRITINGS—All self-illustrated: *Ting Cartoons* (cartoon collections), London Free Press, (nine books published) 1950-83; *The Day Slippery Ran Away* (a juvenile), McClelland & Stewart, 1958; *Storybook Gardens Coloring Book*, Ting Cartoons, 1971, 1974, 1978, 1981.

Self-portrait of Merle R. Tingley with Luke Worm (© Merle R. Tingley, *London Free Press*. Reprinted by permission.)

An editorial cartoon (© 1986, Merle R. Tingley, *London Free Press*. Reprinted by permission.)

EXHIBITIONS: St. Thomas-Elgin Art Gallery, St. Thomas, Canada, 1979; Traveling Show, Southern Ontario, 1980; London Regional Art Gallery, London, Canada, 1986.

SIDELIGHTS: Montreal-born Merle Tingley had one year of art school in his hometown, but he really learned the basics of his future craft, cartooning, during the four-and-a-half years he spent in the Canadian Army during World War II. His apprenticeship on service publications was so fruitful, in fact, that his newly acquired skills landed him a job with the daily *London Free Press*, first as a part-time artist in 1947, and as the first full-time editorial cartoonist on the paper the following year.

Ting—as he signs his cartoons—has enjoyed a long and apparently harmonious relationship with his paper from the first days of his tenure. He draws in a broad style reminiscent of old-time cartoonists like John McCutcheon

and Bill Ireland, and with a great attention to line, perhaps a throwback to his early days as an engineering draftsman. (Of these times the artist likes to recall that he "drew a worm in a building plan and lost [his] first drafting job." In mock repentance he now draws a pipe-smoking worm in each of his cartoons. The varmint, affectionately nicknamed "Luke Worm" by the readers, has become something of a local celebrity—as well as the cartoonist's trademark.)

One reason for Ting's longevity and continuing popularity among newspaper readers in southern Ontario is the attention he pays to local personalities and concerns; but his commentary also extends to Canadian national and international issues. It is this aspect of his work that is best known in the United States, as the many reprintings of his cartoons readily attest. His comments have a conservative bent, and he often take stands against big government (and big labor). He is particularly alert to government's fondness for cant and rosy predictions (one 1976 cartoon, for example, has labor and business trudging over hill after endless hill in search of the elusive goal sign-posted "Recovery Junction"). In Ting's opinion, bureaucrats in the end often stalemate one another, as in a 1985 cartoon where an exasperated official from Environment Canada proposes a simple solution for the disposal of pollutant PCB's: "Mail them!"

One of Ting's major concerns is for the environment and the depredations visited on our planet. After the Three-Mile Island accident one of his cartoons simply (and eloquently) depicted Death roasting a barren globe over a nuclear reactor; in another cartoon a radiation victim exclaims to his equally afflicted family: "Well, thank God. . . the neutron bomb left our home intact!" Humanitarian concerns such as those nicely balance Ting's more acerbic comments to form a well-rounded body of work. His almost forty-year career until his retirement in July, 1986, is remarkable for its consistency and its absence of malice.

BIOGRAPHICAL/CRITICAL SOURCES: Charles Brooks, editor, *Best Cartoons of the Year,* Pelican Publishing, 1976, 1982, 1984; *Portfolio 85: The Year in Canadian Caricature,* Croc Publishing (Montreal), 1985.

*   *   *

TORRES PRAT, Enric   1938-
(Enric, Enrich)

PERSONAL: Born July 21, 1938, in Barcelona, Spain; son of Enric and Antonia (Prat) Torres; married Virginia Caro Diaz in the 1960s; children: Jordi. *Education:* Studied business administration in the 1950s. *Home:* Valencia 564, 08026 Barcelona, Spain. *Agent:* Herb Spiers, S.I. International, 43 E. 19th St., New York, N.Y. 10003.

CAREER: Advertising and graphic artist, 1953-60; graphic designer and staff artist, Selecciones Ilustradas, Barcelona, Spain, 1960-68; free-lance artist and illustrator, 1968—; cover artist for U.S. publishers, 1970—; painter, 1970—.

AWARDS, HONORS: Warren Award, Warren Publishing Co., 1974; "1984" Award (given by the readers of the magazine *1984*), Spain, 1980.

SIDELIGHTS: From the beginning of the 1970s up to 1986 Enric Torres illustrated more than three hundred covers for the American market, some of them for magazines such as *Heavy Metal* and the Warren publications *Creepy, Eerie,* and *Vampirella,* but the bulk of them for such paperback publishers as Avon, Bantam, Dell, Signet, and Berkley. Until the end of the 1970s the artist signed his work "Enrich"; from 1980 on he dropped the final "h" from his signature.

Torres's beginnings as a graphic artist gradually led him to drawing covers for medical textbooks, a specialization that he escaped by also drawing covers for science-fiction novels published in Spain, starting in the mid-1960s. He made this smooth transition without going through the illustrator's usual apprenticeship; and his international fame in this field is derived from his fascination with photography and with all the aspects of chromatic techniques.

Enric paints his covers with oils, but in the 1960s he had widely experimented in the area of color illustration,

A cover illustration (© 1984, Enric Torres Prat. Reprinted by permission.)

manufacturing his own plastic colors from a transparent latex base, "despite the incomprehension of some of my colleagues," he says, "who claimed that plastic could only be used on murals." Such a disposition to devise his own working tools also prompted Enric, as soon as he had his own studio, to set up a color photography laboratory inside it. At the time Barcelona was a city where very few color labs could be found, and Enric developed his own for his personal use. The stylistic connection between his chromatic experiments and his photographic research led the artist into naturally developing his definitive style as an illustrator, a style not far removed from hyperrealism, but allied to a fondness for fantasy. The artist acknowledges Norman Rockwell as his major influence, and he likes to illustrate works in the most varied areas as possible. "I don't want to be typed as a single-theme illustrator," he says, "and furthermore I don't have a preference for one genre over another."

Enric normally first delineates an illustration's general background and setting through a series of color photographs. Working directly from the developed film, the artist then painstakingly refines the precise color range in order to obtain exactly the tones he wants. In addition, he must conform to the instructions of the publishing companies' art directors, and his love of perfection often leads him to design many of his cover illustrations in giant poster size in order to get the smallest detail and color tone just right. One of his major worries is the unavoidable difference in chromatic tonality between the colors of the original and those of the reproduction. The mechanical process that follows his own creative effort, over which he has no control, too often weakens the genuine vigor of his color tones.

According to Enric, his first cover illustration for an American publisher was the one he did for Ace Books' paperback edition of Jack Williamson's science-fiction novel *People Machines* (1971). At the same time in the 1970s that he did covers for Warren's comic magazines, Enric explored new themes—those of gothic and romantic fiction—for a number of novels published by Dell. Among his recent work for the United States (it should be noted that his work is also widely published in Europe), particular mention should be made of the covers he did for the series of *Star Trek* novels published by Bantam.

BIOGRAPHICAL/CRITICAL SOURCES: Comix Internacional (Barcelona), Number 11, 1981.

A poster design (© 1985, Enric Torres Prat. Reprinted by permission.)

U–V

URAM, Lauren 1957-

PERSONAL: Born November 9, 1957, in Hartford, Conn.; daughter of Earl M. (a consulting engineer) and Joan (a librarian; maiden name, Swett) Uram. *Education:* Pratt Institute, B.F.A., 1980. *Home and studio:* 251 Washington Ave., Brooklyn, N.Y. 11205.

CAREER: Free-lance artist and illustrator, 1980—. Clients include AT&T, British American Tobacco, Teradyne Inc., American International Pictures, and other corporations and institutions. Contributor of illustrations to *New York Times, Village Voice, Washington Post, National Review, Life, Redbook,* and other periodicals.

MEMBER: Foundation for the Community of Artists.

AWARDS, HONORS: Awards from *Communication Arts,* 1982, for Boston Musica Viva poster; from New York Art Directors Club, 1982, for portrait of Duke Ellington; from *Communication Arts,* 1985, and from Society of Illustrators, 1986, both for portrait of Peter Lorre.

EXHIBITIONS: Society of Illustrators' Museum of Illustration, New York City, 1978, 1979, and 1986.

WORK IN PROGRESS: A packaging campaign for Polo by Ralph Lauren; a series of puppets based on and named for various locations in New York City.

SIDELIGHTS: "My earlier work was predominantly three-dimensional and done in a variety of media ranging from welded nails to embossed paper," Lauren Uram wrote *CGA.* "I still work with many different kinds of materials and constantly explore new media; most of my illustration work, however, is done with collage, creating images from ripped pieces of paper with different colors, textures, and patterns."

She added this postscript: "I spend a significant amount of time studying Indoda Entsha ("Kingdom Seeker," a form of martial arts based on the revolving circle and concentrating on creative spiritual productivity)."

Lauren Uram has reached a high level of proficiency as well as a broad level of acceptance in a very short time. She had her works exhibited while still in college and received a number of prestigious awards while still in her twenties. She has chosen to work in a medium where pattern and texture form an intricate background to the purely illustrative elements of line and color that go into the depiction of the subject. The result is often striking, adding a rich depth of mood and meaning to the illustration, and is perhaps best exemplified in her posters. For instance, the one for the musical event Boston Musica Viva featured a music director lost in a whirlwind of staves and octaves; or her poster for the 1985 meeting of the American Booksellers Association simply set one arch of the Golden Gate Bridge against the fiery circle of the setting sun, thus creating a sense of place in one paradigmatic image.

Uram's technique is perfectly suited to portrait, and it is for her portraits that she has been most acclaimed. Actor Peter Lorre comes across as a sad, forlorn figure, like many of the roles he played, his face a map of tormented and creased features painfully emerging out of the ripped paper the artist used as a medium. The Reverend Martin Luther King, Jr., pensively poses against a serenely blue sky, a few clouds overlapping his giant figure, and the folds of his suit revealing on close examination newspaper headlines summing up his achievements.

Uram does not restrict her work to collage, however; her pencil and brush drawings of water fowl reveal a delicate

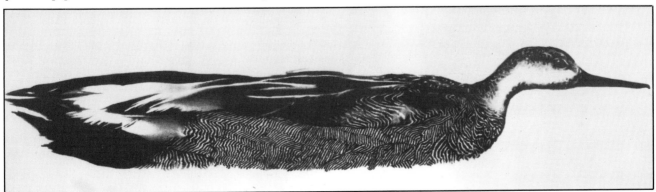

"Wild Duck," a drawing (© 1985, Lauren Uram. Reprinted by permission.)

talent, but also one that is totally grounded in faultless technique. Such thorough professionalism and technical mastery in an artist so young would be uncanny if they weren't also tempered by the exuberance and mischievousness of youth; paradoxically, these qualities are most visible in her corporate promotion work (a young woman's face is refracted in the crystal formed by her intertwining fingers, a human hand stretches toward infinity under the luminescent rays of a bio-medical machine). These are the markings of a major illustration talent for decades to come.

BIOGRAPHICAL/CRITICAL SOURCES: Upper and Lower Case, June, 1981; *American Showcase*, 1983, 1984, 1985, 1986; Les Krantz, *American Artists*, Facts on File, 1985.

* * *

VERA, Nazario Luque
  See LUQUE VERA, Nazario

* * *

VO-DINH, Mai   1933-
  (Vo Dinh)

PERSONAL: Born November 14, 1933, in Hue, Vietnam; came to United States, 1960; naturalized citizen, 1976; son of Thang (a civil servant) and Do-Thi (Hanh) Vo-Dinh. *Education:* Attended the Sorbonne, 1956, Academie de la Grande Chaumiere, 1957, and Ecole Nationale Superieure des Beaux-Arts, 1959, all in Paris. *Studio:* P.O. Box 425, Burkittsville, Md. 21718.

CAREER: Artist, author, translator, 1956—; instructor, Hood College, Frederick, Md., 1978—. Artist-in-residence at Synechia Arts Center, 1974.

Photograph by Hannah L. G. Vo-Dinh. Courtesy of Mai Vo-Dinh.

MAI VO-DINH

The Last Princess, **an acrylic painting, ca. 1984** (© Mai Vo-Dinh. Reprinted by permission.)

MEMBER: Artists Equity Association.

AWARDS, HONORS: Christopher Award, 1975; National Endowment for the Arts Literature Program Fellowship, 1984.

WRITINGS: (Self-illustrated) *The Toad Is the Emperor's Uncle,* Doubleday, 1970; (self-illustrated) *The Jade Song,* Chelsea House, 1970; *Views of a Vietnamese Artist* (lecture), Southern Illinois University Press, 1972; *Xu Samset,* (title means "Thunder Country"), La Boi Press (Paris, France), 1980.

Portfolios: *The Crimson Silk Portfolio,* VDM Editions, 1968; *Unicorn Broadsheet # 4,* Unicorn Press, 1969; *Recent Works by Vo-Dinh,* Suzuki Graphics, 1972; *The Woodcuts of Vo-Dinh,* Hoa-Binh Press, 1974.

Illustrator: *Wind Play,* Unicef, 1964; *Birds, Frogs, and Moonlight,* translation by Sylvia Cassedy and Kunihiro Suetake, Doubleday, 1967; Nhat Hanh, *The Cry of Vietnam,* Unicorn Press, 1968; *All Year Long,* Unicorn Press, 1969; (and translator) Doan Quoc-Sy, *The Stranded Fish,* Sang-Tao Press, 1971; (and translator) Hanh, *The Path of Return Continues the Journey,* Hoa-Binh Press, 1972; James Kirkup, *The Magic Drum,* Knopf, 1973; Helen Coutant, *FirstSnow,* Knopf, 1974; Hanh and Daniel Berrigan, *The Raft Is Not the Shore,* Beacon Press, 1976; (and translator) Hanh, *Zen Poems of Nhat Hanh,* Unicorn Press, 1976; Hanh, *The Miracle of Mindfulness,* Beacon Press, 1976; Ron Roy, *One Thousand Pails of Water,* Knopf, 1978; *The Way of Everyday Life,* Center Publications, 1978.

(And translator) *Fragrance of Zen,* Buddhist Cultural Center, 1981; (and translator) *Tuyet Dau Mua,* LaBoi Press (Paris), 1981; Huyn Quang, *The Land I Lost,* Harper, 1982; *The Brocaded Slipper,* Addison-Wesley, 1982; Eve Bunting,

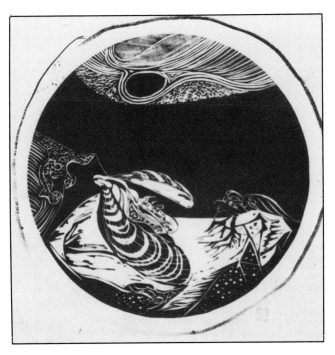

The Mussel, **a woodcut, ca. 1985** (© Mai Vo-Dinh.
Reprinted by permission.)

The Happy Funeral, Harper, 1982; (and translator) Nhat
Hanh, *A Flower for You,* Nam Tuyen Temple, 1983; Gesshin
Myoko Midwer, *A Flash of Lightning,* International Zen
Institute, 1983; Michele Surat, *Angel Child, Dragon Child,*
Carnival Press, 1983; Coutant, *The Gift,* Knopf, 1984; (and
translator) Marguerite Bouvard, editor, *Landscape and
Exile,* Rowan Tree Press, 1985.

Contributor to various Vietnamese cultural publications in
exile in Europe, the United States, and Canada.

EXHIBITIONS: Over forty one-man shows since 1960,
including those at Mars Hill College, Mars Hill, N.C., 1981;
Phoenix Fine Arts Gallery, Frederick, Md., 1981; Washing-
ton International Arts Exposition, Washington, D.C., 1981;
Arsenal Gallery, New York City, 1982; Mills House Visual
Arts Complex, Garden Grove, Calif., 1982; Arts Club of
Washington, Washington, D.C., 1983; Touchstone Gallery,
Washington, D.C., 1983; Phoenix II Gallery, Washington,

D.C., 1983; Paul Rosen Gallery, Washington, D.C., 1983;
Master Eagle Gallery, New York City, 1983; George Mason
University, Arlington, Va., 1984; Arlington County Visual
and Performing Arts, Arlington, Va., 1985.

WORK IN PROGRESS: Translating a selection titled
Vietnamese Short Stories; producing *Basic Yoga,* an illustrated manual in Vietnamese.

SIDELIGHTS: "I am first and foremost a painter and
printmaker," Mai Vo-Dinh wrote *CGA,* "and secondly a
writer and translator; my work as an illustrator comes third.
Born and raised in Vietnam, educated in France, and now a
resident of the United States, I have travelled extensively.
Although my heart has remained in my place of birth, I
consider myself a citizen of the world in the sense that I love
and understand cultures of wide-ranging diversity, which
may help explain why I am so interested in translation:
literature builds the most durable cultural bridges."

Reflecting this cultural diversity, Vo Dinh acknowledges the
influence of a broad range of artists on his work, from early
Chinese masters to Pablo Picasso and Henri Matisse; but he
reserve his greatest admiration for two Englishmen, Francis
Bacon and Graham Sutherland, and for the (very) American
Georgia O'Keeffe. In order to find his own identity he
experimented with a great many different media—oil,
acrylics, collages, woodcuts—but of late he has returned to
the practice of traditional media of the Far East, ink and
watercolors on paper. His landscapes are especially striking
and display a restrained lyricism tinged with mystery.
As can be expected, the war in Vietnam has affected Vo
Dinh strongly. His feelings are reflected in many of his book
illustrations (particularly those done for Vietnamese-lan-
guage publications), and also in some of his paintings, such
as *The Last Princess,* in which the wistful expression on the
face of the forlorn subject epitomizes the poignancy of a way
of life irretrievably gone. A Saigon reviewer may have
summed up the artist's achievements best when he wrote:
"Vo-Dinh is truly a Vietnamese artist. . . . Through his
work non-Vietnamese have a chance to know and respect a
people who has suffered immeasurably, but who is also
endowed with talents and an old and rich culture."

BIOGRAPHICAL/CRITICAL SOURCES: Song Than (Saigon), March 14, 1974; *Something about the Author,* Vol. 16,
Gale, 1979; *Contemporary Authors,* New Revision Series,
Vol. 13, Gale, 1984; *Who's Who in American Art,* Bowker,
1984; Les Krantz, *American Artists,* Facts on File, 1985.

MORT WALKER

WALKER, (Addison) Mort(on)   1923-
(Addison)

PERSONAL: Born September 3, 1923, in El Dorado, Kan.; son of Robin A. (an architect) and Carolyn (a designer and illustrator; maiden name, Richards) Walker; married Jean Suffill, March 12, 1949 (divorced, July, 1985); married Catherine Carty Prentice (an executive administrator), August 24, 1985; children: Greg, Brian, Polly Embree, Morgan, Marjorie, Neal, Roger; stepchildren: Whitney, Cathy II, Priscilla. *Education:* University of Missouri, B.A., 1948. *Politics:* Republican. *Home:* Stamford, Conn. *Syndicate:* King Features Syndicate, 235 E. 45th St., New York, N.Y. 10017.

CAREER: Designer, Hallmark Greeting Cards, Kansas City, Mo., 1941-42; editor, Dell Publishing Co., New York

City, 1948-50; creator of comic strips, *Beetle Bailey*, 1950—, (with Dik Browne) *Hi and Lois*, 1954—, (with Frank Roberge) *Mrs. Fitz's Flats*, 1957-72, (with Jerry Dumas) *Sam's Strip*, 1961-63, (under name "Addison") *Boner's Ark*, 1968—, (with Jerry Dumas) *Sam and Silo*, 1977—, and (with Johnny Sajem) *The Evermores*, 1982—. Founder, Museum of Cartoon Art. Founder and publisher, Comicana Books. Lecturer. Former member of President's Committee for Employing the Handicapped. *Military service:* U.S. Army, 1943-46, served in Europe; became first lieutenant.

MEMBER: National Cartoonists Society (president, 1959-60), Artists and Writers Association, Newspaper Features Council, Cartoonists Guild, Society of Illustrators, Authors League.

AWARDS, HONORS: Reuben Award for best cartoonist, National Cartoonists Society, 1953; Silver Lady award, the Banshees (a New York City club of artists, writers, and editors), 1955; National Cartoonists Society plaques for best cartoonist, 1966 and 1969; Il Secolo XIX award (Italy), 1972; Adamson Award (Sweden), 1975; Power of Printing Award, 1977; Elzie Segar Award, National Cartoonists Society, for outstanding contribution to the profession, 1977; Fourth Estate Award, American Legion, 1978; Jester Award, 1979.

WRITINGS: (With Dik Browne) *Most* (a juvenile), Windmill Books, 1971; (with Browne) *Land of Lost Things* (a juvenile), Windmill, 1973; *Backstage at the Strips*, Mason/Charter, 1975; *The Lexicon of Comicana*, Comicana Books, 1980.

Cartoon books; published by Grosset, except as noted; *Beetle Bailey and Sarge*, Dell, 1958; (with Browne) *Trixie*, Avon, 1960; *Beetle Bailey*, 1968; *Fall Out Laughing, Beetle Bailey*, 1969; *At Ease, Beetle Bailey*, 1970; (with Browne) *Hi and Lois*, 1970; *I Don't Want to Be Here Any More Than You Do, Beetle Bailey*, 1970; (with Jerry Dumas), *Sam's Strip Lives*, Carriage House, 1970; *What Is It Now, Beetle Bailey?*, 1971; (with Browne) *Hi and Lois in Darkest Suburbia*, 1971; *Beetle Bailey on Parade*, 1972; *I'll Throw the Book at You, Beetle Bailey*, 1973; *We're All in the Same Boat, Beetle Bailey*, 1973; *Shape Up or Ship Out, Beetle Bailey*, 1974.

Take Ten, Beetle Bailey, 1975; *I've Got You on My List, Beetle Bailey*, 1975; *Take a Walk, Beetle Bailey*, 1975; *I Thought You Brought the Compass, Beetle Bailey*, 1975; *Is That All, Beetle Bailey?*, 1976; *About Face, Beetle Bailey*, 1976; *I'll Flip You for It, Beetle Bailey*, 1976; *I Just Want to Talk to You, Beetle Bailey*, 1978; *Looking Good, Beetle Bailey*, 1978; *Give Us a Smile, Beetle Bailey*, 1979.

A *Beetle Bailey* **daily strip by Mort Walker** (© 1985, King Features Syndicate. Reprinted by permission.)

Up, Up and Away, Beetle Bailey, 1980; (with Browne) *Hi and Lois, Family Ties*, 1980; *Peace, Beetle Bailey*, Ace, 1981; *Beetle Bailey's Activity Game Challenge*, Ace, 1982; *Who's in Charge Here, Beetle Bailey?*, Ace, 1982; *You're Out of Hup, Beetle Bailey*, Ace, 1982; *Miss Buxley: Sexism in Beetle Bailey?*, Comicana, 1982; (with Browne) *Suburban Cowboys*, Ace, 1982; *Beetle Bailey: Double Trouble*, Tor, 1983; *Beetle Bailey, Rise and Shine!*, Tor, 1983; *Beetle Bailey, Is This Another Complaint?*, Ace, 1983; *Friends*, Dargaud, 1983; *Too Many Sergeants*, Dargaud, 1983; *Would It Help to Say I'm Sorry, Beetle Bailey*, Ace, 1983; (with Browne) *Hi and Lois: How Do You Spell Dad?*, Ace, 1983; (with Browne) *Hi and Lois: American Gothic*, Ace, 1983.

Beetle Bailey in the System, Dargaud, 1984; *Beetle Bailey: Operation Good Times*, Ace, 1984; *The Best of Beetle Bailey*, Holt, 1984; *You Crack Me Up, Beetle Bailey*, Tor, 1984; *You'll Get a Bang Out of This, Beetle Bailey*, Ace, 1984; (with Browne) *Hi and Lois: The Bright Stuff*, Ace, 1984; (with Browne) *Hi Honey, I'm Home*, Tor, 1984; (with Browne) *Is Dinner Ready?*, Tor, 1984; (with Browne) *Saturday Night Fever*, Tor, 1984; *Beetle Bailey: Hard Knocks*, Tor, 1985; *Hey There, Beetle Bailey!*, Tor, 1985; *Potato Pancakes*, Tor, 1985; *Strategic Withdrawal*, Tor, 1985; *You're All Washed Up, Beetle Bailey*, Ace, 1985.

Work is widely anthologized in the United States and abroad. Contributor of cartoons to *Saturday Evening Post, Esquire*, and many other periodicals. Contributor of articles to *Horizon*. Co-editor of *National Cartoonists Society Album*.

EXHIBITIONS: Work included in all major exhibitions of comic art, including "Bande Dessinee et Figuration Narrative," Louvre, Paris, 1967; "75 Years of the Comics," New York Cultural Center, New York City, 1971; "The Art of the Comic Strip," University of Maryland, 1971; "The Cartoon," John F. Kennedy Center, Washington, D.C., 1975; "The Cartoon Art Show," Whitney Museum, New York City, 1983. Work widely exhibited in galleries and museums in the United States and abroad. One-man show: Felicie Gallery, New York City, 1984.

SIDELIGHTS: In 1986 Mort Walker was producing no fewer than five nationally syndicated newspaper strips simultaneously, every day of the week—a record that has no parallel in the entire history of the comics. All of his strips (*Boner's Ark, Sam and Silo, The Evermores*, and the top-ranking *Beetle Bailey* and *Hi and Lois*) are distributed by King Features Syndicate, a fact that has prompted some wags to dub the Walker studio in Connecticut "King Features East." His prodigality of output is only matched by his activities in related fields, such as his association with the Museum of Cartoon Art and the launching of his own small publishing company. It is easy to understand why the name Mort Walker looms large in the annals of contemporary comics and cartoons.

As a child, Walker grew up in an artistic environment—his father was a would-be cartoonist himself, and his mother had been an illustrator with the *Kansas City Journal* before her marriage. With the encouragement of his understanding parents, he started drawing at an early age, selling his first cartoon at eleven to *Child Life* and kept cartooning all through his teenage years, eventually landing a job with Hallmark Cards. Even his being drafted could not stop him: all through his years in military service he sketched hilarious scenes of army life in his diary. "These sources have been a research gold mine for over 25 years," he later wrote.

Back to civilian life, Walker resumed his interrupted studies at the University of Missouri, eventually earning a bachelor's degree in 1948. These college years were also fruitful ones on a more practical level: Walker became editor of the campus magazine (to which he contributed many cartoons) and made his first sales to national magazines such as *Esquire* and the *Saturday Evening Post*. On the strength of these sales he moved to New york City after graduation, took up an editorial position at Dell, and was declared the top-selling gag cartoonist of 1949, an honor that puzzles him to this day, since he had only earned seventy-five hundred dollars that year. "If you're the top seller and that's all you're making," his wife told him, "then it must be a bad business."

In the meantime Walker had doggedly pursued his dream of becoming a nationally syndicated comic strip artist. In 1950 he brought to King Features the samples of a strip that was to become *Beetle Bailey*; it originally took place on a college campus, but poor sales prompted the artist to switch the locale to an army base. The move proved momentous: the feature soon zoomed to dizzying heights of circulation, and it has earned its author many awards and distinctions, as well as a devoted and loyal following.

Beetle Bailey's home base, Camp Swampy, is possibly the best-known U.S. Army outfit anywhere as well as its most

A *Beetle Bailey* **daily strip by Mort Walker** (© 1985, King Features Syndicate. Reprinted by permission.)

unmanageable, peopled as it is by an unlikely congregation of misfits, shirkers, and incompetents. Beetle (whose eyes are permanently hidden under his helmet) is a reluctant draftee, and uses his ineptness to get out of most situations; Killer is the camp's resident Casanova, and Zero is the military equivalent of the village idiot; they and the other denizens of Camp Swampy are kept in some semblance of shape only by Sergeant ("Sarge") Orville Snorkel's iron hand and iron lungs. Most of the officers are no better: Lieutenant Fuzz is a petty sycophant, Lieutenant Flap an afro-coiffed martinet, while General Halftrack, the base commandant, appears well on his way to senility. Finally, mention should be made of the general's secretary, the buxom Miss Buxley, whose innocent sexiness has embroiled Walker more than once with feminist detractors. "Basically the strip is *not* about the army," Walker has averred in his memoir *Backstage at the Strips*, "but about a bunch of funny people who happen to be in the army." In 1986 Walker launched *Beetle Bailey, the Musical* for a pre-Broadway run in regional theaters.

Some people (including Pentagon officials) view *Beetle Bailey* as a satire of the army. Walker denies this interpretation. In reference to his theme he is on the record as stating (perhaps a bit defensively) that it deals with "authority, the abuse of it, the resistance to it, and who's going to get up and turn off the light?" A close analysis of the strip bears him out on this point. The cool and professional Captain Scabbard is actually running the camp, ably assisted by Sarge who is as competent at his job as he is ineffectual in everything else.

Beetle Bailey is Walker's most successful and popular strip, continuously ranking among the top five newspaper features; but it is far from being his only creation in the field. In 1954, in collaboration with Dik Browne, he produced *Hi and Lois*, an endearingly funny feature about a suburban family, Hi and Lois Flagston, and their children, Chip, Dot, Ditto, and Trixie. Among Walker's strips it ranks only second to *Beetle* in popularity. In 1957 came *Mrs. Fitz's Flats*, drawn by Frank Roberge: it dealt with the humorous adventures of a feisty old landlady in Florida, and lasted till 1972. Using his first name, Addison, as his only signature, Walker next brought out *Boner's Ark* in 1968: under the amiably inept stewardship of Captain Boner, this ark and its ill-assorted menagerie of motley animals keeps drifting aimlessly from one hilarious incident to the next.

In 1961 Walker and his assistant Jerry Dumas had created *Sam's Strip*, in which the hero found himself confronted with old-time comic strip characters, such as Popeye, Krazy Kat, and Happy Hooligan. It lasted only until 1963, but in 1977 it was revived as *Sam and Silo*, and as a straight gag strip written and drawn by Dumas it is highly successful. Then in 1982 came *The Evermores*, a strip set in ancient Roman times, the collaboration of Mort Walker and Johnny Sajem. In 1984 Walker put together two old-time cartoon favorites to form *Betty Boop and Felix* [*the Cat*], and it is being produced by four of the Walker children, Brian, Greg, Neal, and Morgan.

In addition to his workload Walker has found time to write a hilarious account of his experiences in the field of comics, *Backstage at the Strips*, and he often writes articles and lectures on the subject. In 1974 he founded the Museum of Cartoon Art, and also served as its first president until 1985 (he is now its board chairman). Originally established in Greenwich, Connecticut, and now located in Rye Brook, New York, the Museum is probably the world's foremost institution of its kind. It houses and maintains an extensive collection of original comic strips and cartoons, as well as thousands of animated films. It has held a number of outstanding exhibitions of comic art, and maintains an extensive research library. The monthly lectures, often given by outstanding personalities in the field, are a Museum feature, as are its frequent retrospectives of animated cartoons. There is no doubt that the Museum owes a great deal of its success to the efforts and personality of its founder, who is also its most able supporter.

BIOGRAPHICAL/CRITICAL SOURCES: Stephen Becker, *Comic Art in America*, Simon & Schuster, 1959; Pierre Couperie and Maurice Horn, *A History of the Comic Strip*, Crown, 1968; *Cartoonist Profiles*, winter, 1969; Reinhold Reitberger and Wolfgang Fuchs, *Comics: Anatomy of a Mass Medium*, Little, Brown, 1970; *Christian Science Monitor*, May 2, 1973; Jerry Robinson, *The Comics: An Illustrated History of Comic Strip Art*, Putnam, 1974; Mort Walker, *Backstage at the Strips*, Mason/Charter, 1975; *The World Encyclopedia of Comics*, Chelsea House, 1976; *Horizon*, July, 1980; *Cartoonist Profiles*, December, 1980; *Contemporary Authors*, New Revision Series, Vol. 3, Gale, 1981; Mort Walker, *The Best of Beetle Bailey*, Holt, 1984.

—*Sketch by Maurice Horn*

WALLMEYER, Dick
See WALLMEYER, Richard

* * *

WALLMEYER, Richard   1931-
(Dick Wallmeyer)

PERSONAL: Born February 1, 1931, in Chicago Ill.; son of Arthur Eugene (a cartographer) and Evelyn (Gronquist) Wallmeyer; married Helen Rachel Fohs Allen, 1953 (divorced, 1963). *Education:* Attended Chicago Academy of Fine Arts, 1948-49; followed correspondence course of Art Instruction Schools, 1959-62. *Politics:* "Middle of the road: has adopted liberal, conservative, and midroad positions during career, depending on the issue." *Religion:* Lutheran. *Office:* Press-Telegram, 604 Pine Ave., Long Beach, Calif. 90844.

CAREER: Proofreader, Newman-Rudolph Lithograph Co., Chicago, Ill., 1948-50; salesman, Montgomery Ward, Chicago Heights, Ill., 1950-51; newscaster, WCHI-FM radio station, Chicago Heights, 1951; art studio apprentice, Bundy Friday Studio, Chicago, 1955; paste-up and line drawing artist, Filmack Studios, Chicago, 1956; shoe salesman, Children's Bootery, Long Beach, Calif., 1956-61; editorial cartoonist, *Press Telegram*, Long Beach, 1961—. *Military service:* U.S. Air Force, 1951-55.

MEMBER: Association of American Editorial Cartoonists.

Photograph by Press-Telegram. Courtesy of Richard Wallmeyer.

RICHARD WALLMEYER

AWARDS, HONORS: National Safety Council Public Interest Award, 1963, for holiday traffic cartoon; California Newspaper Publishers Association Award of Merit, 1982, for editorial cartoon on nuclear war.

WRITINGS: (Contributor) Raymond B. Rajski, editor, *A Nation Grieved: The Kennedy Assassination in Editorial Cartoons*, Tuttle, 1967; (contributor) Roy Paul Nelson, *Cartooning*, Regnery, 1975; (contributor) *Best Editorial Cartoons of the Year* (annual anthologies), Pelican, 1973—. Cartoons reprinted in *Time, Newsweek, U.S. News and World Report*, and other periodicals.

EXHIBITIONS: Graham Gallery, New York, N.Y., 1972; Long Beach, Calif., Public Library, 1983. Represented in Association of American Editorial Cartoonists annual and traveling exhibits.

SIDELIGHTS: Richard Wallmeyer wrote *CGA*: "I do not subscribe to the view of many of my cartoonist colleagues that editorial cartooning is essentially a destructive art. It is true that much of it is biting and critical commentary on various public figures and their activities; and this constitutes a very important part of cartooning. There is no argument that keeping a critical eye on public servants and other movers and shakers is a prime motivation in cartooning. I do think, however, that much cartooning can have an important influence in other ways as well: focusing the reader's attention on various issues of the day, for instance, and getting them to think seriously about these issues is a useful function of the cartoonist.

"The positive aspect of cartooning is as important as its critical function. If you consider, for instance, the tragic effects of drug abuse on our society, and especially on the young, I believe that a cartoon that in some way might influence youngsters to turn away from drugs has made a valuable contribution. The idea that a cartoon by itself or in some capacity can have enough of an impact to accomplish something of that nature may be regarded by some as questionable or even too idealistic; nevertheless it is an appealing idea that should occupy an important place in the cartoonist's arsenal.

"When I comment on politics, the arms race, social issues, the Middle East, and other international, national, and local issues, I try to get a nice mix of criticism, satire, and humor in my weekly output. Occasionally I like to do something a little different just for entertainment and a change of pace. But, whatever the approach or subject matter, the best cartoons always have something to say to the reader."

Wallmeyer certainly practices that which he preaches. A survey of his cartoons over a given period does show a wide range of approaches and a broad concern for seemingly unrelated issues. A humanistic touch is also very often apparent in his commentary; as for instance in the footnote he appends to the famous lines engraved on the Statue of Liberty: "This offer good only when foreign policy, immigration laws, or sanctuary status of cities is not prohibitive"; or when he depicts the implacably growing U.S. and Russian nuclear arsenal that stretches to the crack of doom, in the midst of which a small voice timidly asks: "Are we safe enough yet?"

As befits an artist who has practiced long and hard at his craft, while holding down a variety of mundane jobs, Wallmeyer has a crisp, economical, no-nonsense style. His

An editorial cartoon by Richard Wallmeyer (© 1985, *Press-Telegram*. Reprinted by permission.)

drawings are clear and to the point, and his captions show a predilection for the punch-line. When he has a more elaborate point to make, he frequently draws several panels in succession, comic-strip style, to good effect. Also borrowing from the comics, he sometimes makes witty use of speech ballons instead of captions, as in the cartoon showing three cats of varying sizes on a fence, respectively labeled "rich," "poor," and "middle" (class), each commenting in turn on the promises of tax reform.

BIOGRAPHICAL/CRITICAL SOURCES: John Chase, *Today's Cartoon*, Hauser Press, 1962; *International Who's Who in Art and Antiques*, 2nd edition, Melrose Press, 1976.

*   *   *

WELLER, Don 1937-

PERSONAL: Born August 13, 1937, in Colfax, Wash.; son of Harry Charles (an architect) and Margaret (Mighell) Weller; divorced from first wife, Camille, 1973; married Chikako Matsubayashi (a graphic designer), 1976; children: Anna, Nancy, Julietta, Kathy. *Education:* Washington State University, B.A., 1960. *Home and studio:* 1398 Aerie Dr., Box 726, Park City, Utah 84060. *Agent:* Weller Institute for the Cure of Design, Box 726, Park City, Utah 84060.

CAREER: Graphic designer at various studios and freelance illustrator, 1960-66; proprietor of own studio, 1966-69; partner, Weller & Juett, 1970-73; founder and proprietor, Weller Institute for the Cure of Design, Park City, Utah, 1973—. Teacher of graphic design at University of California at Los Angeles, 1968-70; teacher of illustration at Art Center College of Design, 1972-82. Member of Steering Committee for "The Design Conference That Just Happens to Be in Park City (TDCTJHTBIPC)," 1977—.

MEMBER: Los Angeles Society of Illustrators (president, 1968).

AWARDS, HONORS: Recipient of many awards, including Certificates of Merit, 1963-84, Awards of Distinctive Merit, 1971-73, silver medals, 1966 and 1979, gold medals, 1972-75, Hugo Hammer Memorial Award, 1981, all from Art Directors' Club of Los Angeles; Certificates of Merit, 1964-85, Best of Show Awards, 1964, 1967, 1980, and 1981, Life Time Achievement Award, 1982, all from Society of Illustrators of Los Angeles; Certificates of Merit, 1966-67, 1969-71, 1973-81, 1984-85, Certificate of Distinctive Merit, 1969, all from *Communication Arts*; Certificates of Merit, 1969-79, 1981-85, gold medals, 1971 and 1985, Art Directors' Club of New York; Certificates of Merit, 1967-76, 1978-85, from Society of Illustrators, New York City; *Graphis Annuals*, 1968-72, 1974-81, 1983; Awards of Typographic Excellence, 1970, 1980-85, from Typographic Directors' Club of New

York; Creativity Awards, 1971-81, 1983, from *Art Directors Magazine*; awards from *Modern Publicity*, 1972-82; Certificates of Merit, 1972-75, 1977, 1978, and 1982, Certificate of Distinctive Merit, 1978, silver awards, 1972-73, all from Society of Publication Designers; Desi Awards, 1980-84, from Graphic Design: USA; represented in STA 100 Show, 1980, 1982, 1985, of the Society of Typographic Arts; Alumni Achievement Award from Washington State University, 1986; awards from the American Institute of Graphic Arts in packaging, graphic design, communication graphics, learning materials.

WRITINGS: Work featured in such books as *Two Hundred Years of American Illustration, Graphic Design: Problems, Methods, Solutions, Letterheads 1* and *2, World Trademarks and Logotypes*, and *Package Design 2*, and in many magazines, including *Forbes, Communication Arts, Association, Japan Creators Association (JCA) Annual*, and *Industrial Design Magazine*.

EXHIBITIONS: One-man shows include those at Los Angeles Art Gallery, 1968 and 1969; Washington State University, Pullman, Wash., 1970 and 1973; Ventura College, Ventura, Calif., 1975; Spokane Falls Community College, Spokane, Wash. 1981. Work exhibited in group shows, including "Typomundus 20/2," at International Center for the Typographic Arts, Stuttgart, Germany, 1969; California State University at Los Angeles, 1974; Bienale Uzite Grafik, Brno, Czechoslovakia, 1974, 1982, and 1984; Mead Library of Ideas, New York City, 1975; "Two Hundred Years of American Illustration," New York Historical Society, New York City, 1976; Commercial Photo, Japan, 1976; Clara Eagle Gallery, Murray, Ky., 1977; "AIGA, the Poster Show," American Institute of Graphic Arts, 1978; American Illustrators Gallery, Atlanta, Ga., 1978; Northern Arizona University Art Gallery, Flag-

A fantasy illustration (© 1983, Don Weller. Reprinted by permission.)

staff, Ariz., 1979; Design Council Gallery, Portland, Ore., 1979.

Academy of Art, San Francisco, Calif., 1981; Pierce College Art Gallery, Woodland Hills, Calif., 1981; Peppertree Calabasas, Calabasas, Calif., 1982; Otis Art Institute of Parsons School of Design Art Auction, New York City, 1982; "The New York Illustration Express," Osaka, Tokyo, and Sapporo, Japan, 1982 and 1983; National Art Museum of Sport, University of New Haven, West Haven, Conn., 1983; California State University Northridge Art Gallery, Northridge, Calif., 1983; Western Carolina University, Cullowhee, N.C., 1983; Los Angeles City College, Los Angeles, Calif., 1984; Shoshin Society Peace Poster Project, Hiroshima Museum of Art, Hiroshima, Japan, 1985-86; "First International Triennial of Posters in Toyama," Museum of Modern Art, Toyama, Japan, 1985.

SIDELIGHTS: Don Weller's playful nature is evident in his choice of studio name: the Weller Institute's expressed objective is "the Cure of Design," and with his Japanese-American wife Chikako (whose title is "Design Doctor") he undertakes to improve the state of the art. The enormous range of awards he and his Institute have won on both U.S. coasts, in Europe, and in the Orient bears witness to the success of his efforts. His many prizes include the SanDi Gold Egg, five Andy awards, four LuLu awards, five Desi awards, and gold and silver medals from the New York Art Directors' Club, the Los Angeles Art Directors' Club, and the Western Art Directors' Club. His work has been

DON WELLER

Cover illustration for *Westways* (© 1974, Don Weller. Reprinted by permission.)

exhibited in many cities in the United States, Germany, Czechoslovakia, and Japan, and he has lectured and presented workshops at universities and business organizations in eighteen states and Japan. His work as illustrator has adorned album covers for Warner Brothers and Capitol Records, appeared in *Road and Track* and *Time*, and been used by Datsun Motors and United Airlines. Active in his profession at many levels, Weller has taught illustration and graphic design and been deeply involved with organizations in the field. He is one of the three members of the steering committee that organizes a conference in his home town whimsically called TDCTJHTBIPC ("The Design Conference That Just Happens to Be in Park City"). Weller was one of twelve designers called on for an official "Signature Series" poster for the 1984 Summer Games by the Los Angeles Olympic Organizing Committee.

A typographer of note, Weller has been honored frequently by professional organizations such as the Typographic Directors' Club of New York and the Society of Typographic Arts. His ingenuity and imagination in the design of logotypes has similarly been widely noted, and his trademarks have appeared in *World Trademarks and Logotypes*, published in Japan in 1983, and both the volume on alphabetic designs and the volume on symbolic designs of *Trademarks and Symbols*. But with all the wide range of professional honors he has earned in his field, Weller's name is probably best known to the public at large in the field of watercolor. His illustrations in this medium for many clients have established him as a respected creative artist with a distinct aesthetic voice of his own. His work was exhibited in the Society of Illustrators' 1976 show "Two Hundred Years of American Illustration" at the New York Historical Society and published in the 1977 Random House volume drawn from that show.

Often highly stylized, his watercolors are characterized by elegantly balanced compositions and delicate, luminous colors. His painting *Bull Rider*, for example, is a loosely sketched but naturalistic rodeo scene in vibrant tones, its planes of vivid color combining to produce an animated and dynamic image. His perspectives are sometimes distorted enough to keep his work from photographic realism, but never so much as to render it grotesque or obscure. Even in his more openly fantastic work, like the pen-and-ink drawing "The Dam," the science-fiction note is handled with humor and grace.

BIOGRAPHICAL/CRITICAL SOURCES: Edward Booth-Clibborn, editor, *Two Hundred Years of American Illustration*, Society of Illustrators/Random House, 1977; *Vision: Special Issue on the Work of the Weller Institute for the Cure of Design*, 1979; *Outstanding American Illustrators Today*, I, II, Graphic Sha, 1984, 1985; Les Krantz, *American Artists*, Facts on File, 1985; *Who's Who in the West 1986-87*, Marquis, 1986.

*   *   *

WERNER, Charles George
(Chuck Werner)

PERSONAL: Born in Marshfield, Wis.; son of George and Marie (Tippelt) Werner; married Eloise Robertson; children: David, Jean Louise, Steven. *Education:* Attended special courses at Oklahoma University, Oklahoma City; Northwestern University; Art Institute of Chicago. *Politics:* Republican. *Religion:* Episcopalian. *Home:* 4445 Brown Rd.,

Indianapolis, Ind. 46226. *Office: Indianapolis Star*, 307 N. Pennsylvania St., P.O. Box 145, Indianapolis, Ind. 42206.

CAREER: Staff artist, photographer, reporter, *Springfield News Leader and Press*, Springfield, Mo., 1930-36; editorial cartoonist, *Daily Oklahoman*, Oklahoma City, 1936-41; chief editorial cartoonist, *Chicago Sun*, 1941-47; editorial cartoonist, *Indianapolis Star*, 1947—. Commissioner for Indiana Department of Natural Resources. Instructor and lecturer on the history of the political cartoon.

MEMBER: National Cartoonists Society; Association of American Editorial Cartoonists (president, 1959-60); Sigma Delta Chi (honorary member); Mystic Tie Lodge; Free and Accepted Masons (Thirty-third Degree; Shriner, Jester); Oklahoma City Junior Chamber of Commerce (honorary lifetime member); Columbia Club (Indianapolis); Hillcrest Gold Club; Indianapolis Athletic Club.

AWARDS, HONORS: Recipient of many local and national journalism awards, including Pulitzer Prize for editorial cartoon, 1939; honorable mention for a cartoon on auto safety, 1939; National Safety Council Award, 1940; Sigma Delta Chi Award, 1943; National Headliners Club Award "for consistently outstanding editorial cartoons," 1951; Freedoms Foundation Awards, 1951, 1952, 1953, 1955, 1958, 1962, 1963; National Service Clubs Award, 1955; Dave Roberts Award for contributions to conservationism in Indiana, 1956; National Foundation for Highway Safety Award, 1964; named one of six best caricaturists, Interna-

Self-portrait of Charles George Werner, drawn specially for *Contemporary Graphic Artists* (© 1986, Charles George Werner.)

An editorial cartoon by Chuck Werner (© 1985, *Indianapolis Star*. Reprinted by permission.)

tional Salon of Cartoons, Montreal Pavillion of Humor, Montreal, Canada, 1969.

SIDELIGHTS: Chuck Werner established a national reputation as a perceptive and independent-minded political commentator in the 1930s and has maintained it for nearly a half century with a steady flow of dynamic and expressive editorial cartoons. With no formal art training except a correspondence-school course, he found a job in Springfield, Missouri, as an all-purpose journalist and for six years served the *News Leader and Press* there as reporter, photographer, and staff artist. His gift for drawing and his political insights won him the job of editorial cartoonist at the *Daily Oklahoman* in 1936. In 1939 he won journalism's highest award, the Pulitzer Prize, for a 1938 cartoon forecasting the fate of Czechoslovakia after the Munich Pact, signed a week before. Twenty-eight years old when the cartoon was published, Werner was the youngest cartoonist to win a Pulitzer until then, and one of the very few newspapermen in the United States to recognize the fatal implications of England's appeasement of Nazi Germany.

The year before the United States entered the Second World War, Werner accepted an invitation from Chicago retailing tycoon Marshall Field to become the chief editorial cartoonist of his new paper, the *Chicago Sun*, where Werner remained for the entire seven-year life of that paper. When the *Sun* went bankrupt in 1947, Werner had no trouble

finding another post. He became the *Indianapolis Star*'s editorial cartoonist and has held that position ever since. During his nearly four decades with the *Star* he has received virtually all the awards journalism offers, and bound volumes containing some twelve thousand cartoons he has published—a concise graphic history of our times—line an entire wall of his office.

Werner identifies his political philosophy as "conservative," but over the years he has taken positions that show he is an independent thinker and not bound by any rigid dogma. He has attacked Presidents Nixon and Ford when circumstances called for it (although he admits that his "heart wasn't really in it 100%"), and he takes a notably liberal stand with regard to environmental issues. Like his early influence, cartoonist Jay N. Darling, he has been an articulate champion of wildlife conservation. Among his many honors he numbers the 1956 Dave Roberts Award for his outstanding contribution to conservationism in Indiana in 1955, and a place on the Indiana State Natural Resources Commission. Over the years, no issue or topic has been spared his searching commentary. He has skewered public figures from Indianapolis politicians to presidents and popes without fear or favor. "Nobody's immune from a cartoonist," he asserts.

Indeed Chuck Werner is one of the toughest-minded cartoonists in the business, following his own convictions even when they conflict directly with those of his newspaper.

His years of service and professional prestige have earned him total editorial freedom. He begins his work-day by reading editorials in the morning editions of many papers such as the *Washington Post, New York Times,* and *San Francisco Examiner* and sketching out the idea he extracts for his daily cartoon. Some take less than an hour, others a whole day, but whenever the drawing is finished, it goes straight to the engraving department, with no detour for editorial approval. "The first time the publisher sees a cartoon," Werner reports, "is when it appears in the paper."

His office library consists of a few basic reference books: an unabridged dictionary, a yearbook, Bartlett's *Familiar Quotations,* a Bible, a collection of nursery rhymes, and a complete Shakespeare. He makes extensive use of the Bible, mythology, and Shakespeare in his work, finding these pillars of our culture essential to frame ideas for analogies to current situations.

Several syndicates have offered to distribute Werner's work nationally, but the artist has always refused. Such distribution would require him to keep his attention on national or world affairs and away from issues closer to home. Werner tries to focus at least 40 percent of his cartoons on state or local matters.

Nevertheless, his favorite characters to draw have been international leaders. The features he cites with most pleasure are "the nose and eyes" of Richard Nixon, "the glasses and cigarette holder" of President Franklin D. Roosevelt, the "pear-shaped head" of President Eisenhower, "the big mouth and ears" of Lyndon Johnson, and "the head of hair and toothy grin" of John F. Kennedy. His favorite character was Soviet leader Nikita Khrushchev. "Every cartoonist in the country, I'm sure, misses that fat little bear of the north," he says. "Whenever days were slow, you could always throw something together on Khrushchev."

Werner's undeniable gift for witty and incisive caricature (which he always does from photographs in his paper's library) has not earned him his greatest praise, however. Among his most admired work have been cartoons (such as the simple grave of Czechoslovakia in 1938) in which no human figure appeared and which made their points by the selection of detail and the eloquence of silence. Usually simple in composition, Werner's cartoons are done in bold, heavy strokes, often very dramatically arranged. The impact of a 1979 cartoon showing two sinister vultures watching the fighting in Nicaragua was all the greater for its simplicity and earned the drawing a place in the volume *Best Editorial Cartoons of the Year* for 1979.

Whether featuring human characters or not, Werner's style is in the classic tradition of the first decades of this century. His free, loose attack on his material and powerfully theatrical graphic instinct mark his work unmistakably. Sometimes irresistibly risible, sometimes wrenchingly moving, Werner's daily drawings never fail to affect their readers. In some cartoons the artist uses a personal device, a tiny owl standing on a twig in a lower corner of the panel and making a suitably wise comment on the scene. But with or without the owl, Werner makes his point clearly enough to illuminate, amuse, or infuriate his audience.

Werner is very clear on his objectives as an editorial cartoonist. A political cartoon is, he states, "a ridicule, a jab, a kick in the pants at a person, place, or thing. You have to go after the negative, the controversial, the dark side of life, yet still try to make a reader smile in the process." He believes his trade is essentially a negative one. "A political cartoon should never applaud," he states emphatically. "It should scorn. . . should put the subject in an awkward position." His daily goal, he reports, is "to bring the attention of readers to a specific current event they may have missed had the cartoon not been printed. And, if I can make a reader smile while attempting to get my message across, so much the better." Humor is not always possible, or appropriate, to his subject. A powerful 1981 cartoon showing five nooses forming an Olympic logo and labeled "war crimes against Afghan civilians" made no readers smile, but effectively conveyed the artist's indignation. The range of his palette from such starkly expressive statements to the droll, whimsical jabs at local and national politicians is the mark of his mastery of his craft. His proudest title is the one bestowed on him by the late Bruce Russell of the *Los Angeles Times*: a "cartoonist's cartoonist."

An avid sportsman, Chuck Werner remains very active and continues to produce editorial cartoons with the old verve and vitality. Between his work for such public services as the Natural Resources Commission and his heavy professional load as an editorial cartoonist, he gives no thought to retirement. "As long as Congress keeps holding sessions and politicians keep making promises they know damned well they'll never keep, a cartoonist will never run dry," he writes.

BIOGRAPHICAL/CRITICAL SOURCES: Charles Werner, "Cartoon Must Criticize to Be Good," *Editor & Publisher,* April 20, 1946; Craig Beardsley, "Political Cartoonist Chuck Werner," *Cartoonist Profiles,* March, 1977; *The World Encyclopedia of Cartoons,* Chelsea House, 1980; *National Cartoonists Society Album,* Museum of Cartoon Art, 1980; *Who's Who in America, 1984-85,* Marquis, 1984.

—*Sketch by Dennis Wepman*

* * *

WERNER, Chuck
See WERNER, Charles George

* * *

WIEDEMANN, Dorothea 1930-

PERSONAL: Born September 25, 1930, in Dresden, Germany (now East Germany); emigrated to Brazil as a child; emigrated to the United States, 1961; returned to Brazil, 1978; daughter of Wilhelm (a sociologist) and Hilde (a botanist; maiden name, Joseph) Wiedemann; married Claus Peter Schilsky, August 23, 1953 (divorced, August 5, 1964); married Edward John Long, June 2, 1970 (deceased, 1972). *Education:* University of Recife, B.A., 1949; further studies in art at Atelier Yolanda Mohalyi, Sao Paolo, Brazil, 1949-51; Atelier 17, Paris, France, 1952-53; Atelier Toshi Yoshida, Tokyo, Japan, 1957; and Hamburger Volkshochschule, Hamburg, West Germany, 1958-60. *Home and studio:* Caixa Postal 223, 84160 Castro PR, Brazil.

CAREER: Free-lance artist and print-maker, 1953—; assignments include anthropological illustrating in New Guinea, magazine illustrating in the United States, and limited

DOROTHEA WIEDEMANN

edition woodcuts sold in Europe and the United States. Teacher of printmaking at Grove House School of Art, 1964-72, Coral Gables Learning Center, 1966-69, and Dade County Board of Education, 1968, all in Florida; teacher of art at Colegio Instituto Cristao in Castro, Brazil, 1981—. Research assistant in graphics and layout at University of Miami, 1968-72.

MEMBER: World Print Council (Brazilian correspondent).

WRITINGS: (Illustrator) U. Randall, *Tickey, Totsie, and the Tokolosh*, privately printed, 1968; (illustrator) Hilde Wiedemann, *Der Weg Ist das Ziel*, Deutsche Nachrichten, 1973; (contributor) L. Jaffe and Betty Kjelson, editors, *Vantage Point*, Bright Star, 1979.

Also author of many articles for art journals and reviews, including *Printnews, Central Maandblad, Anuario Evangelico*, and *Joral do Instituto Cristao*.

EXHIBITIONS—One-woman shows: Museum fur Volkerkunde, Hamburg, West Germany, 1958; Galeria Studio, Frankfurt, West Germany, 1969; Barbados Museum, Barbados, West Indies, 1962 and 1963; Village Corner Gallery, Miami, Fla., 1963-64, 1966-68, and 1970; Galeria 167, Sao Paulo, Brazil, 1976; Museu de Arte Contemporanea, Curitiba, Brazil, 1977; Fundaçao Cultural de Curitiba, 1981.

Group shows include those at Print Club of Albany, Albany, N.Y., 1965; Paul Chelko Studio Gallery, Nantucket, Mass.,

1974; Lexington Gallery, New York City, 1974; Miami Art Center, Miami, 1974 and 1975; III, IV SLAC, Sao Paulo, 1975 and 1976; Barbara Gillman Gallery, Miami, 1980; Fundaçao Albares Penteado, Sao Paulo, 1984.

WORKS IN PROGRESS: A comparative study of the symbolic use of colors in primitive and ancient civilizations; a collection of current woodblock prints; continued exploration of the use of wood textures in color prints.

SIDELIGHTS: Few printmakers working today bring to their art an aesthetic sensibility as richly nourished as that of Dorothea Wiedemann, whose work draws from such diverse cultural sources as Europe, tropical America, Japan, and Australasia. The daughter of a distinguished German sociologist and a botanist educated at the University of Chicago, she grew up in a cultivated European family which had fled from the Nazis and settled in rural Brazil. She was drawn to the art of the woodcut as a child, but as the local school had no instruction in it, she had to work out the principles for

Up and Down, **a woodcut** (© 1976, Dorothea Wiedemann. Reprinted by permission.)

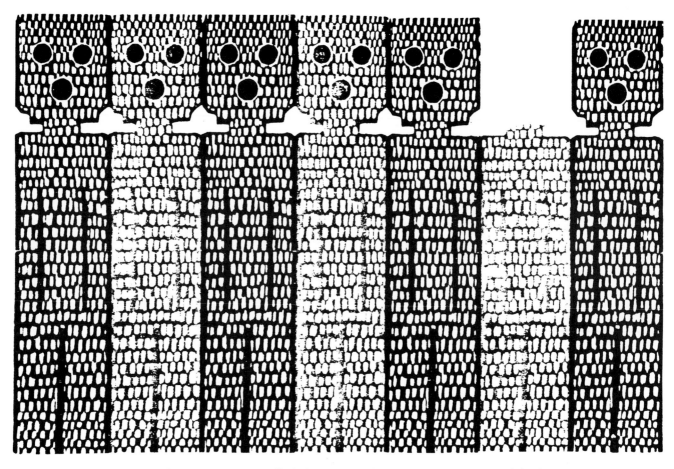

Army Advancing, **a woodcut** (© 1976, Dorothea Wiedemann. Reprinted by permission.)

herself from a book on Albrecht Durer in her father's library. She experimented with wood obtained from a neighboring carpenter and ink from the local newspaper plant. Her first paid commission was not an encouraging one: at age fifteen or sixteen she made a mold for the town baker's marzipan pigs. It was not until she was eighteen or nineteen that she made what she considers her "first real art sale": the owner of an umbrella shop offered her the umbrella of her choice for a watercolor.

In Sao Paulo she studied under the renowned Hungarian watercolorist Yolanda Mohalyi, and later took classes with Karl-Heinz Hansen, who was to become artist-in-residence to Emperor Haile Selassie of Ethiopia. In Paris in 1952 and 1953 she worked in etching and engraving with Stanley Hayter, "the doyen of all printmakers on metal" and author of the standard text *New Ways of Gravure.* A year in Germany studying art history followed, and then three in New Guinea on a special assignment to illustrate anthropological studies. A botanist's daughter, she was fascinated by the exotic flora as well as by the folk art and culture of the natives with whom she lived closely, and did an extensive series of drawings, monotypes, watercolors, and woodcuts. Before returning to Europe she visited Japan, where she spent some months studying Japanese methods of printing woodcuts in watercolor and the art of papermaking.

Wiedemann took up residence in Florida in 1961. There she lectured, taught drawing, silk screen, and woodcuts, and

directed a small gallery. During this period she made illustrations for many magazines, including *Investment Sales Monthly,* which commissioned woodcuts as illustrations and purchased the whole editions for sale to subscribers. During the 1960s and 1970s she exhibited and sold extensively in the United States, England, Germany, and Switzerland, and in 1978 returned to take over the family farm in southern Brazil, where she remains. She teaches art history, drawing, and printmaking at a small college in Castro and maintains a printmaking studio on the farm, where she concentrates on pen-and-ink drawings and woodblock prints.

Although her work has included pen-and-ink, charcoal, watercolor, and most forms of printmaking, Wiedemann still prefers her first love, the woodcut, to any other medium. In her extensive travels, especially to primitive areas, she has chosen it because of its convenience: "Woodcuts can be done anywhere," she points out, "while metal prints require cumbersome presses, acids, and other paraphernalia." But the appeal of the woodcut goes deeper for her, coming from a love for the material itself—"the feeling of wood," as she expresses it, "its smell, its texture." Among the woods of Brazil available to her for block cutting, she especially favors imbuia, a close-grained hardwood of particular beauty, but she uses Brazilian cherry and cedar as well, according to the subject. The different grains of different woods may figure in her work for special effects, and she is as sensitive as a sculptor to each piece of wood she selects to cut. She usually prints with oil pigments on handmade Japanese paper.

Themes underlying Wiedemann's work have ranged as widely as the extraordinary cultural breadth of the artist, but the element of nature has always figured largely among them. Like many artists in all media from tropical climes, she often depicts nature as an aggressive, hostile, even sinister force, although in recent years she has shown it as increasingly serene and poised. When human beings appear in her work, there has usually been a sense of isolation: man and nature have seemed separate, if not actually at odds. In her early work, humans usually appeared, if at all, in situations of stress or pain, and in her urban scenes they were shown as overwhelmed by the city. In recent years, an increasing sense of integration and peace have emerged in her work, with man seeming harmoniously situated in nature.

Wiedemann's early prints showed the influence of the German and Scandinavian Expressionists, and that influence remains apparent. Although she never allows herself their sometimes mannered devices of stylization, she projects the same emotional force as an Edvard Munch or a Kathe Kollwitz. Her style ranges from naturalistic representation to abstraction, but in all her work there is a characteristically powerful interplay of light and dark masses. Increasingly, she has come to use color as an element of design and an integral part of her composition, preferring warm earth colors, indigo, greens and reds. Even one-block prints are sometimes in vibrant, luminous colors.

As fascinated as she has always been by the form and texture of nature—especially leaves, flowers, roots, and tree-trunks—Wiedemann is essentially a philosophical artist, and a complex intellectual content informs even her most abstract work. Haunting and mysterious, her woodcuts often have the same disturbing suggestiveness as the work of Swiss modernist Paul Klee, but with an indefinable cast of Wiedemann's own, derived from her wide exposure to foreign civilizations. As Florida International University philosophy professor T. Kushner has written of her prints, "Their refined sensibility is at times reminiscent of Japanese prints; and like the best of oriental work, the artist successfully uses natural elements to create structures which have. . . harmony, wholeness, and unity."

BIOGRAPHICAL/CRITICAL SOURCES: Hamburger Anzeiger (Hamburg, West Germany), July 15, 1958; *Die Welt* (Hamburg), August 5, 1958; *Advocate* (Barbados, W.I.), August 5, 1963, August 11, 1963; *Barbados Sunday Times*, August 5, 1963; *Miami Herald*, October 2, 1963, May 9, 1965, February 6, 1966, February 7, 1966, February 27, 1966, May 12, 1968; *Art Review*, summer, 1977; *Miami Beach Daily Sun*, November 2, 1966; *Village Post* (Coral Gables, Fla.), May, 1968; *Der Neue Almanach*, Editora Teuto-Braseira, 1976; *Joral de Letras* (Rio de Janeiro, Brazil), January, 1977; L. Jaffe and Betty Kjelson, editors, "Introduction," *Vantage Point*, Bright Star, 1979.

—*Sketch by Dennis Wepman*

* * *

WILSON, Charles Banks 1918-

PERSONAL: Born August 6, 1918, in Springdale, Ark.; son of Charles B. (an interior decorator) and Bertha Juanita (Banks) Wilson; married Edna Frances McKibben, October

CHARLES BANKS WILSON

10, 1941; children: Carrie Vee, Geoffrey Banks. *Education:* Attended Art Institute of Chicago, 1936-41. *Politics:* Democrat. *Religion:* Presbyterian. *Home:* 110 B St. N.E., Miami, Okla. 74534. *Studio:* 100 N. Main St., Miami, Okla. 75354.

CAREER: Artist and magazine and book illustrator in Oklahoma, 1941—; founder and chairman of art department, Northeastern Oklahoma Agricultural and Mechanical College, Miami, Okla., 1945-60. Member of board of directors, Thomas Gilcrease Institute of American History and Art, Tulsa, 1950-60; chairman of Miami Public Library Board, 1957-61.

AWARDS, HONORS: Purchase Award, Chicago Society of Lithographers and Etchers, 1939; National Academy of Design Award, 1943; first prize for prints, second prize for oil painting, Brooklyn Museum of Art, 1943; first prize in painting, Philbrook Art Center, Tulsa, Okla., 1944, 1945, 1954, 1955; art award, Mint Museum of Art, Charlotte, N.C., 1944; art award, Wichita Art Association Annual Exhibition, Wichita, Kan., 1945; first prize, Hendrix College, Conway, Ark., 1946, third prize, 1952, first prize in graphics, 1954, first prize in watercolors, 1955; purchase award, Library of Congress, Washington, D.C., 1953, 1954; first prize, Joslyn Art Museum, Omaha, Neb., 1954; elected Fellow of the International Institute of Arts and Letters, Geneva, Switzerland, 1960.

Awarded Distinguished Service Citation, University of Oklahoma, 1976; first winner, Governor's Art Award, Tulsa, 1976; named "Oklahoma's picture maker," *Orbit* magazine, 1976; inducted into Oklahoma Hall of Fame, 1977; "Charles Banks Wilson Day" proclaimed in Miami, Okla., 1977; Western Heritage Special Trustees' Award, National Cowboy Hall of Fame, 1979; Citation of Honor,

Fishin' Joe's Creek, **a painting** (© 1969, Charles B. Wilson. Reprinted by permission.)

Oklahoma House of Representatives and Senate, 1980; "Charles Banks Wilson Day" proclaimed in Weatherford, Okla., 1980; portrait of Sequoya selected as basis of nineteen-cent stamp, U.S. Postal Department, 1980; many other local and national awards.

WRITINGS—Self-illustrated: *Indians of Eastern Oklahoma*, Buffalo Publishing Co., 1945; *Search for the Purebloods*, Stovall Museum, University of Oklahoma, 1983. Compiled, edited, and illustrated: *Quapaw Agency Indians*, self-published, 1947. Also published art series, including Will Rogers calendars, 1957—, *Ten Little Indians* portfolio, 1957 (published on mugs, Winart Pottery, 1963), and *First Americans* series of black basalt medallions, 1973.

Illustrator: Jim Kjelgaard, *Rebel Siege*, Holiday House, 1943; David Greenhood, *The Hill*, Duell Sloan & Pierce, 1943; Louise Hall Tharp, *Champlain: Northwest Voyager*, Little, Brown, 1944; Robert Davis, Jr., *Gid Granger*, Holiday House, 1945; L. Neyhart, *Henry's Lincoln*, Holiday House, 1945; Tharp, *Company of Adventurers*, Little, Brown, 1946; Carl D. Lane, *River Dragon*, Little, Brown, 1948; Robert Louis Stevenson, *Treasure Island*, Lippincott, 1948; William Marshal Rush, *Red Fox of the Kinapoo*, Longmans Green, 1949; Matt Armstrong, *Turtle River Filly*, Doubleday, 1950; Bruce Lancaster, *Guns in the Forest*, Little, Brown, 1952; Zachary Ball, *Swamp Chief*, Holiday House, 1952; J. Frank Dobie, *The Mustangs*, Little, Brown,

1952; *Oklahoma, Our Home*, Harr Wagoner Co., 1955; Col. Reeder, *Whispering Wind*, Little, Brown, 1955; Ross Taylor, *Chisholm Trail*, Grossett & Dunlap, 1957; Will Henry, *The Texas Rangers*, Random House, 1957; Kjelgaard, *Geronimo*, Grossett & Dunlap, 1958.

FILMS—All concerning the artist: *Names We Never Knew* WKY-TV, Oklahoma City, Okla., 1974; *Trail's End*, NBC, 1980; *Artist Who Never Left Home*, Northeast Oklahoma A. and M. College, 1984; *Portrait of America*, WTBS-TV, 1985; *Charles Banks Wilson*, University of Oklahoma, Stovall Museum, 1986.

EXHIBITIONS: Palace of the Legion of Honor, San Francisco, Calif., 1938-43; City Art Museum, St. Louis, Mo., 1938, 1945, 1946, 1948-51, 1954; U.S. Office of Education, Washington, D.C., 1939; Museum of Fine Arts, Houston, Tex., 1939; Carnegie Institute, Pittsburgh, Pa., 1939; Art Institute of Chicago, 1939 and 1940; Denver Art Museum, Denver, Colo., 1939, 1943, 1948, 1952-54.

Oakland Art Gallery, Oakland, Calif., 1942, 1944, 1945, 1948, 1953; Fine Arts Department, U.S. Department of the Interior, Washington, D.C., 1942; National Academy of Design, New York City, 1942, 1943, 1946, 1949; Metropolitan Museum of Art, New York City, 1942 and 1943; Mint Museum of Art, Charlotte, N.C., 1943-46; Texas Fine Arts Association International Print Show, Austin, Tex., 1943;

Library of Congress, Washington, D.C., 1943-48; Seattle Art Museum, Seattle, Wash., 1943-48; Corcoran Gallery, Washington, D.C., 1944; San Francisco Art Museum, San Francisco, Calif., 1945-48; National Gallery, Smithsonian Institution, Washington, D.C., 1948; Print Club of Rochester, N.Y., 1948; Dallas Museum of Fine Arts, Dallas, Tex., 1948-50, 1954; University of Kansas Art Museum, Lawrence, Kan., 1950; and many others.

WORK IN PROGRESS: The Lithographs of Charles Banks Wilson, a collection to be published by the University of Oklahoma Press; a mural for the U.S. Department of National Monuments and the State of Arkansas.

SIDELIGHTS: Charles Banks Wilson reports that he began drawing at the age of five "on anything flat or empty: bottoms of drawers, backs of pictures or under tables." His dedication to art has not diminished in the more than sixty richly productive years he has devoted to it since then. The son of a professional trombonist-turned-interior decorator and the grandson of a trapeze artist and stagecoach driver, Wilson grew up in a household both artistic and theatrical, and the excitement it generated has remained with him and enriched his art ever since. From his early youth he has directed his extensive artistic energies to capturing and preserving the scenes and faces of his Southwestern childhood, and in the process he has created an impressive monument to the spirit of his region. As painter and printmaker, author and illustrator, Charles Banks Wilson has made a lasting contribution to the record of our national culture.

Wilson's talents were recognized early—he won a National Scholastic Art Award from *Scholastic* magazine at eighteen—and he began his professional career doing movie posters for his hometown theater while still in high school. Like other regionalists in American art, he made the ritual visits to Chicago, where he studied at the Art Institute, and New York, where he had a commission from the Associated American Artists and illustrated his first book. But at nineteen he had already hit upon his true vocation and embarked on what he calls his "lifelong project" of sketching Oklahoma Indians. This was to become the cornerstone of his career and win him a major place in the ranks of spokesmen, both graphic and verbal, for native Americans. He was interviewed on NBC radio, written about as an ethnologist-artist in *Collier's* and *Coronet*, and widely reproduced. In the 1940s he wrote several articles on the Indians of the Southwest. His story of Indians in World War II, "No War Whoops, But!" (syndicated on January 10, 1943, by the United Newspapers Magazine Corp.), was reprinted in eighteen languages and distributed around the world by the U.S. Office of War Information.

Wilson's homespun oils and lithographs of the forties were meticulously executed recollections of the Southwest of his youth. *Ozark Summer*, a 1942 lithograph purchased by the Metropolitan Museum of Art in New York in 1944, was reprinted and distributed to U.S. Army camps to remind our boys of what they were fighting for. Subtitled *Swimmin' Hole*, it shows happy youngsters frolicking in a river and evokes the eternal American Eden-dream of idyllic, pastoral youth. The *New York Herald-Tribune* called it "America's best loved print." From the early 1940s, Wilson's place as a regionalist was secure, both in the art world and the popular market.

In 1943 Wilson returned to Oklahoma, where the focus of his vision was to remain. His 1947 book on the thirteen Indian tribes of Northeast Oklahoma, *Quapaw Agency Indians*, was reprinted in 1957 and again in 1964, and sold 65,000 copies. His art was much in demand, both locally and nationally. Wilson received a one-man show at the Smithsonian Institute in Washington, in 1948, and illustrated many books. His *Henry's Lincoln* was cited among the "Fifty Books of the Year" as the best designed book for children in 1945, and his 1952 illustrations for J. Frank Dobie's *The Mustangs* (for which Wilson used Oklahoma turkey feathers as quill pens) won the Carr P. Collins Award.

During the next decades, prizes and commissions came thick and fast to Wilson. In 1945 he was called upon to design the official emblem of Northeastern Oklahoma Agricultural and Mechanical College, and the same year he joined its faculty to found and head its art department. In 1955 John D. Rockefeller, Jr., commissioned a mural, *Rendezvous*, for Jackson Lake Lodge in Teton National Park. His state entrusted Wilson with a commission to portray its favorite son Will Rogers (Wilson's portraits of showman Rogers were featured on a series of calendars from 1957, installed in the State Capitol Rotunda in Oklahoma City, and used on the cover of all Oklahoma telephone directories). He did a series of watercolors on Oklahoma lake fishing for the Ford Motor Company, painted famed Indian athlete Jim Thorpe for the State Capitol, and in 1970 began a State Legislature commission for four twenty-seven-by-thirteen-foot murals on Oklahoma history for the Capitol Rotunda, the pinnacle of any career as a public artist.

Widely admired as his institutional portraits and historical murals are in his home state, Wilson's wider reputation rests on his Indian studies and regional scenes. The original pencil illustrations for his 1983 book *Search for the Purebloods*—drawings of the last pureblood Indians—went on national tour, and his many series on Indians remain perennial favorites. *Ten Little Indians*, a portfolio of ten Indian children in their tribal costumes, is scrupulously researched and stands as an important piece of ethnographic scholarship as well as a popular and decorative collection. Wilson's 1973 series of black basalt medallions, *First Americans*, done for Josiah Wedgewood in England, portrays twelve prominent Indian chiefs. These intense portraits, with their starkly dramatic modeling, like Wilson's prints with their brilliant use of color and light and their vivid chiaroscuro, stand as valuable national artifacts.

Sometimes folksy in content, Wilson's art never sinks to the sentimentalism of popular Americana printmakers Currier and Ives, but rather invites comparison with the powerful work of George Catlin and Frederick Remington of the Far West and John Steuart Curry, Grant Wood, and Thomas Hart Benton of the Midwest. A long-time friend of Benton, with whom he made many sketching trips, Wilson was the only artist ever to do a life portrait of him. Like Benton, Wilson has been deeply identified with his region during his long working career, and like him he has eloquently celebrated its life in simple, dynamic art. His work has taken its place along with that of his friend as a major part of the cultural history of our nation.

BIOGRAPHICAL/CRITICAL SOURCES: Coronet, October, 1940; *Collier's*, July 25, 1942; *Who's Who in the Western Hemisphere*, Marquis, 1943; *This Week*, January 10, 1943,

Indian Profile, **a painting** (© 1969, Charles B. Wilson. Reprinted by permission.)

July 13, 1947; Hal Borland, *An American Year*, Simon & Schuster, 1946; Henry Pitz, *Treasury of American Book Illustration*, Studio Books, 1946; *Who's Who is the Southwest*, Marquis, 1954; *Tulsa Daily World*, November 6, 1952, November 23, 1952; J. Frank Dobie, *Life and Literature in the Southwest*, Southern Methodist University, 1953; *Daily Oklahoman*, December 6, 1953, October 27, 1976, October 31, 1976, November 7, 1976; *Amarillo News*, September 18, 1955; *American Artist*, November, 1969; Peggy and Harold Samuels, *The Illustrated Biographical Encyclopedia of Artists of the American West*, Doubleday, 1976; *Who's Who in America 1984-85*, Marquis, 1984; *Who's Who in American Art*, Bowker, 1984.

—*Sketch by Dennis Wepman*

* * *

WILSON, Gahan   1930-

PERSONAL: Given name is pronounced "Gay-uhn"; born February 18, 1930, in Evanston, Ill.; son of Allen Barnum (a steel company executive) and Marion (Gahan) Wilson; married Nancy Dee Midyette (a journalist and novelist under the name Nancy Winters), December 30, 1966; stepchildren: Randy Winters, Paul Winters. *Education:* Attended Art Institute of Chicago, 1948-52. *Home:* New York, N.Y. *Office:* C/o Readers Service, 919 N. Michigan Ave., Chicago, Ill. 60611.

CAREER: Cartoonist, illustrator, and author, 1952—; cartoonist and author of *Gahan Wilson's Sunday Comics*, syndicated strip, Register & Tribune Syndicate, 1972-74. Author of fiction review column ("The Dark Corner") in *Fantasy and Science-Fiction*, 1969-72; author of movie review column in *Twilight Zone*, 1983—. Radio commentator, National Public Radio's *All Things Considered*. *Military service:* U.S. Air Force ("brief stretch as airman").

MEMBER: American Society of Illustrators, Cartoonists Guild (president for two years in early 1970s), Cartoonists Association, Mystery Writers of America, Science Fiction Writers of America, honorary member of Wolfe Pack (Rex Stout fan club).

AWARDS, HONORS: Many awards, including the "Clio" for advertising art and awards from the Advertising Directors Society, the American Society of Illustrators, and a special award from the World Fantasy Convention in 1979.

WRITINGS: Collections of cartoons: *Gahan Wilson's Graveside Manner*, edited by Terry Carr, Ace, 1965; *The Man in the Cannibal Pot*, Doubleday, 1970; *I Paint What I See*, Fireside Books/Simon & Schuster, 1971; *Playboy's Gahan Wilson*, Playboy Press, 1973, 1980; *Weird World of Gahan Wilson*, Tempo Books/Grosset & Dunlap, 1975; *Gahan Wilson's Cracked Cosmos*, Tempo Books/Grosset & Dunlap, 1975; *". . . And Then We'll Get Him!"*, Richard Marek Publishers, 1978; *Nuts*, Richard Marek Publishers, 1979; *Is Nothing Sacred?*, St. Martin's Press/Marek, 1982.
Self-illustrated commentary: *Gahan Wilson's America*, Simon & Schuster, 1985.

Self-illustrated children's books: *Harry, the Fat Bear Spy*, Scribner's, 1973; *The Bang Bang Family*, Scribner's, 1974; *Harry and the Sea Serpent*, Scribner's, 1976.

GAHAN WILSON

Illustrator: Jerome K. Beatty, Jr., *Matthew Loonie in the Outback*, William R. Scott, 1969; George Mendoza, *The Good Luck Spider and Other Bad Luck Stories*, Doubleday, 1970; J. Beatty, Jr., *Matthew Loonie and the Space Pirates*, Young Scott Books, 1972; J. Beatty, Jr., *Matthew Loonie's Voyage to the Earth*, Avon, 1972; Felice Holman, *The Future of Hooper Toote*, Scribner's, 1972; Lilian Moore and Lawrence Webster, compilers, *Catch Your Breath: A Book of Shivery Poems*, Gerrard, 1973; Phyllis La Farge, *Granny's Fish Story*, Parents Magazine Press, 1975; Russell Baker, *The Upside-Down Man*, McGraw; 1977; J. Beatty, Jr., *Bob Fulton's Amazing Soda-Pop Stretcher*, Bantam, 1979.

Editor: *Gahan Wilson's Favorite Tales of Horror*, Tempo/Grosset & Dunlap, 1977. *First World Fantasy Collection Anthology*, Doubleday, 1977.

Contributed two short stories to *Playboy Horror Stories*, Playboy; science fiction and fantasy stories in many national periodicals.

EXHIBITIONS: Represented in many exhibits in New York City, San Francisco, and Europe during the 1970s and 1980s, including one-man exhibitions at the Puck Gallery in New York, 1974; the Gallerie Isy Brachot in Brussels, Belgium, 1982; "Humor in Play and Art," Thorpe Intermedia Gallery in New York, 1983; an exhibit in Germany, 1984; and others at the Louis K. Meisel Gallery in New York and the Walton-Gilbert Gallery in San Francisco, Calif.

WORK IN PROGRESS: A novel, "a terribly difficult, very involved book," for Times Books, New York.

SIDELIGHTS: One of the most distinctive and original comic artists of our time, Gahan Wilson has established a secure reputation in cartooning as "the mirthful master of the macabre." Before he was out of swaddling clothes, he was drawing "strange things with amoeboid bodies" which his mother dutifully labeled with explanations like "horrible green monsters coming to attack us all." He blandly explains his "innocent affection for the ghastly and the macabre" by the fact that he was "born dead." Declared stillborn by the doctor who delivered him, the infant Wilson was plunged into a basin of ice water to revive him. "There must have been brain damage," he concludes.

Wilson was a devoted reader of comic books as a child, already favoring "those who drew odder styles such as Basil Wolverton and Dick Briefer." A predilection for the bizarre may have been hereditary: he had an uncle who was a professional lion-tamer and includes legendary showman P. T. Barnum and William Jennings Bryan among his great-uncles.

His first published cartoon, appearing in the journal of the Acme Steel Company where his father was a vice-president, showed Hitler and Tojo being horribly crushed by shovelfuls of steel, but after this promising and characteristic start Wilson was not to publish again regularly until he had served the usual artist's apprenticeship. His art training was thoroughly professional. After two unsatisfactory summer courses in a commercial art school in Chicago, he went on to the Art Institute there, where he was, he remembers, "the only admitted cartoonist in the whole place." He received a

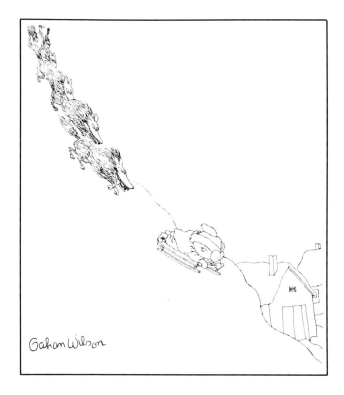

A magazine cartoon (© 1971, Gahan Wilson. Reprinted by permission.)

solid grounding in the techniques and mechanics of art at the Institute. "They had a fine department of graphics," he recalls, "which gave me invaluable hints." After graduating in 1952, he sold a few pieces by mail, but soon realized he had no chance in the field without personal contact. He had to make the rounds on Wednesdays when editors screened new artists, and so moved to New York.

There he lived the life of the starving bohemian in Greenwich Village for a time, selling enough to "dinky markets" to stay afloat but generally meeting with resistance to his highly original approach and subjects. He never made an effort to conform, and while editors were impressed with the rebellious young artist, they were reluctant to run his work, which they found "alarming." "Editors said 'marvelous, wonderful, funny, but the readers won't understand it,'" he recalls. "All of the editors shared this fundamental belief that a great gulf of taste and intelligence separated them from their readers, I don't know on what evidence." It was only when the regular cartoon editor left *Collier's* and an art editor, Bill Chessman, took over temporarily that Gahan Wilson was "discovered."

By the time *Collier's* folded in 1959, he was selling to most of the major markets, and by a fluke (he was looking for Harvey Kurtzman to try to tie in with his magazine *Trump*) he stumbled into the office of *Playboy*. Publisher Hugh Hefner took him up at once, and he has appeared in *Playboy* (where his work is described as "the second most compelling reason teenage boys look at" the magazine) ever since. Other periodicals featuring his work have ranged widely, including *Audubon, Boy's Life, Carte Blanche, Esquire, Fantasy and Science-Fiction, Gourmet*, the *National Lampoon, New York Times* (both the op-ed page and the *Book Review*), *New Yorker, Paris Match, Punch*, and *Voices.*

In the last two decades, Gahan Wilson has become an institution, as firmly placed in the national consciousness as any cartoonist in our history. He has published nine collections of his cartoons and a self-illustrated book of commentary on American life, as well as numerous short stories and reviews, and illustrated nine books for others. He says he will not illustrate other people's books again, however, except for those by close personal friends. It takes as much time, effort, and creativity as doing his own work, without bringing the rewards. His three self-illustrated original children's books have been well received, and he hopes to do more.

Wilson's cartoons, the rock on which his reputation rests most firmly, range from such conventional devices as the old-fashioned visual pun—a man introducing his ankle-high wife as his little woman, or a member of a cult that worships an idol labeled "Nothing" asking another, "Is nothing sacred?"—to some of the most outlandish grotesques ever committed to paper. In some he issues strong political or social statements, as when the last surviving soldier in a total war exclaims amid the rubble, "I think I won!" or two cockroaches reading the chemical contents of a package of food recoil from it in disgust. But in almost all of his work the element of the bizarre predominates. Wilson has been called the heir apparent of *New Yorker*'s macabre Charles Addams, and admits the influence, along with that of Chester Gould, creator of Dick Tracy (whose character Pruneface Wilson names as his "offhand favorite villain"), medieval painter Hieronymus Bosch, and "the slaphappy

A page from *Nuts* (© 1979, Gahan Wilson. Reprinted by permission.)

style" of Fontaine Fox's *Toonerville Trolley*. He also recognizes the influence of W. C. Fields, whose "cluttery, slovenly visual effect" had a formative impact on Wilson's loose, pseudo-sloppy style. But if he has properly filial feelings for his forerunners, he feels somewhat paternal toward cartoonists who have come after him, such as Gary Larson, whom he finds "uneven but sometimes very funny." He is even patient and faintly amused with outright copying. "*Gallery* had a guy who did outrageous imitations," he reports.

"*Playboy* wanted to sue, but it turned out that only France and Italy have laws against drawing in the styles of others." That style—so easy to imitate, so deceptive in its seeming simplicity and tight inner control—may easily be recognized in such disparate periodicals as *Fantasy and Science-Fiction*, where he has appeared in every issue for years, and the *New Yorker*, but he varies the content of his cartoons according to the readership. "When I do something for *National Lampoon*," he says, "I make sure it's in bad taste." But it is in *National Lampoon* that one of Wilson's most imaginative and endearing creations, *Nuts*, appears. This popular strip dealing with "the kid" is dedicated to the profound observation that "those who remember how great it was to be a little kid... don't remember how it was to be a little kid." Drawn in a style and perspective perfect for capturing a kid's-eye view of the terrors, dreams, and stupidities of life, the strip presents an unromanticized picture of childhood. It records its ignorance and credulity as unsparingly as it shows its terrors, frustrations, and fearsome insights. "Remember how confusing it was, being a little kid?" it asks. "Remember trying to make sense out of the weird rules grownups made you follow, and how you always guessed wrong about which ones they'd figure were really important?" Wilson clearly subscribes to William Golding's view of childhood rather than to Robert Louis Stevenson's. In *Nuts* Wilson brings together his twin preoccupations with childhood and the macabre, between which he sees a definite connection. "Kids live in a frightening world. The primordial fears of childhood remain in adults, but they are keenly awake in kids. People who work with horror deal in the existential facts of life." He agrees with the thesis of Sigmund Freud and Bruno Bettelheim that children should be taught to face reality and protect themselves. They should learn that "life is perilous, but it can be dealt with."

Wilson has dealt with fantasy and horror in all of its professional aspects. He has reviewed horror fiction and movies and was instrumental in the organization of the First World Fantasy Convention in 1975. For it he designed the "Howard," an award of a ceramic bust of Howard P. Lovecraft given annually. The sinister, morose, blank face, "like an Easter Island statue," of the noted supernaturalist-writer, stands in three-quarter view on a black cube labeled with a funereal plaque. In his own writing he has created a town like Lovecraft's Arkham "where terrible things happen." His fictitious Lakeside, in the Midwest, is based on his own hometown of Evanston, Illinois, a sunny, prosperous suburb of Chicago. "The Midwest," Wilson states, "is fuller of spooky stuff than the Gothic South or Lovecraft's New England, although they deny it. In fact, it is because they deny it that it is so spooky."

Wilson's syndicated *Sunday Comics*, which ran for a year-and-a-half in the early 1970s, had an estimated readership of fifteen million, but he decided to drop it when he found it was inhibiting. He felt that he was censoring himself for its amorphous mass market and has not regretted giving it up. Various syndicates have offered him deals since, but he has not been seriously tempted.

Although very prolific, Wilson works very slowly and carefully, putting several days into some of his more ambitious cartoons. He uses a pencil for rough sketches and then a crowquill penpoint. For his *Playboy* and *National Lampoon* cartoons, he uses watercolor—"a heritage of my academic training," he calls it—rather than the easier, less subtle liquid aniline dyes, because watercolors are more flexible. Such discipline is very characteristic of Wilson, a humorist who takes his humor very seriously.

BIOGRAPHICAL/CRITICAL SOURCES: Playboy, "Playbill" section, March, 1959; Dick Voll, "Interview with Gahan Wilson," *Graphic Story Magazine*, summer, 1973; *New York News*, November 21, 1974; Mike Ashley, editor, *Who's Who in Horror and Fantasy Fiction*, Elm Tree Press,

A magazine cartoon (© 1971, Gahan Wilson. Reprinted by permission.)

"Oh very well, then—go ahead and set."

1977; *Contemporary Authors*, First Revision, Vol. 25-28, Gale, 1977; Henry Allen, "Gahan Wilson," *International Herald-Tribune*, December 4, 1979; Francis J. Moriarty, "The Mad World of Gahan Wilson," *California Living*, December 9, 1979; *The World Encyclopedia of Cartoons*, Chelsea House, 1980; Mark Jacobs, *Jumping Up and Down on the Roof, Throwing Bags of Water on People*, Dolphin Books/Doubleday, 1980; *Something About the Author*, Vol. 27, Gale, 1980; *Arts Magazine*, September, 1981; Steve Heller, editor, *Man Bites Man: Two Decades of Drawings and Cartoons by 22 Comic and Satiric Artists*, A & W Publications, 1981; *Publisher's Weekly*, April 9, 1982, *Forbes Magazine*, July 5, 1982; *New York Times*, February 27, 1983; *Something About the Author* Vol. 35, Gale, 1984; Barbara Stewart, "Gahan Wilson: The Zen of Cartooning," *New Age Journal*, September, 1984; Les Krantz, *American Art Galleries*, Facts on File, 1985.

—*Sketch by Dennis Wepman*

* * *

WILTON, John 1948-

PERSONAL: Born September 8, 1948, in Portland, Me.; son of Harry J. and Virginia R. Wilton; married Nancy J. Dripps, February 14, 1969; children: Jessica. *Education:* Florida State University, B.A., 1971; Florida International

University, M.S., 1981. *Politics:* "No party affiliation." *Religion:* Christian. *Home:* 2648 Flowing Well Rd., De-Land, Fla. 32720. *Office:* Southeast Center for Photo/ Graphic Studies, Daytona Beach Community College, P.O. Box 1111, Daytona Beach, Fla. 32015.

CAREER: Free-lance designer and illustrator, Miami, Fla., 1973-77; creative director, Michael Sherman advertising, Miami, 1977-80; senior art director, Greenman Advertising, Hollywood, Fla., 1980-81; instructor, Daytona Beach Community College, Daytona Beach, Fla., 1981—, chairman of graphic art-advertising design department of Southeast Center for Photo/Graphic Studies, 1984—; illustrator and designer, 1981—. Instructor in graphic design, Miami Dade Community College, 1979-81. Member of board of DeLand Museum of Art (vice-president, 1984-85); member of board, Volusia Cultural Affairs League.

AWARDS, HONORS: Winner, Summer Music Theater Poster Competition, Daytona Beach, 1983; Award of Merit, for illustration, Art Directors Club of New York, 1983; Merit Award for graphics, DeLand Museum of Art, 1983; winner, DeLand/West Volusia Tourist Advisory Board T-Shirt Design Competition, 1984; Second Place, Mixed Media, DeLand Outdoor Art Festival, 1984.

FILMS—Director and producer of animated films: *Interview with Andrew Gogy*, 1979; *Bad Day for Black Bart at Black Rock*, 1981.

EXHIBITIONS: Bacardi Gallery, Miami, Fla., 1981; Visual Arts Gallery, Florida International University, Miami, 1982; Goddard Center for the Arts, Daytona Beach Community College, 1983, 1984, 1985; (one-man show) "Zoographics," Security First Federal, DeLand, Fla., 1983; Ormond Beach Memorial Art Gallery, Fla., 1983 and 1984; (one-man show) Gallery 300, Orange City, Fla., 1984; Gallery 600, Largo, Fla., 1984; The Village Gallery, Ormond Beach, 1985; G. Sander Gallery of Fine Art, Daytona Beach, Fla., 1985; (one-man show) Halifax Hospital, Daytona Beach, 1985; AAO Gallery, Buffalo, N.Y., 1985.

Self-portrait of John Wilton (© 1985, John Wilton. Reprinted by permission.)

Flamingoes, **a painting** (© 1985, John Wilton. Reprinted by permission.)

WORK IN PROGRESS: "Eyesee" series of portraits of artists; "Down in F.L.A.," a mixed media series; "River/ Florida," a water media series.

SIDELIGHTS: Mixing oil media and watercolors, blending pointillist, surrealist, and expressionist motifs, and using a variety of different techniques (dots, collages, montages, appliques), John Wilton creates an attractive and very personal world revolving around his experiences in Florida. Native flora and fauna (flamingoes, sharks, passion flowers) abound in his prints and his color illustrations (many of them for Florida magazines and concerns); and there is a very appealing luminosity in his compositions. At the same time, however, the artist is intent on transcending the limitations of purely local imagery. His self-portrait, for example, while recording the artist's memories of a carefree boyhood, also addresses more universal themes of loss and longing.

The most characteristic feature of Wilton's art is its openness; he never overloads his symbols with more emotional freight than they can carry. There is also an infectious charm to his depictions: his gorilla doesn't simply look "almost human" (as the cliche goes), he practically winks at us in the complicity of kinship, while his sharks are more winsome than their usual reputation. Now calling the state "his hometown," Wilton is able to see Florida with the eyes of the discoverer and the vision of the artist.

BIOGRAPHICAL/CRITICAL SOURCES: John Wilton, "Fine Art Through Small Dots," *Artist's Magazine*, January, 1985.

WRIGHT, Dick
    See WRIGHT, Richard

* * *

WRIGHT, Richard   1944-
    (Dick Wright)

PERSONAL: Born February 14, 1944, in Los Angeles, Calif.; son of Richard R. (an engineer) and Lettie (Eastman) Wright (a real estate broker); married Susan Colbert, August 8, 1966; children: Jane Suzanne, Anne Catherine. *Education:* Graduated from Pasadena City College, 1965, and from Long Beach State University, 1974. *Politics:* Conservative. *Religion:* Assembly of God. *Home:* 4570 Lynn Forest Dr., Gainesville, Va. 22065.

CAREER: Mechanical designer, Jet Propulsion Lab, 1966-71; free-lance cartoonist, 1971-74; syndicated feature artist for *Sportsquiz*, McNaught Syndicate, Copley News Service, 1974-84; editorial cartoonist, *San Diego Union*, 1974-76; editorial cartoonist, *Providence Journal*, Providence, R.I., 1976-83; chief editorial cartoonist, Scripps-Howard Newspapers, Washington, D.C., 1983-85; editorial cartoonist, *Providence Journal*, 1985—. Editorial cartoons syndicated by United Feature Syndicate, 1981—. *Military service:* U.S. Coast Guard, 1965, played softball on "Sea Hawks" team; Coast Guard Reserves, 1965-71.

Self-portrait of Richard Wright (© Dick Wright. Reprinted by permission.)

MEMBER: Association of American Editorial Cartoonists.

AWARDS, HONORS: Named Best Editorial Cartoonist in New England, United Press International (U.P.I.) 1979, 1981, and 1982; second place, U.P.I. Best Editorial Cartoonist, 1980; runner up, Pulitzer Prize, 1983.

WRITINGS: Wright Editorial Cartoons (collection), Providence Journal, 1980. Also contributor to collections, including *Best Editorial Cartoons of the Year* (Charles Brooks, editor), Pelican Publishing, 1978-83 and 1985, *The 1970s: Best Political Cartoons of the Decade* (Jerry Robinson, editor), McGraw, 1981.

EXHIBITS: Examples of editorial cartooning appear in "Artpac" shows to raise money for the arts, Washington, D.C.; Dryden Gallery, Providence, R.I., group show to celebrate the one hundred and fiftieth birthday of the *Providence Journal*, 1982.

WORK IN PROGRESS: A series of Bible story comics for publication by United Media.

SIDELIGHTS: Educated as a mechanical designer, Dick Wright shows the discipline and control that so technical a training provides. His work is always immaculate in execution and balanced in composition. Only a deficiency in mathematics prevented him from remaining in the aerospace industry and devoting his creative energies to the design of rockets for the government.

Wright graduated from Pasadena City College with a degree in mechanical design in 1965 and for six years worked for the U.S. government Jet Propulsion Lab in Pasadena designing rocket components. In 1967 and 1969 he designed the fuel system for the "Mariner" rocket, but finally realized that he didn't have enough math for a real future in the industry. When he returned to school at Long Beach State University to study finance in 1971, he was twenty-seven and married—a sober, mature adult with a world view unlike that of most of his fellow California undergraduates in the early 1970s. At the peak of student activism, his conservative views were rare enough among his classmates to command attention.

While at Long Beach University, he began drawing cartoons for the school newspaper, *The Fortyniner*, reflecting a position so exotic to the revolutionary spirit of the school that they led to violence. His drawings attacking the liberal heroine Angela Davis so enraged the left-wing Students for Democratic Action that some of their members roughed up the *Fortyniner*'s editor as a warning not to use any more of Wright's material. The heady experience was so exciting to the cartoonist that he began to devote more of his time to drawing, and in time began to sell some of his work to local newspapers. By the time he graduated in 1974, he was hooked, and Dick Wright has been a professional editorial cartoonist ever since.

The first commercial daily to print his work was the *Long Beach Press-Telegram*, but he attempted to extend his range by mail. He sold a few of his drawings, which encouraged him to travel around for a while with his portfolio, seeking a full-time job in the field. At last, in 1975, he found himself back in California, where the *San Diego Union* took him on as a back-up to their regular political cartoonist. After eighteen months on this job he moved up to the regular political cartoonist's chair with the *Providence Journal* in

Rhode Island. Seven years later he went to Washington for two years as chief editorial cartoonist of the Scripps-Howard Newspapers, and, in 1985, returned to the *Journal*, where he remains. Since August, 1981, his work has been distributed nationally by United Feature Syndicate, and appears in one hundred newspapers nationwide. His cartoons appear regularly in the *Baltimore Sun, Dallas Morning News, Detroit Free Press*, and *New York Times*, as well as such magazines as *Time, Newsweek*, and *U.S. News and World Report*.

In 1974 Wright's *Sportsquiz* feature was syndicated by McNaught (later carried by Copley News Service) and ran for ten years. This one-column feature had a cartoon of an athlete above a question about him, and its popularity during its decade of existence has prompted Wright to revive it. The *Journal* is now syndicating a more elaborate version of the feature.

Wright's fertile imagination suggests many ideas, and he is never at a loss for a new project. He is always watching the market for the right moment to try one or another of the features his inventive mind churns up. He is, for example, currently working on a series of trade books, half Bible stories in comic-strip form and half game-puzzle features about the stories.

Although an avowed conservative, Wright draws one of the sharper caricatures of Ronald Reagan in the field: the President's tiny, beady eyes are shown peering suspiciously or unhappily from his long, deeply lined face. However, as unappealing as Reagan appears, the spirit of the Soviet Union is shown as a far more sinister figure. In one cartoon, the shrouded scythe-bearing skeleton of Death stands grinning horribly among the onion-domed structures of Moscow, making the artist's point as eloquently as a thousand words.

Having grown up in Los Angeles, Wright was early exposed to the work of the *Herald Express*'s noted editorial cartoonist Karl Hubenthal, and credits the conservative artist as a major inspiration in his work. The influence of Hubenthal can be observed in many aspects of Wright's work: there is much of the same elegance of design and balance of composition in both, and if the master had a surer sense of human anatomy, the disciple is often more thematically inventive. Like Hubenthal, Wright uses heavy shading, which, against empty or simple, stylized backgrounds, produces a very striking effect. Invariably Wright's clean, clear art is aesthetically pleasing, and the ingenuity with which he wordlessly makes his point is often stunning.

Less obvious influences on Wright's graphic style are Walt Disney, whose work Wright could hardly have avoided in his early youth, and *Mad* magazine's Mort Drucker. The faces of Wright's characters show evidence of the Drucker style, but nothing of the overall form of Wright's cartoons seems to have been influenced by the ubiquitous spirit of *Mad*. In general, for all of the acknowledged sources of Dick Wright's art, the final result is unmistakably his own, both in content and in form.

Wright's work, although very simple in execution, is carefully and meticulously done. The artist reports that he uses a number one red sable brush and Higgins waterproof ink. The paper he usually prefers is Doushade number 232, and he sometimes uses two- or three-ply Strathmore kid. The effect is a richly textured and dramatic figure which is always eye-catching and handsome.

"People are always interested in what kind of 'tools' we cartoonists use," Wright has remarked. "But the *real* tools of an editorial cartoonist are *conviction*, which gives our work punch, *imagination*, from which interesting, clever, and entertaining ideas come, [and] *insight* and *analysis*, which we need for credibility." Finally, the artist lists the obvious necessity, artistic ability. Some editorial cartoonists have succeeded without one or another of these "tools," and many reveal a greater development in one element of their work than in the others. Dick Wright's artistic equipment is striking as much for its balance as for any particular feature; he displays conviction, imagination, insight, and technique in equal measure and in consequence produces a uniformly thought-provoking and attractive body of work.

—Sketch by Dennis Wepman

Z

GEORGE ZEBOT

ZEBOT, George 1944-

PERSONAL: Born Jurij Zebot, November 7, 1944, in Ljubljana, Slovenia, Yugoslavia; given name anglicized to George upon immigration to the United States as a child; son of Frank (an attorney) and Lija (a teacher; maiden name, Pogacnik) Zebot. *Education:* California State University, Long Beach, B.A., 1970, M.A., 1973. *Home:* 888 Bluebird Canyon Rd., Laguna Beach, Calif. 92651. *Office:* P.O. Box 4295, Laguna Beach, Calif. 92652. *Agent:* Bonnie Mateer, Graphic Collaborative, P.O. Box 16931, Irvine, Calif. 92713.

CAREER: Free-lance illustrator, 1973—; instructor in fine art, California State University, Long Beach, 1978—. Adjunct professor, Chapman College, Orange, Cal., 1977-81 and 1983-84. Career counselor for area high schools. Speaker and lecturer.

AWARDS, HONORS: First- and second-place medals, Media Arts Exhibit, Anaheim, Calif., 1978; second- and third-place awards, International Graphics Competition, Washington, D.C., 1978; Special Judges Award, Society of Illustrators, Los Angeles, 1978; third place award, Graphic Arts News National Logo Competition, 1981; Certificate of Commendation from City of Los Angeles, 1981, for Watts Towers Map Project; Gold Medal, Society of Illustrators, Los Angeles, 1982; proclamation from City of Newport Beach, Calif., 1982, for poster for its seventy-fifth anniversary.

EXHIBITIONS: Masters' Exhibit, California State University, Long Beach, 1973; "Slovenian Artists" (a traveling show of Yugoslav-born artists), New York and Cleveland, 1974; "Reproduced Originals" (one-man show), Chapman College, Orange, Calif., 1977; (one-man show) Califor-

An advertising illustration by George Zebot, ca. 1984 (© J. Zebot. Reprinted by permission.)

nia State University, Long Beach, 1977; "Illustration West" annual show of Los Angeles Society of Illustrators, 1977-84; New York Art Directors Show (national traveling exhibition), 1981; Laguna Beach Festival of the Arts, 1981 and 1982; Southern California Photography Exhibition, Saddleback College Art Gallery, Mission Viejo, Cal., 1982 and 1984; Orange County Advertising Federation, Buena Park, Calif., 1983; "Illustrated/Animated," Irvine Fine Arts Center, Irvine, Calif., 1984; Annual International Exhibit, Centre International d'Art Contemporain, Paris, 1986.

WORK IN PROGRESS: Contact: The Dolphins of Monkey Mia, a book about a family of dolphins that share intimate contact with humans on a regular basis; an animal mandala mural; designing labels for a bottled mineral water from Yugoslavia.

SIDELIGHTS: Yugoslav-born George Zebot came to the United States at a young age, and he received his education in this country, culminating in a master's degree from California State. A free-lance illustrator from his day of graduation, he has assimilated within his very personal style elements of Slavic culture with a resolutely American approach and intensity. His attention to animistic and primitive cultures (with which he had contact in his world-wide travels to remote areas of the globe) has resulted in the incorporation of atavistic elements even in his advertising work; for example, he used American Indian motifs and artifacts in promoting a brand of skateboards. Since he himself stated that he sees "dream imagery as a key to creativity," it is no wonder that many (if not most) of his compositions have the fluidity and translucency of half-remembered dreams.

His distinctiveness of treatment has enabled Zebot to work for a varied group of international clients, ranging from Westinghouse and Rolaids in the United States to Carta Blanca beer in Mexico, Radenska mineral water in Yugoslavia, and Maruka/Akiyama, a producer of color printing presses, in Japan. His eclecticism extends to magazines, and he has contributed illustrations to publications as diverse as *Human Behavior, Playgirl, Westways, Surfing, Pacific Skipper, Aquarius*, and *Road and Track*.

As the number of his awards and exhibitions attests, Zebot has gained a solid reputation in the fields of illustration and fine art. *American Artists* said of him that he "has developed

An announcement illustration by George Zebot, ca. 1985
(© J. Zebot. Reprinted by permission.)

a style of illustration that combines fantasy and the real in a careful combination of abstract and representational elements." Even his abstract elements have roots in the outside world, however, deriving their shapes from living creatures, mythical archetypes, or totemic symbols. These forms are often set against familiar, everyday objects (a blanket, a pencil eraser, a sheaf of note-paper) and recognizable human shapes in a shifting, shallow, and illusionary space.

BIOGRAPHICAL/CRITICAL SOURCES: Les Krantz, *American Artists*, Facts on File, 1985.

Cumulative Indexes

Cumulative Artist Index

273

Cumulative Occupation Index

ADVERTISING DESIGNERS AND ILLUSTRATORS

Bindig, Robert Kuhn 1
Browne, Richard Arthur Allen 1
Cassady, John R. 2
Charmatz, Bill 2
Cober, Alan E(dwin) 2
Cornell, Jeff(rey W.) 2
Craft, Kinuko Yamabe 1
Crofut, Robert Joel 1
Cuccio, David 1
Cusack, Margaret 2
Daly, Tom 2
De Cesare, John A. 1
Drucker, Mort 1
Duke, Chris(tine) 2
Emmett, Bruce 1
Garland, Michael 2
Goslin, Charles 2
Hess, Richard 2
Hull, Cathy 2
Lettick, Birney 1
Mandel, Saul 1
McMullan, James (Burroughs) 1
Melgar, Fabian 2
Meyer, Gary 1
Morgan, Jacqui 1
Moss, Donald 1
Nessim, Barbara 1
Outcault, R(ichard) F(elton) 1
Park, W(illiam) B(ryan) 2
Peak, Robert 1
Preiss, Alexandru 2
Seaver, Jeff 1
Smith, Elwood H. 2
Sorel, Edward 1
Tierney, Tom 1
Uram, Lauren 2
Weller, Don 2
Wilton, John 2
Zebot, George 2

ANIMATORS, ANIMATION PRODUCERS AND DIRECTORS

Barbera, Joseph Roland 1
Beckerman, Howard 2
Beiman, Nancy 1
Blechman, R. O. 1
Canemaker, John 1
Clampett, Robert
  Obituary 1

Corben, Richard V(ance) 1
Cruikshank, Sally 1
Ehrlich, David 1
Furukawa, Taku 1
Hubley, Faith Elliot 1
Klein, I(sidore) 1
Mattingly, David B. 1
McCay, Winsor Zenic 1
McLaren, Norman 2
Nakazawa, Keiji 2
Partch, Virgil Franklin II
  Obituary 1
Pojar, Bretislav 2
Reitherman, Wolfgang
  Obituary 2
Sito, Thomas 2
Tezuka, Osamu 1

BOOK AND MAGAZINE DESIGNERS AND ILLUSTRATORS

Bascove 2
Berry, William A(ugustus) 1
Blechman, R. O. 1
Bosch Penalva, Jordi 1
Bowler, Joseph, Jr. 2
Catrow, (David Johnson III) 1
Charmatz, Bill 2
Cleaver, Elizabeth (Mrazik)
  Obituary 2
Clifford, Judy 2
Cober, Alan E(dwin) 2
Colin, Paul
  Obituary 2
Corben, Richard V(ance) 1
Cornell, Jeff(rey W.) 2
Craft, Kinuko Yamabe 1
Creamer, David H. 1
Crockett, Linda 2
Crofut, Robert Joel 1
Cruise, S(haron) 2
Cuccio, David 1
Cusack, Margaret 2
Daumier, Honore (Victorin) 2
Devlin, Harry 1
Di Fate, Vincent 2
Dore, (Louis Christophe Paul)
  Gustave 1
Duke, Chris(tine) 2
Eaton, Tom 1
Emmett, Bruce 1
Enos, Randall 1
Fernandez (Sanchez), Fernando 1

Filippucci, Sandra 2
Foster, Brad W. 1
Fowler, Eric N. 2
Garland, Michael 2
Glaser, Milton 1
Gleason, Paul M. 1
Gonzalez (Navarro), Jose 1
Gorsline, Douglas (Warner) 2
Groth, John 2
Hall, H. Tom 1
Hess, Richard 2
Hoff, Syd(ney) 1
Hogarth, Burne 1
Hogarth, William 2
Holland, Brad(ford) 1
Hull, Cathy 2
Impiglia, Giancarlo 2
Jetter, Frances 2
Johnson, Lonni Sue 2
Kent, John Wellington 1
  Obituary 2
Kipniss, Robert 2
Krigstein, Bernard 2
Lettick, Birney 1
Mandel, Saul 1
Mattingly, David B. 1
McMullan, James (Burroughs) 1
Meyer, Gary 1
Moss, Donald 1
Odom, Mel 2
Oppenberg, Sheldon 1
Park, W(illiam) B(ryan) 2
Peak, Robert 1
Perez Clemente, Manuel 2
Pyle, Howard 2
Quagmire, Joshua 2
Raney, Ken 2
Royo (Navarro), Luis (Fernando) 2
Salerno, Steve 2
Salmon, Donna (Elaine) 1
Seaver, Jeff 1
Segrelles (Sacristan), Vicente 2
Slackman, Chas B. 2
Smilkstein, Harry 1
Sorayama, Hajime 2
Sorel, Edward 1
Sumichrast, Jozef 1
Torres Prat, Enric 2
Veitch, Rick 1
Vo-Dinh, Mai 2
Ward, Lynd (Kendall)
  Obituary 1

Cumulative Occupation Index

Cumulative Subject Index

This index lists important awards, organizations, company names,
titles of works, artistic media, genres, and other key topics.

Cumulative Subject Index

DATE DUE

PRINTED IN U.S.A.